OLYMPIC GAMES OFFICIAL BRITISH GUIDE
BARCELONA 1992
CONTEN

GW00482753

THE SPORTS FILE

An in-depth analysis of the sports on the Olympic programme: the stars; rules; schedules; medals and Britain's chances.

THE FACT PACK

A comprehensive digest of history, schedules, past British "bests", flag bearers, past results and medallists.

THE BIOGRAPHIES

Profiles of some of the people likely to star for Britain at the Games.

Published by **BBC Books**, a division of **BBC Enterprises Limited**
Woodlands, 80 Wood Lane, **LONDON**, W12 0TT
First published 1992:
© British Olympic Association and Desmond Lynam, 1992
ISBN 0 563 36364 9

Editorial assistants: Jill Beagley, Carl Hicks, Jan Paterson and Roxane Still
Designed and printed by: Stonham Baxter, 35 High Street, LEWES, East Sussex, BN7 2LY
Photographs by: Allsport, Colorsport, ASP, Mark Shearman, PJS Photos
Front cover: Kriss Akabusi and Derek Redmond celebrate Tokyo gold (Allsport)

Although this book is the official publication of the **British Olympic Association, 1 Wandsworth Plain, LONDON, SW18 1EH**, the views expressed are not necessarily those of the Association.

Unimaginable really, and yet all that has come to pass. The Soviet Union and East Germany had, of course, been two of the great Olympic powers for many years. Now there is a united German team for the first time since 1936 and a whole host of one-time great Soviet athletes are appearing under different and various banners.

The power houses of world sport had, of course, been undergoing changes before the dramatic political ones had taken place.

China had already emerged as a potential giant, not so much in track and field (although they were amongst the medallists at the 1991 Tokyo World Championships), but most certainly in

Who would have thought there would be no Soviet Union?

diving, gymnastics, badminton and table tennis.

Four years ago the South Koreans also showed expertise of the highest order in sports as varied as archery and hockey as well as the more likely table tennis and boxing. They have since proved, in world championships, that they do not need home advantage to excel.

Africa is the great continent of untapped talent in many sports but just look at the achievement of the track stars from that continent. In last year's Tokyo World Championships only the Americans prevented Kenyan or Algerian athletes from a clean sweep in men's track events.

Their women are beginning to make their mark too. African athletes are bound to feature in some of the great stories of these Games.

Cuba, who have not sent a team since 1980, look like being present this time and their great stars of the boxing ring and their baseball heroes (they have many) will surely be amongst the gold medallists. The USA, always one of the three leading medal-winning nations, could end up top this time. Their track stars and swimmers will show the way.

But when the memories of these

China is a potential sporting giant in 1992 – its divers lead the world.

The Koreans are likely to excel even without home territory.

Barcelona Olympics are recalled in years to come, it will not be the nations that are remembered but the individuals.

It will be the modern-day Jesse Owens, Olga Korbuts, Mark Spitzs and Bob Beamons whose legendary performances will leave a lasting impression on the mind.

Olympic history is about to be made by the stars of '92. This time there are twenty-five sports, two more than four years ago. The additions are baseball and badminton. Each of the twenty-five are dealt with under separate chapters.

The modern Olympics, founded at the end of the last century, were totally amateur in ideal. In those early Games, an athlete who was coached was thought to be bending if not breaking the amateur code. Sport in those days was seen very much as a part-time occupation. It was for the man who, every four years, left his "day-job" behind, put on his

American swimmers – and track stars – could show the way.

Can Carl Lewis emulate Jesse Owens once more?

running vest or unwrapped his shooting pistol and became a very temporary Olympian.

As time went by, some nations, recognising the international status to be gained from success in the Olympics, made it possible for their athletes to concentrate on their sports to the exclusion of almost everything else.

The communist countries in particular followed this course. Strictly they did not break the amateur code because their sportsmen were not paid for their sport - although their army officers, who concentrated on sport, received a normal military pay-packet. The Americans in turn perfected the 'college' system where their sportsmen had little to do but train.

The amateur ideal was being broken in everything but name by the major competing countries.

Now the Games are virtually 'open'. But anomalies galore still exist. For example, the baseball players who earn their living in America's major leagues are excluded but the world's highly paid tennis stars are in. Professional boxers will not be at the Games. But professional footballers will be and, of course, nearly all the major stars of track and field follow their calling full-time and get handsomely paid for it.

And yet competitors will arrive from nearly all the countries at varying levels and take part just as they might have years ago. One thing is for sure, no-one gets paid by the Olympic authorities for performing at the Olympic Games. And make no mistake, nothing in sport can still quite rank as high as winning an Olympic gold medal.

In this television age, the Games will be watched in every corner of the globe and for over three years the plans have been under way to make sure the coverage of all 25 sports in Barcelona will be the best ever.

There will be an international television crew of over 3,000 covering events at 41 venues.

Highly paid tennis stars compete whilst baseball pros are not permitted.

British athletes will be amongst the top track medal winners.

And with the Games falling into our own time zone for the first time since 1980, there will be live coverage on BBC Television of all the main events.

The first television Games had been planned for Melbourne in 1956 but that was the year of the Suez crisis and the Hungarian uprising and in the end there was a television boycott. Not a single moving picture of some of the great British exploits on the track and in the boxing ring emerged till some time later.

By the Rome Olympics of 1960, television had got its act together and viewers were able to watch a good deal of live action, but only in black and white. In those days the pictures came through land lines, like your telephone. Now, of course, the perfect colour pictures are beamed instantly into your home in any corner of the world, by satellite.

THE CHOICE OF CHAMPIONS

Mars

a day helps you

m&m

MILK CHOCOLATE

OFFICIAL SNACKFOOD OF THE 1992 OLYMPIC GAMES

NOT THE PLAIN OLYMPICS
IN SPAIN

Caroline Searle sets the scene as Barcelona begins its Olympic adventure.

HOST CITY

For the Olympic Movement there is always a moment when time seems to stand still. A moment of trembling anticipation. That came, for the prospective host cities of 1992, at 13:30 on October 17, 1986, in the Beaulieu Palace, Lausanne, Switzerland - home town of the International Olympic Committee.

"And the Games of the XXVth Olympiad are awarded to the City of ....". The clock flipped over to 13:31, an envelope seal was broken in the silence of a collectively-held breath ...."to Barcelona, Spain", said the suitably emotional Catalan-accented voice of the IOC President Juan Antonio Samaranch.

Since that moment – almost six years ago – Barcelona has bustled, buzzed and built for the Games. And now it is ready to hold the world's greatest-ever sporting festival.

Over 10,000 representatives of the youth of the world will gather together in the Catalonian capital to compete in 16 days of superlative sport from July 25 – August 9, 1992.

There are more sports – 25 – than ever before. And 257 events. Almost 15,000 media representatives will transmit and translate the action for billions around the world. And TV rights have been sold for over 500 million US dollars for the Games – a Games which will need almost 100,000 volunteers and Organising Committee staff to operate. Spectators and sponsors alike will be treated to a feast of international activity.

HOME AND AWAY

Athletes and officials will be lodged – all bar the rowers and whitewater canoeists who have separate venues at Banyoles and in the Parc de Segre – in an Olympic Village in the Parc de Mar

The Olympic Village will be right on the coast.

The sport itself will be based in four zones of the city interconnected by a sophisticated Games transport network: Parc de Mar, Montjuic, Vall D'Hebron and Diagonal. A good transport system, capable of rapid and secure movement of large numbers of people, will be vital to the Games success.

So, too, will the people and the venues. The former are fiercely Catalan, seeking autonomy and justly proud of their achievement in securing the Games. But they have also proved capable of successful cooperation with the overall Spanish authorities where major infrastructure projects are concerned.

Barcelona has a new airport terminal, the coastal railway has been permanently diverted to make space for the

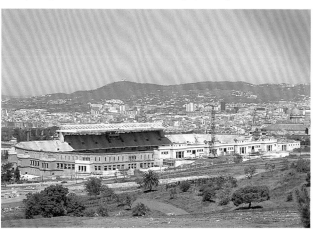

Barcelona has bustled, buzzed and built to be ready for the Games.

9

Vall D'Hebron area facilities include the Olympic Velodrome.

Olympic Village and the motorway sent underground for a long stretch to ease traffic congestion around the port.

For the last few years Barcelona has groaned under the weight of heavy construction. It has now burst forth with sporting venues of breathtaking vision and quality.

A PLACE TO PLAY

The Palau Sant Jordi, home to gymnastics and handball, was designed by a Japanese architect, Isozaki Arada. And it is a technological first. Thousands of interlocking girders were connected at ground level in an intricate, inverse pattern before being tensioned and lifted into a dome-like roof by hydraulic supports. It is a venue capable of staging an infinite variety of events from rock concerts to indoor windsurfing.

Whilst the Palau has brought nothing but praise, the Olympic stadium at Montjuic has incited controversy. There is no doubting its atmospheric appeal. The original 1929 facade of pinkish stone has been preserved. And its setting gives superb views out over the sea and city.

Inside, the stadium has been deepened and re-built to provide a suitable Olympic competition venue. Yet a maximum of 65-70,000 people can sit within its walls. That is very intimate but also very small by Olympic standards.

The 1992 Olympic swimmers will compete on Montjuic, too, in the open-air "Bernat Picornell" pools. Sun-block will be an essential part of the British team kit issue in the soaring Spanish summer temperatures.

Tennis, a relatively new Olympic sport, leads the cluster of activities in the Vall D'Hebron area of the city's northern quarter. Nestled between the hills and the sea the clay-courts complex is bordered by the archery field, cycling velodrome and an indoor-sport complex.

One of Barcelona's most elegant venues, the Diagonal lends its name to the third venue cluster. This plays host to a number of sports including football - at the famous FC Barcelona stadium - equestrian events at the Polo Club, judo and modern pentathlon.

Table tennis and badminton competitors will be able to walk to their venues from the Olympic Village at Parc de Mar. So will the yachtsmen and women competing from the Olympic port across the road.

Boxing and basketball take place just along the coast in the sports-mad suburb of Badalona.

REVERSE PLAY

Barcelona is set to be remembered by a new generation as "Olympic" city. But its history is also one of diversity and complexity - as is its architecture.

Over more than 2000 years this mediterranean city has been influenced by Greeks, Romans, Vizigoths, Arabs and Franks. All of them have left their mark - on the city's walls, language, cuisine and culture. In more recent times the famous names of modernism and the Avantgarde have stamped the city with much of its current character.

Picasso, Miro, Dali and Montserrat Caballe have played a part. But the leading role was cast to Gaudi the architect-genius who designed several private and public buildings but whose life's main work the "Sagrada Familia" remains stunning yet unfinished.

Barcelona has long been a busy port. And Christopher Columbus is commemorated in a statue overlooking the port.

Barcelona – a mixture of old elegance and new-style chic.

Today's Barcelona, though, is also a brave new city. It is an industrial growth area – a city of contrasts: between industrial plants and palm-lined avenues; between old-style elegance and new-style chic; between the clean-cut financial districts and the hard-working, dusty suburbs; between the seaboard and the landlocked.

It is located in the North-east of Spain across the plain bounded by the Llobregat and Besos Rivers, the hills of the Sierra de Collcerola and the mediterranean sea.

'There is an old fisherman's quarter a working port and industrial zone producing textiles, chemicals, paper and graphic arts. Under Franco the locals were forced to speak Castilian Spanish in all public places and at school. But the language and culture are Catalan.

The mixture of hills and sea provide a mild climate although during the period of the Games average temperatures are expected to be 26°C. Barcelona's average rainfall is 600mm a year and 2,500 hours of sunshine.

It is the warmth of that Spanish sun, the vitality of the people and the setting which could spell the best Games yet for Barcelona.

The Games mascot – Cobi.

AN OLYMPIC CORNER OF SPAIN

The essential guide for the best-informed Olympic addict:

Barcelona

Population:	1,700,000 (city itself)
	4,000,000 (metropolitan area)
Location:	North-east Spain
Region:	Catalonia
Languages:	Catalan and Spanish
Industry:	Textiles, chemicals, paper, graphic art and service industry.
Economy:	20% of Spain's gross national product (approx. 165,000 million US dollars) Spain's second ranked Stock Exchange.
International Relations:	60 permanent consulates (including Great Britain) and 23 foreign Chambers of Commerce.
Temperatures:	Winter average 9°C. Summer average 23.5°C. 2,500 hours of sunshine per year.

Olympics

Sports:	archery, athletics, badminton, baseball, basketball, boxing, canoeing, cycling, equestrian, fencing, football, gymnastics, handball, hockey, judo, modern pentathlon, rowing, shooting, swimming, table tennis, tennis, volleyball, weightlifting, wrestling, yachting.
	New sports are baseball and badminton
	Events: 257 of which canoe slalom, women's judo and windsurfing are making their Olympic debuts.
Dates:	Games open 25 July, 1992
	Games close 9 August, 1992
	Awarded the Games October 17, 1986. Decision made in Lausanne, Switzerland, by the International Olympic Committee with 47 votes in Barcelona's favour in the final round.
Athletes:	10,000
Officials:	5,000
Media:	15,000
Volunteers:	100,000
Spectators:	2,000,000
Transport:	11,000 taxis. 4 underground lines 2,000 Olympic-family dedicated cars. New airport terminal.
Medal table leader:	USA with 752 gold, 569 silver, 481 bronze medals.
New Olympic countries in 1992:	Estonia, Latvia, Lithuania, Croatia, Slovenia and Namibia. Soviet Union now called the "Unified Team" (Equipe Unifee)
BBC TV:	Exclusive British rights-holders. Broadcasts planned daily both live and recorded highlights.

SEOUL CITY REVISITED

On the eve of the **XXVth** Olympiad, Caroline Searle takes a glance back to the thrills and spills of Seoul in 1988.

"Do you remember the Kimchi?" Any athlete who tried this pungent South Korean dish during the 1988 Games will have vivid memories of the experience. But the spice of the local cuisine was only part of the flavour of a Games which opened up a new culture to western observers.

Opening Ceremony - Seoul.

The music, the drums, the language, the people, the facilities and the sunny blue skies served the world with a memorable sporting dish. Even Desmond had us learning Korean phrases on the box. And we loved it. But Seoul provided the sporting world with some soul-searching, too. The bell which tolled for big Ben Johnson - disqualified after winning the 100m gold when his drug-test showed steroid use - had its sobering impact on the whole Olympic Movement.

Since that time, more stringent tests have been introduced. And many sports have been forced to put their respective houses in order.

The Olympic Flame comes to life in the Seoul stadium in 1988.

Barcelona, then, will hope to avoid the medical commission summonses, drug labs, media scandals and human agony which also touched the innocent Linford Christie, Dominic Mahony and Graham Brookhouse of the British team and which engulfed their judo colleague Kerrith Brown.

Soul-searching after Johnson steroid scandal.

THE HOME TEAM

It all started well ..... and ended well for Britain four years ago. Three golds were also scored in the middle. Swimmer Adrian Moorhouse showed true Yorkshire grit when he clawed his way back into a gold medal finish down the second length of the 100m breaststroke on day two. He will hope for equal success in Barcelona.

Adrian Moorhouse gave Britain a flying start in 1988.

The early boost to overall team morale was of immeasurable benefit. Malcolm Cooper continued the theme two days later when he successfully defended his small-bore rifle (three position) title. What would have been the unassuming Hampshire man's overall medal tally if the shooters had not boycotted Moscow? Malcolm has now retired.

Steven Redgrave and Andrew Holmes came next. The country's rowing power-houses took gold in the coxless pairs to complete the midddle-Games victories. Redgrave goes for gold once more in 1992.

Redgrave got his second gold.

Britain then held its breath. It waited for a gold on the track which never came. Instead Bryn Vaile and Mike McIntyre proved in a "Star" class of their own down in Pusan - home of the Olympic yachting, 200 miles from Seoul. Finances have ruled them out of a Barcelona title defence.

Finally, on a glorious, sunny final Saturday our eleven men hockey players came through in true "boys own" style with a stunning 3-1 victory over West Germany to take the gold.

Britain's track athletes, meanwhile, provided a six-fold silver lining. Gutsy Peter Elliott overcame the pain of injury to take 1500m silver. Linford Christie, already a silver-medallist in the now-infamous 100m final, fought off his own personal drug-allegations trauma to join a stunning sprint-relay silver.

Hockey had a field day.

Fatima Whitbread, Colin Jackson and Liz McColgan all added to the tally. Some other silver-coloured precious medal also came to Britain via the traditional routes of equestrian, swimming and shooting. More specifically from the horse and riders of the 3-day event team and Ian Stark as an individual horseman; Nick Gillingham in the 200m breaststroke and Alister Allen in the small-bore rifle (3 positions).

Britain took plenty of silver but no gold on the track.

Amongst the bronze medals, perhaps, the pluckiest belonged to the modern pentathlon team - particularly as Dominic Mahony carried a knee injury into the final cross-country section.

THE OPPOSITION

From a worldwide perspective American Gregory Louganis' head took a bashing on the diving board. But he recovered to stitch up two golds against fierce Chinese opposition.

Australian Duncan Armstrong's coach proved over-exuberant in celebration of his protégé's 200m freestyle victory. He gave the kind of playful thump that sent a TV reporter sprawling poolside. Kristin Otto, meanwhile, had six-appeal in the women's event when she took that number of golds.

Korean boxer Byun Jong-il did neither his sport nor himself any good with a 70-minute protest sit-in after being beaten by Bulgarian Alexander Hristov. Mind you, nor did the officials who created chaos out of order at the two-ring venue. Boxing will be hoping to "go straight" in Barcelona.

The United States of America went into national mourning when they lost the men's basketball semi-final to the former Soviet Union. Not even a gold in the women's final event would atone.

Down at the track Ben Johnson stole all the "positive" headlines - both as a victor and a later-exposed cheat. And "Flo-Jo" - Florence Griffith-Joyner - ran away with three golds and a silver. Her sister-in-law Jackie Joyner-Kersee was a double gold medallist in the long jump and heptathlon.

West Germany's women introduced a stunning new style which gave them four fencing medals. And a tiny Turk called Naim Suleymanoglu lifted more than three times his own body weight to smash a string of world records and take his country's first Olympic gold for twenty years.

Tennis made its Olympic re-introduction smoothly and its two eventual individual gold medallists Steffi Graf and Miloslav Mecir, were regularly seen during the fortnight soaking up the atmosphere as spectators at other sports. For Steffi it set the seal on a golden slam - the four majors and Olympic gold in one year.

From riches to rags. Tennis to gymnastics. Eastern-bloc stars Elena Chouchounova, USSR, and Daniela Silvas of Romania battled to become the gymnastics queen of 1988.

But two of Elena's male team-mates stole a fair share of the limelight. Vladimir Artemov, multi gold medallist, proved one of the supreme gymnasts of all time. And Dmitri Bilozertchev created a personal triumph picking up a gold and silver after recovering from a horrific car crash which had left his shin shattered in so many places that surgeons had considered amputation.

BRITAIN ALONE

Britain finished twelfth out of 160 nations on the overall medal table at the Seoul Olympic Games four years ago. As Barcelona beckons, the nation once more expects the best of its world-class athletes.

Conditions, for that kind of success, have to be perfect. Most of Britain's elite in Barcelona will have trained hard over the long winter months. Others will be coming to the peak of a long competitive season preceded by hours of gruelling preparation.

To be a modern sporting hero requires total dedication single-mindedness and finance. But it can also require - for all but exceptional individuals - a support package of any mixture of coaches, doctors, physiotherapists, sports scientists, colleagues, family and friends.

This is the kind of back-up team available to the best competitors around the world. To move higher up the league or, even, to hold firm in its current position on the medal table, Britain must make sure it does not score any financial own goals.

It now costs upwards of £2 million to send a full British team to the Olympic, and Olympic Winter, Games. The British Olympic Association (BOA), raises the money through public Appeal and sponsorship. For that money Britain's 500-strong athlete delegation is clothed, transported, insured, covered medically and administratively.

Vital equipment - including horses, yachts, canoes and boats are transported to the venues. And accommodation is provided for all the back-up team of coaches, doctors, vets, grooms and managers.

But it costs the BOA almost as much again to make sure that its athletes are properly-prepared. "It is no good sending them out to compete with one hand tied behind their backs", explains long-standing BOA general secretary Dick Palmer. "World standards are improving all the time and we must keep pace by all fair means possible."

So the BOA also runs a four-year round programme of elite coaching, sports science and sports medicine services. The aim is to improve performance by the tiny fractions that

The nation expects the best of its world-class athletes.

can make the difference between a medal and a mere placing.

Money available to the individual sports federations from the government, the pools promoters and, potentially, a new national lottery, also has a role to play in this preparation.

But as Britain lines up in Barcelona it will be in a unique position. Britain alone raises its money for Olympic participation independently whilst, at the same time, paying back tax on its sponsorship revenue.

Over the 1988 Olympic campaign that cost the BOA almost £1 million in lost earnings. How much did it cost our individuals' attempts to beat the best in the world. And in Barcelona...?

WHAT IS THE BRITISH OLYMPIC ASSOCIATION?

The BOA is a non profit-making organistion composed of an elected representative of each of the Olympic sports – winter and summer. The Association enters Britain's sportsmen and women for the Games and takes care of all the detail needed to take the team to the Games and manage their participation.

Within the BOA, the sports representatives sit on the National Olympic Committee which decides matters of Olympic policy - for instance how the team is selected.

But sport is also a fast-moving business. So the BOA employs a team of professional managers, coaches, medical and clerical staff to carry out its policy.

The BOA raises its entire funding independently from the public, industry and corporate sponsors. Its base is in London.

Each Olympic Games it runs an Appeal. For 1992 this has been led by Lord Alexander of Weedon QC, Chairman of National Westminster Bank. Nat West employees countrywide have also become deeply involved in local fund-raising.

The British Olympic Association is extremely grateful to the following companies and organisations for their sponsorship of the 1992 Olympic Team:

3M UK Ltd

Adidas (UK) Ltd

Bausch & Lomb UK Ltd

Brooke Bond Foods Ltd

Brother International Europe Ltd

Budget Rent a Car International Inc

Burger King (UK) Ltd

Carlsberg Brewery Ltd

Coca Cola (Great Britain) Ltd

EDS United Kingdom Ltd

EMS

Fisons Plc

Glaxo Pharmaceuticals UK Ltd

Grant Thornton

Harcros Timber & Building Supplies Ltd

Kodak Ltd

MD Foods (UK) Ltd

Mars Confectionery Ltd

Minet Holdings Plc

National Westminster Bank Plc

Next Retail Ltd

Olympus Sport International Ltd

Panasonic Europe Ltd

Philips Electronics

Procter & Gamble Ltd

Rank Xerox (UK) Ltd

Richard Ellis

Ricoh UK Ltd

Royal Mail

Salisburys Ltd

Seat UK Ltd

Seiko UK Ltd

Sportsworld Travel

Stylo Matchmakers International Ltd

Texaco Ltd

Thorn EMI UK Rental Ltd

Time Magazine

Time Management International

Visa International

ARCHERY

D **ES SEZ** In the 1900 Games one of the events was "Shooting the Live Pigeon".
Archery as a sport has developed considerably since those days, not least to the advantage of pigeons.
It had a long absence from the Games - from 1920 to 1972 - but has been ever present since.
The men's individual gold medal has been won by an American on four out of the five occasions since
its re-introduction. However the current world champion is an Australian, Simon Fairweather.
The Koreans had a wonderful time in this sport when they were hosts four years ago. They took both the
men's and women's team events and Kim Soo-Nyung was the women's individual gold medallist. Last year she
won the world championship for the second time and will be a hot favourite to retain her Olympic title.
Way back in 1908 William Dod of Great Britain won a gold medal and his sister Lottie took a silver. Tennis
buffs may recognise that last name because it was the same Lottie Dod who won the Wimbledon singles title
on no fewer than five occasions. She was also a winner of the British women's golf championship and played
hockey for England. Can you imagine what she could earn from sport today?
Britain broke their 80-year medal drought with a splendid bronze medal for Steve Hallard, Richard
Priestman and Leroy Watson in the men's team event in Seoul.

FACT-O-FILE

Archery owes its origins to the use of bows as hunting weapons.
But Robin Hood - or even Kevin Costner in last year's block-
buster film of the same name - might have found the sheriff of
Nottingham easier prey with today's sophisticated competition
bows.

Olympic archers use bows which often retain some wood but can
incorporate glass or carbon-fibre. They also carry stabilisers - the
bits which visibly stick out - as well as sighting aids.

At Barcelona's "Camp de Tir Amb Arc", in the Vall D'Hebron dis-
trict, the world's leading archers will line up in men's and women's
individual and team events. Each nation can enter one team per
event and a maximum of three competitors in the individual
disciplines.

RULES AND TOOLS

There is no limit to the length or weight of bows used for
Olympic competition. Instead bows are regulated by "drawing
strength".

At the outset of competition archers unleash 36 arrows at each of
four targets placed at different distances: 70m, 60m, 50m and 30m
(for women) and 90m, 70m, 50m and 30m (for men). The 32
highest-scoring individuals then go forward to a knock-out tournament where the number of competitors is reduced by half in each
round until the final. At this elimination stage each archer only has
12 arrows to shoot at the 70m target.

Nations for the team event are selected on the basis of scores in
the individual events. Only the 16 top-scoring teams go into an
elimination series where each team member shoots nine arrows at
a 70m target.

The target itself has ten zones depicted in five different colours.
Each colour has an inner and outer ring scoring differently. From
the centre outwards - inner to outer - the points scored are: gold
(10 or 9); red (8 or 7); blue (6 or 5); black (4 or 3); white (2 or 1).

THE OLYMPIC ROUTE

Only the best have made it to Barcelona. FITA (The International
Archery Federation) set some tough qualifying standards. The men
had to record a competition score of 1200 points and the women

1150 in at least two international events between January 1991
and March 25, 1992.

BARCELONA BRITS

Britain's 1988 Olympic bronze medal-winning men's team are once
more in contention in 1992. So, too, are Joanne Edens, neé Franks,
and Pauline Edwards. Franks - a former maths student from
Thetford - came seventh in the individual event four years ago.

How am I doing so far?

ARCHERY

Edwards, meanwhile, is a former world bronze medallist. The British team failed to make the medals at the 1991 world championships in Kracow, Poland, in August. They will be looking to atone that pain in Spain.

DATA-BANK

VENUE:
Camp de Tir Amb Arc in the Vall d'Hebron area, 6 km from the Vila Olimpica.
Competition area is 14,600m^2 and holds 4,000 spectators.

EVENTS:
Individual Grand Round (m+w)
Team Grand Round (m+w)

1988 CHAMPIONS:
Singles	(m)	Jay Barrs (USA)
	(w)	Kim Soo-Nyung (KOR)
Team	(m)	Korea
Team	(w)	Korea

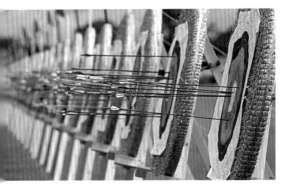

Five colours but ten scoring zones.

Joanne Franks in action in Seoul.

SCHEDULE	
LOCAL SPANISH TIME. SUBTRACT ONE HOUR FOR BRITAIN.	
JULY	
31	70m & 60m qualification (w)	09.00
	90m & 70m qualification (m)	13.00
AUGUST	
1	50m & 30m qualification (w)	09.00
	50m & 30m qualification (m)	13.00
2	70m last 32 & last 16 (w)	09.00
	70m q/f, s/f & **F** (w)	13.00
3	70m last 32 & last 16 (m)	09.00
	70m q/f, s/f & **F** (m)	13.00
4	Team event 70m last 16, q/f, s/f and **F** (w)	09.00
	Team event 70m last 16, q/f, s/f and **F** (m)	13.00

VALL D' HEBRON
⇨ **Details** Capacity 4,000
Distance to Olympic Village 11.5
Distance to CMC 8.5

MEDALS

	Men			Women			
Country	G	S	B	G	S	B	Total
United States	7	5	4	5	3	3	27
France	6	10	6	-	-	-	22
Belgium	10	5	3	-	-	-	18
Korea	1	1	-	3	1	2	8
USSR	-	1	2	1	2	2	8
Great Britain	1	1	1	1	1	1	6
Finland	1	-	1	-	-	1	3
Japan	-	1	1	-	-	-	2
Netherlands	1	-	-	-	-	-	1
China	-	-	-	-	1	-	1
Indonesia	-	-	-	1	-	-	1
Poland	-	-	-	-	1	-	1
Sweden	-	1	-	-	-	-	1
Italy	-	-	1	-	-	-	1
	27[1]	25	19[2]	10	10	9[3]	100

[1] Only a gold medal awarded in two 1920 events.
[2] No bronze medals in one 1900 and six 1920 events.
[3] No bronze medal in 1904 team event.

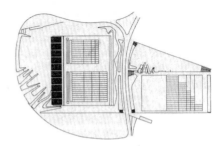

DID YOU KNOW...? The oldest archery gold medallist was Rev Galen Spencer aged 64 years and 2 days in 1904 and the youngest was Seo Hyang Soon of Korea winning in 1984 aged 17 years and 34 days.

Archery is governed internationally by **FITA**, the International Archery Federation, and in Great Britain by the Grand National Archery Society.

THE UK's № 1 SPORTS RETAILER

Meeting the needs of tomorrow's stars.

OFFICIAL SUPPLIERS OF
WINTER SPORTS CLOTHING
TO THE 1992
BRITISH OLYMPIC TEAM

Over 200 stores nationwide.

OFFICIAL SPONSORS OF THE
1992 BRITISH OLYMPIC TEAM

D **ES SEZ** This is the centrepiece of the Olympic Games and the exploits of the great performers here are usually the ones that live most vividly in the memory. Forty-three Olympic track and field titles in all will be won, 24 by men and 19 by women.

Men's track and field, of course, played a prominent part in the Games right from the first modern Olympics in 1896. Women's athletics, however, were included for the first time in 1928 with only five events. It stayed that way until 1972 when the 1500m was introduced and then in 1984 a women's 3000m and marathon were added. In Seoul, women competed over 10,000m for the first time in the Games.

Now women's track events are more or less compatible with the men's - except that their sprint hurdles are over 100m as opposed to 110m, and the 3000m race corresponds to the men's 5000m. Women still do not compete in steeplechase but of course they do at 400m hurdles, which was once described as the "man-killer" event.

Most of the Olympic heroes in track and field are household names but you may not have heard of Ray Ewry. His great feats were in the discontinued "standing" events of long-jump, high-jump and triple-jump and his record of twelve gold medals has never been beaten. These medals, however, were won a long time ago - back in 1904 and 1908.

Linford Christie: a commanding performer.

The great Paavo Nurmi of Finland won twelve medals, nine of them gold, between 1920 and 1928. He established another record in 1924 by winning five gold medals at the one Games. They were in the 1500m, the 5000m (run just an hour-and-a-half later) and three discontinued events - the 3000m team race, the individual cross-country and the team cross-country.

The most individual titles won at a Games is four by Alvin Kraenzlein in 1900 with wins in 110m hurdles, long-jump, 60m dash and the 200m hurdles. The two latter events were discontinued. The legendary Jesse Owens won four titles in Berlin in 1936. Three were at individual events - 100m, 200m and long-jump. His fourth came in the sprint relay.

In 1984 Carl Lewis, probably the greatest current athlete, equalled that record in the same four events.

Four years ago, Lewis defended his long-jump title successfully and ended up with the gold medal in the 100m under infamous circumstances after Ben Johnson had been disqualified for drug abuse. Lewis therefore goes into these Games needing three gold medals to equal Nurmi's haul of nine.

The achievement is certainly not beyond him. Last year at the Tokyo world championships he won the 100m and was part of the winning sprint relay team and was pipped in the long-jump only by that staggering performance by Mike Powell who broke the 23 year old world record of Bob Beamon.

Other famous Olympians of recent times include another Finnish distance runner, Lasse Viren. He is the only man to achieve a double 'double', winning the 5000m and 10,000m in both 1972 and 1976. He also finished fifth in the marathon in Montreal, thereby just missing the target set by the great Czech runner Emil Zatopek, who won all three distance races in 1952.

In the 1980 Games the Ethiopian soldier Miruts Yifter did the 'double' of 5000m and 10,000m In 1976 Cuba's long-striding Alberto Juantorena stunned the world with the amazing double of 400m and 800m. The former Soviet Union's Valeriy Borzov won both 100m and 200m, the last man to complete that feat until Carl Lewis came along.

Other 'Greats':

Ed Moses two gold and a bronze at 400m hurdles. He would surely have had a third gold but for the American boycott of the 1980 Games.

Abebe Bikila (Ethiopia) and Waldemar Cierpinski (GDR), both with two marathon gold medals.

Viktor Sanayev (URS) - three gold and one silver in triple jump between 1968 and 1980.

And Al Oerter (USA) - gold medallist in discus at four Games running from 1956 to 1968.

In the women's events three competitors have won four gold medals. Holland's Fanny Blankers-Koen won all hers in 1948 (100m, 200m, 100m hurdles and 4x100m relay). The other two women to achieve this feat – but at separate Games, are Australia's Betty Cuthbert in 1956 and 1964, and Barbel Wockel (Eckert) (GDR) in 1976 and 1980.

Australia's Shirley Strickland won a record seven medals between 1948 and 1956, of which three were gold. Irena Szewinska (Kirzenstein) equalled that between 1964 and 1976. Tatanya Kazankina (URS) preceded Seb Coe in winning and retaining a 1500m title - 1976 and 1980. Ulrike Meyfarth (FRG) won the women's high-jump at the Munich Games in 1972 at the age of 16 years and 123 days. Twelve years later she won gold again at the Los Angeles Games.

Two big stars of the last Olympics were sisters-in-law. Florence Griffith-Joyner was the sprint sensation, winning gold medals at 100m, 200m and 4x100m. She added a silver medal at 4x400m. Jackie Joyner-Kersee won both the long-jump and heptathlon.

Britain are still third in the all-time Olympic track and field medals table behind the USA and the former Soviet Union. However, in modern times, medal-winning has become a much tougher proposition. The nadir came in 1976 when Britain's only track medal was a bronze in the men's 10,000m won by Brendan Foster.

In 1980, with the Americans and others absent, things looked up. Allan Wells just missed the sprint double, taking the 100m in Britain's first win at the event since Harold ('Chariots of Fire') Abrahams in 1924. Wells was within 2/100ths of a second behind Italy's Pietro Mennea in the 100m. Also in Moscow, Sebastian Coe and Steve Ovett were at their peak.

Ovett won the 800m and was third in the 1500m. Coe won the 1500m and was second at 800m. Daley Thompson won the decathlon and four years on both Coe and Thompson retained their titles. Britain's third gold in Los Angeles came from javelin thrower Tessa Sanderson. Her great rival, Fatima Whitbread, took the silver in Seoul. Britain had a somewhat disappointing Games for athletics there. No golds.

Even so, apart from Whitbread's silver, there were also medals for Linford Christie (silver 100m), Peter Elliott (silver 1500m), Mark Rowland (bronze steeplechase), Colin Jackson (silver 110m hurdles and men's 4x100m silver), Yvonne Murray (bronze 3000m) and Liz McColgan (silver 10,000m).

The Tokyo world championships of August 1991 showed where the current strengths lie. Americans, Carl Lewis (100m), Michael Johnson (200m) Antonio Pettigrew (400m) and Greg Foster (110m hurdles) took the sprint gold medals but apart from the marathon which went to Japan, all the other men's track events were won by athletes from the African continent. The Kenyans took four gold medals - Billy Konchella (800m), Moses Kiptanui (3000m steeplechase), Yobes Ondeiki (5000m) and Moses Tanui (10,000m). Algeria's Nouredine Morceli won the 1500m and his countrywoman, Hassiba Boulmerka, took the women's equivalent.

Katrin Krabbe of Germany was the golden-girl of the meeting, winning the sprint 'double', eclipsing the favourite Merlene Ottey of Jamaica in both races. Her career, though, has since lost some of its glitter. Barring injury most of the other stars are likely to play a prominent role in Barcelona.

For Britain, the strongest gold medal favourite is Liz McColgan. She became 10,000m silver medallist in Seoul and world champion at the Tokyo Championships. Sally Gunnell won silver in Tokyo at 400m hurdles. She has good medal chances. And Peter Elliott, Roger Black, Kriss Akabusi and Steve Backley are all world class. As ever Britain will also have good medal hopes in both men's relays.

But the story of the Games would, undoubtedly, be if Daley Thompson, decathlon god medallast in 1980 and 1984, could return to reclaim his title. That would be one of the all-time great come-backs.

ATHLETICS

Peter Elliott grimaced but got silver.

FACT-O-FILE

Times change. Other things appear more constant.

In 1896 the first 100m final of the modern Olympic era was won in 12 seconds. Almost 100 years later - at the 1991 world athletics championships in Tokyo - four men crossed the line in the 100m final in less than 10 seconds.

An American, Thomas Burke, won the 100m in 1896 in Athens. And Americans start as favourites for the 100m medals at the 1992 Olympic Games in Barcelona. Can they go faster? And can Carl Lewis, the reigning Olympic and world champion, find the pace for a hat-trick of Olympic titles?

Track and field athletics, whatever the outcome, will provide the main focal point of the Games. Its participants come in all shapes and sizes and its breadth and variety of competition adds to the spectator attraction.

The popularity of athletics at the Games stretches back to Ancient Greece where the foot races were a crowd favourite. The earliest recorded races were in 776BC but they may well have been in existence long before that. These races, of course, were only for men. Women were forbidden from even spectating.

In more modern times Britain took the lead in organised athletics competitions and development. The first athletics club, Necton Guild, was formed in 1817. And the inaugural English National championships took place in 1866. Over the next few decades America took over as the dominant international force.

In Barcelona, Britain and the USA will once more be strong nations. So, too, will the athletes from the Unified Team - all from the former Soviet Union - as well as the might of the combined new German team. But the African nations will also lead the way in many track events.

Britain, meanwhile, compete in Barcelona without their longtime team manager Les Jones. This popular figure will be sadly missed after his death from a heart-attack during the European Indoor championships in Genoa in March.

RULES AND TOOLS

Each nation can enter a maximum of three competitors per event and one team in each relay provided they have all met the worldwide qualifying standards set by the International Amateur Athletic Federation between January 1991 and 10 July 1992. If a nation does not have any suitably qualified athletes, it can still enter one person per event in order to gain experience and as an incentive.

Competition for the leading athletes of the world will take place at the Estadi Olimpic at Montjuic - a stadium which positively oozes atmosphere. Perched at the top of a hill overlooking the city and the sea, the stadium was originally built in 1929 but refurbished for the Games. This involved preserving the original facade but lowering the interior ground level by 10m to allow for extra seating capacity.

The 400m, 8-lane track has a Sportflex surface and there are several ancillary jumping and throwing competition areas. Spare a thought, though, for the marathon runners. They will be forced to climb the stadium hill at the end of a gruelling effort bringing them the classic 26 miles and 385 yards from the start at Mataro. So, too, will the race walkers who will compete along the Passeig de la Zona Franca on the seafront.

Competitors in the field events are not permitted to use their own equipment – with the exception, that is, of the pole vaulters' poles. The Organising Committee will supply various stocks of shots, discus, hammer and javelins.

ATHLETICS

DATA-BANK

VENUE:
Track and field events - Edstadi Olimpic, Montjuic area, 6km from Vila Olimpica. Holds 65,000 spectators.
Marathon - From Mataro (30 km from Barcelona) to the Estadi Olimpic.
Walking - On a 2,000m circuit in the Passeig de la Zona Franca (1.5km from Estadi Olimpic), starting on the circuit and finishing in the Estadi Olimpic.

EVENTS:

Field:	Track:
High jump (m+w)	100m (m+w)
Long jump (m+w)	200m (m+w)
Triple jump (m)	400m (m+w)
Pole vault (m)	800m (m+w)
Shot put (m+w)	1,500m (m+w)
Discus (m+w)	3,000m (w)
Javelin (m+w)	5,000m (m)
Hammer (m)	10,00m (m+w)
Road:	100m hurdles (w)
10km walk (w)	110m hurdles (m)
20km walk (m)	400m hurdles (m+w)
50km walk (m)	3,000 m steeple (m)
Marathon (m+w)	4x100m relay (m+w)
Combined:	4x400m relay (m+w)
Decathlon (m)	
Heptathlon (w)	

The men's javelin underwent a technical change in 1986 because the top throwers were reaching distances beyond the bounds of safety. So, the javelin was re-designed with a different centre of gravity to reduce distances. The women's javelin remains the same.

In all three throwing competitions the contestants are given three attempts to qualify for the final. No-throws are recorded if a discus, shot or hammer thrower steps out of the circle or if a javelin thrower steps over the line or if the implement falls outside the designated landing area..

Technique for the high jump was revolutionised in the sixties by a man called Dick Fosbury. He converted the top jumpers from a style where they straddled the bar by swinging one leg over it first – to a style which involved a take-off on one foot backwards over the bar. This is called a Fosbury flop and is now used by all the leading competitors. If a jumper registers three failed attempts at a particular height they are out of the competition.

In the long jump and triple jump (the hop, step and jump) there are three qualifying jumps followed by a final. The pole-vaulters now use fibre-glass poles and inflated landing pits - a gigantic technological leap from the hickory or bamboo poles and sand pits.

Meanwhile, on the track, starting blocks are compulsory in the sprint events because they are wired to detect a false start. Competitors will have several eliminating rounds to complete before reaching the final. All the hurdles races involve ten barriers but they are of differing heights ranging from 106.7 cms in the 110m men's event to 76.2cm in the women's 400m. Athletes can knock down any number of hurdles without being disqualified but they cannot trail their leg around the hurdle.

The 800m and 1500m are considered "middle distance" events. In the 800m competitors start in lanes and then "break" to the inside

after the first bend. For the 1500m they line up on a simple curved starting line. In the steeplechase the barriers are 0.914m high placed at 77.7m intervals. There is also a water jump after the third barrier which requires a different hurdling technique.

A marathon course (26miles 385 yards) equates to 42.19km. Most physical problems for athletes occur after the 17 mile marker when, they come up against a fatigue barrier known as the "wall".

Relays traditionally bring the Games to a close. Smooth changing of the baton is essential. In the sprint relays this must happen within a 20m designated "box" with the incoming athlete given a 10m area to get up to speed before the box. The changeovers in the 4 x 400m relay can prove more chaotic - particularly as the race breaks from lanes on the second leg to the inside of the track.

Multi-events are the most demanding competitions on the

1988 CHAMPIONS:

				Time or Result
100m	(m)	Carl Lewis	(USA)	9.92
	(w)	Florence Griffith-Joyner	(USA)	10.54
200m	(m)	Joe Deloach	(USA)	19.75
	(w)	Florence Griffith-Joyner	(USA)	21.34
400m	(m)	Steve Lewis	(USA)	43.87
	(w)	Olga Bryzguina	(URS)	48.65
800m	(m)	Paul Ereng	(KEN)	1:43.45
	(w)	Sigrun Wodars	(GDR)	1:56.10
1500m	(m)	Peter Rono	(KEN)	3:35.96
	(w)	Paula Ivan	(ROM)	3:53.96
3000m	(w)	Tatyana Samolenko	(URS)	3:26.53
5000m	(m)	John Ngugi	(KEN)	13.11.70
10,000m	(m)	Brahim Boutaib	(MAR)	27:21.46
	(w)	Olga Bondarenko	(URS)	31:05.21
100m hurdles	(w)	Jordanka Donkova	(BUL)	12.38
110m hurdles	(m)	Roger Kingdom	(USA)	12.98
400m hurdles	(m)	Andre Phillips	(USA)	47.19
	(w)	Debbie Flintoff-King	(AUS)	53.17
3000m steeplechase	(m)	Julius Kariuki	(KEN)	8:05.51
4x100m relay	(m)		(URS)	38.19
	(w)		(USA)	41.98
4x400m relay	(m)		(USA)	2:56.16
	(w)		(URS)	3:15.17
High jump	(m)	Guennadi Avdeenko	(URS)	2.38m
	(w)	Louise Ritter	(USA)	2.03m
Long jump	(m)	Carl Lewis	(USA)	8.72m
	(w)	Jackie Joyner-Kersee	(USA)	7.40m
Triple jump	(m)	Hristo Markov	(BUL)	17.61m
Pole vault	(m)	Sergey Bubka	(URS)	5.90m
Shot put	(m)	Ulf Timmermann	(GDR)	22.47m
	(w)	Natalya Lisovskaya	(URS)	22.24m
Discus	(m)	Jurgen Schult	(GDR)	68.82m
	(w)	Martina Hellmann	(GDR)	72.30m
Javelin	(m)	Tapio Korjus	(FIN)	84.28m
	(w)	Petra Felke	(GDR)	74.68m
Hammer	(m)	Serguei Litvinov	(URS)	84.80m
20km walk	(m)	Jozef Pribilinec	(TCH)	1h 19:57
50km walk	(m)	Viacheslav Ivanenko	(URS)	3h 38.29
Marathon	(m)	Gelindo Bordin	(ITA)	2h 10:32
	(w)	Rosa Mota	(POR)	2h 25:40
Decathlon	(m)	Christian Schenk	(GDR)	8488pts
Heptathlon	(w)	Jackie Joyner-Kersee	(USA)	7291pts

⌔ ATHLETICS

Liz McColgan: exhausted superlatives and opponents alike.

MEDALS	Men			Women			
Country	G	S	B	G	S	B	Total
USA	244	186	151	32	21	11	645
USSR	34	35	40	30	20	34	193
Great Britain	43	57	40	4	20	12	176
Germany (FRG)	11	29	34	12	18	15	*119
Finland	47	32	29	-	2	-	110
GDR	14	14	14	24	23	21	110
Sweden	19	24	42	-	-	3	88
Australia	6	9	11	11	8	11	56
France	7	20	19	3	1	3	53
Italy	13	7	18	3	4	2	47
Canada	9	9	16	2	5	6	47
Poland	9	7	4	6	8	7	41
Hungary	6	13	16	3	1	2	41
Kenya	10	8	6	-	-	-	24
Romania	-	-	1	9	8	6	24
Greece	3	9	12	-	-	-	24
Czechoslovakia	6	7	3	3	2	2	23
Jamaica	4	9	4	-	1	3	21
New Zealand	7	1	7	1	-	1	17
South Africa	4	4	4	1	1	1	15
Netherlands	-	2	5	5	2	1	15
Japan	4	4	6	-	1	-	15
Bulgaria	1	-	1	2	6	4	14
Norway	3	2	7	-	1	-	13
Cuba	2	5	1	1	1	2	12
Belgium	2	6	3	-	-	-	11
Ethiopia	5	1	4	-	-	-	10
Brazil	3	2	5	-	-	-	10
Switzerland	-	6	2	-	-	-	8
Ireland	4	1	-	-	-	-	5
Mexico	3	2	-	-	-	-	5
Morocco	2	1	1	1	-	-	5
Argentina	2	2	-	-	1	-	5
Portugal	1	1	1	1	-	1	5
Austria	-	-	-	1	1	3	5
Tunisia	1	2	1	-	-	-	4
Denmark	1	1	1	-	-	1	4
Trinidad	1	1	2	-	-	-	4
Chile	-	1	-	-	1	-	2
India	-	2	-	-	-	-	2
Tanzania	-	2	-	-	-	-	2
Yugoslavia	-	2	-	-	-	-	2
Estonia	-	1	1	-	-	-	2
Latvia	-	1	1	-	-	-	2
Spain	-	1	1	-	-	-	2
Taipei	-	1	-	-	-	1	2
China	-	-	1	-	-	1	2
Panama	-	-	2	-	-	-	2
Philippines	-	-	2	-	-	-	2
Luxembourg	1	-	-	-	-	-	1
Uganda	1	-	-	-	-	-	1
Haiti	-	1	-	-	-	-	1
Iceland	-	1	-	-	-	-	1
Ivory Coast	-	1	-	-	-	-	1
Senegal	-	1	-	-	-	-	1
Sri Lanka	-	1	-	-	-	-	1
Barbados	-	-	1	-	-	-	1
Djibouti	-	-	1	-	-	-	1
Nigeria	-	-	1	-	-	-	1
Turkey	-	-	1	-	-	-	1
Venezuela	-	-	1	-	-	-	1
	533	535	524	155	157	154	2058

* Includes 1 gold, 11 silver and 3 bronzes won by GDR athletes in combined German teams 1956-64.

programme. Daley Thompson used to refuse to give an interview to any journalist who could not name the ten events over the two days of the decathlon in their correct sequence. The female version, the heptathlon (which replaced the pentathlon in 1980), consists of seven events over two days. Both are a mixture of track and field disciplines and are designed to test the all-round athlete.

OLYMPIC ROUTE

The International Amateur Athletics Federation set minimum qualifying standards for all track and field events in Barcelona to be acheived between 1 January 1991 and 10 July 1992.

MONTJUIC

⇨ **Details** Capacity	70,021
Distance to Olympic Village	6
Distance to CMC	1

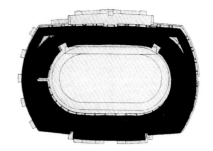

SCHEDULE	
LOCAL SPANISH TIME. SUBTRACT ONE HOUR FOR BRITAIN.	
JULY	
31	100m rd 1 **(w)**	09.30
	Shot put q **(m)**	10.00
	100m rd 1 **(m)**	10.30
	800m rd 1 **(w)**	11.30
	Javelin q **(w)**	18.00
	100m rd 2 **(w)**	18.05
	High jump q **(m)**	18.10
	Shot put **F (m)**	19.00

ATHLETICS

SCHEDULE	
JULY continued	
800m rd I (m)	19.05
20km walk F (m)	(start) 19.15
Javelin q (w)	19.30
3000m rd I (w)	19.50
10,000m 1st heat (m)	20.50
10,000m 2nd heat (m)	21.35
AUGUST	
1 Heptathlon (100m hurdles)	09.30
400m rd I (m)	10.00
Heptathlon (high jump)	10.30
400m hurdles rd I (w)	11.00
Hammer q (m)	11.30
Hammer q (m)	13.00
Heptathlon (shot put)	17.30
Triple jump q (m)	18.00
100m semi-final (w)	18.15
Marathon F (w)	(start) 18.30
100m semi-final (m)	18.35
800m rd 2 (m)	18.55
Javelin F (w)	19.20
800m semi-final (w)	19.25
100m F (w)	19.45
100m F (m)	20.00
Heptathlon (200m)	20.15
10,000m ht I (w)	21.15
10,000m ht 2 (w)	21.55
2 110m hurdles rd I (m)	10.00
Heptathlon (long jump)	10.05
Discus q (w)	10.30

SCHEDULE	
AUGUST continued	
400m rd I (w)	11.00
Discus q (w)	11.30
Hammer F (m)	16.30
High jump F (m)	18.00
Heptathlon (javelin)	18.25
110m hurdles rd 2 (m)	18.30
400m rd 2 (m)	19.15
400m hurdles semi-final (w)	19.50
Heptathlon (javelin)	20.00
800m semi-final (m)	20.20
800m F (w)	20.45
3000m F (w)	21.00
Heptathlon (800m)	21.303
3 Discus q (m)	09.30
200m rd I (w)	09.35
200m rd I (m)	10.20
Discus q (m)	11.00
1500m rd I (m)	11.15
400m hurdles rd I (m)	12.15
110m hurdles semi-final (m)	18.00
200m rd 2 (w)	18.20
200m rd 2 (m)	18.45
Discus F (w)	18.50
400m rd 2 (w)	19.10
Triple jump F (m)	19.30
400m semi-final (m)	19.35
10km walk F (w)	(start) 19.50
110m hurdles F (m)	20.05
3000m steeple rd I (m)	20.45

Relay celebrations in Tokyo.

This is our third Olympic Games running.

This year adidas will again be the official clothing suppliers to the British Olympic Team. In fact, we've been at the Olympics since Jesse Owens won four Berlin gold medals sporting Adi Dassler shoes.

This Summer there'll be a whole range of Olympic clothing available in the shops. So you can team up with adidas for our third Olympic Games running, jumping and throwing.

adidas

ATHLETICS

Steve Backley: world javelin record holder in early '92.

	400m hurdles **F (w)**	21.30
	10,000m **F (m)**	21.45
4	Rest Day	
5	Decathlon (100m)	09.00
	Pole vault q **(m)**	09.30
	1500m rd 1 **(w)**	10.00
	Decathlon (long jump)	10.05
	100m hurdles rd 1 **(w)**	10.45
	Decathlon (shot put)	11.45
	Shot put q **(w)**	17.30
	Decathlon (high jump)	17.35
	100m hurdles rd 2 **(w)**	18.00
	200m semi-final **(w)**	18.30
	Long jump q **(m)**	18.35
	200m semi-final **(m)**	18.50
	400m hurdles semi-final **(m)**	19.15
	Discus **F (m)**	19.30
	400m semi-final **(w)**	19.35
	3000m steeple semi-final	19.50
	400m **F (m)**	20.20
	200m **F (w)**	20.35
	200m **F (m)**	20.50
	800m **F (m)**	21.05
	Decathlon (400m)	21.20
	5000m rd 1 **(m)**	21.45
6	Decathlon (110m hurdles)	09.00
	High jump q **(w)**	09.30
	Decathlon (discus) q	10.00
	Long jump q **(w)**	10.05
	Decathlon (discus) q	11.30
	Decathlon (pole vault)	13.00
	Decathlon (javelin)	17.30

	100m hurdles semi-final **(w)**	18.00
	400m **F (w)**	18.30
	Decathlon (javelin)	18.45
	Long jump **F (m)**	18.50
	400m hurdles **F (m)**	19.00
	1000m semi-final **(w)**	19.20
	1500m semi-final **(m)**	19.45
	100m hurdles **F (w)**	20.10
	5000m semi-final **(m)**	20.30
	Decathlon (1,500m)	21.15
7	50km walk **F (m)**	(start) 07.30
	4x100m relay rd 1 **(m)**	09.30
	Javelin q **(m)**	09.35
	4x100m relay rd 1 **(w)**	10.00
	4x400m relay rd 1 **(m)**	10.30
	Javelin q **(m)**	10.45
	Pole vault **F (m)**	17.00
	Shot put **F (w)**	18.55
	4x100m relay semi-final **(w)**	19.00
	Long jump **F (w)**	19.15
	4x100m relay semi-final **(m)**	19.30
	4x400m relay rd 1 **(w)**	20.00
	4x100m relay semi-final **(m)**	20.30
	3000m steeple **F**	21.00
	10,000m **F (w)**	21.20
8	High jump **F (w)**	18.30
	Javelin **F (m)**	18.55
	4x100m relay **F (w)**	19.00
	4x100m relay **F (m)**	19.20
	1500m **F (w)**	19.50
	1500m **F (m)**	20.15
	5000m **F (m)**	20.40
	4x400m relay **F (w)**	21.25
	4x400m relay **F (m)**	21.40
9	Marathon **F (m)**	(start) 18.30

DID YOU KNOW...? That Ray Ewry - twelve times gold medallist in 1900 and 1908 - turned to athletics despite being a polio victim as a child.

In 1948 Micheline Ostermeyer of France took two golds and a bronze in the shot, discus and long jump respectively. She was also a concert pianist. Emile and Dana Zatopek of Czechoslovakia became the first husband and wife team to win gold medals on the same day at the 1952 Games. Both of them were born on the same day.

Athletics is governed internationally by the International Amateur Athletics Federation and in Great Britain by the British Athletic Federation.

BADMINTON

DES SEZ There is a potential nightmare ahead of the BBC's badminton commentator at these Olympics. She's called Sarwendah Kusumawardhani and she comes from Indonesia. She is almost certain to be in the medal reckoning, too, because she is very good.

This sport enters the Olympic arena for the first time in 1992, although it was a demonstration sport at the Munich Games in 1972. It is interesting to note that as recently as the Los Angeles Olympics eight years ago there were no 'racket-type' sports. Now badminton joins tennis and table tennis.

At the Commonwealth Games, English players usually dominate. But Britain will have a much tougher task at Olympic level. The sport is hugely popular in the Far East and China can boast both the men's and women's world individual champions in Zhao Jianhua and Tang Jiuhong respectively. Indeed that country has won the men's championship four times in a row and the women have gone one better.

Britain's singles hopes - more of the doubles later - include Darren Hall the 1990/1991 European Champion; Fiona Smith, the current Commonwealth champion, back after having a baby, and Helen Troke. A bronze medal or two would be an excellent achievement.

Badminton's introduction to the Olympics has come too late for London-based Dane, Morten Frost, who was the world's leading player for some time. Last year he announced his retirement.

FACT-O-FILE

Badminton begins to write its own Olympic history in Barcelona. That will leave an alphabetic juggling act for the historians and statisticians.

No doubt they will tune their skills to the task just as the people behind the names - many exotic and far-eastern - conjure with the shuttle on court at great speed to mesmerise crowds and opponents alike.

China and the Republic of Korea are the leading nations. But Malaysia and Indonesia are not far behind. Denmark, Sweden, England and the Netherlands lead the way in Europe. Although players from the former Soviet Union are beginning to make their mark.

RULES AND TOOLS

96 men and 96 women will take part in four separate knock-out events - men's and women's singles and doubles - at the Pavello de la Mar Bella in Barcelona.

In the men's singles and both doubles events this sport is played over the best of three games (or sets) up to 15 points. The women's singles is played up to 11 points.

But if the points score is equal at the later stages of any game then a new series of scoring rules called "setting" come into play. For instance at 13-13 in the doubles the players will be asked if they wish to "set to 5 points", meaning they will continue to contest the match with the winner being the pair which first scores five points.

Courts are marked out for singles and doubles play. The singles court uses the full length but a narrower width than the doubles court. The doubles service court is also shorter and fatter than its singles counterpart.

Players can only score a point when they are serving. If the receiver moves before the server strikes the shuttle a "fault" is called. And the server's racket head must be below the level of their hand as they serve. During play the object is to force the shuttle to the floor on the opponent's side of the net - or force them to make an error. Rallies can be fast and furious as players jockey into an attacking position.

Modern badminton rackets have to be strong, flexible and light. Wood has long been ousted as a material in favour of carbon fibre and other alloys and composites. The top shuttles, however, are still made from natural feathers and come in different speeds.

They are discarded if they become damaged. And you may often see players testing shuttle flight between points or asking for the speed to be changed if playing temperatures or conditions change dramatically.

The All England championships, held every year at Wembley, are the "Wimbledon tennis" of badminton. They are joined by the world championships, world cup and grand prix as the premier events.

Indonesia's Ardy Wiranata and Susi Susanti will be strong medal contenders. So, too, will Zhao Jianhua and Tang Jiuhong - the reigning world singles champions. Korean men Park Joo Bong and Kim Moon Soo must be favourites for the men's doubles. And their compatriots, together with the Chinese, will be hard to beat in the women's doubles. It will be a struggle for any Europeans to reach the podium. Britain's best hope of a medal must come in that event from the strong pairings of Gill Clark and Julie Bradbury or Gill Gowers and Sara Sankey.

In the men's singles, hopes will be pinned on Darren Hall, Anders Neilsen and Steve Butler and, for the women, on Helen Troke, Jo Muggeridge and Fiona Smith.

OLYMPIC ROUTE

Qualifying for the Olympic Games was decided on ranking points earned from tournament matches around the world up to April 30, 1992.

DATA-BANK

VENUE:
Pavello de la Mar Bella in the Parc de Mar area, next to the Vila Olimpica. The Pavello holds 4,000 spectators.

The competition area measures 49x22m and contains three courts.

EVENTS:
Singles and doubles (m+w)

BADMINTON

Fiona Smith: multi-Commonwealth medallist.

DID YOU KNOW...? *Zhao Jianhua, current world champion, was nicknamed "Zhao Kapow!" when he first emerged on the world circuit in 1985 because of his dynamic, attacking style.*
Gillian Clark has represented her country more times than any other member of the British Olympic team in Barcelona. She has over 110 caps.

Badminton is governed internationally by the International Badminton Federation and in Britain by the British Badminton Olympic Committee

JULY

28	Singles & doubles rd 1 (m+w)	10.00-14.00
	Singles & doubles rd 1 (m+w)	17.00-21.00
29	Singles & doubles rd 2 (m+w)	10.00-14.00
	Singles & doubles rd 2 (m+w)	17.00-21.00
30	Singles rd 2 (m+w)	
	Doubles rd 1 (m+w)	10.00-14.00
	Singles rd 2 (m+w)	
	Doubles rd 2 (m+w)	17.00-21.00
31	Singles rd 3 (m+w)	
	Doubles rd 2 (m+w)	10.00-14.00
	Singles rd 3 (m+w)	
	Doubles rd 2 (m+w)	17.00-21.00

AUGUST

1	Singles rd 3 (m+w)	
	Doubles rd 2 (m+w)	10.00-14.00
	Singles rd 3 (m+w)	
	Doubles rd 2 (m+w)	17.00-21.00
2	Singles qtr-**finals** (m+w)	
	Doubles qtr-finals (m+w)	10.00-14.00
	Singles qtr-finals (m+w)	
	Doubles qtr-finals (m+w)	17.00-21.00
3	Singles semi-final (m+w)	
	Doubles semi-final (m+w)	10.00-14.00
	Singles semi-final (m+w)	
	Doubles semi-final (m+w)	17.00-21.00
4	1 Singles **F** (m+w)	
	1 Doubles **F** (m+w)	11.00-15.00

PAVELLO MAR BELLA

▷ **Details** Capacity	4,000
Distance to Olympic Village	-
Distance to CMC	-

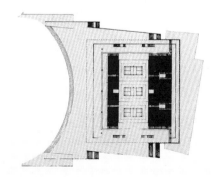

BASEBALL

DES SEZ This sport has been trying to get into the Olympics for years and has finally made it. A gold medal for the United States absolutely guaranteed you would think. However, the problem for them is that their major league players will not be eligible.

In this way the sport is rather like boxing where for example the Evander Holyfields and Mike Tysons cannot compete. It is interesting to note that basketball has taken a different route - their top professionals will be allowed to play in Barcelona. The vagaries of world sport!

So the favourites for the gold medal will be the Cubans. They are the 1990 world and Pan-American champions. It is actually the national sport in that country, too.

Other top teams will come from Nicaragua, the world championship runners-up, Japan and Italy. Although Britain were the first world amateur baseball champions back in 1938, no British team has ever qualified for any of the six demonstration competitions at previous Olympics and they have not made it this time either. In fact the British team has been relegated from Europe's top eight so they were nowhere near.

Eight countries will compete for the medals: the top four from the Pan-American Games, the top two from the Asian Games, Italy, who are the European champions and the host nation, Spain.

By the end of the Games we might just have a clue about 'earned run averages' and what 'top of the inning' means.

FACT-O-FILE

The uninitiated could be forgiven for thinking that the "Minnesota Twins" were, perhaps, the first identical twins to win Olympic medals in the same race. Think again. "They" are the name of a team which once won the world series in one of America's most popular sports. baseball.

Baseball conjures up America, the movies, the top pros and big money. But now it also means the Olympic Games even if the top American professionals are barred from entering.

American baseball has been a demonstration sport no fewer than six times. In 1912 an American team started it all when they beat Sweden 13-3. Since then, the sport has been a popular part of the Olympic fringe. In 1956, for example, 114,000 people watched an American services team beat Australia 11- 5. More recently, the USA won the 1988 8-nation demonstration event by beating Japan in the final - a result which reversed Japan's own win in 1984 in Los Angeles.

RULES AND TOOLS

Compared with its English equivalent of rounders, baseball can appear complex. The pitch is divided between a diamond-shaped in-field containing the four "bases" at each corner and a larger out-field. Two teams of nine players compete over nine innings with the aim of winning by scoring the most runs.

A run is scored when a batter successfully hits the ball safely and runs around the four bases to get "home" before the ball is fielded by the opponents. This does not have to be achieved in one movement. A batter can make any number of bases before stopping and waiting for the next batter on his team to hit the ball and run.

An innings means that both teams are given a chance to bat. A team remains in bat and can keep scoring until three of its members are "out". Batters are either caught-out, run-out or struck-out when the pitcher beats them with three successful throws over the "plate" or strike zone.

A batter scores only when he gets "home". However he can also score more runs if he brings preceding batsmen, already on bases,

home with him. Very rarely he can score a "grand-slam homer". This happens if all three bases are "loaded" and the hit is good enough to bring four people home including the batter.

If the score is level after nine innings, extra innings are played until one team pulls ahead at the end of an innings.

Competition in Barcelona will be under International Baseball Association rules. Eight teams, with a maximum of 20 players per squad, will contest a preliminary stage in which all the teams play each other.

The top four teams will then go through to cross-over semi-finals followed by a final and a bronze medal play-off for the winners and losers respectively.

DATA-BANK

VENUE:
Estadi de Beisbol de l'Hospitalet, holding 7,000 spectators. It is 12km from the Vila Olimpica.
Estadi de Beisbol de Viladecans, holding 4,000 spectators. It is 19km from the Vila Olimpica.

EVENTS:
A men's tournament with eight teams.

SCHEDULE	
LOCAL SPANISH TIME. SUBTRACT ONE HOUR FOR BRITIAN.	

JULY

26-29 & 31	Preliminaries Viladecans and Hospitalet	

AUGUST

1 & 2	Preliminaries Viladecans and Hospitalet	
4	Semi-final (L'Hospitalet)	16.00
	Semi-final (L'Hospitalet)	21.00
5	Final (3rd-4th) (L'Hospitalet)	16.00
	Final (L'Hospitalet)	21.00

Baseball is governed internationally by the International Baseball Association and in Britain by the British Baseball Federation.

 Probably the best sponsor in the world.

BASKETBALL

DES SEZ There are a batch of Olympic silver medals lying in a Munich bank vault that have never been collected. They belong to the United States team that finished runners-up to the Soviet Union in the Games of 1972. The two countries were involved in one of the most infamous basketball matches of all time.

America had gone into the final with an unbeaten Olympic record from 61 matches during which they had collected every gold medal available since 1936. This time, however, they lost 51-50 to the Soviet Union in the final.

The Americans protested that they had been cheated by extra time being played when they were ahead. The protests were long and loud, but in vain and so those medals remain in that bank vault. The Americans felt that the medals they actually won vanished around Soviet necks. In fact the now former Soviet Union are the current Olympic champions, too, with the USA relegated to the bronze medal position behind Yugoslavia four years ago.

This time, though, there will dramatic changes. For the first time, professional players from the NBA will be allowed to compete for the United States. Look out for famous names like Michael Jordan and Larry Bird. The Baltic States, Croatia and Slovenia have all attempted to qualify on their own. The break-up of Yugoslavia will mean the challenge from that particular country may well have disappeared and the Soviet team will almost certainly be reduced in strength by the independence of the Baltic states. Traditionally, many top Soviet players came from those countries.

Get your money on the Americans for the men's gold medal. And probably the women, too. Britain's men will be taking part in the pre-qualifying tournament just before the Games. Four years ago they missed going to Seoul by just two places. Britain's women's team have not qualified.

FACT-O-FILE

Ordinary mortals - and particularly women - might quiver at the thought of growing more than seven feet tall. But those kinds of heights are a valuable tool of the trade for the world's leading basketball players.

Four years ago Arvidas Sabones of the former Soviet Union's gold medal-winning team equalled the record height of seven feet four inches. His compatriot in the 1976 and 1980 women's team, Iuliana Semenova, was seven feet, one and three-quarter inches.

So the bed extensions are already on order for the Olympic Village.

Modern basketball has spread a long way since it was invented in 1891 by Dr James Naismith to add variety to sport lessons at Springfield College, Massachusetts, USA.

Peach boxes were suspended from the ten-foot high balcony of the college gymnasium. Later nets and backboards were added and the twentieth century version was born - a version played from Kamchatka to Alaska via Asia, Australasia, Africa, Europe and South America.

RULES AND TOOLS

There are five players per team on court at any one time in this sport. But a team can also have up to seven substitutes. Players can take as many steps as they like whilst "dribbling" the ball but only one when holding it.

Teams must shoot within 30 seconds of winning possession and they must move the ball from back to front court within ten seconds. These rules make the game fast-moving. Its excitement is measured by the fact that basketball is now one of the most popular sports in the world.

Teams score by shooting the ball into the hooped baskets. Two points can be scored from free play three points from long range and one from a free throw.

Twelve teams will take part in the men's tournament in Barcelona, divided into two preliminary groups of six. The top eight teams will go forward to knock-out quarter-finals, followed by semis, a final and a bronze medal play-off.

Meanwhile the women's tournament will consist of eight teams again divided into two equal preliminary groups. Only the top four teams will go into cross-over semi-finals and a final. The losing semi-finalists will play again to decide the bronze medal winner.

THE OLYMPIC ROUTE

Teams have qualified for Barcelona on world championships results and qualifying tournament.s.

MEDALS	Men			Women			
Country	G	S	B	G	S	B	Total
United States	9	1	1	2	1	-	14
USSR	2	4	3	2	-	1	12
Yugoslavia	1	3	1	-	1	1	7
Brazil	-	-	3	-	-	-	3
Bulgaria	-	-	-	-	1	1	2
Uruguay	-	-	2	-	-	-	2
Canada	-	1	-	-	-	-	1
France	-	1	-	-	-	-	1
Italy	-	1	-	-	-	-	1
Korea	-	-	-	-	1	-	1
Spain	-	1	-	-	-	-	1
China	-	-	-	-	-	1	1
Cuba	-	-	1	-	-	-	1
Mexico	-	-	1	-	-	-	1
	12	12	12	4	4	4	48

BASKETBALL

USA v USSR in 1988.

DATA-BANK

VENUE:
Palau d'Esports de Badalona, 10km from the Vila Olimpica.
12,500 spectators.
The single playing surface measures 28m x 15m.

EVENTS:
One men's and one women's tournament.

1988 CHAMPIONS:
Men   USSR
Women -   USA

SCHEDULE

LOCAL SPANISH TIME. SUBTRACT ONE HOUR FOR BRITAIN.

JULY

26-31	Preliminaries (m+w)	09.30-22.30

AUGUST

1 & 3	Preliminaries (w)	11.00-22.00
2	Preliminaries (m)	09.30-22.30
4	Classification (m)	09.30
		11.30
	Qtr finals (m)	14.30
		16.30
		20.30
		22.30
5	Classification (w)	11.00
	Semi-final (w)	13.00
	Classification (w)	20.00
	Semi-final (w)	22.00
6	Places 11-12 (m)	09.00
	Places 9-10 (m)	11.00
	Classification (m)	14.30
	Semi-final (m)	16.30
	Classification (m)	20.30
	Semi-final (m)	22.30
7	Places 5-6 (w)	11.00
	Places 3-4 (w)	13.00
	Places 7-8 (w)	20.00
	Final (w)	22.00
8	**Final 5-6 (m)**	11.00
	Final 3-4 (m)	13.00
	Final 7-8 (m)	20.00
	Final (m)	22.00

BADALONA
➡️ **Details** Capacity   12,500
     Distance to Olympic Village   8
     Distance to CMC   11

DID YOU KNOW...?

Basketball is governed internationally by **FIBA**, the International Amateur Basketball Federation, and in Great Britain by the **British and Irish Basketball**

⚡ BOXING

D **ES SEZ** A number of Olympic boxing stars have gone on to become the biggest names in international sport of all time. Muhammed Ali(Cassius Clay), George Foreman, Joe Frazier, Floyd Patterson and the Spinks brothers, Leon and Michael,all became world heavyweight champions.

Evander Holyfield was an Olympic bronze medallist and Lennox Lewis,who at the time of writing has his sights on the world championships, was super-heavyweight gold medallist in Seoul.

But the stars have not been confined to the heavier men. Sugar Ray Leonard and Mark Breland were gold medallists who went on to hit the jackpot in the professional ring. Another all-time great Olympian was Teofilo Stevenson of Cuba who won three titles at heavyweight and might have added a fourth but for his country's withdrawal from the 1984 Games.

Laslo Papp of Hungary won three gold medals, one at middleweight and two at light-middleweight. But the first man to retain an Olympic title was British middleweight Harry Mallin who won in 1920 and 1924.

Ingamar Johansson of Sweden, another man to become world heavyweight champion was a finalist at the 1952 Games. He had to wait nearly thirty years to receive his silver medal which had been withheld for alleged 'inactivity' in his final bout.

Cassius Clay won his gold medal at light-heavyweight in the Rome Olympics of 1960 but he was not the recipient that year of the Val Barker award which goes to the best boxers at the Games. That honour fell to Italy's Nino

Richie Woodhall took bronze for Britain in Seoul.

Benvenuti who went on to become middleweight champion of the world. Britain's most successful Games since the war were the Melbourne Olympics in 1956 when Terry Spinks won the gold medal at flyweight and Dick McTaggart became lightweight champion.

There has been only one British gold medal winner since then - Chris Finnegan, middleweight champion in 1968. At the following Games in Munich, Britain's Alan Minter was desperately unlucky to come away with only a silver. Impartial observers were convinced he had beaten West Germany's Dieter Kottysch in the final. He did not get the decision which even Kottysch disagreed with. The two boxers have remained friends down the years. Minter was another who went on to become a world champion. Britain has claimed one bronze medal in each of the last four Games - the most recent by Richie Woodhall at light-middleweight in Seoul.

The Cubans have boycotted the last two Olympics but they plan to be present this time and put your money on them for around four gold medals. Roberto Bolado, who is the top super-heavyweight in the world and Felix Savon, who has been world amateur heavyweight champion three times are amongst their stars. The Unified Team, and the Americans who always peak well for the Games, will be the main threat to Cuban domination. But medallists can come from almost anywhere in the world.

The sport has been put under the microscope by the IOC for medical reasons and boxing desperately needs to avoid the kind of disgraceful behaviourh shown by South Korean officials in Seoul when a decision went against them, or the kind of bad decisions that have sometimes appeared politically based in the past. Nonetheless, some of the best Olympic action will come from the boxing ring.

There are twelve weight categories from light-flyweight to super-heavyweight. For the first time, boxers have had to pre-qualify to take part.

BOXING

FACT-O-FILE

Boxing was part of the Ancient Games. Contestants squared up with simple leather straps on their hands. Since then it has been a sport of raw and enduring popularity.

But boxing's history has also been one of turmoil. At times the sport has been rendered illegal. At others there has been no agreement over format, rules, fees and material.

In Britain boxing has passed through several phases including fairground entertainment and bare-knuckle fights. Gloves were first used in 1743. The late 1700s and early 1800s formed the era of the prize-fight. Then the sport faced a period of illegality in all its forms.

In 1865 the Marquess of Queensberry drew up his famous rules to standardise competition and ensure fairness and safety. The Amateur Boxing Association - governing the sport in Britain - was set up in 1880.

Modern boxing suffers from a plethora of professional ruling organisations each with their own set of world titles. But Olympic - and, therefore, amateur - boxing is more cohesive.

RULES AND TOOLS

The sport in Barcelona will take place under AIBA (International Amateur Boxing Association) rules. Each nation can enter one boxer per weight category of between 17 and 32 years of age, as long as they have pre-qualified.

Bouts are of three rounds each lasting three minutes with a one-minute rest between rounds. Boxers can win on points or a knock out. They wear gloves, headguards (introduced in 1984) and gumshields. The Olympic competition will take place at the Pavello Club Joventut in Badalona.

Boxing referees do not judge bouts but are there to control the action and stop a boxer if he is outclassed or hurt of if the rules are broken. He can also call for a standing count for a boxer who is under pressure.

Boxers can only score points by landing punches with the correct part of their gloves on the target area. This includes the opponent's torso above the waist as well as the front and side of the head. Five ringside judges, all of a different nationality, score the bouts. There can be no draw.

DATA-BANK

VENUE:
Pavello Club Joventut, Barcelona, 10km from the Vila Olimpica.
The competition area has one ring and holds 5,500 spectators.

EVENTS:

Light flyweight	up to 48kg
Flyweight	over 48kg up to 51kg
Bantamweight	over 51kg up to 54kg
Featherweight	over 54kg up to 57kg
Lightweight	over 57kg up to 60kg
Light welterweight	over 60kg up to 63.5kg
Welterweight	over 63.5kg up to 67kg
Light middleweight	over 67kg up to 71kg
Middleweight	over 71kg up to 75kg
Light heavyweight	over 75kg up to 81kg
Heavyweight	over 81kg up to 91kg
Super heavyweight	over 91kg

Boxing is one of the few Olympic sports where there is no seeding when the tournament draw is made. It is possible, therefore, for the two main favourites to meet in the first round

1988 CHAMPIONS:

Light flyweight	Ivailo Hristov (BUL)
Flyweight	Kim Kwang-Sun (KOR)
Bantamweight	Kennedy McKinney (USA)
Featherweight	Giovanni Parisi (ITA)
Lightweight	Andreas Zuelow (GDR)
Light welterweight	Vyacheslav Janovski (URS)
Welterweight	Robert Wangila (KEN)
Light middleweight	Park Si-Hun (KOR)
Middleweight	Henry Maske (GDR)
Light heavyweight	Andrew Maynard (USA)
Heavyweight	Ray Mercer (USA)91kg
Super heavyweight	Lennox Lewis (CAN)

SCHEDULE

LOCAL SPANISH TIME. SUBTRACT ONE HOUR FOR BRITAIN.

JULY

26	First rounds	13.00
		19.00
31	Second rounds	13.00
		19.00

AUGUST

1 & 2	Last 16	13.00
		19.00
3 & 4	Qtr-finals	13.00
		20.00
6 & 7	Semi-final (6)	13.00
8 & 9	**Finals** (6)	10.00

PAVELLO CLUB JOVENTUT

⇨ **Details** Capacity	5,500
Distance to Olympic Village	8
Distance to CMC	11

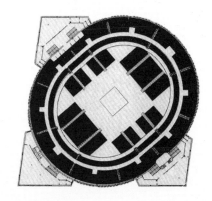

BOXING

OLYMPIC ROUTE

The Barcelona boxers have all qualified through a series of ranking tournaments around the world. This is the first time boxers have had to qualify for the Games and it should mean a reduction in numbers competing.

BARCELONA BRITS

Ex-Guyanan Adrian Carew - now transformed by deed poll to Adrian Dodson - could be the only boxer to make waves for Britain in 1992. He is tipped for a medal after fighting for Guyana in the 1988 Games.

Britain has won at least a bronze in the last five Games.

MEDALS — Men

Country	G	S	B	Total
United States	45	20	28	93
USSR	14	19	18	51
Great Britain	12	10	20	42
Poland	8	9	25	42
Italy	14	12	13	39
Cuba	12	8	5	25
Argentina	7	7	9	23
German (FRG)	4	10	9	23
South Africa	6	4	9	19
Romania	1	8	10	19
Hungary	9	2	4	15
Canada	3	5	6	14
GDR	5	2	6	13
Korea	3	5	5	13
France	3	4	6	13
Finland	2	1	10	13
Bulgaria	3	2	6	11
Yugoslavia	3	2	6	11
Mexico	2	3	6	11
Denmark	1	5	5	11
Sweden	-	5	6	11
Kenya	1	1	5	7
Ireland	-	2	5	7
Czechoslovakia	3	1	2	6
Norway	1	2	2	5
Venezuela	1	2	2	5
Australia	-	2	3	5
North Korea	1	2	1	4
Belgium	1	1	2	4
Netherlands	1	-	3	4
Uganda	-	3	1	4
Puerto Rico	-	1	3	4
Japan	1	-	2	3
Chile	-	1	2	3
Ghana	-	1	2	3
Nigeria	-	1	2	3
Philippines	-	1	2	3
Thailand	-	1	2	3
Colombia	-	-	3	3
New Zealand	1	1	-	2
Cameroon	-	1	1	2
Algeria	-	-	2	2
Turkey	-	-	2	2
Estonia	-	1	-	1
Bermuda	-	-	1	1
Brazil	-	-	1	1
Dominican Rep	-	-	1	1
Egypt	-	-	1	1
Guyana	-	-	1	1
Mongolia	-	-	1	1
Morocco	-	-	1	1
Niger	-	-	1	1
Pakistan	-	-	1	1
Tunisia	-	-	1	1
Uruguay	-	-	1	1
Zambia	-	-	1	1
	168	168	274[1]	610

[1] From 1952 both losing semi-finalists have been awarded a bronze medal.

Looking for an opening.

DID YOU KNOW...? *Two bronze medals are awarded in each weight category in boxing so that potentially tired or damaged boxers are not forced into yet another bout.*

Boxing doctors use a mixture of 1/1000th adrenalin to control bleeding. Viewers may have thought they were witnessing a first ever when Korean Byun Jong-Il staged his sit-in protest in 1988 after losing. But Byun's compatriot Dong Kih Choh had done it all before 24 years earlier. In 1964 Dong refused to leave the ring for a full 51 minutes after a decision went against him.

Boxing is governed internationally by AIBA, International Amateur Boxing Association, and in Great Britain by the British Amateur Boxing Association.

CANOEING

DES SEZ Medals were first won in canoeing at the Berlin Games in 1936 and women took part for the first time in London in 1948. There are kayak races in which the competitors sit in the craft in normal fashion and the paddles used have two blades. And there are Canadian races in which the paddlers kneel and switch the one-bladed paddle from side to side. So races are designated K or C. A K2 race is for a kayak with two on board, a C1 is a race for Canadian canoe with one on board.

There are twelve Olympic titles to win in canoe racing. In addition, for only the second time (the last was at the Munich Games of 1972) there are slalom events. Four Olympic titles will be at stake here. In these events, the competitor is timed over the course - there are no head-to-head races as such.

Flatwater canoeing is a sport in which Britain has a poor Olympic record. The main reason is that British canoeists are better at slalom events which featured only in those Munich Games. Britain has produced world champions in these events in the past. In the flatwater canoe racing, medallists can come from anywhere but Germany was particularly strong in the kayak races at the last world championships. The former Soviet Union and Hungary won most medals in the Canadian-style races. If you are wondering whether canoeists or rowers are faster, the answer is that the rowers would nearly always have the edge. But in the Games, the canoe racers travel just half the rowers distance of 2000 metres.

FACT-O-FILE

Canoeing, of course, is a sport which owes its origins to an early form of human transport. The eskimos are credited with developing the kayak whilst the North American Indians perfected canadian-style canoes. But many cultures have records of similar craft.

The sport was popularised in Britain by John 'Rob Roy' MacGregor who organised the first recorded regatta on the Thames in 1867. By 1870 the American Canoe Association had been formed and the British version followed in 1887.

Canoeing's inaugural world championships were held in 1930. And the sport made its Olympic debut in 1936 for men and 1948 for women - having been a demonstration event in 1924.

SLALOM

Britons Gareth Marriott, Shaun Pearce and Richard Fox have all tasted major championship honours in their chosen discipline of slalom (sometimes called white-water) canoeing. Fox, in particular, has been several times world champion.

All three will be hoping to convert their expertise into Olympic medals at La Seu d'Urgell on 1st and 2nd August. The Spaniards have built an artificial course for the occasion in the mountains of the Parc del Segre.

Each nation is allowed to enter three boats in the slalom. And competition is over two runs with only the better of the two counting towards the result. There are both Canadian and Kayak events.

The course is 340m long with a drop of 6.5m and a maximum water flow rate of 15m3/second. Canoeists have to negotiate a series of gates defined by poles hanging over the course. Time penalties are added for any missed gates where a competitor does

Slalom canoeists search for control in fast water.

CANOEING

GB sprint canoe squad in training for Barcelona.

not succeed in getting at least their head and shoulders between the poles without touching them.

SPRINT

Whilst the slalom exponents seek control of fast water, sprint canoeists covet raw speed.

Ideal canoe-racing conditions are on the type of man-made regatta course which exists for the Games at Castelldefels. Sprint canoeists can reach speeds of over 20kmph.

Modern racing canoes are highly specialised and completely enclosed apart from a small cockpit in which the canoeist sits. Foot rests and contoured seats provide control of the boat, along with a foot-operated rudder.

DATA-BANK

VENUE:
Flat Water Canoeing
Canal Olimpic de Castelldefels, 18km from Barcelona and 21km from the Vila Olimpica.Competition canal is 1,200m long, 118m wide and 3.5m deep. There is room for 8,000 spectators.

Slalom Canoeing
Parc del Segre in La Seu d'Urgell,
180km from Barcelona and 187km from the Vila Olimpica.
Slalom canal has a competition section 340m long, its width varying between 5m and 15m. Maximum flow rate is 15m3/sec, and the total difference in level is 6.5m. There is room for 5,000 spectators.

EVENTS:

Flat water		Slalom	
k1 500m	(m+w)	k1	(m+w)
k2 500m	(m+w)	c1	(m)
k4 500m	(w)	c2	(m)
k1 1000m	(m)		
k2 1000m	(m)		
k4 1000m	(m)		
c1 500m	(m)		
c1 1000m	(m)		
c2 1000m	(m)		

As its rowing counterpart, canoe racing consists of heats, a semi-final and a final. There is a repechage system which gives heat losers a second chance to qualify.

Competition in Barcelona will be in both canadian and kayak disciplines. Canoeists from the former East Germany are likely to do well. So are the Americans and New Zealanders.

BARCELONA BRITS

Britain was disappointed with its showing in Seoul in 1988. The squad was plagued with injuries prior to the Games despite a good showing at the pre-Olympics in 1987.

Britain has always been strong in canoe marathon racing. But this is not an Olympic discipline.

Britain are whitewater specialists.

CANOEING

1988 CHAMPIONS:

Men

k1	500m	Zsolt Gyulay (HUN)
k1	1000m	Greg Barton (USA)
k2	500m	New Zealand
k2	1000m	United States
K4	1000m	Hungary
c1	500m	Olaf Heukrodt (GDR)
c1	1000m	Ivan Klementyev (URS)
c2	500m	USSR
c2	1000m	USSR

Women

k1	500m	Vania Guecheva (BUL)
k2	500m	GDR
k4	500m	GDR

MEDALS

Country	Men			Women			Total
	G	S	B	G	S	B	
USSR	21	11	7	8	2	3	52
Hungary	7	16	12	-	3	4	42
FRG	6	8	8	2	6	2	32
GDR	8	5	8	6	2	1	30
Romania	8	8	8	1	1	3	29
Sweden	11	7	2	2	1	-	23
France	1	5	10	-	-	-	16
Canada	3	5	3	-	1	1	13
Austria	3	4	4	-	1	1	13
USA	4	2	3	-	1	1	11
Denmark	2	3	4	1	-	1	11
Czechoslovakia	6	3	1	-	-	-	10
Bulgaria	1	1	4	1	2	1	10
Finland	3	2	3	1	-	-	9
Netherlands	-	1	3	-	2	2	8
New Zealand	5	1	1	-	-	-	7
Poland	-	2	3	-	-	2	7
Yugoslavia	2	2	1	-	-	-	5
Australia	-	2	3	-	-	-	5
Norway	1	1	2	-	-	-	4
Spain	-	2	2	-	-	-	4
Italy	-	1	-	-	-	-	1
	92	92	92	22	22	22	342

LA SEU D'URGELL

⊳ **Details** Capacity 5,000
  Distance to Olympic Village 152
  Distance to CMC 145

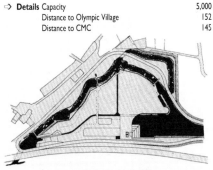

SCHEDULE	
LOCAL SPANISH TIME. SUBTRACT ONE HOUR FOR BRITAIN.	

AUGUST

Flatwater

3	500m k1, c1, k2, c2 heats (m+w)	09.00-11.50
	500m k1, c1, k2, c2 repechages (m+w)	17.00-19.00
4	1000m k1,c1,k2,c2,k4 heats (m)	
	500m k4 heats (w)	09.00-11.50
	1000m k1,c1,k2,c2,k4 repechages (m)	
	500m k4 repechages (w)	17.00-19.00
5	500m k1, c1, k2, c2 semi-finals (m+w)	09.00-11.30
6	1000m k1,c1,k2,c2,k4 semi-finals (m)	
	500m k4 semi-finals (w)	09.00-11.30
7	500m k1, c1, k2, c2 **F** (m+w)	09.00-11.30
8	1000m k1,c1,k2,c2,k4 **F** (m)	
	500m k4 **F** (w)	09.00-11.30

Slalom

1	K1 **F** (w)	
	C1 **F** (m)	09.00
2	K1 **F** (m)	
	C2 **F** (m)	09.00

CASTELLDEFELS

⊳ **Details** Capacity 8,000
  Distance to Olympic Village 21.5
  Distance to CMC 19

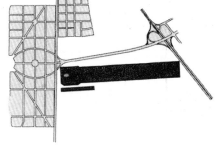

DID YOU KNOW...? Britons Ivan Lawler and Graham Burns won the International Fair Play Award in 1991. In a canoe-marathon race they were in the lead when their main rivals from Denmark developed rudder trouble.

The British duo stopped to help out and then both crews resumed the race with the Danes winning a close finish.

The most successful canoeing competitor ever at the Games was Gert Frederiksson of Sweden with six gold, one silver and one bronze medal between 1948 and 1960 - all in kayaks.

Canoeing is governed internationally by the International Canoe Federation (FIC) and in Great Britain by the British Canoe Union.

The BOC Group is proud to be a supporter
of the 1992 British Olympic Team.

THE BOC GROUP

CYCLING

D **ES SEZ** The Los Angeles Games of 1984 saw the first 'low profile' bicycles with solid graphite-sheeted wheels for better drag-coefficient (to cut down air-resistance) and aerodynamic headgear for the riders. That is all now commonplace and you, or your children, may well own the kind of machinery that was a technological breakthrough only eight years ago.

Advanced machines like these are used on the track. On the road, machines are of a more traditional design. Men's cycling has been part of every modern Olympics except one (1904) and Britain stands third in the all-time medal winners list. However, success has been hard to come by in recent Games.

Britain's last medal, a bronze, was won in the team pursuit in 1976 and you have to go back twenty years to find the last won by an individual - a bronze won by Alan Jackson in the road race at the Melbourne Games. Before that Reg Harris won two silver medals in 1948 and was still good enough to win the British sprint title in 1974 at the age of 54. This time there are possible medal hopes in the individual pursuit with national champion Chris Boardman and in the team pursuit again.

The former Soviet Union and the new Germany are likely to compete as top dogs in this sport. In Bill Huck and Jens Fiedler the Germans have two of the best sprint cyclists in the world. Spain who do well in professional cycling - Miguel Indurain for example has been a recent winner of the Tour de France - rarely have success in Olympic Games. They do currently have a top track star in Jose Moreno. But he will be returning after a suspension for testing positive for steroids.

Women's cycling was first introduced in 1984 with just a road race. A sprint title was added in 1988 and this time there will also be an individual pursuit. One of the names to look out for is Ingrid Haringa of Holland. A former speed skater, she shot to prominence at the last world championships. Holland won a gold medal in women's cycling in Seoul.

Of the seven titles contested in men's cycling in the last Olympics, only one went outside either the Soviet Union or East Germany. Dan Frost of Denmark won the points race.

Look out for the 1,000m sprint - the 'blue riband' of the sport on the track. Two cyclists compete over three races against each other, over three laps. Riders often play 'cat and mouse' often slowing to a dead stop. An event for brain as well as brawn. Not to mention nerves of steel.

Low profile and high tech on the track.

CYCLING

FACT-O-FILE
In Seoul, four years ago, Britain's Eddie Alexander came within a whisker of a bronze medal in the men's sprint, taking fourth place on a tense night at the track.

Maria Blower, meanwhile, was the most successful British woman with a sixth place in the road race. In that same race all three of the British women finished in the top 12. And Louise Jones, current Commonwealth champion, was seventh in the sprint.

Any repeat of those performances in Barcelona may prove difficult. Top riders, particularly amongst the men, are constantly lost to the professional ranks. Equally, Britain does not have a covered velodrome for year-round training - although Manchester Olympic Bid Committee plans might change that in time for 1996.

Whatever the British success rate, cycling as a sport is sure to be an Olympic winner once more. It is fast and exciting. And, on the track the tactical battles can prove fascinating.

RULES AND TOOLS
Each country can enter a maximum of 20 cyclists for the Olympic Games in 1992 - 15 men and 5 women. This permits each nation one competitor per track event, three per road race and four per road and track team events. All of them must be at least 17 years old.

On both the road and track, the time trial races mean just that - the fastest recorded time wins. The time of the third cyclist to cross the line decides the team events.

For the pursuit races - whether team or individual - cyclists start on opposite sides of the track and try to overtake their opponents. If they do not succeed the fastest time wins.

Finally, in the points races cyclists score points on each lap if they cross the line first with double points available for the last lap.

VELODROM
⇨ **Details** Capacity 6,400
Distance to Olympic Village 10.5
Distance to CMC 9.5

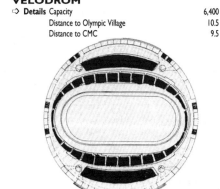

Team GB on the 100km time trial circuit.

THE OLYMPIC ROUTE
Cyclists are selected for the Games by their individual national federations with the sanction of the National Olympic Committee.

DATA-BANK

VENUES:
Track events:- Velodrom in the Vall d'Hebron area, 10.5km from the Vila Olimpica. The stands hold 6,400 spectators. The track is built of wood, with a circumference of 250m and is 7m wide.

Individual road events:- Circuit de Sant Sadurni d'Anoia, 45km from Vila Olimpica.

100km team trial:- Circuit de l'A-17, starting and finishing at the Circuit Automobilistic de Catalunya, 25km from the Vila Olimpica.

EVENTS:
Track events:	Road events:
1km time trial **(m)**	Ind. road race 194.40km **(m)**
Sprint **(m+w)**	Ind. road race 81km **(w)**
Ind. pursuit **(m+w)**	100km team trial **(m)**
Team pursuit **(m)**	
Ind. points race **(m)**	

1988 CHAMPIONS:
1km time trial **(m)**	Alexandr Kiritchenko (URS)
1000m sprint **(m)**	Lutz Hesslich (GDR)
4000m ind. pursuit **(m)**	Gintoautas Umaras (URS)
4000m team pursuit **(m)**	USR
Ind. points race **(m)**	Dan Frost (DEN)
Road race team trial **(m)**	German Democratic Rep.
Ind. road race **(m)**	Olaf Ludwig (GDR)
Sprint **(w)**	Erika Saloumae (URS)
Ind. road race **(w)**	Monique Knol (HOL)

SCHEDULE
LOCAL SPANISH TIME.SUBTRACT ONE HOUR FOR BRITAIN

JULY

26	100km team time trial **F (m)**	09.00-13.30
	Ind. road race **F (w)**	17.30-20.00
27	Ind pursuit elim rd 1 **(m)**	18.00-19.45
	1km time trial **F (m)**	20.00-21.45
28	Sprint elim rd 1 **(m+w)**	10.00-11.20
	Ind. pursuit elim rd 2 **(m)**	18.00-19.00
	Sprint elim rd 2 **(m+w)**	19.05-19.50
	Ind. points race elim rd 1 **(m)**	20.00-20.45
	Sprint repechage **(m+w)**	20.50-21.20
	Ind. points race elim rd 2 **(m)**	21.35-22.20
29	Ind. pursuit s/f **(m)**	18.00-18.15

SCHEDULE

JULY continued

29	Sprint elim rd 3 (m)	18.20-18.40
	Sprint q/f (w)	18.40-18.55
	Sprint repechages (m)	18.55-19.10
	Sprint q/f (w)	19.10-19.25
	Ind. pursuit **F** (m)	19.30-19.40
	Sprint q/f (m)	20.00-20.15
	Sprint q/f (possible tie break) (w)	20.15-20.30
	Sprint q/f (m)	20.30-20.45
	Sprint q/f (possible tie break) (m)	20.50-21.00
30	Team pursuit elim rd 1 (m)	18.00-20.20
	Ind. pursuit elim rd 2 (w)	20.20-21.00
	Sprint s/f (m+w)	21.10-21.30
	Sprint s/f (m+w)	21.30-21.50
	Team pursuit q/f (m)	21.50-22.20
	Ind. pursuit q/f (w)	22.20-22.45
	Sprint s/f (possible tie break) (m+w)	22.45-23.00
31	Team pursuit s/f (m)	18.00-18.30
	Ind. pursuit s/f (w)	18.30-18.40
	Sprint Final 1st heat (m+w)	18.50-19.00
	Sprint Final 5-8 (m&w)	19.00-19.05
	Sprint Final 2nd heat (m+w)	19.05-19.15
	Sprint F (possible tie break) (m+w)	19.20-19.30
	Team pursuit **F** (m)	20.00-20.10
	Ind. pursuit **F** (w)	20.30-20.35
	Ind. points race (50km) **F** (m)	21.00-22.10

AUGUST

2	Ind. road race **F** (m)	08.30-14.15

DID YOU KNOW...? Christa Rothenburg Luding of the former German Democratic Republic won a women's cycling sprint silver at the Olympic Games in Seoul in 1988. But Christa had earlier taken gold in the 1000m speed skating in Calgary in that same year to add to a 500m skating gold won in 1984. She was also world cycling sprint champion in 1986.

Tandem races were last seen in the Olympic Games in 1972. Now there are no "bicycles made for two" in the Games.

Four Swedish brothers - Gosta, Sture, Erik and Tomas - took the silver medal in the road team time trial in 1968. Nothing like keeping it in the family!

Cycling is governed internationally by **FIAC**, the International Amateur Cyling Federation, and in Great Britain by the British Cycling Federation.

MEDALS	Men			Women			
Country	G	S	B	G	S	B	Total
France	27	15	20	-	-	-	62
Italy	26	14	6	-	-	-	46
Great Britain	8	21	14	-	-	-	43
USA	10	9	12	1	1	1	34
FRG	6	11	12	-	1	1	31
USSR	10	4	8	1	-	1	24
Netherlands	8	11	4	1	-	-	24
Belgium	6	6	9	-	-	-	21
Denmark	6	6	7	-	-	-	19
GDR	7	5	4	-	1	-	17
Australia	5	6	4	-	-	-	15
Sweden	3	2	8	-	-	-	13
South Africa	1	4	3	-	-	-	8
Poland	-	5	3	-	-	-	8
Czechoslovakia	2	2	2	-	-	-	6
Switzerland	1	3	2	-	-	-	6
Greece	1	3	1	-	-	-	5
Austria	1	-	2	-	-	-	3
Canada	-	2	1	-	-	-	3
Norway	1	-	1	-	-	-	2
Jamaica	-	-	1	-	-	-	1
Japan	-	-	1	-	-	-	1
Mexico	-	-	1	-	-	-	1
	129	129	126*	3	3	3	393

* No bronzes in 1896 100km, 1972 road team trial and ind. road race.

Road race start '88 style. Britain's women all finished in top 12.

1.05 seconds faster, and he's back in the team.
Anything less, and he's back on the bench.

SEIKO

Official Timer of the Games of the XXV Olympiad

EQUESTRIAN

D ES SEZ Apart from some yachting and shooting events, this is the only current Olympic sport in which men and women compete together. No distinction is made between male and female horses either (or indeed neutered ones).

There are three distinct competitions - dressage, show-jumping and three-day eventing. Two of the three disciplines within eventing are dressage and show-jumping but they are quite different from the pure dressage and show-jumping competitions.

In the separate dressage competition, Britain has never won a medal, but can boast the oldest ever competitor. Lorna Johnstone was 70 years of age when she finished 12th in the 1972 Games. The sport is a sort of ballet for horses requiring the highest degree of co-ordination between horse and rider. It tests their ability in patterns of movement and is the direct outcome of the exercises taught in the early French and Italian riding academies.

In show-jumping, a familiar sport on our television screens, Britain has surprisingly never won an individual gold medal but Marian Cokes on Stroller in 1968 and Ann Moore on Psalm in 1972 both won silver. David Broome has won two bronze medals - 1960 and 1968 and is in contention once more for the team in Barcelona. Britain did win the team gold medal in 1952.

Eventing is a gruelling sport for both horse and rider. Both have to be complete all-rounders. They have to cope with both dressage and show-jumping and sandwiched between is the speed and endurance section (commonly known as cross-country) where the courses are long and the obstacles imaginative and fixed. Only Richard Meade, in 1972, has won an individual gold medal for Britain. But there have been three team golds. First in 1956 and then back-to-back in 1968 and 1972. Meade was in both. More recently, Virginia Holgate won an individual bronze in 1984. With Lucinda Green, Diana Clapham and Ian Stark, the British team won a silver medal that year.

At the last Games Virginia, now better known as Ginny Leng, won another individual bronze. Ian Stark finished ahead of her to take the silver and, along with Mark Phillips and Karen Straker, they took the team silver. Britain has high hopes of success again. But New Zealand's Mark Todd will be seeking his hat-trick of individual gold medals.

FACT-O-FILE

Chariot-racing provided horses with an introduction to the Olympic Games. That was back in Ancient Times.

Now horse-riding is the basis of all the modern Olympic equestrian disciplines in a sport which, on a worldwide basis, has a great variety and depth of competitive forms. Olympic riders have honed the skills used by generations of their ancestors for survival, farming, hunting, travel, battle and sporting pleasure.

The equestrian events - which appeared in the modern Games briefly in 1900 before reappearing permanently in 1912 - form one of the most colourful and exciting spectacles. They could also provide Britain once more with a fertile vein of medals.

RULES AND TOOLS

Each nation at the Games can enter a maximum of 14 riders and 22 horses across the three disciplines. Riders must be at least 18 years old and their horses at least seven years old. Barcelona's Real Club de Polo will play host to all the disciplines except the dressage and endurance test section of eventing.

Dressage riders, unlike the other two disciplines, aim to score maximum possible points. The show-jumpers and eventers, meanwhile, will be looking to avoid picking up penalty points.

A country can enter four horses for all three individual competitions. The three best scores then count towards the team result. However, in the show-jumping and dressage competions only a maximum of three competitors from one nation may go forward to the individual event.

Showjumping fences reach heights of 1.70m. Horses and riders are also asked to show their paces against the clock in the jump off.

Eventing, though, is probably the most complete test of all-round ability. Two days of dressage are followed hard by a steeple chase

Jo Turi slays the dragons.

EQUESTRIAN

course, two sections of roads and tracks and a cross country course; a total of around 26km. Finally, the contestants are asked to compete in a show-jumping contest.

THE OLYMPIC ROUTE
National Olympic Committees can only enter competitors who have a valid International Equestrian Federation (FEI) licence. Selection in Britain is based on performance at a series of international and national championships. There are also stringent veterinary controls.

BARCELONA BRITS
Show-jumping: David Broome could clock up his fifth Olympic Games for Britain in Barcelona if selected. He could be joined by Whitaker brothers, John and Michael. The former will compete if the owners of his horse, Henderson Milton, the current world cup winner, allow the horse to travel. He also has Dollar Girl to ride.

Dressage: Former world bronze medallist Jennie Loriston Clarke heads Britain's lists for this demanding event. Annie McDonald Hall, Laura Fry, Carl Hester, Richard Davison and Ferdi Alberg are also amongst the front runners for places.

Three-day event: Britain are the current European team champions and took all three individual medals at the same champi-

onships in 1991. Badminton winner, Rodney Powell, is out of contention because he has sold his horse. That leaves Ian Stark, Richard Walker, Ginny Leng, Karen Straker, Mary Thomson and Lorna Clarke to fight for team places.

MEDALS

Country	G	S	B	Total
Germany (FRG)	24	15	18	57
Sweden	17	8	14	39
France	11	12	9	32
United States	8	15	9	32
Italy	7	9	7	23
Great Britain	5	7	9	21
Switzerland	4	8	7	19
USSR	6	5	4	15
Belgium	4	2	5	11
Netherlands	5	3	1	9
Mexico	2	1	4	7
Poland	1	3	2	6
Australia	2	1	2	5
Denmark	-	4	1	5
Canada	1	1	2	4
New Zealand	2	-	1	3
Portugal	-	-	3	3
Spain	1	1	-	2
Austria	1	-	1	2
Chile	-	2	-	2
Romania	-	1	1	2
Czechoslovakia	1	-	-	1
Japan	1	-	-	1
Argentina	-	1	-	1
Bulgaria	-	1	-	1
Norway	-	1	-	1
Hungary	-	-	1	1
	103[1]	101	101[2]	305

[1] Two gold medals in 1900 high jump.
[2] no bronze in 1932 3-day team event.

DATA-BANK

VENUES:
Real Club de Polo, 8km from the Vila Olimpica - Individual dressage and jumping, and dressage and jumping in the 3-day event. Its stadium holds 16,000 spectators.
El Circuit d'Hipica, 49km from Vila Olimpica - Endurance test of the 3-day event.

EVENTS:
3-day event (ind. and team)
Dressage (ind. and team)
Show jumping (ind. and team)

Team silver for the eventers four years ago.

Ginny Leng on Master Craftsman.

EQUESTRIAN

⇨ **Details** Capacity 16,000
Distance to Olympic Village 8
Distance to CMC 4

1988 CHAMPIONS:

Three-day event		Mark Todd (NZL)
Three-day event	(Team)	FRG
Dressage		Nichole Uphoff (FRG)
Dressage	(Team)	FRG
Show-Jumping		Pierre Durand (FRA)
Show-Jumping	(Team)	FRG

SCHEDULE

LOCAL SPANISH TIME. SUBTRACT ONE HOUR FOR BRITAIN.

JULY

27	3-day event: dressage	08.30-13.30
		15.30-19.20
28	3-day event: dressage	08.30-13.30
29	3-day event: endurance	08.30-17.30
30	3-day event: jumping **F**	17.00-20.00

AUGUST

2	Team dressage	08.00-13.30
		16.00-19.30
3	Team dressage	08.00-13.30
	Final	16.00-19.30
4	Team show-jumping	08.00-14.00
	Final	15.00-20.00
5	Individual dressage - **Final**	09.00-13.30
7	Individual show-jumping - qualifying	09.30-13.30
		16.30-19.30
9	Individual show-jumping - **Final** (course A)	09.00-12.30
	Individual show-jumping - **Final** (course B)	13.30-15.00

The formality of dressage.

DID YOU KNOW...? *Reiner Klimke of Germany won five golds in separate Games over a 24 year period between 1964 and 1988 in the dressage.*

The oldest gold medallist was Josef Neckermann (FRG) in 1968 aged 56 years and 141 days. The youngest was Edmund Coffin (USA) in 1976 aged 21 years and 77 days.

Equestrian events are governed internationally by the FEI (International Equestrian Federation) and in Great Britain by the British Equestrian Federation.

47

FENCING

DES SEZ It's a long time since Britain won a medal in fencing - 28 years to be exact since Bill Hoskyns took a silver in the epee in Tokyo. Hoskyns competed in six successive Games. Gillian Sheen won Britain's only gold back in 1956 in women's foil.

In men's fencing, three weapons are used: foil, epee and sabre. And there are individual and team titles contested in each. Women compete only in foil both individually and as teams. Traditionally France, Italy and Hungary have been the strongest countries but the former Soviet Union are currently the world team champions in epee and have the individual champions in epee and sabre, Grigoriy Kirienko and Andrei Chouvalov respectively. In foil, Cuba are the current world team champions while Ingo Weissenborn of Germany is the individual champion. Women's foil has recently been dominated by Italy. The sport, which has been included in every Games since 1896, has on occasions been taken so seriously that arguments have led to real life duels. In 1924 a judge called Kovacs and an Italian fencer Puliti fought a duel.

Reigning women's foil champion Anja Fichtel.

Both men suffered wounds. After an hour honour was deemed restored, they shook hands and made up.

One of the most successful swordsmen of all time was Edoardo Mangiarotti of Italy who won 13 medals, six of them gold between 1936 and 1960. He was a natural right-hander but was forced by his father, a fencing master, to fence left-handed which is thought by some to be an advantage.

Electronic apparatus registers hits in epee and foil and sabre. In sabre, it is not just the point of the sword that can score a hit.

Best British hopes are for a top ten place in women's foil.

FACT-O-FILE

Picture a small town on the Hungarian border just as dawn breaks. Two men prepare to duel with sabres. Battle is joined and one man falls to the ground clutching a bad head wound. The seconds call proceedings to a close. Honour is satisfied.

It might be a scene from the normal swashbuckling movie associated in many people's minds with fencing. Instead it was a real-life drama after the 1924 Olympics at which the Italian-born Hungarian team coach, Italo Santelli, had been accused of lying by the Italian team captain, Adolfo Contronei.

Olympic fencing might be a world away with its white suits, body-protectors and masks but it still has drama. And it requires great speed, courage and reflexes.

Fencing has been part of the modern Games since the outset in 1896. The men's epee was added to the foil and sabre events in 1900. Women's foil came onto the scene in 1924 with a team event from 1960 onwards.

RULES AND TOOLS

A maximum of 12 fencers per nation - nine men and three women - will take part in the 1992 Olympic Games. The competition format is the same for all weapon categories.

Opening round-robin pools are followed by two eliminating rounds with a repechage second chance for initial losers. The top 32 move into a knock-out stage. Only the top eight then contest the final.

At all stages of the individual events matches are decided as the best of three rounds of five hits in six minutes.

Initial pools are seeded according to FIE (International Fencing Federation) rankings. A fencer cannot be dropped from a competition until he/she has suffered two defeats.

Target areas vary according to the weapons. The torso only is the scoring area for the foil exponents whilst the sabre fencers can also score by hitting the arms. Epeeists can legitimately score by hitting any area of the torso, head or limbs.

In the foil and epee hits are only recorded with the point of the weapon whereas the cutting edge also counts in the sabre events. The foil and epee are similar weapons although the latter is a little stiffer and thicker. Sabres, however, have flattened v-shaped blades.

DATA-BANK

VENUE:
Palau de la Metal-lurgia, in the Montjuic area, 5.5km from the Vila Olimpica. There is space for 3,500 spectators.
The competition area has 15 pistes.

EVENTS:
Foil - team and individual **(m+w)**
Sabre and epee - team and individual **(m)**

FENCING

Swashbuckling stuff from the sabre specialists.

BARCELONA BRITS

Steven Paul, Bill Gosbee, Donnie McKenzie and Fiona McIntosh are some of the names who could lead Britain's challenge in Barcelona.

1988 CHAMPIONS:

Foil (m)	Stefano Cerioni (ITA)		
Foil (w)	Anja Fichtel (FRG)		
Sabre (m)	Jean Francois Lamour (FRA)		
Epee (m)	Arnd Schmitt (FRG)		
Team foil (m)	USSR	Team sabre (m)	Hungary
Team foil (w)	FRG	Team epee (m)	France

MEDALS

Country	Men			Women			Total
	G	S	B	G	S	B	
France	32	31	24	2	1	2	92
Italy	30	31	19	2	2	3	87
Hungary	26	11	19	5	6	5	72
USSR	13	12	14	5	3	2	49
FRG	6	9	3	5	4	3	30
USA	2	6	11	-	-	-	19
Poland	4	6	6	-	-	1	17
Belgium	5	3	5	-	-	-	13
Great Britain	-	6	-	1	3	-	10
Greece	3	3	2	-	-	-	8
Romania	1	-	2	-	2	3	8
Netherlands	-	1	7	-	-	-	8
Sweden	2	3	2	-	-	-	7
Austria	-	1	3	1	-	2	7
Cuba	5	1	-	-	-	-	6
Denmark	-	1	1	1	1	2	6
Switzerland	-	2	3	-	-	-	5
Bohemia (Czech)	-	-	2	-	-	-	2
China	-	-	-	1	-	-	1
GDR	-	1	-	-	-	-	1
Mexico	-	-	-	-	1	-	1
Argentina	-	-	1	-	-	-	1
Portugal	-	-	1	-	-	-	1
	129	128	125	23	23	23	451

THE OLYMPIC ROUTE

Twelve nations have qualified for the team event at the Games. These include Spain, the top eight nations from the world championships and three more from a special qualifying tournament.

SCHEDULE		
LOCAL SPANISH TIME. SUBTRACT ONE HOUR FOR BRITAIN.		
JULY		
30	Ind. foil preliminaries (w)	09.00
	Ind. foil F (w)	20.00
31	Ind. foil preliminaries (m)	09.00
	Ind. foil F (m)	20.00
AUGUST		
1	Ind. epee preliminaries (m)	09.00
	Ind. epee F (m)	20.00
2	Ind. sabre preliminaries (m)	09.00
	Ind. sabre F (m)	20.00
3	Team foil qualifying pool (w)	11.00
4	Team foil qualifying (m)	09.00
	Team foil elimination (w)	11.00
	Team foil F (w)	20.00
5	Team epee qualifying pool (m)	09.00
	Team foil straight elimination (m)	11.00
	Team foil F (m)	20.00
6	Team sabre qualifying (m)	09.00
	Team epee elimination (m)	11.00
	Team epee F (m)	20.00
7	Team sabre elimination (m)	11.00
	Team sabre F (m)	20.00

PALAU METAL-LURGIA

⇨ **Details** Capacity	3,500
Distance to Olympic Village	5.5
Distance to CMC	0.1

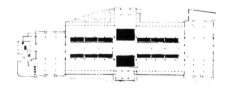

DID YOU KNOW...? A new style adopted by the West German women in Seoul in 1988 took the world by surprise - and gave the country the team gold as well as all three individual medals.

Kerstin Palm of Sweden competed over seven Games from 1964 - 1988. This is a record attendance for any female in any sport at the Games.

Fencing is governed internationally by the FIE, the International Fencing Federation, and in Great Britain by the Amateur Fencing Association.

FOOTBALL

DES SEZ You may be wondering why there is no British football team in the Olympic Games. The reason is that the sport in the UK is organised by the Football Associations of England, Scotland, Wales and Ireland. They all operate national teams in World and European competitions. There is a reluctance to come together to produce a British team because, it is felt, this could jeopardise the separate existence of the home countries in future World Cups. It might create a costly precedent.

Interestingly, the Republic of Ireland have entered under the guidance of one Jack Charlton.

Qualifications for players have continually changed. Once they had to be unpaid amateurs. But those days have long since gone. In recent Games, playing in World Cup matches disbarred players from the Olympics. This time there is an age barrier. Players must be under 23.

In the past, Olympic champions have gone on to be World Cup winners two years later. Both Uruguay and Italy achieved this before the second world war. In 1952 Hungary won the gold medal, the first of three since the war. And their team included the famous names of Puskas, Hideguti and Boszik all of whom came to Wembley the following year and inflicted the first home defeat on England by a country outside the British Isles.

In 1972 in Munich, Poland, who won the gold medal, paraded the team that - almost to a man - knocked England out of the World Cup the following year. The Soviet Union won the gold medal in Seoul beating Brazil in the final. That was the second silver medal running for the Brazilians. In 1984 in Los Angeles France beat them in the final. Over 100,000 people saw that match. Who says there is no audience for soccer in the United States?

Sixteen countries will take part but, unlike some other Olympic team sports, there is no women's event.

FACT-O-FILE

Of all the Olympic sports this is, perhaps, the one which needs the least introduction to a British audience. Football is, after all, one of the world's best-known and most-played sports. And in 1994 it will attempt to penetrate the North American barrier when the World Cup is staged stateside.

Football made its unofficial Olympic debut in 1896 in Athens when two local Greek sides played-off for the right to face a Danish team in the final. Four years later football established itself officially - and has remained there, bar 1932, ever since. Great Britain were the first Olympic champions.

FIFA, the world governing body, was formed in 1904. But football at Olympic level has always been plagued by controversy over eligibility and selection criteria.

RULES AND TOOLS

The Barcelona football tournament will consist of 16 teams split into four round-robin groups. Teams will win two points for a victory, one for a draw and none for a loss. The top two teams in

DATA-BANK

VENUES:

Estadi del FC Barcelona in Diagonal Olympic Area, 8km from Vila Olimpica. It holds 114,763 spectators.

Estadi del RCD Espanyol, Barcelona, 7km from the Vila Olimpica. It holds 42,000 spectators.

Estadi del la Nova Creu Alta de Sabadell. Sabadell is 24km from the Vila Olimpica. It holds 16,000 spectators.

Estadio La Romareda de Zaragoza. Zaragoza is 326km from the Vila Olimpica. It holds 43,349 spectators.

Estadi Luis Casanova de Valencia. Valencia is 368km from the Vila Olimpica. It holds 49,398 spectators.

EVENTS:

The final phase of the Olympic tournament will be a men's tournament of 16 teams.

Football: a horizontal hold on sporting popularity.

each group will go into the knock-out stage of quarter-finals, semi-finals and then a final.

From the quarter-finals onwards extra time will be played if there is a draw at full-time. And, just to add spice, a penalty shoot-out will follow if there is still no result.

OLYMPIC ROUTE

Teams are selected through continental zone qualifying tournaments.

BARCELONA BRITS

Britain will not compete in Barcelona. The individual home countries have not attempted to qualify for more than two decades.

1988 CHAMPIONS:
USSR

In the heat of the moment.

FOOTBALL ⚽

SCHEDULE

LOCAL SPANISH TIME. SUBTRACT ONE HOUR FOR BRITAIN.

JULY

24-30	Preliminaries		19.00 & 21.00

AUGUST

1	Qtr final	1stB-2ndA (26) Valencia	19.00
		1stA-2ndB(25) Barcelona (Estadi del FC)	21.30
2	Qtr final	1stD-2ndC(28) Zaragoza	19.00
		1stC-2ndD(27) Barcelona (Estadi del FC)	21.30
3 & 4			Rest days
5	Semi-final	W26-W28(30) Valencia	19.00
		W25-W27(29) Barcelona (Estadi del FC)	21.30
6		Rest Day	
7	**Final** 3-4	Barcelona (Estadi del FC)	20.00
8	**Final**	Barcelona (Estadi del FC)	20.00

CLUB F. C. BARCELONA

Details Capacity · 120,000
Distance to Olympic Village · 8
Distance to CMC · 4

MEDALS

Country	G	S	B	Total
Hungary	3	1	1	5
USSR	2	-	3	5
Denmark	1	3	1	5
Yugoslavia	1	3	1	5
Great Britain	3	-	-	3
GDR	1	1	1	3
Sweden	1	-	2	3
Netherlands	-	-	3	3
Uruguay	2	-	-	2
Czechoslovakia	1	1	-	2
France	1	1	-	2
Poland	1	1	-	2
Belgium	1	-	1	2
Italy	1	-	1	2
Brazil	-	2	-	2
Bulgaria	-	1	1	2
Greece	-	1	1	2
USA	-	1	1	2
FRG	-	-	2	2
Canada	1	-	-	1
Argentina	-	1	-	1
Austria	-	1	-	1
Spain	-	1	-	1
Switzerland	-	1	-	1
Japan	-	-	1	1
Norway	-	-	1	1
	20	20	21*	61

* Third place tie in 1972

Denmark – a long tradition of Olympic football.

DID YOU KNOW...? *Four Britons, all named Whittal, were in a Danish side which won in 1906. If they were all brothers that would be an Olympic record.*

Britain's Vivian Woodward, meanwhile, is the oldest gold medallist ever at 33 years and 32 days in 1912. The youngest was Pedro Petrone (URS) in 1924 two days short of his 19th birthday.

Football is governed internationally by **FIFA**, the International Federation of Association Football, and in Great Britain by the **Football Association**.

FOOTBALL

VISA MAKES THE WORLD GO ROUND.

Visa's sponsorship is helping athletes from around the world prepare for the Olympics.

WORLDWIDE SPONSOR
1992 OLYMPIC GAMES

GYMNASTICS

DES SEZ This is one of the most popular Olympic sports for television viewers and in the TV age women gymnasts have become far more famous than the men. In 1972 it was Olga Korbut of the Soviet Union who captivated the watching millions. In Montreal, the Romanian Nadia Comaneci, also just 4ft 11ins tall, took over. The Americans found Mary Lou Retton in 1984 and then in Seoul the star billing was shared between Daniela Silivas of Romania and Yelena Chouchounova of the Soviet Union.

In Barcelona look out for a tiny new super-star. She is fifteen years old, stands just 4ft 5ins. She is from North Korea and her names is Kim Gwang Suk. In last year's world championships in Indianapolis, Kim wowed the crowd with a perfect 'ten' on asymmetric bars to win the gold medal. However it was another Kim, Kim Zmeskal of the USA, who took the overall individual championship.

The men, by comparison, are less well-known but their standards go higher and higher and the athleticism on show will be quite breathtaking. The Japanese domination of men's gymnastics has waned. The gymnasts of the Unified Team are the masters now. They are both world and Olympic team champions. Grigori Misutin is the overall individual champion.

There are eight Olympic gold medals at stake for the men. One for the team championships, the overall individual championship and then separate titles at stake for each piece of apparatus, floor, pommel horse, parallel bars, horizontal bar, vault and rings.

There are six Olympic titles for women: team event, overall individual, and the disciplines of vault, asymmetric bars, beam and floor. In addition there is rhythmic gymnastics with balls, hoops and ribbons, the sort of 'synchronised swimming' of the sport. The standard of gymnastics in Britain is improving and the men's team has qualified for the Games, led by British number one Neil Thomas.

You may be interested to know that back in 1904 an American, George Eyser, won a total of five medals in the sport - not bad considering George had a wooden leg.

FACT-O-FILE

A group of western observers sat entranced in the stands high above the activity at the Romanian gymnastics championships in Bucharest. One girl, in particular, caught the eye. Perhaps because she was taller than the rest. But also as she was the best. That girl was Nadia Comaneci. Despite appearances she stood a mere 4'11" tall. And she had just mesmerised the world at the Montreal Olympic Games by scoring the first-ever perfect tens to take gold. All of that before her fifteenth birthday.

Such grace, artistry, stamina and strength have made gymnastics one of the most popular Olympic sports. It has been part of the

James May in action. GB men have qualified against the odds.

Games since 1896 although the women joined in 1928 with a team event and in 1952 as individuals.

But gymnastics, itself, dates back beyond even the Ancient Games. Some cultures - such as the Chinese with Wushu as organised mass exercise - have used gymnastics since time immemorial.

In the late 1800s and early 1900s Germany and Scandinavia took the lead in founding modern gymnastics. Britain, meanwhile, despite the formation of the British Amateur Gymnastics Association in 1888, remained hooked on team sports at school. So gymnastics did not take off until the post-TV age.

The scene is set in Barcelona for a tough battle between the top nations - a return of the fierce rivalry witnessed in Seoul.

RULES AND TOOLS

Over one hundred men and a equal number of women will take part in the 16 medal events at the Games of the XXVth Olympiad. All male competitors must be 16, all female artistic participants 15 and the rhythmic gymnasts, 14.

The team event comes first in the artistic competition. Six gymnasts per team complete 12 exercises across the apparatus. Six are compulsory and six optional. Four judges mark each exercise out of ten. The top and bottom marks are discarded and the middle two are averaged to give the score.

Gymnasts scoring within the top 36 of the team event then contest an all-round final. This involves one optional exercise on each of the apparatus. The highest combined score wins.

Finally, there is a final on each of the individual apparatus contested by the top eight scoring gymnasts on each piece in the team event. Once more the gymnasts are required to complete one optional exercise.

GYMNASTICS

DATA-BANK

VENUES:
Artistic gymnastics - Palau Sant Jordi in the Montjuic area, 6km from the Vila Olimpica. The competition hall holds 15,000 spectators.
Rhythmic gymnastics - Palau d'Esports de Barcelona in the Monjuic area, 5.5km from the Vila Olimpica. The competition hall holds 6,500 spectators.

EVENTS:
Artistic gymnastics:
Team, all-round individual and apparatus finals:
floor exercises **(m)**
pommel horse **(m)**
rings **(m)**
vault **(m+w)**
parallel bars **(m)**
asymmetric bars **(w)**
horizontal bar **(m)**
beam **(w)**
floor exercises **(w)**

Rhythmic gymnastics:
General multiple competition

1988 CHAMPIONS:
Men:

Team	USSR
Ind. all-round	Vladimir Artemov (URS)
Floor exercises	Sergey Kharikov (URS)
Parallel Bars	Vladimir Artemov (URS)
Pommel horse	Lyubomir Gueraskov (URS)
	Zsolt Borkai (HUN)
	Dmitry Bilozertchev (URS)
Rings	Holger Behrendt (GDR)
	Dmitry Bilozertchev (URS)
Horizontal bar	Vladimir Artemov (URS)
	Valeriy Lioukine (URS)
Horse vault	Lou Yun (CHN)

Women:

Team:	USSR
Ind. all-round	Yelena Chouchounova (URS)
Asymmetric bars	Daniela Silivas (ROM)
Floor exercises	Daniela Silivas (ROM)
Horse vault	Svetlana Boguinskaya (URS)
Modern Rhythmic	Marina Lobatch (URS)

SANT JORDI
⇨ **Details** Capacity 15,000
Distance to Olympic Village 6
Distance to CMC 1

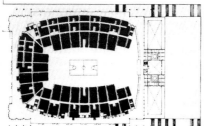

Rhythmic gymnasts face a preliminary competition using each piece of equipment. Only the top 12 go through to the final.

THE OLYMPIC ROUTE
Gymnasts were selected for the Olympic Games on results at the 1991 world championships in Indianapolis (the same event will be held at Birmingham's Indoor Arena in 1993). The top twelve men's and women's teams qualified automatically. Then three gymnasts were selected from the teams finishing 13-15 and two from those placing 16-18.
The technical committee of the International Gymnastics Federation added a further nine gymnasts at their discretion with the blessing of the relevant National Olympic Committees.

BARCELONA BRITS
British gymnastics is on a high after the 1991 world championships in which the British men achieved a top twelve placing - and Olympic selection - for the first time in decades.
Neil Thomas, James May, David Cox and Terry Bartlett should be amongst the names to follow.

Rhythmic gymnasts add grace and artistry.

GYMNASTICS

Women gymnasts have stolen recent TV limelight.

MEDALS

Country	Men G	Men S	Men B	Women G	Women S	Women B	Total
USSR	40	38	18	34	29	27	186
Japan	27	27	28	-	-	1	83
USA	21	15	19	1	3	5	64
Switzerland	15	19	13	-	-	-	47
Hungary	7	5	6	6	5	10	39
Romania	-	-	2	13	10	11	36
Czechoslovakia	3	7	9	9	6	1	35
GDR	3	3	9	3	10	7	35
FRG	11	7	11	1	1	-	31
Italy	12	7	9	-	1	-	29
Finland	8	5	12	-	-	-	25
France	4	7	9	-	-	-	20
China	5	4	2	1	-	1	13
Yugoslavia	5	2	4	-	-	-	11
Sweden	5	2	-	1	1	1	10
Greece	3	2	4	-	-	-	9
Norway	2	2	1	-	-	-	5
Denmark	1	3	1	-	-	-	5
Bulgaria	1	-	2	-	1	1	5
Austria	2	1	-	-	-	-	3
Great Britain	-	1	1	-	-	1	3
Belgium	-	1	1	-	-	-	2
Poland	-	1	-	-	-	-	2
Canada	-	-	-	1	-	-	1
Netherlands	-	-	-	1	-	-	1
Korea	-	-	1	-	-	-	1
	175	159	163	71	67	66	701

SCHEDULE

LOCAL SPANISH TIME. SUBTRACT ONE HOUR FOR BRITAIN.

JULY

26	Compulsory exercises - team (w)	11.30
		20.00
27	Compulsory exercises - team (m)	11.00
		15.00
		20.00
28	Optional exercises - team (w)	11.30
	Final	20.00
29	Optional exercises - team (m)	11.00
		15.00
	Final	20.00
30	All-round ind. - F (w)	20.00
31	All-round ind. - F (m)	20.00

AUGUST

1	Apparatus - F (w)	20.00
2	Apparatus - F (m)	20.00
6 & 7	Rhythmic - prel. (w)	16.00
8	Rhythmic - F (w)	16.00

Gymnastics is governed internationally by FIG, the International Gymnastics Federation, and in Great Britain by the British Amateur Gymnastics Association.

GYMNASTICS

HANDBALL

DES SEZ First of all there are two international sports of handball. One is played predominantly in Ireland and the USA and is a game rather like squash in that it is played by two (or four in doubles) against a wall. Instead of using a racket, players simply use their hands. This sport, which has a world championship, has nothing to do with Olympic handball.

The version seen in the Games is played between two teams of seven players, a sort of cross between basketball and football where the players shoot into a soccer-like goal. It was introduced into the 1936 Olympics by the Germans as an eleven-a-side game played indoors (A competition which the Germans duly won). The current indoor version was re-introduced when the Games returned to Germany in 1972 and the women's event started in 1976.

European teams have largely dominated the men's competition. The silver medal for Korea in Seoul was one of only fifteen ever awarded not to have been won by a European country. Likewise with the women's game, except that the Koreans have produced the best results of recent Games - a silver medal in 1984 and gold on home soil last time.

In the latest world championships, the surprise winners of the men's event were Sweden. They have never won an Olympic medal in this sport. The Swedes will obviously be leading contenders this time but, as usual, the Unified Team, Czechoslovakia, Romania and Germany will have very strong teams as well as the Koreans.

The German side will still primarily be made up of players from the East. In the women's competition, the Koreans are fancied to retain their crown.

No British team has ever qualified for Olympic competition, but take a look at your local sports centre and you may well see that the game is taking a hold and some budding young stars are developing.

FACT-O-FILE

Barcelona's magnificent Palau Sant Jordi awaits the handball teams who reach the semi-finals and final of the Olympic tournament. Perched on the same hill as the Montjuic Olympic Stadium, the space-age Palau is a testament to the imagination and skill of a Japanese architect.

Its roof was created by tensioning a matrix of thousands of metal girders and lifting them into place in one action withl hydraulic supports. The Palau can be used for anything from indoor windsurfing to ice-skating as well as normal court sports.

RULES AND TOOLS

Before the teams get through to the Palau there are preliminary stages. Twelve men's and eight women's teams will do battle in two groups each of six and four teams respectively. Teams will score two points for a win, one for a draw and none for a loss.

The top two from each group will go through to cross-over semi-finals and the winners will play the final. A play-off is also scheduled for the bronze medal and all other classification places.

Handball is a fast-moving sport. Players can only hold the ball for three seconds. "Dribbling" is allowed and the aim is to attack the football-like goal from around the 6m goal semi-circle. Midfield possession is not important as the game swings from end to end.

Unlike football, players are not permitted to use their body below the knees to control the ball - a ball which is smaller than a basketball or football.

If matches in the final stage are drawn after the normal period of two 30 minute halves, extra time of ten minutes is played. The rules also permit a further ten-minute extension of extra time before penalty shoot-outs are used as the ultimate decider.

OLYMPIC ROUTE

Spain, as host nation, will play in both the men's and women' tournament. In the men's tournament the winner of the African, American and Asian continental qualifying championships will join Sweden, the Unified Team, Romania, Hungary, Czechoslovakia,

Swedish defence penetrated.

HANDBALL

HANDBALL

DATA-BANK

VENUES:
Palau d'Esports in Granollers, 30km from Barcelona and 20km from the Vila Olimpica, which holds 5,500 spectators. For all days except last day. Finals: Palau Sant Jordi, in the Montjuic area, 6km from the Vila Olimpica, which holds 15,000 spectators.

EVENTS
One men's and one women's tournament.

1988 CHAMPIONS:
Men USSR
Women Korea

MEDALS

Country	Men G	S	B	Women G	S	B	Total
USSR	2	1	-	2	-	1	6
Yugoslavia	2	-	1	1	1	-	5
Romania	-	1	3	-	-	-	4
GDR	1	-	-	-	1	1	3
Korea	-	1	-	1	1	-	3
FRG	1	1	-	-	-	-	2
Austria	-	1	-	-	-	-	1
Czechoslovakia	-	1	-	-	-	1	1
Norway	-	-	-	-	1	-	1
China	-	-	-	-	-	1	1
Hungary	-	-	-	-	-	1	1
Poland	-	-	1	-	-	-	1
Switzerland	-	-	1	-	-	-	
	6	6	6	4	4	4	30

SCHEDULE

LOCAL SPANISH TIME. SUBTRACT ONE HOUR FOR BRITAIN.
(NB: All preliminary events are at 10.00, 11.30, 14.30, 16.00, 19.00 and 20.30 each day.)

JULY
| 27 | Prel. (m) | |

JULY 29 & 31, AUGUST
| | Prel. (m) | |

JULY 30, AUGUST 1 & 3
| | Prel. (w) | |

AUGUST
6	Semi-finals (w)	**14.00 – 16.00**
	Semi-finals (m)	**19.00 – 21.00**
7	Final 7-8 (w)	09.00
	Final 5-6 (w)	11.00
	Final 11-12 (m)	14.00
	Final 9-10 (m)	16.00
	Final 7-8 (m)	19.00
	Final 5-6 (m)	21.00
8	Final 3-4 (w)	10.00
	Final (w)	12.00
	Final 3-4 (m)	15.00
	Final (m)	17.00

Germany and France. It is not sure yet how Yugoslavia will be replaced in the line-up for either the men's or women's events. The same tournament winners will be added to the Unified Team, Germany and Austria in the women's event.

1988 USA v Czechoslovakia.

PALAU D'ESPORTS, GRANOLLERS

⇨ **Details** Capacity 5,500
  Distance to Olympic Village 24
  Distance to CMC 32

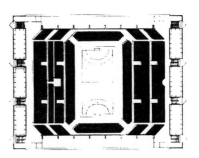

Handball is governed internationally by the Inernational Handball Federation, and in Great Britain by the British Handball Association.

57

HOCKEY

That golden moment...

DES SEZ If hockey had a 'Pele', he would come from the sub-continent. As Brazil are considered the 'true artists' of football, the Indian sub-continent has provided the most skilful players in this sport.

However, like the Brazilian footballers, India and Pakistan, whilst still producing wonderfully talented players have been caught up by perhaps less gifted teams but who are better prepared and tactically more sound.

India have been the Olympic champions on no fewer than eight occasions with an unbeaten run from 1928 to 1956. Pakistan have won three times. But at the Seoul Games, of course, there was a thrilling win for the British team, with players like Sean Kerly and Ian Taylor becoming household names.

They had built on the success of 1984, when invited to play only after the Soviet withdrawal, the British team finished third for their first hockey medal since 1952. Since the triumph of 1988, the team has fallen in world standings and now ranks outside the top four. A repeat of the Seoul gold medal might be a little too much to expect for. Holland, Germany, Australia, plus of course India and Pakistan, will all by vying strongly to take over as Olympic champions.

Women's hockey became part of the Games in 1980, with Zimbabwe taking the gold medal on that occasion. Members of the team were rewarded with an ox by a grateful Zimbabwean Minister for Sport.

Britain finished fourth in Seoul and have once again qualified for the Games. Australia are currently the best women's team and a British medal of any colour would be excellent.

FACT-O-FILE

It was a glorious September Saturday in Seoul when Great Britain's hockey men won gold with a 3-1 win over Germany and her women finished fourth in their tournament. Emotions ran even higher than those of four years previously when the men took bronze in Los Angeles as last-minute replacements for the boycotting Soviet Union.

Back on the windy, often rainswept playing fields of Britain, a sporting lifetime has since passed. Some of the key British players have retired. And other nations have been quick to make up the gap.

So a successful title defence will be tough in Barcelona. Certainly both the men and women have had torrid times - as well as some triumphs - on the international scene in the last four years. The men have failed to win a medal at the last four "Champions Trophies" And the women lost to Canada, Argentina and Australia in the Olympic qualifying in 1991.

But the Olympic Games is a different atmosphere. Perhaps it will provide the catalyst needed for Britain to prove themselves once more.

In the men's tournament, the players of the Unified Team will be an early focus of attention. Last year they vowed to stay together - one step ahead of their own authorities. But with crumbling finance they may find the going tough. New Zealand have also qualified for both events and could give the established nations some problems.

Hockey, meanwhile, made its Olympic debut in 1908 in a tournament won by England with Ireland, Scotland and Wales all amongst the medallists. The sport has since been part of every Games except 1912 and 1924. Women, however, did not join in until 1980. Since 1928 the men's Olympic tournament has often been dominated by India and Pakistan. Only New Zealand, West Germany and Britain have broken that run.

RULES AND TOOLS

Teams are 11-a-side (with two substitutes) and matches last 70 minutes - in two 35 minute halves. Extra time can be added when the tournament gets to the knock-out stage if the score is level at full-time.

The rules are similar to soccer except that goals cannot be scored from outside the "circle". Penalty, or "short" corners, can be awarded for deliberately playing the ball over the goal line, an offence in the circle or a deliberate foul within the 25 yard line. Only the "flat" side of the stick may be used for play.

OLYMPIC ROUTE

The men's tournament includes: Great Britain (as 1988 champions); Spain (as hosts); Pakistan (as Asian champions); the Unified Team; Holland (as World cup winners); Malaysia; New Zealand; Germany, Australia, Argentina, India and Egypt.

Sherwani sidesteps Germany in the 1988 final.

GB women looking for a medal against teams like South Korea.

HOCKEY

DATA-BANK

VENUE:
Estadi d'Hoquei de Terrassa, 35km from Barcelona. The competition area has two pitches.
The main stadium holds 10,200 spectators. The second stadium can accommodate 4,200.

EVENTS:
One men's and one women's tournament.

1988 CHAMPIONS:
Men	Great Britain
Women	Australia

MEDALS

Country	Men G	S	B	Women G	S	B	Total
India	8	1	2	-	-	-	11
Great Britain	3	2	4	-	-	-	9
Pakistan	3	3	1	-	-	-	7
FRG	1	3	2	-	1	-	7
Netherlands	-	2	3	1	-	1	7
Australia	-	2	1	1	-	-	4
Spain	-	1	1	-	-	-	2
USSR	-	-	1	-	-	1	2
USA	-	-	1	-	-	1	2
New Zealand	1	-	-	-	-	-	1
Zimbabwe	-	-	-	1	-	-	1
Czechoslovakia	-	-	-	-	1	-1	
Denmark	-	1	-	-	-	-	1
Japan	-	1	-	-	-	-	1
Korea	-	-	-	-	1	-	1
Belgium	-	-	1	-	-	-	1
	16	16	17*	3	3	3	58

* 2 bronzes in 1907.

Britain's Jane Sixsmith should sparkle in GB Barcelona attack.

SCHEDULE
LOCAL SPANISH TIME. SUBTRACT ONE HOUR FOR BRITAIN.

(NB: For the Pool phase, the men's games will be at 10.00, 17.00 and 19.00 each day and the women's at 17.00 and 19.00)

JULY 26, 28, 30, **AUGUST** 1, 3
Pool (m)	

JULY 27, 29, **AUGUST** 2
Pool (w)	

AUGUST

4	Classification (w)	09.30 & 18.15
	Semi-final (w)	17.00 & 19.30
5	Classification (m)	09.30, 17.00, 19.30
	Semi-final (m)	09.30, 17.00, 19.30
6	Final 5-8 (w)	09.30
	Final 5-12 (m)	17.00
	Final 5-8 (w)	18.15
	Final 5-12 (m)	19.30
7	Final 5-12 (m)	09.30
	Final 3-4 (w)	17.00
	Final 5-12 (m)	18.15
	Final (w)	19.30
8	Final 3-4 (m)	17.00
	Final (m)	19.30

TERRASSA
⇨ **Details** Capacity   10,200 – main stadium / 4,200 sec. stadium
    Distance to Olympic Village   34
    Distance to CMC   39

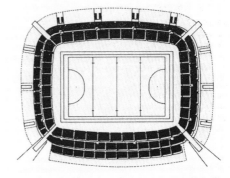

DID YOU KNOW...? The youngest ever hockey gold medallist was Britain's Russell Garcia in 1988 at the age of 18 years and 103 days. Abdul Rashid of Pakistan was the oldest at 38 years and 100 days in 1960.

India hold the record for the highest international score. They beat the United States 24 - 1 in 1932.

Hockey is governed internationally by the FIH, the International Hockey Federation, and in Great Britain by the Great Britain Hockey Board.

JUDO

D **ES SEZ** This is the sport that without question is the greatest test of the art of radio commentary.

Judo players in the Olympic Games do not go flying through the air (like Kato in those Pink Panther films). So, to the non-expert, you end up with what seems to be an exercise in the removal of two sets of pyjamas. Of course the pyjamas are 'judogi' and the players are 'judokas' and the variations of throws and holds take years to learn. To make it all a bit more difficult, all terminology is in Japanese.

There are seven weight categories and for the first time women's judo is included in the Games. (It had previously been demonstrated.) This may be very good news for Britain because at the last world championships, which were actually held in Barcelona, Britain's women ended up with five medals. Karen Briggs, Sharon Rendle and Diane Bell have all been world champions and will compete strongly for gold medals at the Games.

Men's judo has been part of the Olympics since 1964 (with one exception) and of course the Japanese dominated. Britain has a fine haul of medals but has never won gold. Neil Adams twice won silver medals (1980 and 1984). On the latter occasion momentary lack of concentration cost him the gold when he was hot favourite.

Angelo Parisi won a medal in 1972 and added gold and silver four years later. Unfortunately for Britain, by the time of the 1976 Games, he was living in France having married there and was competing for that country. By the end of the competition in Barcelona, you may well have acquired a grasp of such terms, as **IPPON** – full-point, **HARAI-GOSHI** - sweeping lion throw or **YUSHI-GACHI** - won on superiority (referees decision), but if you get a chance, listen to the judo commentary on the radio. It's quite an experience.

Gargantuan Gordon going for gold.

FACT-O-FILE

Britain's judo men went to Seoul in 1988 as genuine medal contenders in several weight categories. Their morale was sky-high when Kerrith Brown took lightweight bronze. It plummeted beyond retrieval when he was disqualified on a drug-abuse charge. And the team came home empty-handed except for a courageous bronze from Dennis Stewart.

Barcelona is the perfect setting to blow away the bad memories. The men will find the opposition tough. But the women's squad - in the Games for the first time - will hope to repeat the 1988 "dry-run". In the Seoul demonstration event both Sharon Rendle and Diane Bell took gold. And Britain's squad groups together a number of current world medallists.

South Korea, France and, of course, Japan could prove the main rivals. Japan has often been accused of "copycat" technology but in judo they are the acknowledged original masters. And they have opened their craft to the rest of the world - nowadays often to their detriment.

Back in the late 1800s Dr Jigoro Kano moulded the unarmed sections of the ancient Chinese art of Ju-Jitsu (a combat art which was part of Samurai training until they were forbidden to carry swords) into a new school called Kodokan judo.

The Japanese founder of modern judo then proceeded to export the sport to the rest of the world through travelling pupils. A century later some westerners have assimilated the art expertly enough to be able to beat its top Japanese exponents.

The transition, however, was a slow one. A Kano pupil first visited Europe in 1889. The first British club - the Budokwai in Westminster - was formed in 1918 and clubs followed in Africa, America and Australia. But Judo did not really blossom as a competitive sport until after the Second World War. Both the

JUDO

DATA-BANK

VENUE:
Palau Blaugrana, which is part of the FC Barcelona in the Diagonal Area, 8km from the Vila Olimpica. It holds 6,400 spectators.
There will be two tatamis on a 50cm high raised platform in the 16m x 30m competition area.

EVENTS:

Men	extra lightweight	up to 60kg
	half-lightweight	up to 65kg
	lightweight	up to 71kg
	half-middleweight	up to 78kg
	middleweight	up to 86kg
	half-heavyweight	up to 95kg
	heavyweight	over 95kg
Women	extra lightweight	up to 48kg
	half-lightweight	up to 52kg
	lightweight	up to 56kg
	half-middleweight	up to 61kg
	middleweight	up to 66kg
	half-heavyweight	up to 72kg
	heavyweight	over 72kg

1988 CHAMPIONS:

Up to 60kg	Kim Jae-Yup (KOR)
Up to 65kg	Lee Kyung-Keun (KOR)
Up to 71kg	Marc Alexandre (FRA)
Up to 78kg	Waldemar Legien (POL)
Up to 86kg	Peter Seisenbacher (AUT)
Up to 95kg	Aurelio Miguel (BRA)
Over 95kg	Hitoshi Saito (JPN)

MEDALS

Country	G	S	B	Total
USSR	5	5	13	23
Japan	14	2	6	22
Korea	4	4	5	13
France	3	2	8	13
Great Britain		4	7	11
FRG	1	5	4	10
GDR	1	2	6	9
USA	-	2	4	6
Netherlands	3	-	2	5
Poland	1	2	2	5
Brazil	1	1	3	5
Cuba	1	3	-	4
Austria	2	-	1	3
Italy	1	1	1	3
Switzerland	1	1	1	3
Hungary	-	-	3	3
Belgium	1	-	1	2
Bulgaria	-	1	1	2
Canada	-	1	1	2
Mongolia	-	1	1	2
Romania	-	-	2	2
Yugoslavia	-	-	2	2
Egypt	-	1	-	1
Australia	-	-	1	1
Czechoslovakia	-	-	1	1
Iceland	-	-	1	1
North Korea	-	-	1	1
	39	38*	78	155

* 1972 silver withheld due to disqualification.

Take that! Japan throws the GDR.

European Judo Union and British Judo Association were formed in 1948 and the International Judo Federation followed in 1951.

The first world championships were held in 1957 but the Japanese, with a participation base of around eight million, were still dominant. Only in 1961 was the mould broken with massive Dutchman Anton Geesink (6'6" and 18-stones) winning the World Open title. His victory paved the way for hitherto unknown weight divisions in competitions. Geesink is now an IOC member. At the request of the Japanese hosts, judo made its Olympic debut in 1964 in Tokyo. It missed out in 1968 but has been in every Games since with its mixture of stamina, skill, art and aggression.

RULES AND TOOLS

The aim of judo is to throw an opponent cleanly on to his/her back or hold him/her there for thirty seconds or force a submission through pressure of an arm or stranglehold or gain a decision from the two judges and referee.

Each nation in Barcelona can enter a maximum of 14 judokas (players) - one per weight category. The Palau Blangrana will host the competitions which are knock-out draws with a repechage system giving a second chance. Medallists in the preceding world championships are seeded to avoid each other in the early part of the draw.

JUDO

SCHEDULE		
LOCAL SPANISH TIME. SUBTRACT ONE HOUR FOR BRITAIN.		
(NB: The timings of the phases are the same each day.)		
JULY		
27	Heavyweight preliminary (m+w)	16.30
	double repechage (m+w)	
	semi-final (m+w)	21.30
	finals repechage 3-5 (m+w)	21.54
	F	22.23
28	Half-heavyweight (m+w) F	16.30-22.23
29	Middleweight (m+w) F	16.30-22.23
30	Half-middleweight (m+w) F	16.30-22.23
31	Lightweight (m+w) F	16.30-22.23
AUGUST		
1	Half-lightweight (m+w) F	16.30-22.23
2	Extra lightweight (m+w) F	16.30-22.23

Sharon Lee (top) in action.

Rendle on the Seoul podium.

Each judoka must weigh within the category limit on the morning of the competition. Most judokas are skilled at the art of arriving at just the correct body weight at the right moment. Bouts in the men's event last 5 minutes whilst the women fight for a minute less. All the contests in one weight category are decided in one day - quite a test of stamina.

THE OLYMPIC ROUTE

Competitors are selected by their individual federations and ratified by their National Olympic Committees.

BARCELONA BRITS

Britain has a wealth of world-class talent in this sport. Many of its women are several-times world champions, including the indomitable Karen Briggs. She has returned from a series of injuries to remain at the top of her sport. In Barcelona, though, she will have to watch out for Cecile Nowak of France who beat her in the 1991 world championships.

Elvis Gordon - gargantuan former world silver medallist - should also add a sparkle to the squad.

PALAU BLAUGRANA

⇨ **Details** Capacity 6,400
Distance to Olympic Village 8
Distance to CMC 4

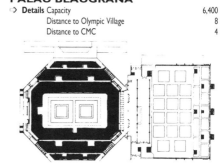

Judo is governed internationally by the International Judo Federation and in Great Britain by the British Judo Association.

Keeping the world in touch

BT would like to wish the British Olympic Team every success in the 1992 Summer Olympic Games.

It is a reassuring thought that, thanks to BT's international telephone network, friends and relatives can keep in touch with the Team and its supporters at anytime, throughout the Games.

MODERN PENTATHLON

D ES SEZ This is the sport that fits the Olympic bill perfectly. There are five disciplines involved: fencing, swimming, shooting, running and riding. It originally appealed almost exclusively to the military.

For Barcelona, the order of the disciplines has changed. On the first day there is fencing, with the epee, and all competitors meet each other. On the second day there is both 300m swimming and pistol shooting. Day three is for 4,000m cross-country run. And the riding, which used to be the first discipline at recent Games, now comes last - on day four. The riding is always highly contentious and something of a lottery. Unlike other equestrian sports competitors do not ride horses belonging to them but draw 'lots' for animals they will not have seen before.

A West German athlete had to be dragged away by his team-mates from attacking his mount which had three times refused at one fence in the 1972 Games. Sweden is synonymous with the sport. The individual gold medal has gone to that country nine times. In the team event, included since 1952, Hungary and the former Soviet Union have won four times each, Hungary being the reigning champions, while Italy won in 1984 (Eastern European Boycott) and Britain enjoyed a tremendous victory in 1976.

The team of Jim Fox, Danny Nightingale and Adrian Parker lay in fifth place going into the final discipline which was then the cross-country run. Parker was the hero, running a phenomenal 12m 9secs, 17 seconds faster than any other runner and still an Olympic best.

Those Games are remembered for the Boris Onishenko incident. The Soviet star, who had won both the individual and team gold medals at the previous Games, had cunningly tampered with the electronic equipment so that his epee would register a hit even if no contact was made. He and the Soviet team were disqualified in shame. Jim Fox's suspicions had raised doubts about Onishenko's performances.

Britain had further success in Seoul in 1988 when Richard Phelps, Dominic Mahony and Graham Brookhouse won the team bronze. The same three will be in contention again. Medal favourites will be the Unified Team, the Poles and the Hungarians who finished in that order in the last world championships.

Individually, Peter Steinmann of Switzerland and Richard Phelps, if he can get his shooting right, could give the leading athletes from those three countries a run for their money.

By the way, a certain George Patten (USA) came fifth in the 1912 Games. He later became famous of course as the second world war general. He would have won an Olympic medal ... but his shooting let him down!

Bronze in ''88, gold in ''76. Barcelona next stop..

MODERN PENTATHLON

FACT-O-FILE

The five elements of modern pentathlon, so the legend goes, emerged from the story of a soldier who starts out on horseback to deliver his general's orders. His horse is killed behind enemy lines but he fights his way clear first with a sword, then with a pistol before swimming across a river and finally running to his destination.

The sport-like the multi-event track and field disciplines – equates to a desire to find the perfect all-round sportsman. Skills are tested across five disciplines as well as stamina and steadiness under pressure.

Modern pentathlon went Olympic in 1912. A team event was added in 1952. The UIPMB (International Modern Pentathlon and Biathlon Union) was formed in 1948 during the Olympic Games of London.

The sport now has a recognised female competitive structure but this is not represented at the Games.

RULES AND TOOLS

A maximum of 66 competitors will take part in the sport in Barcelona.

Each country can enter four men of which only three will eventually line up at the start.

Fencing comes first with two-minute long bouts. The fencer recording a hit first wins. When no hit is registered both fencers have a "loss" marked on their scoresheet. Points at the end of the competition are awarded for the number of wins - i.e. 70% wins carries 1000pts etc.

For the 300m swimming event, 1000 points are awarded for a time of 3 minutes 54 seconds. Four extra points are added or deducted for every half-second below or above this time. Top Olympic swimmers would cover this course in half the time - but, then, can Matt Biondi shoot and fence, too?

50cm wide targets are used for the shooting discipline. There are six scoring zones. A maximum 10 points is given for hitting the inner 10cm circle from a distance of 25m. Each pentathlete fires four rounds of five shots.

On the third day pentathletes take on the cross-country course of 4000m. There is a staggered start so they merely race against the clock.

1000pts are scored for a time of 14 minutes and 15 seconds with additions and deductions of three points for every second below and above.

First is now last. And the pentathletes in Barcelona conclude with a show-jumping contest on unfamiliar horses. The 600m course has 15 obstacles including a double and a triple with a time limit of 1 minute 43 seconds.

A maximum 1100 points can be scored by jumping a clear round in less than the time limit.

THE OLYMPIC ROUTE

To qualify for the Olympic Games pentathletes must have recorded a score of at least 4,700 points in a UIPMB-recognised international competition.

DATA-BANK

VENUES:

Fencing:Palau de la Metal-lurgia, 3.5km from the Vila Olimpica. It holds 3,500 spectators.
Swimming:Piscines Bernat Picornell, 6km from the Vila Olimpica. It holds 10,700 spectators.
Shooting:Camp de Tir Olimpic de Mollet, 20km from the Vila Olimpica. It holds 800 spectators.
Cross-Country:Circuit de Cros, 6km from the Vila Olimpica. It holds 20,000 spectators.
Riding:Real Club de Polo, 8km from the Vila Olimpica. It holds 15,300 spectators.

EVENTS:

Fencing:	epee
Swimming:	300m freestyle
Shooting:	.22 calibre pistol or revolver.
Cross-country:	4,000m cross-country.
Riding:(jumping)	15 obstacles over a 600m course.

1988 CHAMPIONS:

Individual :	Janos Martinek (HUN)
Team:	Hungary

MEDALS — Men

Country	G	S	B	Total
Sweden	9	7	5	21
Hungary	8	6	3	17
USSR	5	5	5	15
USA	-	5	3	8
Italy	2	2	2	6
Finland	-	1	4	5
FRG	1	-	1	2
Great Britain	1	-	1	2
Czechoslovakia	-	1	1	2
France	-	-	2	2
Poland	1	-	-	1
	27	27	27	81

SCHEDULE

LOCAL SPANISH TIME. SUBTRACT ONE HOUR FOR BRITAIN.

JULY

26	Fencing	09 00 – 20.00
27	Swimming	12.00 – 13.30
	Shooting	16.30 – 19.30
28	Cross-country	11.00 – 12.30
29	Riding	10.00 – 13.00 17.00 – 20.00

DID YOU KNOW...? The pentathlon of Ancient times included javelin, discus, jumping, running and wrestling.

Unlike the Barcelona competition, the modern pentathlon is normally held over five days.

The most gold medals have been won by Andras Balczo of Hungary. He took the team title in 1960 and 1968 and added an individual gold in 1972 making a hat-trick.

Modern Pentathlon is governed internationally by the **UIPMB, the International Union of Modern Pentathlon and Biathlon**, and in Great Britain by the **Modern Pentathlon Association of Great Britain.**

ROWING

DES SEZ peer of the realm once described rowing as an activity 'the French rightly reserved for their convicts and the Romans for their slaves'.

More gold to come in Barcelona?

The British in general decided it was a good sport and as often, the rest of the world followed. It is ironic that being the best in the world at one sport, such as tennis, can make you a multi-millionaire, while being best in the world at a sport like rowing might earn you considerable kudos but not a penny piece. It's a thought that may just have crossed Steven Redgrave's mind. In 1984 with Martin Cross, Richard Budgett and Andy Holmes, not forgetting the cox Adrian Ellison, Redgrave won a gold medal in the coxed fours. In 1988 with Holmes, he won a gold in the coxless pairs. And this time with Matthew Pinsent, Redgrave is a gold medal favourite again. These two are the reigning world champions.

There are eight events for men from single sculls up to eights. Women's rowing, which entered the Olympics in 1976, has six events. They do not compete in coxed pairs or coxless fours.

Britain has won a good crop of medals in this sport down the years and may well earn another three or four here. But one of the gold medal favourites are the famous Italian brothers Carmine and Giuseppe Abbagnale. With passenger Giuseppe Dicapua they have taken the gold medal at the last two Games in the coxed pairs. They are also the reigning world champions.

Incidentally a coxless pair or four will usually record faster times than equivalent 'coxed' boats. Why then have a cox, you may ask? The reason is historical. The sport of rowing began with coxes and the practice is continued mostly for the sake of tradition. However, in 'eights' the little passenger at the back (or front) will play an important role in terms of encouragement and tactics.

One other historical note. John Kelly of the United States who won three gold medals in the twenties was the father of Grace Kelly, the film actress who became Princess Grace of Monaco. Her brother, also John, was an Olympic medallist in rowing, too.

FACT-O-FILE

If Steven Redgrave wins gold at the 1992 Olympic Games he will join a very elite club - of only five rowers to have won three golds in successive Games.

For Redgrave, then, a gold might seem old hat. But it will be a new trick for his partner Matthew Pinsent - a 21 year-old Oxford student who is title favourite with Redgrave in the coxless pairs. The likeable Pinsent, whose father is a rector in Portsmouth, had not even considered rowing when Redgrave was winning his first gold eight years ago.

The duo face tough opposition, of course, as well as a tough internal decision - whether to row in both the coxed and coxless pairs or to concentrate their effort on one discipline. Perhaps the new coach Jurgen Grobler, from the all-powerful former East Germany, will have some advice to give.

Rowing made its Olympic debut in 1900 - for men only - over a course on the River Seine. Women's rowing was introduced in 1976 over a 1000m course which changed to a 2000m course from 1988 onwards.

RULES AND TOOLS

In the meantime, each country at the Barcelona Games - a misnomer for the rowers who compete at Banyoles 124km from the Catalonian capital - has the right to enter one crew per event. A country can also carry a certain number of reserves even after the heats of an event if there is a genuine illness or injury.

Amongst the eight events for men and the six for women there are two distinct categories: sweep rowing and sculling. For the former - used for the coxed and coxless pairs and fours and the eight - rowers use a single oar two-handed. In sculling a rower, or sculler, uses two oars.

Boats vary in size from 9m-20m and a repechage system operates for crews beaten in the early heats. In the "coxed" boats the cox steers and shouts out the stroking rate - i.e. the number of

Redgrave and Pinsent out of context but making a splash.

ROWING

Redgrave (left) and Andy Holmes receive gold from The Princess Royal in Seoul.

"pulls" per minute. For the coxless events one of the rowers has rudderlines attached to a pivoting shoe which he or she steers. The seats in the boat are fitted on rails and slide back and forth in unison with the rowing motion.

Rowing is one of the most aerobically demanding Olympic sports. But rowers have to be supple as well as strong.

OLYMPIC ROUTE

Britain's rowers have been selected for the Games through a series of trials and consideration of their international results

BARCELONA BRITS

Rowing has a strong tradition in Britain. It is a well-established sport on the curriculum of a large number of schools. Even so, the coxed fours gold in Los Angeles ended a medal famine of almost forty years.

In Barcelona, Britain must have strong chances of making the final in nearly all the men's sweep-oar disciplines. Martin Cross is likely

to lead one of the fours boats. Britain took fourth place in both the coxed and coxless fours, as well as the eights, finals in Seoul in 1988.

For the women, the opposition - particularly from the former Soviet Union and East Germany - should prove difficult. Britain has a number of "lightweight" rowing world medallists but has not had the same measure of success in the Olympic disciplines – except at the 1991 World Championships with a bronze in the coxless pairs.

BANYOLES

> **Details** Capacity 24,000
Distance to Olympic Village 130
Distance to CMC 136

DATA-BANK

VENUE:
Estany de Banyoles (Girona Province), 124km from Barcelona.
The competition area has six lanes, each 2000m long x 13.5m wide, running from south to north. It holds 24,000 spectators.

EVENTS:
Single sculls (m+w) Quadruple sculls (m+w)
Double sculls (m+w) Coxless fours (m+w)
Coxless pairs (m+w) Coxed fours (m)
Coxed pairs (m) Eights (m+w)

1988 CHAMPIONS:
Men
Single sculls Thomas Lange (GDR)
Double sculls HOL
Coxless quadruple
 sculls ITA
Coxless pairs GBR
Coxed pairs ITA
Coxless fours GDR
Coxed fours GDR
Eights FRG
Women
Single sculls Jutta Behrendt (GDR)
Double sculls GDR
Coxed quadruple
 sculls GDR
Coxless pairs ROM
Coxed fours GDR
Eights GDR

MEDALS	Men			Women			
Country	G	S	B	G	S	B	Total
USA	27	18	14	1	4	1	65
GDR	20	4	7	13	3	1	48
USSR	11	14	7	1	6	4	43
FRG	17	12	11	-	-	2	42
Great Britain	16	15	6	-	-	-	37
Italy	12	10	8	-	-	-	30
France	4	13	9	-	-	-	26
Canada	3	6	9	-	2	1	21
Romania	1	3	1	7	3	5	20
Switzerland	4	7	9	-	-	-	20
Netherlands	4	4	5	-	1	1	15
Denmark	3	3	6	-	-	1	13
Australia	3	4	4	-	-	1	12
New Zealand	3	2	5	-	-	1	11
Bulgaria	-	-	1	2	3	4	10
Czechoslovakia	2	1	7	-	-	-	10
Norway	1	3	6	-	-	-	10
Poland	-	1	7	-	1	-	9
Belgium	-	6	1	-	-	1	8
Finland	3	-	3	-	-	-	6
Yugoslavia	1	1	3	-	-	-	5
Greece	1	2	1	-	-	-	4
Argentina	1	1	2	-	-	-	4
Austria	-	2	2	-	-	-	4
Uruguay	-	1	3	-	-	-	4
Hungary	-	1	2	-	-	-	3
Sweden	-	2	-	-	-	-	2
China	-	-	-	-	1	1	2
Spain	-	1	-	-	-	-	1
	137	137	139	24	24	24	485

ROWING

World silver medallist Katie Brownlow (front) could stroke the women's eight in Barcelona.

SCHEDULE

LOCAL SPANISH TIME. SUBTRACT ONE HOUR FOR BRITAIN.

JULY

27	Heats	Coxless fours (w)	08.00
		Double sculls (w)	
		Coxless pairs (w)	
		Coxed fours (m)	
		Double sculls (m)	
		Coxless pairs (m)	
		Single sculls (m)	
28	Heats	Single sculls (w)	08.00
		Quadruple sculls (w)	
		Eights (w)	
		Coxed pairs (m)	
		Coxless fours (m)	
		Quadruple sculls (m)	
		Eights (m)	
29	Repechage	Coxless fours (w)	08.00
		Double sculls (w)	
		Coxless pairs (w)	
		Coxed fours (m)	
		Double sculls (m)	
		Coxless pairs (m)	
		Single sculls (m)	
	Repechage	Single sculls (w)	17.30
		Quadruple sculls (w)	
		Eights (w)	
		Coxed pairs (m)	
		Coxless fours (m)	
		Quadruple sculls (m)	
		Eights (m)	

(For events with less than 13 entries, the repechage will be held on the morning of Friday, 31 July)

30	Semi-final	Coxless fours (w)	08.00
		Double sculls (w)	
		Coxless pairs (w)	
		Coxed fours (m)	
		Double sculls (m)	
		Coxless pairs (m)	
		Single sculls (m+w)	
31	Semi Final	Single sculls (w)	08.00
		Quadruple sculls (w)	
		Eight oars with coxswain (w)	
		Coxed pairs (m)	
		Coxless fours (m)	
		Quadruple sculls (m)	
		Eights (m+w)	
		(See timing note under July 29 section)	

SCHEDULE

AUGUST

1	**Final** B	Coxless fours (w)	07.50
		Double sculls (w)	
		Coxless pairs (w)	
		Coxed fours (m)	
		Double sculls (m)	
		Coxless pairs (m)	
		Single sculls (m+w)	
	Final A	Coxless fours (w)	09.10
		Double sculls (w)	
		Coxless pairs (w)	
		Coxed fours (m)	
		Double sculls (m)	
		Coxless pairs (m)	
		Single sculls (m)	
2	**Final** B	Single sculls (w)	07.50
		Quadruple sculls (w)	
		Eights (w)	
		Coxed pairs (m)	
		Coxless fours (m)	
		Quadruple sculls (m)	
		Eights (m)	
	Final A	Single sculls (w)	09.10
		Quadruple sculls (w)	
		Eights (w)	
		Coxed pairs (m)	
		Coxless fours (m)	
		Quadruple sculls (m)	
		Eights (m+w)	

DID YOU KNOW...? If a cox falls overboard during a race a crew is disqualified but if a rower falls overboard the crew can continue the race.

One of the most famous father and son Olympic partnerships comes from the sport of rowing. Julius Beresford took a rowing silver in 1912 and his son, Jack, won three golds in 1924, 1932 and 1936.

Another British pair - Charles (1908) and Richard (1948) Burnell are the only father and son in Olympic rowing history to have both won gold medals.

Rowing is governed internationally by **FISA**, the International Amateur Rowing Federation, and in Great Britain by the Amateur Rowing Association.

Pulling for Manchester
and for Britain

Slater Heelis
SOLICITORS

71 Princess Street, Manchester M2 4HL
Telephone 061-228 3781

SHOOTING

D **ES SEZ** Happily for the pigeon community, shooting the live pigeon has not been part of the Olympic Games since 1900.

Nowadays, the pigeons are strictly clay and in Barcelona thirteen gold medals will be available; seven for men, four for women and two in 'open' events - Olympic trap and skeet.

Medallists can come from anywhere but as in so many Olympic sports, the former Soviet Union has been the recent dominant force. Britain has had considerable success in recent Games. Malcolm Cooper won gold medals in both Los Angeles and Seoul in the small bore rifle (three position) event. Alister Allen took bronze and silver behind him. Cooper has since won two world championship events, but has now retired from Olympic competition.

Prior to Cooper, Britain's last gold medal was won by Robert Braithwaite in 1968. His event was Olympic Trap, this sport has provided the oldest gold medallist in Oskar Swahn of Sweden who was 64 in 1912. In 1920 at 72 he became the oldest silver medallist. An extraordinary champion was Hungary's Karoly Takacs. European pistol shooting champion in the thirties, he then lost his right hand in an army accident. Remarkably, he taught himself to shoot left-handed and went on to win gold medals at both the 1948 and 52 Games.

FACT-O-FILE

Shooting has a unique Olympic claim to fame. It was the sport practised by Baron Pierre de Coubertin, founder of the modern Games. And, fittingly, it has been on the programme since 1896 with the exception of 1904 and 1928.

Britain's team in 1992 will miss Malcolm Cooper. The quiet Hampshire double gold-medallist has called it a day. The shooting British will, no doubt, hope that someone will step in to take his place.

Shooting has had its lighter Olympic moments. Take Cooper in 1988, for instance. The media-shy champion agreed to hold a pre-competition press conference at the range only to be repaid by a BBC radio reporter knocking over and breaking his favourite rifle. Full points to Cooper for temper-control under the circumstances

and for carrying on to win a gold two days later.

In 1956 a Canadian, Gerald Ouellette, was ecstatic at taking the small-bore rifle prone event title with a maximum possible score of 600points. His delight was not quite so evident when his world record was taken away because the range was later discovered to be 1.5m short.

RULES AND TOOLS

440 of the world's leading exponents will group in Barcelona for the Games. Each nation has a quota of shooters who have pre-qualified up to a maximum of two per rifle, pistol and running target event and three per trap and skeet event. Shooters can compete in more than one event.

All shooting competitions have preliminary or qualifying rounds followed by a semi-final and final. A varying number of shooters per discipline can move through to the final. Competitors draw for start numbers and firing stations.

Target size, distance and permitted shooting time vary across the disciplines. One of the fastest is the rapid-fire pistol where five targets turn from side-on to face the shooter for between eight and four seconds depending on the stage of the competition.

The air-pistol, meanwhile, is more a test of precision. Competitors have 90 minutes to fire 60 shots (for men) and 40 shots (for women) at a target placed 10m away. But the inner,

Take aim...

1988 CHAMPIONS:

Men

Air pistol	Taniou Kiriakov (BUL)
Free pistol 50m	Sorin Babii (ROM)
Rapid fire pistol	Afanasi Kouzmine (URS)
Small-bore rifle prone	Miroslav Varga (TCH)
Small-bore rifle - 3 positions	Malcolm Cooper (GBR)
Running game target	Tor Heiestad (NOR)
Olympic trap	Dmitri Monakov (URS)
Skeet	Axel Wegner (GDR)
Air rifle	Goran Maksimovic (YUG)

Women

Sport pistol	Nino Saloukvadze (URS)
Standard rifle	Silvia Sperber (FRG)
Air pistol	Jasna Sekaric (YUG)
Air rifle	Irina Chilova (URS)

SHOOTING

MEDALS	Men			Women*			
Country	G	S	B	G	S	B	Total
United States	42	23	17	1	1	1	85
Sweden	13	23	18	-	-	-	54
USSR**	15	15	16	2	1	3	52
Great Britain	13	14	19	-	-	-	46
France	12	15	12	-	-	-	39
Norway	16	7	10	-	-	-	33
Switzerland	11	9	10	-	-	-	30
FRG	5	6	5	1	2	-	19
Greece	5	7	6	-	-	-	18
Denmark	3	8	6	-	-	-	17
Finland	3	5	9	-	-	-	17
Italy	6	3	6	-	1	-	16
GDR	3	8	5	-	-	-	16
Hungary	6	3	6	-	-	-	15
Romania	5	4	3	-	-	-	12
Canada	3	3	2	1	-	-	9
China	2	1	3	1	-	2	8
Czechoslovakia	3	3	1	-	-	-	7
Belgium	2	3	2	-	-	-	7
Poland	2	1	3	-	-	-	6
Austria	1	1	3	-	-	-	5
Bulgaria	1	1	3	-	1	-	4
Japan	1	-	2	-	1	-	4
Yugoslavia	1	-	-	1	-	1	3
Brazil	1	1	1	-	-	-	3
Peru	1	1	-	-	-	-	2
Colombia	-	2	-	-	-	-	2
Netherlands	-	1	1	-	-	-	2
Spain	-	1	1	-	-	-	2
Australia	-	-	1	-	-	1	2
North Korea	1	-	-	-	-	-	1
Argentina	-	1	-	-	-	-	1
Chile	-	1	-	-	-	-	1
Korea	-	1	-	-	-	-	1
Mexico	-	1	-	-	-	-	1
Portugal	-	1	-	-	-	-	1
South Africa	-	1	-	-	-	-	1
Cuba	-	-	1	-	-	-	1
Haiti	-	-	1	-	-	-	1
New Zealand	-	-	1	-	-	-	1
Venezuela	-	-	1	-	-	-	1
	177	175	173	7	7	7	546

* Excluding female medallists prior to 1984.
** Including a silver and bronze for Russia in 1912.

SCHEDULE

LOCAL SPANISH TIME. SUBTRACT ONE HOUR FOR BRITAIN.

JULY

26	10m air rifle (w) prelims & F	08.30
	Skeet (o) prelims	09.00
	50m free pistol (m) prelims & F	11.30
27	Skeet (o) prelims	09.00
	25m sport pistol (w) prelims	09.00
	Final	14.00
	10m air rifle (m) prelims	09.00
	Final	12.30
28	Skeet (o) s/f	09.00
	Final	14.00
	10m air pistol (m) prelims	09.00
	Final	14.00
29	50m free rifle (m) prelims	09.00
	Final	12.30
	25m rapid fire pistol (m) prelims	09.00
30	25m rapid fire pistol (m) prelims	09.00
	Final	14.00
	50m standard rifle (w) prelims	09.00
	Final	12.30
31	50m free rifle (m) prelims	09.00
	Final	15.30
	Prel. 10m running target (slow) run (m) prelims	09.00
	Prel. trap (o) prelims	09.00

AUGUST

1	10m air pistol (w) prelims	09.00
	Final	12.00
	10m running target (m) prelims	09.00
	Final	14.30
	Prel. trap (o) prelims	09.00
2	Trap (o) s/f	09.00
	Final	14.00

Smoke with fire. Skeet shooter in action.

highest-scoring, ring is only a quarter of an inch wide.

For the small-bore rifle events the target is set at a distance of 50m. Each competitor gets two hours to fire 60 shots. Only the top eight scorers go through to the final of just 10 shots. For the three-position category, shooters have 40 shots from each of the prone, kneeling and standing positions.

Olympic trap and skeet are similar to clay-pigeon shooting. Each contestant has 150 clays to target over two days. The top 24 go through to a semi-final of 50 clays and then the top six to a final of 25 clays. Skeet is the same as trap except that competitors have to shoot from a number of different firing stations.

BARCELONA BRITS

To be considered for selection to a national team for the Games, shooters have to meet UIT (International Shooting Union) standards for their chosen discipline. This means scoring a set number of points in the world championships, continental cups or world cups under UIT rules before 10 July 1992.

DID YOU KNOW...? In 1932 Antonis Lemberkovits of Hungary hit the bullseye of the wrong target during his round. Nobody else noticed but he admitted the error. Without his honesty he would have won the gold medal.

Shooting is governed internationally by UIT, the International Shooting Union, and in Great Britain by the Great Britain Shooting Federation.

SHOOTING

71

SHOOTING

Gold and silver last time round.

⇨ **Details** Capacity   2,500 (F.y Skeet) – 1,800 (S. Finals)
          Distance to Olympic Village   28
          Distance to CMC   28

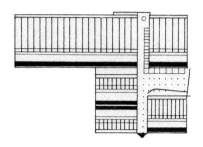

DATA-BANK

VENUE:
Camp de Tir Olimpic del Mollet, 35km from the Vila Olimpica. The competition area measures 342,000m². It holds 5,140 spectators.

EVENTS:

25m rapid-fire pistol **(m)**	25m sport pistol **(w)**
50m free pistol **(m)**	10m air pistol **(w)**
10m air pistol **(m)**	10m air rifle **(w)**
10m running target **(m)**	50m standard rifle **(w)**
10m air rifle **(m)**	
50m free rifle (3 pos'ns) **(m)**	Skeet **(o)**
50m free rifle (prone) **(m)**	Trap **(o)**

SWIMMING

DES SEZ This has been one of the central Olympic sports since the Games were reintroduced in 1896. Women's events began in 1912. In the early Games swimming took place in natural surroundings. Twice it was held in the sea, once in a lake and once in the River Seine. Underwater swimming was one of the events in the Paris Games. Not very pleasant one would have thought.

The now-established 50m pool was first used in 1924. In Barcelona there are 31 gold medals to be won in swimming, 16 for men and 15 for women. That is as far as racing is concerned. In addition, there will be two gold medals in synchronised swimming - women only - and there are four gold medals in diving and one for water polo.

No country dominates a major Olympic sport to the extent that the USA does in swimming and diving events. In swimming they have won more than a third of all medals, and in diving more medals than all other countries put together.

Once again, in 1992, the USA will be the dominant force in the pool but their superiority has been threatened in diving at the past two Games with the emergence of the Chinese. They have won three of the last four women's titles and only the brilliance of the great American Greg Louganis has denied the Chinese men. Swimming, of course, has produced some of the greatest Olympic names.

In 1924 and 1928 the blue riband 100m freestyle event was won by Johnny Weissmuller. He won five gold medals in total before becoming the most famous Tarzan in Hollywood history. In 1972 the same title was won by Mark Spitz. It was one of seven won by the American in Munich - a record at one Games in any sport. Spitz had earlier won two gold medals in 1968. In early 1992 there was talk of an extraordinary Olympic comeback for Spitz. But he could not produce fast enough times to make the Olympic trials.

The last Olympics produced the finest ever women's swimming performance with the East German Kristin Otto becoming the first woman to win six gold medals at one Games. She also became the first woman to win Olympic titles at three different strokes: freestyle, butterfly and backstroke.

Britain has maintained a good record in the sport. In recent years there have been three golden heroes at breaststroke. In 1976 David Wilkie became Britain's first male swimming gold medallist for 68 years when he won the 200m breaststroke. He also took silver in the 100m.

In 1980 when American swimmers were not present, Duncan Goodhew won gold at 100m breaststroke and at the last Games Adrian Moorhouse repeated that success while Nick Gillingham took silver over 200m.

In women's events, Britain has not had a 'golden girl' since Anita Lonsborough won the 200m breaststroke in Rome in 1960. Since that Games the only individual medallists are Sharron Davies (silver 400m medley, 1980), Sarah Hardcastle and June Croft (silver and bronze 400m freestyle, 1984) and Hardcastle (bronze 800m freestyle also in 1984).

Britain's best hopes for medals will be Moorhouse and Gillingham, both still going strong and both medallists at the 1991 world championships (silver and bronze). The Americans of course will take some beating in most events and Hungary has two outstanding stars in Norbert Rosza who has taken the world record that Moorhouse held and Tamas Darnyi who is the first man to go under two minutes for the 200m medley. They also have a star in women's swimming in Krisztina Egerszegi who has set world record times in backstroke.

Matt Biondi and Janet Evans, of the USA, also return to defend only some of their 1988 titles.

East Germany used to produce most of the medal winners in women's swimming - but since the Berlin Wall came down, their standards have plummeted. 'Too much junk food' according to former West German gold medallist Michael Gross. Incidentally, freestyle is the fastest swimming stroke, breaststroke the slowest. Butterfly came about as a result of a loophole in the breaststroke rules and backstroke swimmers are the only ones who start in the pool. And if you are wondering about medley races. This is where all four strokes are employed by either an individual or in relay.

Matt Biondi triumphs in the 1988 50m free.

 SWIMMING

FACT-O-FILE

What a difference four years looks set to make. Matt Biondi, Kristin Otto and Janet Evans were the super-heroes of 1988. As the Berlin wall tumbled, however, Otto, recently retired, found herself partially villified instead of glorified.

Biondi and Evans, meanwhile, look unlikely to repeat their multi-medal feats. They ducked out in all except a few distances at the USA Olympic trials.

The world awaits some new faces. Adrian Moorhouse will be hoping that they are not Hungarian. He lost his world record to Norbert Rosza last year and will be looking for revenge in attempting to defend his title.

The swimming events will be held under open Spanish skies at the Bernat Picornell pool nestled next to the Olympic stadium at Montjuic. Unlike Seoul most events will have their heats and finals on the same day.

RULES AND TOOLS

FINA (International Amateur Swimming Federation) rules will apply and each country can enter two swimmers (up to a maximum of 26 men and 26 women) or divers and one relay team per event. In the synchronised swimming each nation is only permitted one competitor in the solo event.

The first Olympic swimming events were held in 1896 in the Bay of Zea near Piraeus. The sport did not have a purpose-built "tank" until 1908 in the centre of the White City stadium. Women joined in from 1912 onwards and the sport moved indoors for the first time at Wembley in 1948.

DATA-BANK

VENUE:
Piscines Bernat Picornell, 6km from the Vila Olimpica.
Consists of two 50m x 25m pools: a covered pool for warm-up and the open-air competition pool. The stands hold 10,700 spectators.
Piscina de Montjuic in the Montjuic area, 6km from the Vila Olimpica. Two open-air pools, one for diving (25m x 25m) and the other for water polo (33.3m x 25m). The stands hold 6,498 spectators.

EVENTS:
Swimming
:50m free (m+w)
100m free (m+w)
200m free (m+w)
400m free (m+w)
800m free (w)
1500m free (m)
100m back (m+w)
200m back (m+w)
100m breast (m+w)
200m breast (m+w)
100m fly (m+w)
200m fly (m+w)
200m medley (m+w)
400m medley (m+w)
4x100m free relay (m+w)
4x200m free relay (m)
4x100m medley relay (m+w)

Diving
Platform (m+w)
Springboard (m+w)

Sychronised swimming
Solo (w)
Duet (w)

Water polo:
Team (m)

Adrian Moorhouse seeks a golden defence.

SWIMMING MEDALS

Country	Men			Women			Total
	G	S	B	G	S	B	
USA	91	69	48	63	41	36	368
Australia	23	18	27	14	12	9	103
GDR	6	7	5	32	25	17	92
FRG	12	15	14	2	5	13	61
USSR	9	14	18	4	7	8	60
Great Britain	10	12	12	4	9	12	59
Hungary	10	11	10	5	5	3	44
Japan	12	17	11	2	1	1	44
Netherlands	-	-	2	9	13	10	34
Canada	5	7	5	1	5	10	33
Sweden	7	7	9	-	2	2	27
France	2	5	7	-	1	2	17
Denmark	-	2	1	2	3	3	11
Austria	2	3	5	-	-	1	11
Greece	1	4	3	-	-	-	8
New Zealand	1	-	2	-	-	1	4
South Africa	-	-	-	1	-	3	4
China	-	-	-	-	3	1	4
Brazil	-	1	3	-	-	-	4
Italy	-	-	1	-	1	2	4
Belgium	-	1	1	-	-	1	3
Romania	-	-	-	-	1	2	3
Argentina	1	-	-	-	1	-	2
Yugoslavia	-	-	-	1	1	-	2
Mexico	1	-	-	-	-	1	2
Bulgaria	-	-	-	-	1	1	2
Finland	-	2	-	-	-	-	2
Philippines	-	2	-	-	-	-	2
Poland	-	-	1	-	-	1	2
Spain	-	2	-	-	-	-	2
Surinam	1	-	-	-	-	-	1
Costa Rica	-	-	-	-	1	-	1
Switzerland	-	1	-	-	-	-	1
Venezuela	-	-	1	-	-	-	1
	194[1]	193	193	140[2]	138	140[3]	998

1 Double counting of Australia/New Zealand relay team in 1912.
2 Two golds in 1984 100m free.
3 Two bronzes in 1988 50m free.

SWIMMING

LOCAL SPANISH TIME. SUBTRACT ONE HOUR FOR BRITAIN.

SWIMMING

JULY

26	Heats	100m free (w)	10.00
		100m breast (m)	
		400m medley (w)	
		200m free (m)	
	Finals	100m free (w)	18.00
		100m breast (m)	
		400m medley (w)	
		200m free (m)	
27	Heats	100m fly (m)	09.30
		200m free (w)	
		400m medley (m)	
		200m breast (w)	
		4x200m free (m)	
		100m fly (m)	18.00
		200m free (w)	
		400m medley (m)	
		200m breast (w)	
		4x200m free (m)	
28	Heats	400m free (w)	10.00
		100m free (m)	
		100m back (w)	
		200m back (m)	
		4x100m free (w)	
	Finals	400m free (w)	18.00
		100m free (m)	
		100m back (w)	
	Finals	200m back (m)	
		4x100m free (w)	
29	Heats	400m free (m)	10.00
		100m fly (w)	

SCHEDULE			

JULY 29 continued

		200m breast (m)	
		100m breast (w)	
		4x100m free (m)	
		800m free (w)	
	Finals	400m free (m)	18.00
		100m fly (w)	
		200m breast (m)	
		100m breast (w)	
		4x100m free (m)	
30	Heats	200m fly (m)	10.00
		200m medley (w)	
		100m back (m)	
		4x100m medley relay (w)	
		50m free (m)	
		1500m free (m)	
	Finals	200m fly (m)	18.00
		200m medley (w)	
		50m free (m)	
		800m free (w)	
		100m back (m)	
		4x100m medley (w)	
31	Heats	200m fly (w)	10.00
		200m medley (m)	
		200m back (w)	
		4x100m medley (m)	
		50m free (w)	
	Finals	200m fly (w)	18.00
		200m medley (m)	
		50m free (w)	
		1500m free (m)	
		200m back (w)	
		4x100m medley (m)	

Nick Gillingham surges forward.

SWIMMING

DIVING

Diving made its Olympic debut in 1904 for men and 1912 for women. Perhaps one of the greatest divers of all-time was Greg Louganis. He took double gold in both 1984 and 1988 fending off a strong Chinese challenge.

His 1988 victories were all the more remarkable for having been achieved after a horrific incident in which he hit the back of his head on the board during one dive and required stitches to his head before he could continue.

Competition order in diving is decided by draw and the top 12 from the preliminaries compete in the final in reverse order of placing.

In the men's highboard each competitor performs seven dives in the preliminaries and ten in the final.

For the springboard event they must execute one extra dive in the final. The women complete six and seven preliminary dives and six and ten final dives in the highboard and springboard respectively.

Seven judges mark each dive out of ten points. There are over 80 recognised competition dives and each carries a different "degree of difficulty" grading.

Great Britain has never won a diving gold medal. Brian Phelps and Liz Ferris were the nation's last medallists in 1960 when both took bronze. Britain's top two divers are currently Robert Morgan and Tony Ali.

DIVING MEDALS

Country	Men G	S	B	Women G	S	B	Total
USA	26	19	19	19	20	19	122
Sweden	4	5	4	2	3	3	21
FRG	3	5	5	3	1	1	18
USSR	2	1	3	2	3	3	14
China	-	3	2	3	1	-	9
Italy	3	4	2	-	-	-	9
Mexico	1	3	4	-	-	-	8
GDR	1	-	-	1	2	3	7
Great Britain	-	-	2	-	1	2	5
Czechoslovakia	-	-	-	1	1	-	2
Canada	-	-	-	-	-	1	2
Denmark	-	-	-	1	-	1	2
Egypt	-	1	1	-	-	-	2
Australia	1	-	-	-	-	-	1
France	-	-	-	-	1	-	1
Austria	-	-	1	-	-	-	1
	41	41	43	33	33	33	224

1 Two bronzes awarded in a 1904 and a 1908 event.

SCHEDULE
LOCAL SPANISH TIME. SUBTRACT ONE HOUR FOR BRITAIN.
SYNCHRONISED SWIMMING

AUGUST

2 & 3	Solo and duet - prelims.	15.00
5	Figures	08.00
6 & 7	**Finals** solo and duet	15.00

SYNCHRONISED SWIMMING MEDALS

Country	Women G	S	B	Total
Canada	2	2	-	4
USA	2	2	-	4
Japan	-	-	4	4
	4	4	4	12

PICORNELL

⇨ **Details** Capacity — 10,700
Distance to Olympic Village — 6
Distance to CMC — 1.5

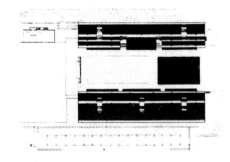

SCHEDULE
LOCAL SPANISH TIME. SUBTRACT ONE HOUR FOR BRITAIN.
DIVING

JULY

26	Platform (w) prelims	10.00 & 15.00
27	**Final** platform (w)	15.00
28	Prel.round springboard (m)	10.00 & 15.00
29	**Final** springboard (m)	15.00

AUGUST

2	Springboard (w) prelims.	10.00 & 15.00
	Platform (m) prelims.	10.00 & 14.30
3	**Final** springboard (w)	14.30
4	**Final** platform (m)	15.00

SYNCHRO

The USA, Canada and Japan are the strongest nations in the world.

In 1988 Great Britain finished seventh in the duet and sixth, with Nicola Shearn, in the solo event. Kerry Shacklock is Britain's current leading exponent.

Synchronised swimming suffers its fair share of ridicule but it requires hours of training and dedication mixed with stamina and the strength to put the body through its paces for long periods underwater. There is a solo event in two parts - compulsory figures and a free routine.

Only the top swimmers make it into the final. Like diving, synchro is marked by judges out of a maximum ten points.

British synchro duet.

1988 CHAMPIONS:
SWIMMING
Men:

50m free	Matt Biondi (USA)
100m free	Matt Biondi (USA)
200m free	Duncan Armstrong (AUS)
400m free	Uwe Dassler (GDR)
1500m free	Vladimir Salnikov (URS)
100m back	Daichi Suzuki (JPN)
200m back	Igor Polianski (URS)
100m breast	Adrian Moorhouse (GBR)
200m breast	Jozsef Szabo (HUN)
100m fly	Anthony Nesty (SUR)
200m fly	Michael Gross (FRG)
200m ind. medley	Tamas Darnyi (HUN)
400m ind. medley	Tamas Darnyi (HUN)
4x100m free	USA
4x200m free	USA
4x100m medley	USA

Women

50m free	Kristin Otto (GDR)
100m free	Kristin Otto (GDR)
200m free	Heike Friedrich (GDR)
400m free	Janet Evans (USA)
800m free	Janet Evans (USA)
100m back	Kristin Otto (GDR)
200m back	Krisztina Egerszegi (HUN)
100m breast	Tania Dangalakova (URS)
200m breast	Silke Horner (GDR)
100m fly	Kristin Otto (GDR)
200m fly	Kathleen Nord (GDR)
200m ind. medley	Daniela Hunger (GDR)
400m ind. medley	Janet Evans (USA)
4x100m free	German Democratic Rep.
4x100m medley	German Democratic Rep.

DIVING:
Men:

Spring	Greg Louganis (USA)
High	Greg Louganis (USA)

Women:

Spring	Gao Min (CHN)
High	Xu Yanmei (CHN)

SYNCHRONISED SWIMMING

Solo	Carolyn Waldo (CAN)
Duet	Canada

WATER POLO

	Yugoslavia

WATER POLO
MEDALS

Country	Men G	S	B	Total
Hungary	6	3	3	12
USA	1	3	4	8
Yugoslavia	3	4	-	7
USSR	2	2	3	7
Belgium	-	4	2	6
Great Britain	4	-	-	4
Italy	2	1	1	4
FRG	1	2	1	4
France	1	-	2	3
Sweden	-	1	2	3
Netherlands	-	-	2	2
	20	20	20	60

WATER-POLO

Britain has not qualified for the Games. In Barcelona 12 teams will be drawn to compete in two round-robin groups. From these, the bottom eight teams will move into two classification groups to play off for placings from 5-12.

Meanwhile the top four teams will play in cross-over semi-finals and a final for the medals and fourth place.

Greg Louganis – master diver.

SCHEDULE	

LOCAL SPANISH TIME. SUBTRACT ONE HOUR FOR BRITIAIN.

WATER POLO:

AUGUST

1,2 & 3	Prelims. Piscines Bernat Picornell	09.30
	Piscina de Montjuic	18.30
5 & 6	Prelims. Piscina de Montjuic	09.30 & 17.30
	(NB remaining matches at Piscines Bernat Picornell)	
8	Classification 3 matches	09.30
	Classification 1 match	17.30
	Semi-finals	17.30
9	Classification 3 matches	09.00
	Classification 1 match	14.00
	Final (3-4)	14.00
	Final	14.00

◾ TABLE TENNIS

D ES SEZ This is the sport that almost everyone has played at some time or another. It's fun, fast and splendid exercise. But, at the very highest level, the standards of skill are almost unbelievable.

The first ever Olympic men's final four years ago between two Koreans, Yoo Nam Kyu and Kim Ki Taik provided television viewers with thrills galore.

The four gold medals on offer in 1988 were shared between the host nation and China. However, the balance of power in the game has changed. At the 1991 world championships in Tokyo, Sweden won the Swaythling Cup and became the team champions. They also won it the previous time in 1989. On both these occasions Sweden produced the singles winner, too, in Jan-Ove Waldner and Jorgen Persson.

The women's world team champions are Korea who broke a Chinese winning streak of nine titles running. Deng Yaping is the reigning world singles champion for China.

Britain's long-time number one Desmond Douglas has now retired from international competition. But had there been table tennis in the Olympics of 1928 or 1948, Britain would have had hot gold medal prospects. Fred Perry and Johnny Leach were both world champions around that time. Fred, of course, went on to be the world's number one tennis star as well, winning the Wimbledon singles title three times. He was the last British man to do so.

FACT-O-FILE

Britain tried to solve a Chinese puzzle to make sure they had their best player in Barcelona. They would appear to have failed - barring a last-minute reprieve.

Current English champion Chen Xinhua was born in China, won the world cup for that country in 1985 and has helped them to a world team title. That was all before Chen fell in love with, and married, a British girl from Huddersfield.

The Chinese maestro now has a British passport and residence qualifications. He has played several internationals for his newly-adopted country and is a popular member of the squad.

But the Chinese NOC, despite a lot of approaches, will not release him to play for Britain in Barcelona. That means Britain will be relying on Carl Prean, Matthew Syed and Alan Cooke amongst its men and Alison Gordon, Lisa Lomas and Andrea Holt in the women's squad.

Table tennis was recognised as an Olympic sport in 1977. Fittingly, it made its debut in the Far East in Seoul in 1988. South Korea provided the men's singles and women's doubles champions whilst China collected the other two titles.

But China's pre-eminence, established from the time the "bamboo curtain" was lifted for a second time in the early 1970s, has dwindled in recent years. Sweden's men, in particular, have made major in-roads into international honours. The decline is, perhaps, due to a shift away from table tennis as the national sport under Chairman Mao and to Europeans being quick to close the gap.

RULES AND TOOLS

Competition in Barcelona will be under ITTF (International Table Tennis Federation) rules. Sets, or games, in table tennis are played up to 21 points - or beyond if at least a two-point margin has not

Far eastern dominance has been eroded. The Europeans have caught up.

ESTACIO DEL NORD

▢ **Details** Capacity — 5,100
Distance to Olympic Village — 1
Distance to CMC — 4

TABLE TENNIS

THE OLYMPIC ROUTE

A series of qualifying tournaments for the Olympic Games have been held on a zonal basis. Some players also pre-qualified on the strength of their worldwide ranking.

MEDALS	Men			Women			
Country	G	S	B	G	S	B	Total
China	1	-	-	1	2	1	5
Korea	1	1	1	1	-	-	4
Yugoslavia	-	1	-	-	-	1	2
Sweden	-	-	1	-	-	-	1
	2	2	2	2	2	2	12

been secured. The Olympic group matches will be over the best of three sets and the later knock-out stages will be the best of five sets.

The men's and women's singles tournaments will include 64 players divided into groups of four. Each doubles draw will include 32 pairs also divided initially into groups of four. Every competing nation can enter a maximum of three singles players and two doubles pairs per event as long as they have pre-qualified.

In each event the group winners will progress to a knock-out stage leading to semi-finals and a final. Bronze medals will be awarded to both losing semi-finalists.

Over the last few decades table tennis has been plagued by controversy over equipment. In the 1940s and 1950s bats were simple wood covered with rubber. Then came the advent of a sponge layer between the wood and the rubber. This increased the speed of the ball and the players' ability to impart spin. Rallies were reduced and many felt the sport lost its spectator appeal.

The trend deepened with increasingly varied rubber surfaces which could deceive the eye over the type of spin delivered. Players took to putting two different surfaces of the same colour rubber on either side of the bat and then "twiddling" the bat under the table to confuse opponents. International rules put a stop to this by insisting the bats had two different colour rubbers (red and black) on either side.

And despite all this, the sport is still very fast, dynamic and exciting with a mixture of styles and tactics. Players need lightning reflexes as well as physical speed, strength and agility.

DATA-BANK

VENUE:
Polisportiu Estacio del Nord in the Parc de Mar area, 1km from the Vila Olimpica. The competition area is 36x36m and eight tables will be set up. There is room for 5,100 spectators.

EVENTS:
Singles (m+w)
Doubles (m+w)

1988 CHAMPIONS:
Singles (m) — Yoo Nam-Kyu (KOR)
Doubles (m) — (CHN)
Singles (w) — Chen Jing (CHN)
Doubles (w) — (CHN)

SCHEDULE		
LOCAL SPANISH TIME. SUBTRACT ONE HOUR FOR BRITAIN.		
JULY		
28	Doubles (m+w) groups	20.00
29	Singles (w) groups	10.00
	Doubles (m+w) groups	20.00
30	Singles (m+w) groups	09.00
	Doubles (m+w) groups	19.00
	Singles (m) groups	21.40
31	Singles (m+w) groups	09.00
	Doubles (w) q/f	19.00
	Doubles (m) groups	20.00
	Singles (w) groups	21.20
AUGUST		
1	Singles (m) groups	09.00
	Singles (w) last 16	11.00
	Singles (m) groups	12.00
	Doubles (m) q/f	19.00
	Doubles (w) s/f	21.00
2	Singles (m) last 16	11.00
3	**Final - Doubles (w)**	11.00
	Singles (w) q/f	19.00
	Doubles (m) s/f	21.00
4	**Final - doubles (m)**	11.00
	Singles (w) q/f	19.00
	Singles (w) s/f	21.00
5	**Final - singles (w)**	11.00
	Singles (m) s/f	20.00
6	**Final - singles (m)**	11.00

DID YOU KNOW...? Britain's many-times former national champion Desmond Douglas developed his close-to-the-table style by learning to play in a garage without enough run-back. His rapier-like counter-attack brought his country innumerable wins.

Table tennis is governed internationally by the International Table Tennis Federation and in Great Britain by the British Olympic Table Tennis Committee.

TENNIS

D **ES SEZ**   This is the only current Olympic sport in which Britain has won more medals than any other country. The reason, of course, is that tennis was included in the early Olympics when British players were still amongst the best in the world.

The sport was dropped from the Games in 1924 until its reappearance in 1988. Famous names of the past who have won gold medals include Suzanne Lenglen and Helen Wills (Moody). And a famous name of the present is the reigning Olympic champion Steffi Graf who beat Gabriela Sabatini in the 1988 final.

The men's champion in Seoul was Miloslav Mecir of Chechoslovakia who beat that year's Wimbledon champion, Stefan Edberg, in the semi-final and then the American, Tim Mayotte, for the gold medal.

American pairings took both the men's and women's doubles. There are no mixed doubles in the Olympics.

Some of the wealthiest sportsmen and women will be present in this sport. They will, of course, be taking part. Not for money but for the glory of winning an Olympic medal.   Many of the leading players will be there but the most notable omission will be the 1991 women's number one Monica Seles - winner of the Grand Slam tournaments last year. But she did not play at Wimbledon. Monica refused to represent her country, Yugoslavia, in the Federation Cup and is therefore ruled out. The same is likely to happen to Gabriela Sabatini, the Seoul silver medallist.

It could be Germany for both singles gold medals. Becker, Stich and Graf are a formidable team.

A most interested viewer will be Kitty Godfree who as Kitty McKane won five Olympic medals for Britain in the twenties. She was also a Wimbledon champion and, now in her nineties, still enjoys the occasional set at the All-England club.

FACT-O-FILE

If Steffi Graf, several times Wimbledon champion, had not turned to tennis she might well have represented her country - so rumour has it - at the 800m on the track. Such is the athleticism of the woman who won a golden slam - all grand slams plus the Olympic title - in 1988.

Since then illness, alleged family scandals and the rising standards of her opponents have put Steffi's influence into decline. But in Barcelona she will be helped in attempting a title defence by the absence of current world no. 1 Monica Seles. Germany are also strong in the men's event. But Jim Courier, Ivan Lendl and Stefan Edberg cannot be ruled out if they compete.

Britain, meanwhile, are not likely to feature in the final stages. That is a far cry from the situation at the first Olympic Games of the modern era in 1896 when Irish-born John Pius Boland took the men's singles gold. Four years later Charlotte Cooper became the first female to win a title in any Olympic sport when she won the women's singles gold.

Re-introduced in 1988, tennis made its last full appearance before that in 1924. It was also a demonstration event in 1968 and 1984.

RULES AND TOOLS

96 men and 96 women will contest the four tennis events - men's and women's singles and doubles - in Barcelona. The stadium has eight competition and four practice courts as well as the "show" or centre court. The playing surface is clay.

Each nation can enter a maximum of four men and four women as long as they are pre-qualified. The men will play best of five sets and the women best of three. Tie-breaks come at six-all to decide all sets except the final one. The draw will be made on 24 July and players must wear predominantly white - Andre Agassi please take note. Technology has revolutionised modern tennis. Today's stars hit the ball with greater power using carbon fibre, graphite or alloy rackets rather than the wooden frames of yesteryear. The racket

head surface area is bigger, too, and players use increased top-spin to control the ball and give greater consistency.

THE OLYMPIC ROUTE

Some players have pre-qualified on the basis of their world rankings. Others will arrive in Barcelona hot foot from zonal qualifying tournaments.

Steffi Graf, looking to recover her golden ways.

French Davis Cup hero Henri Leconte in Olympic action.

THE BARCELONA BRITS

Jo Durie and Monique Javer have pre-qualified. The situation amongst the men is not as clear cut but Jeremy Bates, Andrew Castle, Chris Broad and Chris Wilkinson are all in the running for places.

1988 CHAMPIONS:

Singles	**(m)**	Miloslav Mecir (TCH)
Doubles	**(m)**	USA
Singles	**(w)**	Steffi Graf (FRG)
Doubles	**(w)**	USA

SCHEDULE

LOCAL SPANISH TIME. SUBTRACT ONE HOUR FOR BRITAIN.

JULY

28 & 29	Singles **(m+w)** rd 1	10.00
30 & 31	Singles **(m+w)** rd 2	10.00
	Doubles **(m+w)** rd 1	

AUGUST

1 & 2	Singles **(m+w)** rd 3	10.00
	Doubles **(m+w)** rd 2	
3 & 4	Singles and doubles **(m+w)** q/f	11.00
5 & 6	Singles and doubles **(m+w)** s/f	11.00
7	**Final** - doubles **(m)**	11.00
	Final - singles **(w)**	14.00
8	**Final** - doubles **(w)**	11.00
	Final - singles **(m)**	14.00

VALL D'HEBRON

⊏⊃ Details	Capacity	13,500
Distance to Olympic Village		11.5
	Distance to CMC	8.5

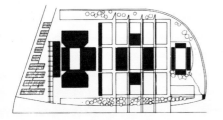

TENNIS

DATA-BANK

VENUE:
Tennis de la Vall d'Hebron, 14km from the Vila Olimpica.
The competition area is 38,000m2 with eight courts. There is space for a total of 15,000 spectators.

EVENTS:
Singles   (m + w)   Doubles (m + w)

MEDALS

Country	G	S	B	Total
Great Britain	16	13	15	44
France	8	7	6	21
USA	9	5	6	20
Greece	1	5	2	8
Czechoslovakia	1	1	6	8
FRG	3	2	2	7
Sweden	-	2	5	7
South Africa	3	1	-	4
Japan	-	2	-	2
Argentina	-	1	-	1
Austria	-	1	-	1
Denmark	-	1	-	1
Spain	-	1	-	1
Australia	-	-	1	1
Bulgaria	-	-	1	1
Italy	-	-	1	1
Netherlands	-	-	1	1
New Zealand	-	-	1	1
Norway	-	-	1	1
	41	42	48	131*

* Two-country pairs counted as two medals.

Stefan Edberg will find clay-courts tough going.

DID YOU KNOW...? *When Kitty Godfree (nee McKane) lost her haul of Olympic medals - one gold, two silver and two bronzes - from 1920 and 1924 - four years ago, IOC President Juan Antonio Samaranch came to the rescue with some replacements.*

Tennis is governed internationally by the International Tennis Federation and in Great Britain by the Lawn Tennis Association.

VOLLEYBALL

DES SEZ This is the sport that is great to play indoors or outdoors but at the highest level has sometimes demanded great sacrifice from its star players.

The Polish team who won the 1976 gold medal spent weeks jumping over 4' 6" barriers wearing 20 and 30lb weights. 400 or so jumps in a day was the norm. It must have been agonizing but obviously effective.

Twelve years earlier, when the sport entered the Games for the first time, the women's gold medal went to the host country, Japan. Ten of the squad worked at the Nichibo spinning mill near Osaka. They were trained by the notorious Horofumi Daimatsu whose methods included hitting his players on the head, kicking them on their hips, insulting and goading them. Daimatsu later went from sport to politics and entered the Japanese parliament. And, in 1972,another Japanese coach Jiji Kojima was the recipient of a writ issued by a West German viewer for 'Inhumane Treatment' of his players.

Whatever their preparation, the athletes of the Unified Team will remain favourites for the men's gold medal this time. (In this sport, the Baltic states wil go their own way after the Olympic Games.) The former Soviets are the current european champions, having beaten the world champions, Italy, in the final. Italy became world champions in 1990 in Rio de Janeiro, beating Brazil first and then Cuba in the final. It was a tremendous performance which augurs well for their hopes in Barcelona.

The USA, winners of the last two Olympic titles, are not quite as strong now but are still medal propects. The South American nations could also do well. Brazil, Argentina and Peru have all been recent Olympic medallists in this sport. The former Soviet Union will be even stronger favourites for the women's gold medal. They are the reigning Olympic, world and european champions.

FACT-O-FILE

If you are a TV "soap" addict you will be familiar with the popularity of volleyball's beach version. It would appear that every self-respecting, sun-drenched hollywood hero is a good player.

But volleyball, indoors, is also a top competitive sport - one which made its Olympic debut in 1964. And only football outstrips its participation levels on a global basis.

The sport is thought to have been devised originally by William G Morgan - a physical training instructor at Hoylake YMCA, near Boston. It became popular in the USA and then spread, via teachers, to the Far East. In Europe its inception and growth was due to

US troops stationed on the continent after the second world war. The FIVB (International Volleyball Federation) was not formed until 1947.

Volleyball had its first world championships - for men only - in 1949. Three years later, the women had their inaugural world championships.

Olympic volleyball has been dominated in recent decades by the former Soviet Union. Their men played 39 matches between 1964 and 1980, dropping only four matches. And the Soviet women have had an equally impressive record over the same period, losing only two in 28 matches.

It's mine – a blanket Soviet defence.

VOLLEYBALL

VOLLEYBALL

RULES AND TOOLS

Each volleyball team consists of six players. Teams face their opponents on the 20m x 9m court across a net 2.43m high. The aim is to get the ball on the floor in the opposing half. A team can only score a point when serving.

Once the ball is in play a team has a maximum of three "touches" of the ball on their side of the net. So the third touch is nearly always an attacking play. Matches are the best of five sets up to 15 points. Competition in Barcelona will consist of 12 men's and eight women's teams. They will be split into groups of six and four respectively. In the men's event the top four in each group go through to the quarter-finals. The top three women's groups will qualify for the later stages with the second and third-placed teams playing off for the right to meet the group winners in the semi-finals.

There will also be bronze medal play-offs and classification matches after the final.

OLYMPIC ROUTE

Teams qualified for the Olympic Games by winning certain world, Olympic and continental titles or through special pre-qualifying tournaments.

BARCELONA BRITS

Britain has not qualified to play in Barcelona.

PALAU ESPORTS

⇨ **Details** Capacity 6,500
Distance to Olympic Village 5.5
Distance to CMC 0.3

DATA-BANK

VENUE:
Palau Sant Jordi, Montjuic area, 6km from the Vila Olimpica, holding 15,000 spectators.
Palau d'Esports de Barcelona, Montjuic area, 5.5km from the Vila Olimpica, holding 6,500 spectators.
Pavello de la Vall d'Hebron, 14km from the Vila Olimpica, holding 2,500 spectators.

EVENTS:
A men's and a women's tournament.

MEDALS	Men			Women			
Country	G	S	B	G	S	B	Total
USSR	3	2	1	4	2	-	12
Japan	1	1	1	2	2	1	8
USA	2	-	-	-	1	-	3
Poland	1	-	-	-	-	2	3
China	-	-	-	1	-	1	2
GDR	-	1	-	-	1	-	2
Bulgaria	-	1	-	-	-	1	2
Czechoslovakia	-	1	1	-	-	-	2
Brazil	-	1	-	-	-	-	1
Peru	-	-	-	-	1	-	1
Argentina	-	-	1	-	-	-	1
Cuba	-	-	-	-	-	1	1
Italy	-	-	1	-	-	-	1
Korea	-	-	-	-	-	1	1
North Korea	-	-	-	-	-	1	1
Romania	-	-	1	-	-	-	1
	7	7	7	7	7	7	42

SCHEDULE	
LOCAL SPANISH TIME. SUBTRACT ONE HOUR FOR BRITAIN.	
JULY 26, 28-31 & **AUGUST** 1-3 - Prelims. (m+w)	10.30-21.30
AUGUST	
4	Final 7-8 (w)	16.30
	Q/f (w)	19.00
	Q/f (w)	21.30
5	Q/f(m)	10.30
	Final 11-12 (m)	15.00
	Final 9-10 (m)	17.30
	Q/f (m)	19.00
	Q/f (m)	21.30
6	Final 5-6 (w)	10.30
	Class.(5/8) (m)	13.00
	Class.(5/8) (m)	16.30
	S/f (w)	19.00
	S/f (w)	21.30
7	S/f (m)	10.30
	Final 3-4 (w)	13.00
	Final 7-8 (m)	15.00
	Final 5-6 (m)	17.30
	S/f (m)	19.00
	Final (w)	21.30
9	Final 3-4 (m) Palau Sant Jordi	10.30
	Final (m) Palau Sant Jordi	13.00

DID YOU KNOW...? The oldest volleyball gold medallist was Ludmila Buldakova aged 34 years and 105 days in 1972 and the youngest was another Ludmila, Borozna, also in 1972 and also of the USSR aged 18 years 249 days.

Volleyball is governed internationally by **FIVB**, the International Volleyball Federation, and in Great Britian by the **British Volleyball Federation**.

VOLLEYBALL

UNITED KINGDOM

NETHERLANDS

BELGIUM

LUXEMBOURG

BARBADOS

CAYMAN ISLANDS

GRENADA

GUADELOUPE & MARTINIQUE

TRINIDAD & TOBAGO

VIRGIN ISLANDS

CAMEROON

NIGERIA

GUATEMALA

MEXICO

NICARAGUA

PANAMA

COLOMBIA

ECUADOR

PARAGUAY

TEXACO. FUELLING IN 39 COU

GREECE

IRELAND

ANTIGUA

BAHAMAS

HAITI

JAMAICA

PUERTO RICO

ST. VINCENT

BELIZE

COSTA RICA

DOMINICAN REPUBLIC

EL SALVADOR

ARGENTINA

BOLIVIA

BRAZIL

CHILE

PERU

URUGUAY

UNITED STATES

THE OLYMPIC SPIRIT
NTRIES.

TEXACO
A brighter star
OFFICIAL SPONSOR OF THE BRITISH OLYMPIC TEAM.

WEIGHTLIFTING

Taking the strain – David Morgan.

D ES SEZ On the face of it, there would not seem to be much attraction in watching competitors lifting weights above their heads. In fact the sport makes superb television. The strain, concentration, the 'psyching up', the failures, successes and the many idiosyncrasies of the lifters, fascinates viewers.

The best competitors will come from the former Soviet Union and Bulgaria. At the world championships in Germany in 1991, the Soviets won the five heaviest categories, with Bulgaria winning two gold medals. A fourth world title was claimed by the outstanding Naim Suleymanoglu of Turkey.

It was his second for that country and he had previously won two championships for Bulgaria. Suleymanoglu defected to Turkey in 1986 when required by the Bulgarian authorities to forego his Turkish ethnic ancestry. He is the reigning Olympic champion and a hot prospect to retain his title.

Ben Johnson made all the headlines as far as drug abuse was concerned at the Seoul Olympics but weightlifting had the worst record of all. No fewer than three Bulgarians in gold medal positions were disqualified. Hopefully the sport will have got its house in order for Barcelona.

In the early modern Games, there were both one-arm and two-arm lifting. However, for many years, the programme has been confined to two-arm lifting and is now judged on the aggregate weight lifted by two separate methods, the 'snatch' and the 'clean and jerk'.

Very simply, the snatch is where a lifter takes the weight up in one movement whereas in the clean and jerk, as the name would imply, there are two movements. First the weight is taken to a position at the shoulders before being extended above the head. The sport has developed so much that modern bantamweights (56kg) lift heavier weights than the heavyweights (110kg) of the pre-second world war period.

Britain's only gold medal came way back in those one-arm days. Launceston Elliot won the first ever competition in 1896. Since then Louis Martin has had the best record for Britain. The four-times world champion picked up a bronze medal in 1960 and silver in 1964.

Perhaps the most famous of all lifters was the giant Soviet, Vassily Alexeyev. He was super-heavyweight champion in 1972 and 1976. He set eighty world records between 1970 and 1977 and attempted to win a third Olympic crown in 1980 but failed with his opening 'snatch'.

A point of interest: Harold Sakata (USA) won a silver medal at the 1948 Games in London. You may have seen him since. He became the actor who played that sinister character 'Oddjob' in the James Bond film "Goldfinger".

FACT-O-FILE

Weightlifting was part of the first modern Olympic Games in 1896. It then disappeared only to return in 1920 under a more standardised format. By that time, too, the International Weightlifting Federation (IWF) had been formed with encouragement from the IOC.

Between 1928 and 1972 all Olympic competitions were decided on an aggregate of two-handed lifts: the press; snatch and clean and jerk. In 1976 the press was eliminated as it proved difficult to judge clearly. Since that time results have been decided on the total lifted in the latter two lifts.

An international competition framework now exists for female weightlifters but they do not compete at the Games.

RULES AND TOOLS

Weightlifting has ten weight divisions. Each country is allowed ten lifters with a maximum of two in any one division. One division will be decided every day at Barcelona's Pavello L'Espanya Industrial between July 26 and August 4, 1992.

Lifters will be placed in groups according to their previous personal best. That means the best lifters will compete together and starting order within the group will be drawn. Each lifter is allowed three attempts to lift to their maximum potential. Any increase between the first and second, and second and third, lifts must be in multiples of 2.5 kilos. Competitors can decide exactly how much.

Weightlifters can choose when to enter the competition.

This tactic is often used as a psychological weapon with lifters starting only when the bar is close to their personal best. But it is also a risky tactic if a lifter fails to start well.

The weightlifting bar, discs and collars must all meet IWF specifications. The discs are different colours according to weight– red being the heaviest and chrome the lightest.

BARCELONA BRITS

David Morgan came close to taking a bronze for Britain in the weighlifting in 1988. No other medals were forthcoming and the opposition will be as tough in Barcelona.

MEDALS — Men

Country	G	S	B	Total
USSR	39	21	3	63
USA	15	16	10	41
Bulgaria	9	11	3	23
Poland	4	2	16	22
FRG	5	4	10	19
Hungary	2	7	8	17
France	9	2	4	15
Italy	5	5	5	15
Austria	5	5	2	12
Japan	2	2	8	12
GDR	1	5	6	12
China	4	3	4	11
Egypt	5	2	2	9
Romania	2	6	1	9
Iran	1	3	5	9
Czechoslovakia	3	2	3	8
Estonia	1	3	3	7
Great Britain	1	3	3	7
Korea	-	1	4	5
Greece	2	-	2	4
Belgium	1	2	1	4
Switzerland	-	2	2	4
Sweden	-	-	4	4
Denmark	1	2	-	3
Australia	1	1	1	3
Finland	1	-	2	3
Trinidad	-	1	2	3
Netherlands	-	-	3	3
Cuba	1	-	1	2
Canada	-	2	-	2
Argentina	-	1	1	2
North Korea	-	1	1	2
Norway	1	-	-	1
Turkey	1	-	-	1
Lebanon	-	1	-	1
Luxembourg	-	1	-	1
Singapore	-	1	-	1
Iraq	-	-	1	1
Taipei	-	-	1	1
	122[1]	118	122[2]	362

[1] Tie for gold in 1928 and 1936 lightweight class.
[2] Triple tie for bronze in 1906 heavyweight class.

1988 CHAMPIONS:

Up to:

52kg	Sevdalin Marinov (BUL)
56kg	Oxen Mirzoyan (URS)
60kg	Naim Suleymanoglu (TUR)
67.5kg	Joachim Kunz (GDR)
75kg	Borislav Guidikov (BUL)
82.5kg	Israil Arsmakov (URS)
90kg	Anatoly Khrapatiy (URS)
100kg	Pavel Kuznetsov (URS)
110kg	Yuriy Zakharevich (URS)
Over 110kg	Alexandr Kurlovich (URS)

DATA-BANK

VENUE:

Pavello L'Espanya Industrial, in the Montjuic area, 6km from the Vila Olimpica.
The hall is 8379 m² and holds 3,500 spectators.

EVENTS:

Up to 52kg	
52.01kg to 56kg	82.51kg to 90kg
56.01kg to 60kg	90.01kg to 100kg
60.01kg to 67.5kg	100.01kg to 110kg
67.51kg to 75kg	Over 110kg
75.01kg to 82.5kg	

Weightlifting is governed internationally by the International Weightlifting Federation and in Great Britain by the British Amateur Weightlifting Association.

WEIGHTLIFTING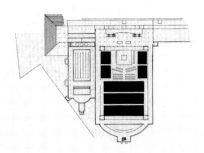

SCHEDULE
LOCAL SPANISH TIME. SUBTRACT ONE HOUR FOR BRITAIN.

(NB: The timings for each group, shown on day 1,
are the same throughout the contest.)

JULY

26	Up to 52kg Group C	12.30
	Up to 52kg Group B	15.00
	Up to 52kg Group A F	18.30
27	52.01kg to 56kg,	
28	56.01kg to 60kg	
29	60.01kg to 67.5kg	
30	67.51kg to 75kg	
31	75.01kg to 82.5kg	

AUGUST

1	82.51kg to 90kg	
2	90.01kg to 100kg	
3	100.01kg to 110kg	
4	Over 110kg	

It's no good ...

PAVELLO L'ESPANYA INDUSTRIAL

⇨ Details	Capacity	3,500
	Distance to Olympic Village	6
	Distance to CMC	1.2

Every Success to
The British Olympic Team

Unilever

Part of everyday life around the world

WRESTLING

DES SEZ First of all put everything out of your mind about that showbiz razzmatazz that you might occasionally see on your television screen from the United States. Professional wrestling has nothing whatsoever to do with the Olympic sport except that the word 'wrestling' is used for both.

And in Olympic wrestling, there are two distinct categories: greco-roman and freestyle. The basic difference is that holds below the hips are not allowed in the greco-roman style. Bouts last five minutes. This was not always so. Before 1924 there were no time limits and in 1912 one bout lasted 11 hours and 40 minutes. The aim is to win through a submission by pinning your opponent to the floor or by scoring more points (actually fewer penalty points) than your opponent.

Britain competes in freestyle wrestling only at the Games. The last home medal success was Noel Loban's bronze in 1984. In Barcelona, best hopes would appear to rest with lightweight Calum McNeil and middleweight Fitzlloyd Walker. There are ten gold medals at stake in each category from light-flyweight up to super-heavyweight.

Wrestlers from the former Soviet Union will almost certainly dominate. In freestyle they have four current world champions. One of them, Arsen Fadzayev, won his sixth world title last year and is the reigning Olympic lightweight champion.

The Americans are strong, too, and in the plain-named John Smith have the current Olympic featherweight champion who has claimed four world freestyle titles. He like Fadzayev is odds-on to win in Barcelona.

Most famous British wrestler was Ken Richmond, a medallist in the 1952 Games who became a familiar figure to cinema-goers. He was the man who bashed the gong at the start of films produced by the J Arthur Rank Company.

FACT-O-FILE

Wrestling in Barcelona shares the Montjuic site with athletics, gymnastics, handball and swimming. Its home will be amongst the mock greco-roman pillars of the National Physical Education Institute.

The pseudo-historical setting could not be more fitting for one of the oldest Olympic sports. Every civilization has had its wrestling heroes and the sport was first recorded at the Games in 704bc. It made its modern Olympic debut in 1896.

In 1900 wrestling at the Games was of the freestyle variety only. But since 1908 both types have been permanently on the programme. Britain wrestle in the freestyle category only. In 1908 British wrestlers took three golds but there have been no golds since then.

RULES AND TOOLS

There are ten weight categories for both styles. Each nation can enter a maximum of 20 competitors - one per weight category. All the wrestlers must be at least 17 years old and possess a valid FILA (International Amateur Wrestling Association) licence.

Wrestlers must also be within the weight limit for their chosen category on three occasions - on the eve of competition and at the end of each day's fighting. Contestants are drawn into two groups.

Bouts last five minutes without a rest. The wrestler who has scored the most points wins. The object is to "pin" the opponent's shoulders to the mat. Few bouts, because of the skill of modern wrestlers, are decided in this way.

Points can be scored on a scale of 1-5 for various holds and throws. Once the competition is over these are converted into penalty points ranging from zero, if the opponent has been "pinned", to a half point for an emphatic win and continuing down the scale. No wrestler can be eliminated until he has been

defeated twice.

Elimination continues throughout the competition until three wrestlers remain. They then dispute the medals taking into account penalty points collected from previous bouts.

There are three officials - a chairman, referee and judge - who all play a role in deciding the contest scores.

DATA-BANK

VENUE:
In the INEFC, in the Montjuic area, 6km from the Vila Olimpica. There will be three mats on a 42x15m podium, 0.85m high. There is room for 4,000 spectators.

EVENTS:
The wrestling competition will consist of greco-roman and freestyle. The weight categories are:

Up to:

48kg	74kg
52kg	82kg
57kg	90kg
62kg	100kg
68kg	130kg

1988 CHAMPIONS:

Up to:	FREESTYLE	GRECO-ROMAN
48kg	Takashi Kobayashi (JPN)	Vincenzo Maenza (ITA)
52kg	Mitsuru Sato (JPN)	Jon Ronningen (NOR)
57kg	Sergey Beloglazov (URS)	Andras Sike (HUN)
62kg	John Smith (USA)	Kamandar Madjidov (URS)
68kg	Arsen Fadzayev (URS)	Levon Djoulfalakian (URS)
74kg	Kenneth Monday (USA)	Kim Young-Nam (KOR)
82kg	Han Myung-Woo (KOR)	Mikhail Mamiachvili (URS)
90kg	Makharbek Khadartsev (URS)	Atanas Komchev (BUL)
100kg	Vasile Puscasu (ROM)	Andrzej Wronski (POL)
130kg	David Gobedjichvili (URS)	Aleksandr Kareline (URS)

WRESTLING

THE OLYMPIC ROUTE
For the first time wrestlers have had to qualify for the Games through continental championships.

SCHEDULE
LOCAL SPANISH TIME. SUBTRACT ONE HOUR FOR BRITAIN.

Greco-Roman Wrestling

JULY

26	52, 68, & 100kg - elimination	10.00-13.00
		17.00-20.00
27	48, 52, 68, 74, 100 & 130kg elimination	10.00-13.00
		17.00-20.00
28	48, 52, 57, 62, 68, 74, 90, 100 & 130kg	10.00-13.00
	elimination	17.00-20.00
	52, 68 & 100kg **F**	19.00
29	48, 57, 62, 74, 82, 90, & 130kg	10.00-13.00
	elimination	17.00-20.00
	48, 74, & 130kg **F**	19.00
30	57, 62, 82 & 90kg. elimination	10.00-13.00
	57, 62, 82 & 90kg **F**	17.00-19.00

Freestyle Wrestling

AUGUST

3	52, 68, & 100kg - elimination	10.00-13.00
		17.00-20.00
4	48, 52, 68, 74, 100 & 130kg elimination	10.00-13.00
		17.00-20.00
5	48, 52, 57, 62, 68, 74, 82, 90, 100 & 130kg	10.00-13.00
	elimination	17.00-20.00
	52, 68 & 100kg **F**	19.00
6	48, 57, 62, 74, 82, 90, & 130kg	10.00-13.00
	elimination	17.00-20.00
	48, 74, & 130kg **F**	19.00
7	57, 62, 82 & 90kg. elimination	10.00-13.00
	57, 62, 82 & 90kg **F**	17.00-19.00

INEFC, MONTJUIC
⇨ **Details** Capacity — 12,500
Distance to Olympic Village — 6
Distance to CMC — 1

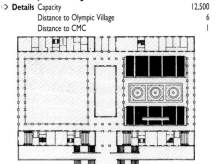

Pre-Games training for Britain.

MEDALS	Freestyle			Greco-Roman			
Country	G	S	B	G	S	B	Total
USSR	28	15	13	34	19	10	119
USA	38	30	20	2	1	2	93
Finland	8	7	10	19	19	18	81
Sweden	8	10	8	19	15	17	77
Bulgaria	6	14	8	8	14	7	57
Hungary	3	4	7	13	9	11	47
Turkey	15	10	5	8	3	2	43
Japan	16	9	6	4	4	2	41
FRG	1	3	5	4	14	8	35
Romania	1	-	4	6	8	12	31
Iran	3	7	9	-	1	1	21
Korea	3	3	6	2	1	4	19
Italy	1	-	-	5	3	9	18
Great Britain	3	4	10	-	-	-	17
Yugoslavia	1	1	2	3	5	4	16
Poland	-	1	3	2	5	5	16
Czechoslovakia	-	1	3	1	6	4	15
Switzerland	4	4	5	-	-	1	14
France	2	2	3	1	1	2	11
Denmark	-	-	-	1	3	7	11
Estonia	2	1	-	3	-	4	10
Greece	-	-	1	1	3	4	9
Mongolia	-	4	4	-	-	-	8
Canada	-	3	5	-	-	-	8
GDR	-	2	1	2	1	1	7
Austria	-	-	1	1	2	1	5
Egypt	-	-	-	1	2	2	5
Norway	-	1	-	1	1	1	4
Belgium	-	3	-	-	-	1	4
North Korea	-	2	1	-	-	-	3
Australia	-	1	2	-	-	-	3
Lebanon	-	-	-	-	1	2	3
Latvia	-	-	-	-	1	-	1
Mexico	-	-	-	-	1	-	1
Syria	-	1	-	-	-	-	1
India	-	-	1	-	-	-	1
Pakistan	-	-	1	-	-	-	1
	143	143	144[1]	141[2]	143	142	856

[1] Two bronzes in 1920 heavyweight class.
[2] No gold in 1912 light-weight class.

DID YOU KNOW...? Wrestling at the 1896 Games was won by Carl Schuhmann of Germany who also won the gymnastics gold. He beat Britain's Launceston Eliot - the weightlifting champion.
The oldest gold medallist was Anatoliy Roschin (URS) in 1972 at 40 years and 184 days. The youngest was Saban Trstena of Yugoslavia in 1984 aged 19 years and 222 days.

Wrestling is governed internationally by the **FILA** (International Amateur Wrestling Federation) and in Great Britain by the British Amateur Wrestling Association.

YACHTING

DES SEZ The first medals were won in Olympic yachting in 1900. In that year the boats sailed were huge. There was a 10-20 ton class and an 'open' class where the size of the vessel was left up to you. Over the years the classes of boat have changed constantly and there is no exception this time. For these games there will be ten gold medals available.

For men only there are Finn, 470 and Board Sailing (windsurfing) competitions. For women only there are 470, Finn, Europe and Board Sailing. There are four 'open' classes, Flying Dutchman, Star, Tornado and Soling.

Board Sailing, Finn and the new Europe class are all for one-person crew. The other boats are sailed by two people except for Soling, the largest boat in the Olympics, which has a crew of three. In each class, except Board Sailing there are seven races and the competitors count their best six results. In Board Sailing nine out of ten races count.

This is a sport in which Britain has a long Olympic tradition and are second in the all-time medal list. the most successful British competitor has been Naval Officer, Rodney Pattison, who won gold medals in the Flying Dutchman in 1968 with Iain MacDonald-Smith and defended the title in 1972 with Christopher Davies. Four years later he had to settle for silver with a third partner, Julian Brooke-Houghton.

The 1968 victory was also an Olympic best performance with Pattison winning five races and finishing second in the other to pick up just 3.0 penalty points. The feat was all the more remarkable for the fact that he had been disqualified after finishing first in the opening race. At the time of writing, Pattison was once again trying to qualify for the Olympics.

Britain's most recent gold medallists were Bryn Vaile and Mike McIntyre. They won the Star class, the oldest in the Olympics dating from 1932, four years ago. Sadly Vaile and McIntyre will not be in Barcelona as they have been unable to find the financial backing to support their efforts in qualifying.

There are British medal chances, particularly in 470, Finn and men's and women's board sailing. Penny Way was the women's board sailing champion in 1991.

Incidentally, yachting produced one of the greatest longtime and successful competitors in Paul Elvstrom of Denmark. He won the single-handed (now Finn) class four times in succession from 1948 to 1960 and as recently as 1984 came fourth with his daughter, Trine, in the Tornado class.

FACT-O-FILE

The "yachties" at the 1992 Olympic Games are bound to find things a little strange at first. After all, this is the first Games in several decades where they have competed at the heart of the action.

Mike McIntyre and Bryn Vaile.

Normally they are confined to a port far removed from Olympic city. In Barcelona they set sail from the shores of the Olympic village itself. No expense has been spared in creating the Olympic port at Nova Icaria. Whether the yachtsmen and women find the atmosphere a distraction or an incentive is yet to be seen.

Yachting stuttered on its intended Olympic debut in 1896. A regatta was planned for the Bay of Salamis but was cancelled due to bad weather. Since 1900, however, the sport has been an exciting part of the programme - even if the classes and boats have changed dramatically.

RULES AND TOOLS

Competition will take place under International Yacht Racing Union (IYRU) rules in Barcelona. Each nation can enter one yacht per race. For all the classes bar the Finn, Europe and Lechner, competitors use their own boats.

Barcelona's organising committee, however, is mandated to supply hulls to the Finn and Europe class competitors and all equipment to the Lechner class. In the other classes the competitors' boats are subject to stringent regulations and measurements.

THE BOATS

Tornado: Regarded as the speed machine of Olympic sailing, the Tornado is a fast and very exciting catamaran. This two-handed boat was designed in 1967 by the British naval architect Rodney March.

YACHTING

Olympic yachting action.

470: A strict design with few variations permitted, the 470 is an ideal dinghy for competitive sailing. Designed in 1963 by the French architect Andre Cornu, it became an Olympic class in 1976. Since that date its popularity has grown enormously and the 470 fleet is the largest Olympic class in Britain. There will be separate classes for men and women at the Barcelona Olympics.

Flying Dutchman: With a length of nearly 20ft and a large fore-sail, the power and speed of the Flying Dutchman make it the fastest Olympic mono-hull. Designed in 1951 by the Dutch architect Vilke Van Essen in 1951, it is a highly technical boat that is difficult to sail well.

Soling: This one design boat is the largest of the Olympic classes. With a crew of three, a fixed keel and alternative spinnakers, the Soling is a sea-going racing boat. It was designed in 1967 by the Norwegian architect Jan Linge and became an Olympic class in 1972.

Lechner: The Lechner is the only windsurfing class in the Olympics. In 1992 it will be the first separate women's Olympic windsurfing class. It is a one design board with a retractable fin and separate skeg. It became a male Olympic class in 1984. This most athletic of all the sailing events requires a high degree of physical fitness.

Europe: The Europe is an international, one design, singlehanded racing dinghy, recommended for sailors in the 45-57kg range. Designed in 1960 by the Belgian architect Alois Roland it becomes a women's Olympic class for the first time in 1992. It is possible to adjust the rig to suit a sailor's height, weight and experience. Weight jackets are banned in the Europe class.

Finn: The Finn is a one design boat for the men's singlehanded class. It was designed in 1950 by the Finnish architect Richard Sarby for the 1952 Olympic Games, which were hosted by Finland. The large sail area and relatively heavy hull calls for strength, stamina and plenty of determination. The recommended

weight for the helmsman is 85-95 kilos. He must be fit enough to hike for the whole race while wearing water bottles or a weight jacket for maximum ballast.

Star: This one design fixed keel boat was first used for an Olympic class in 1932. The two-man boat was designed by the North American architect William Gadner and its tall mast and large mainsail make it instantly recognisable.

BARCELONA BRITS

The 470 is perhaps our strongest class for both men and women. Paul Brotherton and Andy Hemmings came third in the World Championships in Brisbane before Christmas, whilst in the women's events, Debbie Jarvis has teamed up with her old crew Sue Carr in a bid for an Olympic place.

Britain also has two major Olympic hopes in the Lechner class. Penny Way is currently ranked top in the world and is the only British athlete to be pre-selected for the Olympics. Barrie Edgington is the new Lechner World Champion, breaking a record held by France for the last nine years.

DATA-BANK

VENUE:
Port Olimpic and Parc de Mar Olympic Area, near the Vila Olimpica. The competition area consists of six areas located on the waters off the Parc de Mar.

EVENTS:

Lechner A-390	(m+w)
470	(m+w)
Finn	(m)
Europe	(w)
Soling	(o)
Flying Dutchman	(o)
Star	(o)
Tornado	(o)

A scene from Pusan in 1988.

YACHTING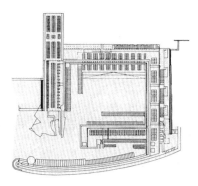

PORT OLIMPIC

⇨ **Details** Capacity	2,500
Distance to Olympic Village	0
Distance to CMC	5.5

1988 CHAMPIONS:

Men:

Olympic monotype	Jose Luis Doreste (ESP)
Windglider class	Bruce Kendall (NZL)
Soling	GDR
470	FRA
Tornado	FRA
Star	Bryn Vaile/Mike McIntyre (GBR)
Flying Dutchman	DEN

Women:

470	USA

SCHEDULE

LOCAL SPANISH TIME. SUBTRACT ONE HOUR FOR BRITAIN.

JULY

27	Lechner (m+w) Race 1&2	13.00
	Europe, Finn, 470, (m+w) Race 1	
	Flying Dutchman, Star, Soling & Tornado (o) Race 1	
28	Lechner (m+w) Race 3&4	13.00
	Europe, Finn, 470, (m+w) Race 2	
	Flying Dutchman, Star, Soling & Tornado (o) Race 2	
29	Lechner (m+w) Race 5&6	13.00
	Europe, Finn, 470, (m+w) Race 3	
	Flying Dutchman, Star, Soling & Tornado (o) Race 3	
30	Lechner (m+w) Race 7&8	13.00
	Europe, Finn, 470, (m+w) Race 4	
	Flying Dutchman, Star, Soling & Tornado (o) Race 4	
31	Lechner (m+w) reserve	13.00
	Europe, Finn, 470, (m+w) reserve	
	Flying Dutchman, Star, Tornado (o) reserve	
	Soling (o) Race 5	

AUGUST

1	Lechner (m+w) Race 9	13.00
	Europe, Finn, 470, (m+w) Race 5	
	Flying Dutchman, Star, Tornado (o) Race 5	
	Soling (o) Race 6	
2	Lechner (m+w) Race 10	13.00
	Europe, Finn, 470, (m+w) Race 6	
	Flying Dutchman, Star, Tornado (o) Race 6	
	Soling (o) reserve	
3	Soling (o) match race	13.00
	Europe, Finn, 470, (m+w) Race 7 **F**	
	Flying Dutchman, Star, Tornado (o) Race 7 **F**	
4	Soling (o) Match race **F**	13.00

MEDALS

Country	Men G	S	B	Total
Great Britain	15	8	7	30
Sweden	9	11	9	29
Norway	14	11	1	26
France	9	8	8	25
Denmark	8	8	3	19
FRG	4	5	6	15
USSR	4	5	4	13
Netherlands	4	3	5	12
New Zealand	5	1	2	8
Australia	3	1	4	8
Brazil	2	1	5	8
Italy	2	1	5	8
Finland	1	1	6	8
Belgium	2	3	2	7
GDR	2	2	2	6
Canada	-	2	4	6
Spain	3	1	1	5
Greece	1	1	1	3
Switzerland	1	1	1	3
Austria	-	3	-	3
Portugal	-	2	1	3
Bahamas	1	-	1	2
Argentina	-	2	-	2
Cuba	-	1	-	1
Ireland	-	1	-	1
Netherlands Antilles	-	-	1	1
Virgin Islands	-	1	-	1
Estonia	-	-	1	1
Hungary	-	-	1	1
	105	98*	91*	294

* Some events in the early Games had no silver and/or bronze medals.

Yachting is governed internationally by the International Yacht Racing Union, and in Great Britain by the Royal Yachting Association.

Royal Mail
Delivering
for
British Sports

Royal Mail Sports Awards

GIVING BRITISH SPORT A WINNING CHANCE

DEMONSTRATION SPORTS

A n early tradition of the modern Olympic Movement was to encourage host countries to display sports of local tradition which did not, necessarily, have a worldwide participation base.

These sports added colour but did not carry medal status. Over the decades the true rationale behind the "demonstration sport" has been lost. That is, perhaps, why the custom will be dropped after 1992.

Meanwhile, Barcelona spectators and TV audiences alike, will be served up a fringe Games dish which includes pelota, roller hockey and taekwondo.

The latter, of course, was also a demonstration sport at the 1988 Games. Britain competed then and is likely to have two representatives in Barcelona. Taekwondo is a sport which has a strong following in the Far East, particularly Korea. It is a dramatic form of unarmed combat permitting its competitors to make flying leaps to score points with their feet. Headguards and chest protectors are "de rigueur" equipment.

Both men and women will take part in the Barcelona taekwondo tournament over eight weight categories each between 3 and 5 August at the Palau Blaugrana. Competition will be under World Taekwondo Federation rules on a straight knock-out competition basis.

Roller (or rink) hockey is a sport of increasing popularity. It is a sport of "presidents". IOC head Juan Antonio Samaranch played this sport for his local team. In Barcelona 12 men's teams each of 5 players will compete in two preliminary round groups of six.

The top three teams from each group then go into a final group from which the leading two teams go into the final and the next two teams play off for the bronze.

Finally, Pelota, of all three demonstration sports, reflects tradition the most. A native sport of the Basque regions, Pelota is a "squash-type" ball game played against two walls with curved bats or quite simply with unprotected hands.

This sport, which dates back to the 16th Century, can also be called Fronton. Scoring varies but is often the first to score 21 points.

136 men and 16 women will take part in the competition which consists of men's singles and doubles and women's singles in varying formats of court and equipment. France, Spain, Mexico, Cuba, Uruguay, Venezuela, Argentina and the United States of America will be represented.

TAEKWONDO

DATA-BANK

VENUE:
Palau Blaugrana, Diagonal Area, 8km from the Vila Olimpica. It holds 6,400 spectators.
Two competition courts, each with a 12mx12m competition area, covered with an elastic mat

TAEKWONDO SCHEDULE	
Local Spanish time. Subtract one hour for Britain.	
AUGUST	
3 Bantam, welter and heavyweight **(m+w) F**	10.00-20.00
4 Fly, light and middleweight **(m+w) F**	10.00-20.00
5 Fin and featherweight **(m+w) F**	11.00-18.30

Taekwondo is governed internationally by the World Taekwondo Federation and in Great Britain by the British Taekwondo Control Board.

Taekwondo competitors are permitted to make flying kicks.

Taekwondo exponents wear chest protectors and helmets – they need them!

ROLLER-HOCKEY

DATA-BANK

VENUES:
Pavello del Club Pati Vic, 69km from Vila Olimpica, holding 1,730 spectators.
Pavello de l'Ateneu de Sant Sadurni, 42km from Vila Olimpica, holding 1,320 spectators.
Pavello d'Esports de Reus, 113km from Vila Olimpica, holding 3,416 spectators.
Palau Blaugrana, 6km from Vila Olimpica, holding 6,400 spectators.

PALAU BLAUGRANA
⊏▷ **Details** Capacity 6,400
Distance to Olympic Village 8
Distance to CMC 4

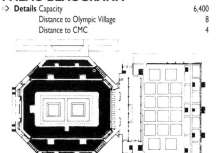

ROLLER-HOCKEY SCHEDULE	
LOCAL SPANISH TIME. SUBTRACT ONE HOUR FOR BRITAIN.	
JULY	
26-30 Preliminary League	Pavello del Club Pati Vic
	Pavello de l'Ateneu de Sant Sadurni
AUGUST	
1 - 5 Semi-finals	Pavello d'Esports de Reus
7 **Final** 3-4 and **Final**	Palua Blaugrana

Roller Hockey is governed internationally by the FIPR, the International Roller Hockey Federation.

BASQUE PELOTA

DATA-BANK

VENUES:
Pavello de la Vall d'Hebron, 6 km from the Vila Olimpica, with three courts and holding 3,300 spectators.
Fronto Colom, 3 km from Vila Olimpica in the Montjuic area, with one court and holding 600 spectators will be used for Frontenis events.

VALL D'HEBRON
⊏▷ **Details** Capacity 3,300
Distance to Olympic Village 11.5
Distance to CMC 8.5

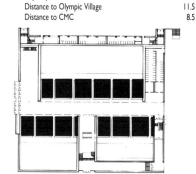

BASQUE PELOTA SCHEDULE	
LOCAL SPANISH TIME. SUBTRACT ONE HOUR FOR BRITAIN.	
JULY	
25-31 classifying matches (**m+w**)	
AUGUST	
2 & 3 semi-final matches (**m+w**)	
3 & 4 **Final** matches (**m+w**)	

Basque pelota is governed internationally by the International Basque Pelota Federation.

anchester for the Millenium. The mouthwatering prospect, in the words of the Prime Minister of Britain. Hosting the 2000 Olympic Games in Manchester is an ambition which commands national support. As the British team prepares for the Games in Barcelona, Manchester is on course to build a series of sports facilities which will be vital to the development of our Olympic athletes for generations to come.

Manchester 2000 took a giant leap forward at the beginning of this year with the commitment of the Government to provide an immediate £53 million towards the creation of:

a National Stadium of the North with up to 80,000 seats

a major indoor arena with up to 20,000 seats

Britain's first indoor velodrome which could become the national cycling centre.

More than that, the Government has pledged to throw its full financial weight behind the building of all the other facilities which we will need to stage the Games if they are awarded to Manchester by the International Olympic Committee (IOC) in September 1993. Over the next 18 months, Manchester 2000's international team – sportsmen and sportswomen, government ministers, diplo-

mats and businessmen – will travel the world to spread the Manchester message.

The Prime Minister declared: "You should be clear about our objective. We are going for gold – not least because in this competion there are no medals for coming second."

The resonance of that undertaking shows the determination of Britain to be awarded the Games for the first time as a result of bidding. Twice before this century, the IOC asked Britain to host the Games in London – in 1908 when Rome pulled out at short notice, and in 1948 in the immediate aftermath of war.

That they chose Britain is an affirmation of our commitment to the Olympic Movement and of our ability to stage Olympic competitions with verve, style and efficient organisation. This time, Manchester is Britain's choice – unanimously supported by the British Olympic Association and backed financially by an increasingly impressive list of national and international companies in the UK, and by

every local authority in the North West of England.

Manchester's vision is to produce for the Millenium not just a Games which will take the Olympic Movement into the next century but that the creation of the best sports facilities in the world will act as a driving force in the renaissance of one of out great cities.

The history of Manchester is studded with firsts. As the crucible of the Industrial Revolution Manchester was the city where Mr Rolls met Mr Royce, where the first commercial computer was developed, where the atom was first split, where flash photography was first used. The city where the first British plane flew, is the home of Europe's fastest-growing airport.

In recent years, while the people continue to indulge an unparalleled passion for sport – not least with the world's most famous football club – the city has emerged once more a major European commercial and cultural centre.

While establishing itself as the leading financial centre outside London, the city is building Britain's most modern

Manchester are hoping for cause to celebrate next year.

We are delighted to support the

Manchester 2000 Bid

Arthur Andersen
Bank House
9 Charlotte Street
Manchester M1 4EU

ARTHUR ANDERSEN & CO. SC

Best Wishes to
The British Olympic Team *from*

BUILDING DESIGN PARTNERSHIP

Europe's major multi-professional design practice

Concept Designers for The British 1996 Bid & one of the Design Consultants for The 2000 Bid to Bring the Games to Manchester

BDP MANCHESTER
SUNLIGHT HOUSE QUAY STREET MANCHESTER M60 3JA 061 834 8441

The Olympic logo towers over Manchester City centre.

concert hall, as a home for the country's longest-established international orchestra, The Halle. Europe's most modern public transport system – the Metrolink supertram – took to the streets this spring.

The best motorway system in the country, and arguably in Europe, means that the Olympic competitions can be staged in several towns and cities in the North West as well as Manchester – allowing competitors swift and comfortable access during the Games and leaving a legacy of new sports facilities to serve our sports stars of the future.

Barcelona has shown the way in which a proud industrial city, with a firm identity of its own within a nation, can harness established values and the vision of the Olympic Games with its physical modernisation.

Britain applauds Barcelona 1992 and looks forward to welcoming the world to Manchester 2000.

FORTE

FORTE
HOTELS

EXCLUSIVE
HOTELS

FORTE
RESTAURANTS

Whatever you wish to say;
Thank You; Well Done; Good Luck –
Forte Leisure Cheques
are the perfect gift anyone can buy or receive.

CAFÉ ROYAL
EST 1865
One of London's Finer Traditions

FORTE
GRAND

They are redeemable for goods and services
throughout the extensive Forte group, including
over 800 hotels and 1,000 restaurants.
Forte Leisure Cheques open up a wide variety
of opportunities from a weekend of
leisure or activity, to a range of
superb wines and hampers.

Wheelers
OF ST JAMES'S

FORTE
Heritage

HARVESTER
RESTAURANTS

FORTE
CREST

So, if you are looking for new and different ideas
for gifts, call Susannah Donne on **0753 573266.**
Available in denominations of £1, £5, £10
and £50 you may place your order by
credit card, or send a cheque to:

FORTE
Posthouse

FORTE
Travelodge

RING & BRYMER
Caterers of excellence for over 300 years.

Forte Leisure Cheques Dept.,
St. Martin's House, 20 Queensmere, Slough,
Berkshire SL1 1YY.

Happy Eater

FORTE
Leisure Breaks

FOR HOTEL RESERVATIONS CALL 0345 40 40 40

FORTE WORLD OF GOLF

Lillywhites

Wine Growers
Association

THE OLYMPIC
FACT PACK

OLYMPIC RESULTS
MEDAL TABLES
HISTORY
CHAMPIONS
FLAG BEARERS
STARS AND SCHEDULES

ALL-TIME MEDAL TABLE

*OLYMPIC MEDALS TABLE BY COUNTRY — 1896–1988

COUNTRY	GOLD	SILVER	BRONZE	TOTAL	COUNTRY	GOLD	SILVER	BRONZE	TOTAL
United States	752	569	481	1802	Pakistan	3	3	3	9
Soviet Union[1]	397	323	304	1024	Uruguay	2	1	6	9
Great Britain	172	221	206	599	Chile	-	6	2	8
FRG[2]	153	206	208	567	Venezuela	1	2	5	8
France	153	170	175	498	Trinidad & Tobago	1	2	4	7
Sweden	132	142	167	441	Philippines	-	1	6	7
GDR[3]	154	131	126	411	Morocco	3	1	2	6
Italy	147	121	123	391	Uganda	1	3	1	5
Hungary	125	112	137	374	Tunisia	1	2	2	5
Finland	97	75	110	282	Colombia	-	2	3	5
Japan	87	75	82	244	Lebanon	-	2	2	4
Australia	71	67	87	225	Nigeria	-	1	3	4
Romania	55	64	82	201	Puerto Rico	-	1	3	4
Poland	40	56	95	191	Peru	1	2	-	3
Canada	39	62	73	174	Latvia	-	2	1	3
Switzerland	41	63	58	162	Ghana	-	1	2	3
Netherlands	43	46	65	154	Taipei	-	1	2	3
Bulgaria	35	62	49	146	Thailand	-	1	2	3
Czechoslovakia[4]	45	48	48	142	Luxembourg	1	1	-	2
Denmark	25	50	49	124	Bahamas	1	-	1	2
Belgium	35	46	42	123	Tanzania	-	2	-	2
Norway	41	33	33	107	Cameroon	-	1	1	2
Greece	22	40	39	101	Haiti	-	1	1	2
Yugoslavia	26	29	28	83	Iceland	-	1	1	2
Austria	19	27	33	79	Algeria	-	-	2	2
Korea (South)	19	22	29	70	Panama	-	-	2	2
China	20	19	21	60	Surinam	1	-	-	1
New Zealand	26	6	23	55	Zimbabwe	1	-	-	1
Cuba	22	19	12	53	Costa Rica	1	-	-	1
South Africa[5]	16	15	20	51	Indonesia	-	1	-	1
Turkey	24	13	10	47	Ivory Coast	-	1	-	1
Argentina	13	19	14	46	Netherlands Antilles	-	1	-	1
Mexico	9	12	18	39	Senegal	-	1	-	1
Brazil	7	9	21	37	Singapore	-	1	-	1
Kenya	11	9	11	31	Sri Lanka	-	1	-	1
Iran	4	11	15	30	Syria	-	1	-	1
Spain	4	12	8	24	Virgin Island	-	1	-	1
Jamaica	4	10	8	22	Barbados	-	-	1	1
Estonia	6	6	9	21	Bermuda	-	-	1	1
Egypt	6	6	6	18	Djibouti	-	-	1	1
India	8	3	3	14	Dominican Republic	-	-	1	1
Ireland	4	4	5	13	Guyana	-	-	1	1
Portugal	2	4	7	13	Iraq	-	-	1	1
North Korea[6]	2	5	5	12	Niger Republic	-	-	1	1
Mongolia	-	5	6	11	Zambia	-	-	1	1
Ethiopia	5	1	4	10					

[1] Includes Czarist Russia
[2] Germany 1896-64, West Germany 1968-1990
[3] 1968-1988 only
[4] Includes Bohemia
[5] South Africa up until 1960
[6] From 1964.

*These totals include all first, second and third places, including those events no longer on the current (1992) schedule. The 1906 Games, which were officially staged by the International Olympic Committee (IOC), have also been included. However, medals won in the Art Competitions (1912-1948) have not been included. Medals won in 1896, 1900 and 1904 by mixed teams from two countries have been counted twice, for both countries.

Procter&Gamble Limited

Manufacturer of
ARIEL
DAZ
BOLD
FAIRY NON-BIOLOGICAL
TIDE
DREFT
LENOR
BOUNCE
(Sheet fabric conditioner)
FAIRY LIQUID
FLASH
VORTEX
PAMPERS
and
ALWAYS

*PROUD TO BE SPONSORING THE BRITISH
OLYMPIC TEAM*

**OFFICIAL SPONSOR
OF THE BRITISH
OLYMPIC TEAM**

BRITAIN'S 1988 MEDALLISTS

ARCHERY

Bronze	Steven Hallard	Richard Priestman	Leroy Watson	968	Team (m)

ATHLETICS

Silver	Linford Christie			9.97	100m (m)
Silver	Peter Elliott			3:36.15	1500m (m)
Silver	Colin Jackson			13.28	110m hurdles (m)
Silver	Elizabeth McColgan			31:08.44	10,000m (w)
Silver	Fatima Whitbread			68.44	Javelin (w)
Silver	Elliott Bunney	Linford Christie	Michael McFarlane	John Regis	38.28	4x100m relay (m)
Bronze	Yvonne Murray			8:29.02	3000m (w)
Bronze	Mark Rowland			8:07.96	3000m steeplechase (m)

BOXING

Bronze	Richard Woodhall	5:00.00	Light-middleweight (71kg)

EQUESTRIAN

Silver	Virginia Leng	62.00	3-day event - team (o)
	Mark Phillips	*	
	Ian Stark	52.80	
	Karen Straker	142.00	
Silver	Ian Stark	52.80	3-day event - ind on Sir Wattie (o)
Bronze	Virginia Leng	62.00	3-day event - ind on Master Craftsman (o)
	* Withdrew after Dressage section.		

HOCKEY

Gold	Paul Barber	Stephen Batchelor	Kulbir Bhaur	Robert Clift	Team (m)
	Richard Dodds	David Faulkner	Russell Garcia	Martyn Grimley	
	Sean Kerly	James Kirkwood	Richard Leman	Stephen Martin	
	Veryan Pappin	Jonathan Potter	Imran Sherwani	Ian Taylor	

JUDO

Bronze	Dennis Stewart	Up to 95kg (m)

MODERN PENTATHLON

Bronze	Graham Brookhouse	Dominic Mahony	Richard Phelps	15,276	Team (m)

ROWING

Gold	Andrew Holmes	Steven Redgrave		6:36.84	Coxless pairs (m)
Bronze	Andrew Holmes	Steven Redgrave	Patrick Sweeney	7:01.95	Coxed pairs (m)

SHOOTING

Gold	Malcolm Cooper	1279.3	Smallbore rifle (3 pos) (m)
Silver	Alister Allan	1275.6	Smallbore rifle (3 pos) (m)

SWIMMING

Gold	Adrian Moorhouse	1:02.04	100m breaststroke (m)
Silver	Nicholas Gillingham	2:14.12	200m breaststroke (m)
Bronze	Andrew Jameson	53.30	100m butterfly (m)

YACHTING

Gold	Michael McIntyre	Bryn Vaile	64.70 & 45.70	Star (m)

BEST BRITISH PERFORMANCES

GREAT BRITAIN'S BEST-EVER MEDAL PERFORMANCES IN ALL CURRENT AND PAST OLYMPIC EVENTS.

ARCHERY

Event	Medal	Name	Year
York Round (m)	Gold	William Dod	1908
National Round (w)	Gold	Queenie Newall	1908
Men's team	Bronze	Steven Hallard	
		Richard Priestman	
		Leroy Watson	1988

ATHLETICS

Event	Medal	Name	Year
100m (m)	Gold	Harold Abrahams	1924
	Gold	Allan Wells	1980
200m (m)	Silver	Walter Rangeley	1928
	Silver	Allan Wells	1980
400m (m)	Gold	Wyndham Halswelle	1908
	Gold	Eric Lidell	1924
800m (m)	Gold	Alfred Tysoe	1900
	Gold	Albert Hill	1920
	Gold	Douglas Lowe	1924
	Gold	Douglas Lowe	1928
	Gold	Thomas Hampson	1932
	Gold	Steve Ovett	1980
1500m (m)	Gold	Charles Bennett	1900
	Gold	Arnold Jackson	1912
	Gold	Albert Hill	1920
	Gold	Sebastian Coe	1980
	Gold	Sebastian Coe	1984
5000m (m)	Silver	Gordon Pirie	1956
10,000m (5 miles) (m)	Gold	Henry Hawtrey	1906
	Gold	Emil Voigt	1908
Steeplechase (m) (4000m)	Gold	John Rimmer	1900
(3200m)	Gold	Arthur Russell	1908
(3000m)	Gold	Percy Hodge	1920
	Gold	Chris Brasher	1956
Marathon (m)	Silver	Sam Ferris	1932
	Silver	Ernest Harper	1936
	Silver	Tom Richards	1948
	Silver	Basil Heatley	1964
110m hurdles (m)	Silver	Grantley Goulding	1896
	Silver	Alfred Healey	1906
	Silver	Don Finlay	1936
	Silver	Colin Jackson	1988
400m hurdles (m)	Gold	Lord Burghley	1928
	Gold	David Hemery	1968
4x100m relay (m)	Gold		1912
4x400m relay (m)	Gold		1920
	Gold		1936
20km walk (m)	Gold	Ken Matthews	1964
50km walk (m)	Gold	Thomas Green	1932
	Gold	Harold Whitlock	1936
	Gold	Don Thompson	1960
High jump (m)	Gold	Con Lea	1906
Long jump (m)	Gold	Lynn Davies	1964
Triple jump (m)	Gold	Peter O'Connor	1906
	Gold	Tim Ahearne	1908
Shot (m)	Silver	Dennis Horgan	1908
Hammer (m)	Bronze	Malcolm Nokes	1924
Javelin (m)	Silver	David Ottley	1984
Decathlon (m)	Gold	Thomas Kiely	1904
	Gold	Daley Thompson	1980
	Gold	Daley Thompson	1984

ATHLETICS
Discontinued Events

Event	Medal	Name	Year
3000m team (m)	Silver		1920
	Silver		1924
3 miles team (m)	Gold		1908
5000m team (m)	Gold		1900
Cross-country (m)	Silver		1920
3550m walk (m)	Gold	George Larner	1908
10,000m walk (m)	Silver	Ernest Webb	1012
	Silver	Gordon Goodwin	1924
10 mile walk (m)	Gold	George Larner	1908

Event	Medal	Name	Year
100m (w)	Silver	Dorothy Manley	1948
	Silver	Dorothy Hyman	1960
200m (w)	Silver	Audrey Williamson	1948
400m (w)	Silver	Ann Packer	1964
	Silver	Lillian Board	1968
800m (w)	Gold	Ann Packer	1964
3000m (w)	Bronze	Yvonne Murray	1988
10,000m (w)	Silver	Liz McColgan	1988
100m hurdles (w)	Silver	Maureen Gardner	1948
	Silver	Carol Quinton	1960
	Silver	Shirley Strong	1984
4x100m relay (w)	Silver		1936
	Silver		1956
4x400m relay (w)	Bronze		1980
High jump (w)	Silver	Dorothy Odam	1936
	Silver	Dorothy Tyler	1948
	Silver	Sheila Lerwill	1952
	Silver	Thelma Hopkins	1956
	Silver	Dorothy Shirley	1960
Long jump (w)	Gold	Mary Rand	1964
Javelin (w)	Gold	Tessa Sanderson	1984

ATHLETICS
Discontinued Event

Event	Medal	Name	Year
Pentathlon (w)	Gold	Mary Peters	1972

BOXING

Event	Medal	Name	Year
Light fly (m)	Bronze	Ralph Evans	1972
Flyweight (m)	Gold	Terry Spinks	1956
Bantamweight (m)	Gold	Henry Thomas	1908
Featherweight (m)	Gold	Richard Gunn	1908
Lightweight (m)	Gold	Fred Grace	1908
	Gold	Dick McTaggart	1956
Light welter (m)	Bronze	Tony Willis	1980
Welterweight (m)	Silver	Alexander Ireland	1920
Light middle (m)	Bronze	John McCormack	1956
	Bronze	William Fisher	1960
	Bronze	Alan Minter	1972
	Bronze	Richie Woodhall	1988
Middleweight (m)	Gold	John Douglas	1908
	Gold	Henry Mallin	1920
	Gold	Henry Mallin	1924
	Gold	Chris Finnegan	1968
Light heavy (m)	Gold	Harry Mitchell	1924
Heavyweight (m)	Gold	Albert Oldham	1908
	Gold	Ronald Rawson	1920
Super heavy (m)	Bronze	Robert Wells	1984

GREAT BRITAIN'S BEST-EVER MEDAL PERFORMANCES IN ALL CURRENT AND PAST OLYMPIC EVENTS.

CYCLING

1km time trial (m)	Silver	Herbert Crowther	1906
Sprint (m)	Silver	HC Bouffler	1906
	Silver	H Thomas Johnson	1920
	Silver	Reg Harris	1948
4000m team pursuit (m)	Gold		1908
Road race - ind (m)	Silver	Frederick Grubb	1912
	Silver	Frank Southall	1928

CYCLING
Discontinued Events

2000m tandem (m)	Gold		1906
	Gold		1920
Team road race (m)	Silver		1912
	Silver		1928
	Silver		1948
	Silver		1956
600yds (m)	Gold	Victor Johnson	1908
5000m track (m)	Gold	Benjamin Jones	1908
20km track (m)	Gold	William Pett	1906
	Gold	Charles Kingsbury	1908
50km track (m)	Silver	Cyril Alden	1920
	Silver	Cyril Alden	1924
100km track (m)	Gold	Charles Bartlett	1908
12hrs track (m)	Silver	F Keeping	1896

EQUESTRIAN

Jumping - ind (o)	Silver	Marion Coates (Stroller)	1968
	Silver	Ann Moore (Psalm)	1972
Jumping - team (o)	Gold		1952
3-day - ind (o)	Gold	Richard Meade (Lauriston)	1972
3-day - team (o)	Gold		1956
	Gold		1968
	Gold		1972

FENCING

Epee - ind (m)	Silver	Allan Jay	1960
	Silver	Bill Hoskyns	1964
Epee - team (m)	Silver		1906
	Silver		1908
	Silver		1912
	Silver		1960
Foil - ind (w)	Gold	Gillian Sheen	1956

FOOTBALL

(m)	Gold		1900
	Gold		1908
	Gold		1912

GYMNASTICS

Ind combined exercises (m)	Silver	SW Tysal	1908
Team (m)	Bronze		1912
(w)	Bronze		1928

HOCKEY

(m)	Gold	England	1908
	Gold	England	1920
	Gold	Great Britain	1988

JUDO

60kg (m)	Bronze	Neil Eckersley	1984
71kg (m)	Silver	Neil Adams	1980
78kg (m)	Silver	Neil Adams	1984
86kg (m)	Bronze	Brian Jacks	1972
95kg (m)	Silver	David Starbrook	1972
Open (m)	Silver	Keith Remfry	1976

MODERN PENTATHLON

Team (m)	Gold		1976

ROWING

Single sculls (m)	Gold	Harry Blackstaffe	1908
	Gold	William Kinnear	1912
	Gold	Jack Beresford	1924
Double sculls (m)	Gold		1936
	Gold		1948
Coxless pairs (m)	Gold		1908
	Gold		1932
	Gold		1948
	Gold		1988
Coxless fours (m)	Gold		1908
	Gold		1924
	Gold		1928
	Gold		1932
Coxed fours (m)	Gold		1984
Coxed pairs	Bronze		1988
Coxed eights (m)	Gold		1908
	Gold		1912

SHOOTING

Free pistol (m)	Bronze	Charles Stewart	1912
Small-bore rifle (prone) (m)	Gold	AA Carnell	1908
Small-bore Rifle (3-pos) (m)	Gold	Malcolm Cooper	1984
	Gold	Malcolm Cooper	1988
Olympic trap (single shot) (m)	Gold	Gerald Merline	1906
Trap (double shot) (m)	Gold	Sidney Merlin	1906
	Gold	Bob Braithwaite	1968
Running game (m)	Bronze	John Kynoch	1972

HERE'S

. . . and that

HOPING THE

Manchester

BRITISH

reigns in the

REIGN IN

2000

SPAIN.

Olympics.

GREAT BRITAIN'S BEST-EVER MEDAL PERFORMANCES IN ALL CURRENT AND PAST OLYMPIC EVENTS.

SHOOTING

Discontinued Events

Free rifle (m)	Gold	Jerry Millner	1908
Military rifle team (m)	Silver		1908
	Silver		1912
Small-bore rifle (moving target) (m)	Gold	AF Fleming	1908
(disappearing target)	Gold	William Styles	1908
Small-bore rifle - team (m)	Gold		1908
	Gold		1912
Live pigeon (m)	Bronze	C Robinson	1900
Clay pigeon - team (m)	Gold		1908
Running deer (m)	Gold	Ted Ranken	1908
	Gold	CW Mackworth-Praed	1924
Running deer - team (m)	Gold		1924
	Gold		1908
Team event (m)	Gold		1912

SWIMMING

100m free (m)	Silver	Bobbie McGregor	1964
400m free (m)	Gold	Henry Taylor	1906
1500m free (m)	Gold	John Jarvis (1000m)	1900
	Gold	Henry Taylor (1 mile)	1906
	Gold	Henry Taylor	1908
100m back (m)	Bronze	Herbert Haresnape	1908
100m breast (m)	Gold	Duncan Goodhew	1980
	Gold	Adrian Moorhouse	1988
200m breast (m)	Gold	Frederick Holman	1908
	Gold	David Wilkie	1976
100m butterfly (m)	Bronze	Andrew Jameson	1988
200m butterfly (m)	Silver	Martyn Woodruff	1968
	Silver	Phil Hubble	1980
200m I/M (m)	Bronze	Neil Cochran	1984
4x100m medley relay (m)	Bronze		1980
4x100m free relay (m)	Gold		1908
100m free (w)	Bronze	Jennie Fletcher	1912
	Bronze	Joyce Cooper	1928
	Bronze	Natalie Steward	1960
400m free (w)	Silver	Sarah Hardcastle	1984
800m free (w)	Bronze	Sarah Hardcastle	1984
100m back (w)	Gold	Judy Grinham	1956
200m breast (w)	Gold	Lucy Morton	1924
	Gold	Anita Longsbrough	1960
400m I/M (w)	Silver	Sharron Davis	1980
4x100m medley relay (w)	Silver		1980
4x100m free relay (w)	Gold		1912

SWIMMING

Discontinued Events

200m obstacle (m)	Bronze	Peter Kemp	1900
400m breast (m)	Bronze	Percy Courtman	1912
4000m free (m)	Gold	John Jarvis	1900

DIVING

Highboard (m)	Bronze	Harold Clarke	1924
	Bronze	Brian Phelps	1960
Highboard (w)	Silver	Eileen Armstrong	1920
Springboard (w)	Bronze	Liz Ferris	1960

WATERPOLO

(m)	Gold		1900
	Gold		1908
	Gold		1912
	Gold		1920

WEIGHTLIFTING

Bantamweight (m)	Silver	Julian Creus	1948
Lightweight (m)	Bronze	James Halliday	1948
Middle heavy (m)	Silver	Louis Martin	1964
Heavyweight (m)	Gold	Launceston Eliot (one-hand)	1896
90kg (m)	Bronze	David Mercer	1984

WRESTLING

Bantamweight free (m)	Silver	William Press	1908
Featherweight free (m)	Silver	James Slim	1908
Lightweight free (m)	Gold	George de Relwyskow	1908
Middleweight free (m)	Gold	Stanley Bacon	1908
Heavyweight free (m)	Gold	George O'Keilly	1908
90kg free (m)	Bronze	Noel Loban	1984

YACHTING

Dragon	Bronze	1956
5.5m	Silver	1956
6m	Gold	1908
	Gold	1936
7m	Gold	1908
	Gold	1920
8m	Gold	1908
12m	Gold	1908
0.5-1 ton	Gold	1900
2-3 ton	Gold	1900
3-10 ton	Bronze	1900
10-20 ton	Bronze	1900
Open	Gold	1900
Star	Gold	1988

Until they come up with a way to fax people.

BRITISH AIRWAYS
The world's favourite airline.

One of the greatest Olympic honours is to be selected to carry the flag for your country at the Opening Ceremony of the Olympic Games.
Here is a *list of those who have been elected by the team managers to do just that for Britain in the past. The list also gives the name of the overall Great Britain team manager - called a "Chef de Mission" - at each Games.

1924 PARIS
Commandant	Brig.-Gen. R.J. Kentish
(No Chef de Mission)	
Flag Bearer	Philip Noel-Baker

1928 AMSTERDAM
Chef de Mission	Evan A Hunter
Flag Bearer	Malcolm Noakes

1932 LOS ANGELES
Chef de Mission:	Evan A Hunter
Flag Bearer:	The Lord Burghley

1936 BERLIN
Chef de Mission	Evan A Hunter
Flag Bearer	Jack Beresford

1948 LONDON
Chef de Mission	Evan A Hunter
Flag Bearer	Emrys Lloyd

1952 HELSINKI
Chef de Mission	Sandy Duncan
Flag Bearer	Harold Whitlock

1956 STOCKHOLM *(Equestrian Only)*
Chef de Mission	Col T D S Williams
Flag Bearer	Lt. Cmdr. J S K Oram

1956 MELBOURNE
Chef de Mission	Sandy Duncan
Flag Bearer	George MacKenzie

1960 ROME
Chef de Mission	Sandy Duncan
Flag Bearer	Richard McTaggart

1964 TOKYO
Chef de Mission	Sandy Duncan
Flag Bearer	Anita Lonsbrough *(Opening Ceremony)*
	Allan Jay *(Closing Ceremony)*

1968 MEXICO CITY
Chef de Mission	Sandy Duncan
Flag Bearer	Lynn Davies *(Opening Ceremony)*
	David Hemery *(Closing Ceremony)*

1972 MUNICH
Chef de Mission	Sandy Duncan
Flag Bearer	David Broome *(Opening Ceremony)*
	Richard Meade *(Closing Ceremony)*

1976 MONTREAL
Chef de Mission	Christopher G V Davidge
Flag Bearer	Rodney Pattisson

1980 MOSCOW
Chef de Mission	Richard Palmer
Flag Bearer	Richard Palmer *(Opening Ceremony)*
	Richard Palmer *(Closing Ceremony)*

(No GB athletes marched at either ceremony due to the political climate surrounding the games).

1984 LOS ANGELES
Chef de Mission	Richard Palmer
Flag Bearer	Lucinda Green *(Opening Ceremony)*
	Sebastian Coe *(Closing Ceremony)*

1988 SEOUL
Chef de Mission	Richard Palmer
Flag Bearer	Ian Taylor *(Opening Ceremony)*
	Malcolm Cooper *(Closing Ceremony)*

Don Thompson in 1964 (Tokyo).

* British Olympic Association records are not complete – particularly for the early Games. If you can help fill the gaps please write to: **The British Olympic Association, 1 Wandsworth Plain, London, SW18 1EH.**

Don't forget to support your
team at the 1992 Olympics.

The British Olympic Association,
1 Wandsworth Plain, London SW18 1EH. Tel: 081-874 8978. Fax: 081-871 9104.

ARCHERY — TIME/POINTS

Open - Men

1	Jay Barrs	USA	2605	
2	Park Sung-Soo	KOR	2614	
3	Vladimir Echeev	URS	2600	
18 (q/f)	Leroy Watson	GBR		
21 (1/8f)	Steven Hallard	GBR		
57 (open rd)	Richard Priestman	GBR		

Open - Women

1	Kim Soo-Nyung	KOR	1352	NOR
2	Wang Hee-Kyung	KOR	2612	
3	Yung Young-Sook	KOR	2603	
7	Joanne Franks	GBR	2557	
17 (q/f)	Pauline Edwards	GBR		
51 (open rd)	Cheryl Sutton	GBR		

Team - Men

1	Chun In-Soo		
	Lee Han-Sup		
	Park Sung-Soo	KOR	986
2	Jay Barrs		
	Richard McKinney		
	Darrell Place	USA	972
3	Steven Hallard		
	Richard Priestman		
	Leroy Watson	GBR	968

Team - Women

1	Kim Soo-Nyung		
	Wang Hee-Kyung		
	Yun Young-Sook	KOR	982
2	L Hankdyani		
	N Saiman		
	Kusuma Wardhani	INA	952
3	Debra Ochs		
	Denise Parker		
	M Skillman	USA	952
5	Pauline Edwards		
	Joanne Franks		
	Cheryl Sutton	GBR	933

ATHLETICS — TIME/POINTS

Men

100 metres

1	Carl Lewis	USA	9.92	NOR
2	Linford Christie	GBR	9.97	
3	Calvin Smith	USA	9.99	
7 (rd2)	Barrington Williams	GBR	10.55	
4 (rd1)	John Regis	GBR	10.76	

200 metres

1	Joe Deloach	USA	19.75	NOR
2	Carl Lewis	USA	19.79	
3	Robson Silva	BRA	20.04	
4	Linford Christie	GBR	20.09	
7	Michael Rosswess	GBR	20.51	
7 (s/f)	John Regis	GBR	20.69	

400 metres

1	Steven Lewis	USA	43.87
2	Harry (Butch) Reynolds	USA	43.93
3	Danny Everett	USA	44.09
8 (s/f)	Brian Whittle	GBR	46.07
6 (rd2)	Todd Bennett	GBR	45.96
	Derek Redmond	GBR	NS

800 metres

1	Paul Ereng	KEN	1:43.45
2	Joaquim Cruz	BRA	1:43.90
3	Said Aouita	MAR	1:44.06
4	Peter Elliott	GBR	1:44.12
4 (rd2)	Tom McKean	GBR	1:46.40
6 (rd2)	Steve Cram	GBR	1:46.47

1500 metres

1	Peter Rono	KEN	3:35.96
2	Peter Elliott	GBR	3:36.15
3	Jens-Peter Herold	GDR	3:36.21
4	Steve Cram	GBR	3:36.24
9 (s/f)	Steve Crabb	GBR	3:39.55

5000 metres

1	John Ngugi	KEN	13:11.70
2	Dieter Baumann	FRG	13:15.52
3	Hansjoerg Kunze	GDR	13:15.73
6	Jack Buckner	GBR	13:23.85
13	Gary Staines	GBR	13:55.00
9 (s/f)	Eamonn Martin	GBR	13:26.26

10,000 metres

1	Brahim Boutaib	MAR	27:21.46
2	Salvatore Antibo	ITA	27:23.55
3	Kipkemboi Kimeli	KEN	27:25.16
AB	Eamonn Martin	GBR	
13 (rd1)	Steve Binns	GBR	28:25.88
AB (rd1)	Michael McLeod	GBR	

Marathon

1	Gelindo Bordin	ITA	2h10:32
2	Douglas Wakiihuri	KEN	2h10:47
3	Houssein Ahmed Saleh	DJI	2h10:59
6	Charlie Spedding	GBR	2h12:19
21	Dave Long	GBR	2h16:18

110 metres hurdles

1	Roger Kingdom	USA	12.98	NOR
2	Colin Jackson	GBR	13.28	
3	Anthony Campbell	USA	13.38	
5	Jonathan Ridgeon	GBR	13.52	
6	Tony Jarrett	GBR	13.54	

400 metres hurdles

1	Andre Phillips	USA	47.19	NOR
2	El Hadj Dia Ba	SEN	47.23	
3	Edwin Moses	USA	47.56	
6	Kriss Akabusi	GBR	48.69	
5 (rd1)	Max Robertson	GBR	50.67	
5 (rd1)	Philip Harries	GBR	50.81	

3000 metres steeplechase

1	Julius Kariuki	KEN	8:05.51	NOR
2	Peter Koech	KEN	8:06.79	
3	Mark Rowland	GBR	8:07.96	
10 (s/f)	Eddie Wedderburn	GBR	8:28.62	
8 (rd1)	Roger Hackney	GBR	8:39.30	

Decathlon

1	Christian Schenk	GDR	8,488
2	Torsten Voss	GDR	8,399
3	Dave Steen	CAN	8,328
4	Daley Thompson	GBR	8,306
24	Alex Kruger	GBR	7,623
30	Greg Richards	GBR	7,237

20km Walk

1	Jozef Pribilinec	TCH	1h19:57
2	Ronald Weigel	GDR	1h20:00
3	Maurizio Damilano	ITA	1h20:14
13	Ian McCombie	GBR	1h22:03
24	Chris Maddocks	GBR	1h23:46

50km Walk

1	Viacheslav Ivanenko	URS	3h38:29
2	Ronald Weigel	GDR	3h38:56
3	Hartwig Gauder	GDR	3h39:45
27	Leslie Morton	GBR	3h59:30
28	Paul Blagg	GBR	4h00:07

The best of British

British Gas wishes the British
Olympic team every success at the
Olympic Games, Barcelona 1992.

British Gas

4x100 metres

1	Victor Bryzgine			
	Vladimir Krylov			
	Vladimir Mouraviev			
	Vitali Savine	URS	38.19	
2	Elliot Bunney			
	John Regis			
	Michael McFarlane			
	Linford Christie	GBR	38.28	
3	Bruno Marie-Rose			
	Daniel Sangouma			
	Giles Queneherve			
	Max Moriniere	FRA	38.40	

4x400 metres

1	Danny Everett			
	Steven Lewis			
	Kevin Robinzine			
	Harry Reynolds	USA	2:56.16	NWR
2	Howard Davis			
	Devon Morris			
	Winthrop Graham			
	Bertland Cameron	JAM	3:00:30	
3	Norbert Dobeleit			
	Edgar Itt			
	Jorg Vaihinger			
	Raif Lubke	FRG	3:00.56	
5	Brian Whittle			
	Kriss Akabusi			
	Todd Bennett			
	Philip Brown	GBR	3:02.00	

Long Jump

1	Carl Lewis	USA	8.72	
2	Mike Powell	USA	8.49	
3	Larry Myricks	USA	8.27	
12	Mark Forsythe	GBR	7.54	
13 (q)	Stewart Faulkner	GBR	7.74	
23 (q)	John King	GBR	7.57	

Triple Jump

1	Hristo Markov	BUL	17.61	NOR
2	Igor Lapchine	URS	17.52	
3	Alexandre Kovalenko	URS	17.42	
13 (q)	Vernon Samuels	GBR	16.28	
16 (q)	John Herbert	GBR	16.18	
23 (q)	Jonathan Edwards	GBR	15.88	

High Jump

1	Guennadi Avdeenko	URS	2.38	NOR
2	Hollis Conway	USA	2.36	
=3	Rudolf Povarnistyne	URS	2.36	
=3	Patrik Sjoberg	SWE	2.36	
=7	Dalton Grant	GBR	2.31	
16	Geoff Parsons	GBR	2.15	
=20 (q)	Floyd Manderson	GBR	2.19	

Pole Vault

1	Sergey Bubka	URS	5.90	
2	Radion Gataullin	URS	5.85	
3	Grigori Egorov	URS	5.80	
(q)	Andrew Ashurst	GBR	X	

Javelin

1	Tapio Korjus	FIN	84.28	
2	Jan Zelezny	TCH	84.12	
3	Seppo Raty	FIN	83.26	
11	David Ottley	GBR	76.96	
20 (q)	Michael Hill	GBR	77.20	
25 (q)	Roald Bradstock	GBR	75.96	

Hammer Throw

1	Serguei Litvinov	URS	84.80	NOR
2	Yuriy Sedykh	URS	83.76	
3	Iouri Tamm	URS	81.16	

22 (q)	Michael Jones	GBR	70.38	
23 (q)	David Smith	GBR	69.12	
28 (q)	Matt Mileham	GBR	62.42	

Discus

1	Jurgen Schult	GDR	68.82	NOR
2	Romas Oubartas	URS	67.48	
3	Rolf Danneberg	FRG	67.38	
20 (q)	Paul Mardle	GBR	58.28	

Shot Put

1	Ulf Timmerman	GDR	22.47	NOR
2	Randy Barnes	USA	22.39	
3	Werner Guenthor	SUI	21.99	
19 (q)	Paul Edwards	GBR	17.28	

Women

100 metres

1	Florence Griffith-Joyner	USA	10.54	NOR
2	Evelyn Ashford	USA	10.83	
3	Heike Drechsler	GDR	10.85	
5 (rd2)	Simmone Jacobs	GBR	11.31	
5 (rd2)	Paula Dunn	GBR	11.37	
6 (rd1)	Helen Miles	GBR	11.88	

200 metres

1	Florence Griffith-Joyner	USA	21.34	NWR
2	Grace Jackson	JAM	21.72	
3	Heike Dreschler	GDR	21.95	
6 (s/f)	Paula Dunn	GBR	23.14	
5 (rd2)	Simmone Jacobs	GBR	23.38	
8 (rd2)	Louise Stuart	GBR	23.59	

400 metres

1	Olga Bryzguina	URS	48.65	NOR
2	Petra Mueller	GDR	49.45	
3	Olga Nazarova	URS	49.90	
5 (rd2)	Linda Keough	GBR	51.91	
7 (rd2)	Loreen Hall	GBR	53.42	
5 (rd1)	Pat Beckford	GBR	54.39	

800 metres

1	Sigrun Wodars	GDR	1:56.10	
2	Christine Wachtel	GDR	1:56.64	
3	Kim Gallagher	USA	1:56.91	
8	Diane Edwards	GBR	2:00.77	
5 (s/f)	Kirsty Wade	GBR	2:00.86	
6 (s/f)	Shireen Bailey	GBR	1:59.94	

1500 metres

1	Paula Ivan	ROM	3:53.96	NOR
2	Lailoute Baikauskaite	URS	4:00.24	
3	Tatiana Samolenko	URS	4:00.30	
4	Christina Cahill	GBR	4:00.64	
7	Shireen Bailey	GBR	4:02.32	
6 (rd1)	Kirsty Wade	GBR	4:08.37	

3000 metres

1	Tatiana Samolenko	URS	8:26.53	NOR
2	Paula Ivan	ROM	8:27.15	
3	Yvonne Murray	GBR	8:29.02	
7	Wendy Sly	GBR	8:37.70	
8 (rd1)	Jill Hunter	GBR	8:57.28	

10,000 metres

1	Olga Bondarenko	URS	31:05.21	NOR
2	Elizabeth McColgan	GBR	31:08.44	
3	Elena Joupieva	URS	31:19.82	
11 (q)	Jane Shields	GBR	32:46.07	
16 (q)	Angela Tooby	GBR	33.26.57	

Marathon

1	Rosa Mota	POR	2h25:40	
2	Lisa Martin	AUS	2h25:53	
3	Kathrin Doerre	GDR	2h26:21	
10	Angela Pain	GBR	2h30:51	
12	Susan Tooby	GBR	2h31:33	
32	Susan Crehan	GBR	2h36:57	

100m hurdles

1	Jordanka Donkova	BUL	12.38	NOR
2	Gloria Siebert	GDR	12.61	
3	Claudia Zackiewicz	FRG	12.75	
6 (s/f)	Sally Gunnell	GBR	13.13	
6 (s/f)	Lesley-Ann Skeete	GBR	13.23	
6 (rd2)	Wendy Jeal	GBR	13.32	

400m hurdles

1	Debra Fintoff-King	AUS	53.17	NOR
2	Tatiana Ledovskaia	URS	53.18	
3	Ellen Fiedler	GDR	53.63	
5	Sally Gunnell	GBR	54.03	
6 (s/f)	Elaine McLaughlin	GBR	55.91	
7 (rd1)	Simone Laidlow	GBR	59.28	

Heptathlon

1	Jackie Joyner-Kersee	USA	7291	NWR
2	Sabine John	GDR	6897	
3	Anke Behmer	GDR	6858	
17	Kim Hagger	GBR	5975	
19	Joanne Mulliner	GBR	5746	
29	Judy Simpson	GBR	1951	

Long Jump

1	Jackie Joyner-Kersee	USA	7.40	NOR
2	Heike Dreschler	GDR	7.22	
3	Galina Tchistiakova	URS	7.11	
6	Fiona May	GBR	6.62	
17 (q)	Kim Hagger	GBR	6.34	
29 (q)	Mary Berkeley	GBR	5.04	

High Jump

1	Louise Ritter	USA	2.03	NOR
2	Stefka Kostadinova	BUL	2.01	
3	Tamara Bykova	URS	1.99	
8	Diana Davies	GBR	1.90	
12	Janet Boyle	GBR	1.90	
13 (q)	Jo Jennings	GBR	1.90	

4x100 metres

1	Alice Brown			
	Sheila Echols			
	Florence Griffith-Joyner			
	Evelyn Ashford	USA	41.98	
2	Silke Moeller			
	Kerstin Behrendt			
	Ingrid Lange			
	Marlies Goehr	GDR	42.09	
3	Lioudmila Kondratieva			
	Galina Maltchougina			
	Marina Jirova			
	Natalia Pomochtchnikova	URS	42.75	
6 (s/f)	Sallyanne Short			
	Beverly Kinch			
	Simmone Jacobs			
	Paula Dunn	GBR	43.50	

4x400 metres

1	Tatiana Ledovskaia			
	Olga Nazarova			
	Maria Piniguina			
	Olga Bryzguina	URS	3:15.18	
2	Denean Howard			
	Diane Dixon			
	Valerie Brisco			
	Florence Griffith-Joyner	USA	3:15.51	
3	Dagmar Neubauer			
	Kirsten Emmelmann			
	Sabine Busch			
	Petra Mueller	GDR	3:18.29	
6	Linda Keough			
	Jennifer Stoute			
	Angela Piggford			
	Sally Gunnell	GBR	3:26.89	

Javelin

1	Petra Felke	GDR	74.68	NOR
2	Fatima Whitbread	GBR	70.32	
3	Beate Koch	GDR	67.30	
21 (q)	Tessa Sanderson	GBR	56.70	
25 (q)	Sharon Gibson	GBR	56.00	

Discus

1	Martina Hellmann	GDR	72.30	NOR
2	Diana Gansky	GDR	71.88	
3	Tzvetanka Hristova	BUL	69.74	
18 (q)	Jacqueline McKernan	GBR	50.92	

Shot Put

1	Natalia Lisovskaya	URS	22.24	
2	Kathrin Neimke	GDR	21.07	
3	Li Meisu	CHN	21.06	
16 (q)	Judy Oakes	GBR	18.34	
17 (q)	Myrtle Augee	GBR	17.31	
20 (q)	Yvonne Hanson-Nortey	GBR	15.13	

BASKETBALL
TIME/POINTS

Team - Men

1	USSR	URS	76-63
2	Yugoslavia	YUG	
3	USA (v AUS)	USA	78-49

Team - Women

1	USA	USA	77-70
2	Yugoslavia	YUG	
3	USSR (v AUS)	URS	68-53

BOXING
TIME/POINTS

Light Fly   **48kg**

1	Ivailo Hristov	BUL	5:0
2	Michael Carbajal	USA	
3	Robert Isaszegi	HUN	
	Leopoldo Serantes	PHI	
rd2	Mark Epton	GBR	

Flyweight   **51kg**

1	Kim Kwang-Sun	KOR	4:1
2	Andreas Tews	GDR	
3	Mario Gonzalez	MEX	
	Timofei Skriabin	URS	
rd1	John Lyon	GBR	

Flyweight   **54kg**

1	Kennedy McKinney	USA	5:0
2	Alexandar Hristov	BUI	
3	Phajol Moolsan	THA	
	Jorge E Julio Rocha	COL	
rd2	Michael Deveney	GBR	

Feather-weight   **57kg**

1	Giovanni Parisi	ITA	RSC
2	Daniel Dumitrescu	ROM	
3	Abdelhak Achik	MAR	
	Lee Lae-Hyuk	KOR	
rd3	David Anderson	GBR	

Light   **60kg**

1	Andreas Zuelow	GDR	5:0
2	George Cramne	SWE	
3	Nerguy Enkhbat	MGL	
	Romallis Ellis	USA	
q/f	Charles Kane	GBR	

TOP THREE FINISHERS AND GB RESULTS ONLY

Light Welter		63.5kg	
1	Viatcheslav Janovski	URS	5:0
2	Grahame Cheney	AUS	
3	Reiner Gies	FRG	
	Lars Myrberg	SWE	
rd2	Mark Elliott	GBR	
Welter		**67kg**	
1	Robert Wangila	KEN	KO
2	Laurent Boudouani	FRA	
3	Jan Dydak	POL	
	Kenneth Gould	USA	
Light Middle		**71kg**	
1	Park Si-Hun	KOR	3:2
2	Roy Jones	USA	
3	Raymond Downey	CAN	
	Richard Woodhall	GBR	
Middle		**75kg**	
1	Henry Maske	GDR	5:0
2	Egerton Marcus	CAN	
3	Chris Sande	KEN	
	Hussain Shah Syed	PAK	
Light Heavy		**81kg**	
1	Andrew Maynard	USA	5:0
2	Nourmagomed Chanavazov	URS	
3	Henryk Petrich	POL	
	Damir Skaro	YUG	
Heavy		**91kg**	
1	Ray Mercer	USA	KO
2	Baik Hyun-Man	KOR	
3	Andrzei Golota	POL	
	Arnold Vanderlijde	HOL	
rd3	Henry Akinwande	GBR	
Super Heavy		**+91kg**	
1	Lennox Lewis	CAN	RSC
2	Riddick Bowe	USA	
3	Alexandre Mirochnitchenko	URS	
	Janusz Zarenkiewicz	POL	

CANOEING — TIME/POINTS

Men
Kayak 1
500m

1	Hungary	HUN	1:44.82
2	German Democratic Republic	GDR	1:46.38
3	New Zealand	NZL	1:46.46
5 (s/f)	Great Britain	GBR	1:46.65

Kayak 2
500m

1	New Zealand	NZL	1:33.98
2	Soviet Union	URS	1:34.15
3	Hungary	HUN	1:34.32
6 (s/f)	Great Britain	GBR	1:37.75

Kayak 1
1000m

1	United States	USA	3:55.27
2	Australia	AUS	3:55.28
3	German Democratic Republic	GDR	3:55.55
5 (rep)	Great Britain	GBR	3:59.69

Kayak 2
1000m

1	United States	USA	3:32.42
2	New Zealand	NZL	3:32.71
3	Australia	AUS	3:33.76
6 (s/f)	Great Britain	GBR	3:31.65

Kayak 4
1000m

1	Hungary	HUN	3:00.20
2	Soviet Union	URS	3:01.40
3	German Democratic Republic	GDR	3:02.37
6 (s/f)	Great Britain	GBR	3:17.54

Canadian - 1
500m

1	German Democratic Republic	GDR	1:56.42
2	Soviet Union	URS	1:57.26
3	Bulgaria	BUL	1:57.27
9	Great Britain	GBR	2:02.27

Canadian - 2
500m

1	Soviet Union	URS	1:41.77
2	Poland	POL	1:43.61
3	France	FRA	1:43.81
4 (s/f)	Great Britain	GBR	1:50.31

Canadian - 1
1000m

1	Soviet Union	URS	4:12.78
2	German Democratic Republic	GDR	4:15.83
3	Bulgaria	BUL	4:18.94
9	Great Britain	GBR	4:39.60

Canadian - 2
1000m

1	Soviet Union	URS	3:48.36
2	German Democratic Republic	GDR	3:51.44
3	Poland	POL	3:54.33
5 (s/f)	Great Britain	GBR	3:59.22

Women
Kayak - 1
500m

1	Bulgaria	BUL	1:55.19
2	German Democratic Republic	GDR	1:55.31
3	Poland	POL	1:57.38
5 (s/f)	Great Britain	GBR	2:04.95

Kayak - 2
500m

1	German Democratic Republic	GDR	1:43.46
2	Bulgaria	BUL	1:44.06
3	Holland	HOL	1:46.00
4 (s/f)	Great Britain	GBR	1:58.70

Kayak - 4
500m

1	German Democratic Republic	GDR	1:40.78
2	Hungary	HUN	1:41.88
3	Bulgaria	BUL	1:42.63
5 (s/f)	Great Britain	GBR	1:46.18

CYCLING — TIME/POINTS

Men
100km Team Time Trial

1	German Democratic Republic	GDR	1h57:47.7
2	Poland	POL	1h57:54.2
3	Sweden	SWE	1h59:47.3
20	Great Britain	GBR	2h08:07.8

1km Ind. Time Trial

1	Alexandre Kiritchenko	URS	1:04.499
2	Martin Vinnicombe	AUS	1:04.784
3	Robert Lechner	FRG	1:05.114

4000m Ind. Pursuit

1	Gintautas Umaras	URS	4:32.00
2	Dean Woods	AUS	4:35.00
3	Bernd Dittert	GDR	4:34.17
4	Colin Sturgess	GBR	4:34.90

Once you've launched the most advanced rescue service in the UK, how much further can you go?

REFLEX
E U R O P E

Since its launch, the RAC Reflex Service has had one simple quest. To provide the finest motoring assistance available on the roads of Britain.

It's a proud ambition. But it did have one limitation.

Its horizons ended at Dover.

So the RAC has broadened the horizons of Reflex rather dramatically.

Right across Europe, in fact.*

For a mere £30 supplement above the normal Reflex price, you can receive a full year's membership of our new Reflex Europe service.

Your motoring will be covered from Aberdeen to Athens, whenever you travel.

In the UK, you will receive the service for which Reflex is already renowned. Once across the Channel, you will find the same commitment to give you the very best emergency assistance.

If Reflex Europe can't get you moving in your car, it can hire you another. And ship yours home if necessary.

It will find spare parts, put you up overnight, and cover you for theft, damage and legal expenses.

And remember, you'll have this cover for a full twelve months, for business or pleasure. So perhaps we'll all be going a little further this year.

For more information on Reflex and Reflex Europe, or to join, ring us free of charge now on 0800 550 550.

*Excluding USSR and Albania.

RAC
THE NEW KNIGHTS OF THE ROAD

Sprint

1	Lutz Hesslich	GDR	
2	Nikolai Kovche	URS	
3	Gary Neiwand	AUS	
4	Edward Alexander	GBR	

50km Points Race

1	Dan Frost	DEN	038
2	Leo Peelen	HOL	026
3	Marat Ganeev	URS	046

4000m Team Pursuit

1	Soviet Union	URS	4:13.31
2	German Democratic Republic	GDR	4:14.09
3	Australia	AUS	4:16.02
13 (q)	Great Britain	GBR	4:25.87

Ind. Road Race

1	Olaf Ludwig	GDR	4h32:22
2	Bernd Groene	FRG	4h32:25
3	Christian Henn	FRG	4h32:46
18	Neil Hoban	GBR	G
36	Paul Curran	GBR	G
62	Mark Gornall	GBR	G

Women

Ind. Road Race

1	Monique Knol	HOL	2h00:52
2	Jutta Niehaus	FRG	G
3	Laima Zilporitee	URS	G
6	Maria Blower	GBR	G
9	Sally Hodge	GBR	G
11	Lisa Brambani	GBR	G

Sprint

1	Erika Saloumiae	URS	
2	Christa Luding Rothenburg	GDR	
3	Connie Paraskevin-Young	USA	
7	Louise Jones	GBR	

3-Day Event

Team

1	Claus Erhorn (Justyn Thyme)		
	Matthias Baumann (Shamrock II)		
	Thies Kaspareit (Sherry 42)		
	Ralf Ehrenbrink (Uncle Todd)	FRG	225.95
2	Mark Phillips (Cartier)		
	Karen Straker (Get Smart)		
	Ginny Leng (Master Craftsman)		
	Ian Stark (Sir Wattie)	GBR	256.80
3	Mark Todd (Charisma)		
	Marges Knighton (Enterprise)		
	Andrew Bennie (Grayshott)		
	Tinks Pottinger (Volunteer)	NZL	271.20

3-Day Event

Individual

1	Mark Todd (Charisma)	NZL	42.60
2	Ian Stark (Sir Wattie)	GBR	52.80
3	Ginny Leng (Master Craftsman)	GBR	62.00
19	Karen Straker (Get Smart)	GBR	142.00
AB	Mark Phillips (Cartier)	GBR	

Dressage

Team

1	Federal Republic of Germany	FRG	4302
2	Switzerland	SUI	4164
3	Canada	CAN	3969
10	Jenny Loriston-Clarke (Dutch Gold)		
	Barbara Hammond (Krist)		
	Diana Mason (Prince Consort)		
	Tricia Gardiner (Wily Imp)	GBR	3797

Dressage

Individual

1	Nicole Uphoff (Rembrandt)	FRG	1521
2	Margitt Otto-Crepin (Corlandus)	FRA	1462
3	Chris Stueckelberger		
	(Gauguin De Lully Ch)	SUI	1417
14	Jenny Loriston-Clarke		
	(Dutch Gold)	GBR	1304

Jumping

Individual

1	Pierre Durand (Jappeloup)	FRA	1.25
=2	Greg Best (Gem Twist)	USA	4.00
=2	Karsten Huck (Neopmuk 8)	FRG	4.00
=4	David Broome (Countryman)	GBR	8.00
=7	Nicholas Skelton (Apollo)	GBR	12.00
14	Joseph Turi (Vital)	GBR	12.25

Jumping

Team

1	Federal Republic of Germany	FRG	17.25
2	United States of America	USA	20.50
3	France	FRA	27.50
6	Nicholas Skelton (Apollo)		
	Joseph Turi (Vital)		
	Malcolm Pyrah (Anglezarke)		
	David Broome (Countryman)	GBR	40.00

Men

Foil Ind.

1	Stefano Cerioni	ITA	10-7
2	Udo Wagner	GDR	
3	Alexandre Romankov	URS	
5th Series	Pierre Harper	GBR	
4th Series	Willaim Gosbee	GBR	
1st Series	Donald McKenzie	GBR	

Sabre Ind.

1	Jeanfrancois Lamour	FRA	10-4
2	Janusz Olech	POL	
3	Giovanni Scalzo	ITA	

Epee Ind.

1	Arnd Schmidt	FRG	10-9
2	Philippe Riboud	FRA	
3	Andrei Chouvalov	URS	
rd3	John Llewellyn	GBR	
rd1	Hugh Kernohan	GBR	

Team Foil

1	Soviet Union	URS	9-5
2	Federal Republic of Germany	FRG	
3	Hungary	HUN	
10	Great Britain	GBR	

Team Sabre

1	Hungary	HUN	8(67)-8(64)
2	Soviet Union	URS	
3	Italy	ITA	

Team Epee

1	France	FRA	8-3
2	Federal Republic of Germany	FRG	
3	Soviet Union	URS	

Women

Foil Ind.

1	Anja Fichtel	FRG	8-5
2	Sabine Bau	FRG	
3	Zita Funkenhauser	FRG	
17	Elizabeth Thurley	GBR	
24	Fiona McIntosh	GBR	
28	Linda Martin	GBR	

Foil Team

1	Federal Republic of Germany	FRG	9-4
2	Italy	ITA	
3	Hungary	HUN	
11	Great Britain	GBR	

FOOTBALL

1	Soviet Union	URS	2-1
2	Brazil	BRA	
3	Federal Republic of Germany (v Italy)	FRG	3-0

GYMNASTICS   TIME/POINTS

Men
All-Around Ind.

1	Vladimir Artemov	URS	119.125
2	Valeri Lioukine	URS	119.025
3	Dmitri Bilozertchev	URS	118.975

Floor Exercises

1	Serguei Kharikov	URS	19.925
2	Vladimir Artemov	URS	19.900
3	Lou Yun	CHN	19.850

Pommel Horse

1	Lyubomir Gueraskov	BUL	19.950
2	Zsolt Borkai	HUN	19.950
3	Dmitri Bilozertchev	URS	19.950

Rings

1	Holger Behrendt	GDR	19.925
2	Dmitri Bilzertchev	URS	19.925
3	Sven Tippelt	GDR	19.875

Vault

1	Lou Yun	CHN	19.875
2	Sylvio Kroll	GDR	19.862
3	Park Jong-Hoon	KOR	19.775

Parallel Bars

1	Vladimir Artemov	URS	19.925
2	Valeri Lioukine	URS	19.900
3	Sven Tippelt	GDR	19.750

Horizontal Bars

1	Vladimir Artemov	URS	19.900
2	Valeri Lioukine	URS	19.900
3	Holger Behrendt	GDR	19.800

Team

1	Soviet Union	URS	593.350
2	German Democratic Republic	GDR	588.450
3	Japan	JPN	585.600
75	Terry Bartlett	GBR	112.950
81	Andrew Morris	GBR	112.050

Women
Team

1	Soviet Union	URS	395.475
2	Romania	ROM	394.125
3	German Democratic Republic	GDR	390.875
82	Karen Hargate	GBR	74.400
89	Karen Kennedy	GBR	36.775

All-Around Ind.

1	Elena Chouchounova	URS	79.662
2	Daniela Silivas	ROM	79.637
3	Svetlana Boguinskaia	URS	79.400

Asymmetric Bars

1	Daniela Silivas	ROM	20.000
2	Dagmar Kersten	GDR	19.987
3	Elena Chouchounova	URS	19.962

Vault

1	Svetlana Boguinskaia	URS	19.905
2	Gabriela Potorac	ROM	19.830
3	Daniela Silivas	ROM	19.818

Beam

1	Daniela Silivas	ROM	19.924
2	Elena Chouchounova	URS	19.875
3	Gabriela Potorac	ROM	19.837

Floor Exercises

1	Daniela Silivas	ROM	19.937
2	Svetlana Boguinskaia	URS	19.887
3	Diana Doudeva	BUL	19.850

Rhythmic

1	Marina Lobatch	URS	60.000
2	Adriana Dounavska	BUL	59.950
3	Alexandra Timochenko	URS	59.875
38	Lisa Black	GBR	36.400

HANDBALL   TIME/POINTS

Team - Men

1	Soviet Union	URS	32-25
2	Korea	KOR	
3	Yugoslavia (v Hungary)	YUG	27-23

Team - Women

1	Korea	KOR	
2	Norway	NOR	
3	Soviet Union (v Yugoslavia)	URS	

HOCKEY

Team - Men

1	Great Britain	GBR	3-1
2	Federal Republic of Germany	FRG	
3	Holland (v Australia)	HOL	2-1

Team - Women

1	Australia	AUS	2-0
2	Korea	KOR	
3	Holland (v Great Britain)	HOL	3-1

JUDO

Men
Extra-light -60kg

1	Kim Jae-Yup	KOR	
2	Kevin Asano	USA	
3	A Tetikachvili	URS	
rd3	Neil Eckersley	GBR	

Half-Light -65kg

1	Lee Kyung Keun	KOR	
2	J Powlowski	POL	
3	Bruno Carabetta	FRA	
rd1	Mark Adshead	GBR	

Light -71kg

1	Marc Alexandre	FRA	
2	Sven Loll	GDR	
3	Michael Swain	USA	
D/q	Kerrith Brown	GBR	

Half-Middle -78kg

1	Waldemar Legien	POL	
2	Frank Wieneke	FRG	
3	Bachir Varaev	URS	
rd3	Neil Adams	GBR	

Middle	-86kg		
1	P Seisenbacher	AUT	
2	V Chestakov	URS	
3	Ben Spikjers	HOL	
qf (repA)	Densign White	GBR	
Half-Heavy	**-95kg**		
1	Aurelio Miguel	BRA	
2	Marc Meiling	FRG	
3	Dennis Stewart	GBR	
Heavy	**+95kg**		
1	Hitoshi Saito	JAV	
2	Henry Stoehr	GDR	
3	Cho Young-Chul	KOR	
rd2	Elvis Gordon	GBR	

MODERN PENTATHLON   POINTS

Team - Men			
1	Janos Martinek		
	Attila Mizser		
	Laszlo Fabian	HUN	15,886
2	Carlo Massullo		
	Daniele Masala		
	Gianluca Tiberti	ITA	15,571
3	Richard Phelps		
	Dominic Mahony		
	Graham Brookhouse	GBR	15,276
Individual			
1	Janos Martinek	HUN	5,404
2	Carlo Massullo	ITA	5,379
3	Vakhtang Iagorachvili	URS	5,367
6	Richard Phelps	GBR	5,229
16	Dominic Mahony	GBR	5,047
21	Graham Brookhouse	GBR	5,000

ROWING   TIME/POINTS

Men			
Single Sculls			
1	German Democratic Republic	GDR	6:49.86
2	Federal Republic of Germany	FRG	6:54.77
3	New Zealand	NZL	6:58.66
Double Sculls			
1	Holland	HOL	6:21.13
2	Switzerland	SUI	6:22.59
3	Soviet Union	URS	6:22.87
Quadruple Sculls			
1	Italy	ITA	5:53.37
2	Norway	NOR	5:55.08
3	German Democratic Republic	GDR	5:56.13
Coxless Pairs			
1	Great Britain	GBR	6:36.84
2	Romania	ROM	6:38.06
3	Yugoslavia	YUG	6:41.01
Coxed Pairs			
1	Italy	ITA	6:58.79
2	German Democratic Republic	GDR	7:00.63
3	Great Britain	GBR	7:01.95
Coxless Four			
1	German Democratic Republic	GDR	6:03.11
2	United States of America	USA	6:05.53
3	Federal Republic of Germany	FRG	6:06.22
4	Great Britain	GBR	6:06.74

Coxed Four			
1	German Democratic Republic	GDR	6:10.74
2	Romania	ROM	6:13.58
3	New Zealand	NZL	6:15.78
4	Great Britain	GBR	6:18.08
Eights			
1	Federal Republic of Germany	FRG	5:46.05
2	Soviet Union	URS	5:48.01
3	United States of America	USA	5:48.26
4	Great Britain	GBR	5:51.59
Women			
Single Sculls			
1	German Democratic Republic	GDR	7:47.19
2	United States of America	USA	7:50.28
3	Bulgaria	BUL	7:53.65
Double Sculls			
1	German Democratic Republic	GDR	7:00.48
2	Romania	ROM	7:04.36
3	Bulgaria	BUL	7:06:03
3rd B final	Great Britain	GBR	8:15.70
Quadruple Sculls			
1	German Democratic Republic	GDR	6:21.06
2	Soviet Union	URS	6:23.47
3	Romania	ROM	6:23.81
Coxless Pairs			
1	Romania	ROM	7:28.13
2	Bulgaria	BUL	7:31.95
3	New Zealand	NZL	7:35.68
2nd B final	Great Britain	GBR	8:15.20
Coxed Four			
1	German Democratic Republic	GDR	6:56.00
2	China	CHN	6:58.78
3	Romania	ROM	7:01.13
6	Great Britain	GBR	7:10.80
Eights			
1	German Democratic Republic	GDR	6:15.17
2	Romania	ROM	6:17.44
3	China	CHN	6:21.83

SHOOTING   TIME/POINTS

Men			
Free Pistol			
1	Sorin Babii	ROM	660.0
2	Ragnar Skanaker	SWE	657.0
3	Igor Bassinski	URS	657.0
34	Paul Leatherdale	GBR	546
SB Free Rifle, Prone			
1	Mirsolav Varga	TCH	703.9
2	Cha Young-Chul	KOR	702.8
3	Attila Zahonyi	HUN	701.9
5	Alister Allan	GBR	700.9
=36	Malcolm Cooper	GBR	592
Olympic Trap Open			
1	Dmitri Monakov	URS	222
2	Miloslav Bednarik	TCH	222
3	Frans Peeters	BEL	219
=25	Ian Peel	GBR	142
Air Rifle			
1	Goran Maksimovic	YUG	695.6
2	Nicolas Berthelot	FRA	694.2
3	Johann Riederer	FRA	694.0
	Alister Allan	GBR	DNS
	Malcolm Cooper	GBR	DNS
SB Rifle 3 positions			
1	Malcolm Cooper	GBR	1279.3
2	Alister Allan	GBR	1275.6
3	Kirill Ivanov	URS	1275.0

Good luck to the competitors
from the world's best all-rounder.

CABLE & WIRELESS

TOP THREE FINISHERS AND GB RESULTS ONLY

Rapid Fire Pistol

1	Afansi Kouzmine	URS	698.0
2	Ralf Schumann	GDR	696.0
3	Zoltan Kovacs	HUN	693.0
=24	Adrian Breton	GBR	596.0

Running Game Target

1	Tor Heiestad	NOR	689.0
2	Huang Shiping	CHN	687.0
3	Guennadi Avramenko	URS	686.0

Olympic Skeet

1	Axel Wegner	GDR	222
2	Alfonso De Iruarrizaga	CHI	221
3	Jorge Guardiola	ESP	220
=27	Ken Harman	GBR	144

Air Pistol

1	Taniou Kiriakov	BUL	687.9
2	Erich Buljung	USA	687.9
3	Xu Haifeng	CHN	684.5
=34	Paul Leatherdale	GBR	569.0

Women
Air Rifle

1	Irina Chilova	URS	498.5
2	Silvia Sperber	FRG	497.5
3	Anna Maloukhina	URS	495.8
=33	Sarah Cooper	GBR	383.0

Sport Pistol

1	Nino Saloukvadze	URS	690.0
2	Tomoko Hasegawa	JPN	686.0
3	Jasna Sekaric	YUG	686.0
11	Margaret Thomas	GBR	582.0

SB Standard Rifle - 3 position

1	Silvia Sperber	FRG	685.6
2	Vessela Letcheva	BUL	683.2
3	Valentina Tcherkassova	URS	681.4
36	Sarah Cooper	GBR	557.0

Air Pistol

1	Jasna Sekariac	YUG	489.5
2	Nino Saloukvadze	URS	487.9
3	Marina Dobrantcheva	URS	485.2
=34	Margaret Thomas	GBR	365.0

SWIMMING

TIME/POINTS

Men
50m Freestyle

1	Matthew Biondi	USA	22.14	NWR
2	Thomas Jager	USA	22.36	
3	Gennadi Prigoda	URS	22.71	
2 (ht)	Mike Fibbens	GBR	23.67	
6 (ht)	Mark Foster	GBR	23.51	

100m Freestyle

1	Matthew Biondi	USA	48.63	NOR
2	Christopher Jacobs	USA	49.08	
3	Stephan Caron	FRA	49.62	
6 (ht)	Andrew Jameson	GBR	51.18	
7 (ht)	Roland Lee	GBR	51.20	

200m Freestyle

1	Duncan Armstrong	AUS	1:47.25	NWR
2	Anders Holmertz	SWE	1:47.89	
3	Matthew Biondi	USA	1:47.99	
8 (B Final)	Paul Howe	GBR	1:51.99	
6 (ht)	Michael Green	GBR	1:53.03	

400m Freestyle

1	Uwe Dassler	GDR	3:46.95	NWR
2	Duncan Armstrong	AUS	3:47.15	
3	Artur Wojdat	POL	3:47.34	
7	Kevin Boyd	GBR	3:50.16	
4 (ht)	Tony Day	GBR	3:57.91	

1500m Freestyle

1	Vladimir Salnikov	URS	15:00.40
2	Stefan Pfeiffer	FRG	15:02.69
3	Uwe Dassler	GDR	15:06.15
7	Kevin Boyd	GBR	15:21.16
7 (ht)	Tony Day	GBR	15:38.75

4x100m Freestyle

1	Christopher Jacobs			
	Troy Dalbey			
	Thomas Jager			
	Matthew Biondi	USA	3:16.53	NWR
2	Gennadi Prigoda			
	Iouri Bachkatov			
	Nikolai Evseev			
	Vladimir Tkashenko	URS	3:18.33	
3	Dirk Richter			
	Thomas Flemming			
	Lars Hinneburg			
	Steffen Zesner	GDR	3:19.82	
7	Michael Fibbens			
	Mark Foster			
	Roland Lee			
	Andrew Jameson	GBR	3:21.71	

4x200m Freestyle

1	Troy Dalbey			
	Matthew Cetlinski			
	Douglas Gjertson			
	Matthew Biondi	USA	7:12.51	NWR
2	Uwe Dassler			
	Sven Lodziewski			
	Thomas Flemming			
	Steffen Zesner	GDR	7:13.68	
3	Erik Hochstein			
	Thomas Fahrner			
	Rainer Henkel			
	Michael Gross	FRG	7:14.35	
5 (ht)	Kevin Boyd			
	Paul Howe			
	Jonathan Broughton			
	Roland Lee	GBR	7:29.77	

100m Breaststroke

1	Adrian Moorhouse	GBR	1:02.04
2	Karoly Guttler	HUN	1:02.05
3	Dmitri Volkov	URS	1:02.20
6 (ht)	James Parrack	GBR	1:04.23

200m Breaststroke

1	Jozsef Szabo	HUN	2:13.52
2	Nick Gillingham	GBR	2:14.12
3	Sergio Lopez	ESP	2:15.21
6 (ht)	Adrian Moorhouse	GBR	2:18.51

100m Butterfly

1	Anthony Nesty	SUR	53.00
2	Matthew Biondi	USA	53.78
3	Andy Jameson	GBR	53.30
8 (B final)	Neil Cochran	GBR	55.22

200m Butterfly

1	Michael Gross	GDR	1:56.94
2	Benny Nielson	DEN	1:58.24
3	Anthony Mosse	NZL	1:58.28
2 (B final)	Tim Jones	GBR	2:00.32
4 (B final)	Nick Hodgson	GBR	2:01.09

100m Backstroke

1	Daichi Suzuki	JPN	55.05
2	David Berkoff	USA	55.18
3	Igor Polianski	URS	55.20
2 (ht)	Neil Harper	GBR	58.02
2 (ht)	Neil Cochran	GBR	58.25

200m Backstroke

1	Igor Polianski	URS	1:59.37	
2	Frank Baltrusch	GDR	1:59.60	
3	Paul Kingsman	NZL	2:00.48	
8 (B final)	Gary Binfield	GBR	2:04.90	
D/q ht	John Davey	GBR		

200m Ind. Medley

1	Tamas Darnyi	HUN	2:00.17	NWR
2	Patrick Kuehl	GDR	2:01.61	
3	Vadim Izarochtchouk	URS	2:02.40	
2 (B final)	John Davey	GBR	2:04.17	
3 (B final)	Neil Cochran	GBR	2:05.44	

400m Ind. Medley

1	Tamas Daryni	HUN	4:14.75	NWR
2	David Wharton	USA	4:17.36	
3	Stefano Battistelli	ITA	4:18.01	
2 (B final)	Paul Brew	GBR	4:26.77	
D/q ht	John Davey	GBR		

4 x 100m Medley Relay

1	David Berkoff			
	Richard Schroeder			
	Matthew Biondi			
	Christopher Jacobs	USA	3:36.93	NWR
2	Mark Tewksbury			
	Victor Davis			
	Thomas Ponting			
	Donald Goss	CAN	3:39.28	
3	Igor Polianski			
	Dmitri Volkov			
	Vadim Iarochtchouk			
	Gennadi Prigoda	URS	3:39.96	
D/q	Neil Harper			
	Adrian Moorhouse			
	Andy Jameson			
	Mark Foster	GBR		

Women

50m Freestyle

1	Kristin Otto	GDR	25.49	NOR
2	Yang Wenyi	CHN	25.77	
3	Katrin Meissner	GDR	25.71	
4 (ht)	Annabelle Cripps	GBR	27.17	
8 (ht)	Alison Sheppard	GBR	27.14	

100m Freestyle

1	Kristin Otto	GDR	54.93
2	Zhuang Yong	CHN	55.47
3	Catherine Plewinski	FRA	55.49
3 (ht)	Annabelle Cripps	GBR	57.81
5 (ht)	June Croft	GBR	58.19

200m Freestyle

1	Heike Friedrich	GDR	1:57.65
2	Silvia Poll	CRC	1:58.67
3	Manuela Stellmach	GDR	1:59.01
2 (B final)	Ruth Gilfillan	GBR	2:01.66
7 (ht)	June Croft	GBR	2:03.63

400m Freestyle

1	Janet Evans	USA	4:03.85	NWR
2	Heike Friedrich	GDR	4:05.94	
3	Anke Moehring	GDR	4:06.62	
7 (ht)	Ruth Gilfillan	GBR	4:16.66	
7 (ht)	June Croft	GBR	4:21.98	

800m Freestyle

1	Janet Evans	USA	8:20.20	NOR
2	Astrid Strauss	GDR	8:22.09	
3	Julie McDonald	AUS	8:22.93	
2 (ht)	Tracey Atkin	GBR	9:00.04	
5 (ht)	Karen Mellor	GBR	8:44.64	

4 x 100m Freestyle Relay

1	Kristin Otto			
	Katrin Meissner			
	Daniela Hunger			
	Manuela Stellmach	GDR	3:40.63	NOR
2	Marianne Muis			
	Mildrid Muis			
	Cornelia Van Bentum			
	Karin Brienesse	HOL	3:43.39	
3	Mary Wayte			
	Mitzi Kremer			
	Laura Walker			
	Dara Torres	USA	3:44.25	
5 (ht)	Annabelle Cripps			
	June Croft			
	Linda Donnelly			
	Joanna Coull	GBR	3:50.84	

100m Breaststroke

1	Tania Dangalakova	BUL	1:07.95	NOR
2	Antoaneta Frenkeva	BUL	1:08.74	
3	Silke Hoerner	GDR	1:08.83	
8 (B final)	Susannah Brownsdon	GBR	1:11.95	
8 (ht)	Margaret Hohmann	GBR	1:12.67	

200m Breaststroke

1	Silke Hoerner	GDR	2:26.71	NWR
2	Huang Xiaomin	CHN	2:27.49	
3	Antoaneta Frenkeva	BUL	2:28.34	
4 (ht)	Helen Frank	GBR	2:41.12	
8 (ht)	Susannah Brownsdon	GBR	2:36.14	

100m Butterfly

1	Kristin Otto	GDR	59.00	NOR
2	Birte Weigang	GDR	59.45	
3	Qian Hong	CHN	59.52	
6 (ht)	Caroline Foot	GBR	1:02.76	
6 (ht)	Annabelle Cripps	GBR	1:03.34	

200m Butterfly

1	Kathleen Nord	GDR	2:09.51
2	Birte Weigang	GDR	2:09.91
3	Mary Meagher	USA	2:10.80
7 (B final)	Helen Bewley	GBR	2:17.11
7 (ht)	Lynne Wilson	GBR	2:17.28

100m Backstroke

1	Kristin Otto	GDR	1:00.89
2	Krisztina Egerszegi	HUN	1:01.56
3	Cornelia Sirch	GDR	1:01.57
8 (B final)	Katharine Read	GBR	1:04.27
8 (ht)	Sharon Page	GBR	1:04.75

200m Backstroke

1	Krisztina Egerszegi	HUN	2:09.29	NOR
2	Kathrin Zimmermann	GDR	2:10.61	
3	Cornelia Sirch	GDR	2:11.45	
4 (B final)	Katharine Read	GBR	2:18.20	
7 (ht)	Helen Slater	GBR	2:21.66	

200m Ind. Medley

1	Daniela Hunger	GDR	2:12.59	NOR
2	Elena Dendeberova	URS	2:13.31	
3	Noemi Ildiko Lung	ROM	2:14.85	
3 (B final)	Jean Hill	GBR	2:19.20	
6 (ht)	Zara Long	GBR	2:22.64	

400m Ind. Medley

1	Janet Evans	USA	4:37.76
2	Noemi Idiko Lung	ROM	4:39.46
3	Daniela Hunger	GDR	4:39.76
5 (ht)	Susannah Brownsdon	GBR	4:54.66
6 (ht)	Tracey Atkin	GBR	5:01.34

4 x 100m Medley Relay

1	Kristin Otto			
	Silke Hoerner			
	Birte Weigang			
	Katrin Meissner	GDR	4:03.74	NOR
2	Beth Barr			
	Tracey McFarlane			
	Janel Jorgensen			
	Mary Wayte	USA	4:07.90	
3	Lori Melien			
	Allison Higson			
	Jane Kerr			
	Andrea Hugent	CAN	4:10.49	
4 (ht)	Katharine Read			
	Susannah Brownsdon			
	Caroline Foot			
	Joanna Coull	GBR	4:16.18	

SYNCHRONISED SWIMMING — TIME/POINTS

Women
Solo

1	Carolyn Waldo	CAN	200.150
2	Tracie Ruiz-Conforto	USA	197.633
3	Mikako Kotani	JPN	191.850
6	Nicola Shearn	GBR	181.933

Duet

1	Michelle Cameron		
	Carolyn Waldo	CAN	197.717
2	Sarah Josephson		
	Karen Josephson	USA	197.284
3	Miyako Tanaka		
	Mikako Kotani	JPN	190.159
7	Nicola Shearn		
	Lian Goodwin	GBR	179.075

DIVING — TIME/POINTS

Men
Springboard

1	Gregory Louganis	USA	730.80
2	Tan Liangde	CHN	704.88
3	Li Deliang	CHN	665.28
26 (prelims)	Graham Morris	GBR	476.74
29 (prelims)	Robert Morgan	GBR	457.65

Platform

1	Gregory Louganis	USA	638.61
2	Xiong Ni	CHN	637.47
3	Jesus Mena	MEX	594.39
15 (prelims)	Robert Morgan	GBR	489.27
21 (prelims)	Jeffrey Arbon	GBR	450.18

Women
Springboard

1	Gao Min	CHN	580.23
2	Li Qing	CHN	534.33
3	Kelly McCormick	USA	533.19
18 (prelims)	Carolyn Roscoe	GBR	399.87
26 (prelims)	Naomi Bishop	GBR	349.44

Platform

1	Xu Yanmei	CHN	445.20
2	Michele Mitchell	USA	436.95
3	Wendy Williams	USA	400.44
18 (prelims)	Carolyn Roscoe	GBR	322.35

WATERPOLO — TIME/POINTS

Men

1	Yugoslavia	YUG	9-7
2	United States of America	USA	
=3	Federal Republic of Germany	FRG	
=3	Soviet Union	URS	

TABLE TENNIS — TIME/POINTS

Men
Singles

1	Yoo Nam Kyu	KOR	17-21, 21-19 21-11, 23-21
2	Kim Ki Taik	KOR	
3	Erik Lindh	SWE	14-21, 21-17
	(v Tibor Klampar, HUN)		21-17, 21-16
q/f	Desmond Douglas	GBR	1-3
	(v Jiang Jialiang, CHN)		
4 (gp)	Carl Prean	GBR	

Doubles

1	Chen Longcan		
	Wei Qingguang	CHN	20-22, 21-8, 21-9
2	Ilija Lupulesku		
	Zoran Primorac	YUG	
3	Ahn Jae Hyung		
	Yoo Nam Kyu	KOR	21-13, 21-16
3 (grp B)	Desmond Douglas		
	Skylet Andrew	GBR	
4 (grp A)	Carl Prean		
	Alan Cooke	GBR	

Women
Singles

1	Chen Jing	CHN	21-17, 21-16 21-23, 15-21 21-15
2	Li Huifen	CHN	
3	Jiao Zhimin	CHN	

Doubles

1	Hyun Jung Hwa		
	Yang Young Ja	KOR	21-19, 16-21 21-10
2	Chen Jing		
	Jiao Zhimin	CHN	
3	Jasna Fazlic		
	Gordana Perkucin	YUG	

TENNIS

Men
Singles

1	Miloslav Mecir	TCH	3-6; 6-2; 6-4; 6-2
2	Tim Mayotte	USA	
=3	Stefan Edberg	SWE	
=3	Brad Gilbert	USA	
last 32	Jeremy Bates	GBR	
last 32	Andrew Castle	GBR	

With
Best Wishes
from ✹
BET

BET is a specialist support services company. It offers a broad range of contract staff and equipment to provide the support services required by its customers. BET's main activities cover business services, plant services and distribution services.

For further information
about BET please contact:
Andrew Mills B.Sc., M.B.A.
Director of corporate affairs
BET Public Limited Company
Stratton House, Piccadilly
London W1X 6AS
Telephone 071-629 8886

Doubles

I	Ken Flach		6-3; 6-4; 6-7;
	Robert Seguso	USA	6-7; 9-7
2	Emilio Sanchez		
	Sergio Casal	ESP	
=3	Stefan Edberg		
	Anders Jarryd	SWE	
=3	Miloslav Mecir		
	Milan Srejber	TCH	
last 16	Jeremy Bates		
	Andrew Castle	GBR	

Women
Singles

I	Steffi Graf	FRG	6-3; 6-3
2	Gabriela Sabatini	ARG	
=3	Zina Garrison	USA	
=3	Manuela Maleeva	BUL	
last 32	Sara Gomer	GBR	
last 32	Clare Wood	GBR	

Doubles

I	Pam Shriver		
	Zina Garrison	USA	4-6; 6-2; 10-8
2	Jana Novotna		
	Helena Sukov	TCH	
=3	Elizabeth Smylie		
	Wendy Turnbull	AUS	
=3	Steffi Graf		
	Claudia Kohde-Kilsch	FRG	

Men

I	United States of America	USA	3-1
2	Soviet Union	URS	
3	Argentina	ARG	

Women

I	Soviet Union	URS	3-2
2	Peru	PER	
3	People's Republic of China	CHN	

Men
52kg

I	Sevdalin Marinov	BUL	270.0	NWR
2	Chun Byung-Kwan	KOR	260.0	
3	He Zhuoqiang	CHN	257.7	

56kg

I	Oxen Mirzoian	URS	292.5	NOR
2	He Yingqiang	CHN	287.5	
3	Liu Shoubin	CHN	267.5	

60kg

I	Naim Suleymanoglu	TUR	342.5	NWR
2	Stefan Topourov	BUL	312.5	
3	Ye Huanming	CHN	287.5	

67.5kg

I	Joachim Kunz	GDR	340.0
2	Joachim Militossian	URS	337.5
3	Li Jinhe	CHN	325.0

75kg

I	Borislav Guidikov	BUL	375.0	NOR
2	Ingo Steinhoefel	GDR	360.0	
3	Alexander Varbanov	BUL	357.5	
7	Dean Willey	GBR	332.5	
II	Ricky Chaplin	GBR	320.0	

82.5kg

I	Israil Arsamakov	URS	377.5
2	Istvan Messzi	HUN	370.0
3	Lee Hyung-Kun	KOR	367.5
4	David Morgan	GBR	365.0

90kg

I	Anatoli Khrapatyi	URS	412.5	NOR
2	Nail Moukhamediarov	URS	400.0	
3	Slawomir Zawada	POL	400.0	
6	David Mercer	GBR	357.5	
8	Keith Boxell	GBR	350.0	

100kg

I	Pavel Kouznetsov	URS	425.0	NOR
2	Nicu Vlad	ROM	402.5	
3	Peter Immesberger	FRG	395.0	
12	Andrew Saxton	GBR	352.5	
13	Peter May	GBR	350.0	

110kg

I	Yuri Zakharevitch	URS	455.0	NWR
2	Jozsef Jacso	HUN	427.5	
3	Ronny Weller	GDR	425.0	
12	Mark Thomas	GBR	360.0	
	Andrew Davies	GBR	EL	

110kg+

I	Alexandre Kourlovitch	URS	462.5	NOR
2	Manfred Nerlinger	FRG	430.0	
3	Martin Zawieja	FRG	415.0	
9	Matthew Vine	GBR	352.5	

Men
Freestyle 48kg

I	Takashi Kobayshi	JPN	16
2	Ivan Tzonov	BUL	4
3	Sergei Karamtchakov	URS	3

Freestyle 52kg

I	Mitsuru Sato	JPN	13
2	Saban Trstena	YUG	2
3	Vladim Togouzov	URS	14

Freestyle 57kg

I	Serg Beloglazov	URS	5
2	Ask Mohammadian	IRN	I
3	Noh Kyung-sun	KOR	9

Freestyle 62kg

I	John Smith	USA	4
2	Stepan Sarkissian	URS	0
3	Simeon Chterev	BUL	5
rd2	Ravi Singh Ravinder	GBR	

Freestyle 68kg

I	Arsen Fadzaev	URS	6
2	Park Jang-soon	KOR	0
3	Nate Carr	USA	5

Freestyle 74kg

I	Kenneth Monday	USA	5
2	Adlan Varayev	SOV	2
3	Rakhmad Sofiadi	BUL	8
rd2	Fitzlloyd Walker	GBR	0

Freestyle 82kg

I	Han Myung-woo	KOR	4
2	Necmi Gencalp	TUR	0
3	Josel Lohyna	CZE	PI

Freestyle 90kg

I	Makharbek Khadartsev	URS	16
2	Akira Ota	JPN	0
3	Kim Tae-woo	KOR	I

WITH EVERY GOOD WISH
FROM
ALFRED DUNHILL

SOUGHT AFTER SINCE 1893

TOP THREE FINISHERS AND GB RESULTS ONLY

Freestyle   100kg
1	Vasile Puscasu	ROM	1
2	Leri Khabelov	URS	0
3	William Scherr	USA	fall

Freestyle   130kg
1	David Gobedjichvili	URS	3
2	Bruce Baumgartner	USA	1
3	Andreas Schroder	GDR	PI

Greco-Roman 48kg
1	Vicenzo Maenza	ITA	3
2	Andrej Glab	POL	0
3	Bratan Tzenov	BUL	PI

Greco-Roman 52kg
1	Jon Ronningen	NOR	12
2	Atsuji Miyahara	JPN	7
3	Lee Jae-suk	KOR	4

Greco-Roman 57kg
1	Andras Sike	HUN	1
2	Stoyan Balov	BUL	
3	Haralambos Holidis	GRE	6

Greco-Roman 62kg
1	Kamandar Madzhidov	URS	6
2	Zhivko Vanguelov	BUL	2
3	An Dae-hyun	KOR	PI

Greco-Roman 68kg
1	Levon Dzhulfalakyan	URS	9
2	Kim Sung-Moon	KOR	3
3	Tapio Sipila	FIN	7

Greco-Roman 74kg
1	Kim Young-nam	KOR	2
2	Daulet Turlykhanov	URS	1
3	Jozef Tracz	POL	2

Greco-Roman 82kg
1	Mikhail Mischler	URS	10
2	Tibor Komaromi	HUN	1
3	Kim Sang-Kyu	KOR	6

Greco-Roman 90kg
1	Atanas Komchev	URS	6
2	Harri Koskela	FIN	0
3	Vladimir Popov	URS	F

Greco-Roman 100kg
1	Andrzej Wronski	POL	3
2	Gerhard Himmel	FRG	1
3	Dennis Koslowski	USA	6

Greco-Roman 130kg
1	Alexandre Kareline	URS	5
2	Ranguel Guerovski	BUL	3
3	Tomas Johansson	SWE	PI

YACHTING

TIME/POINTS

Men
Soling Class
1	Jochen Schuemann		
	Thomas Flach		
	Bernd Jaekel	GDR	23.40
2	John Kostecki		
	William Baylis		
	Robert Billingham	USA	24.00
3	Jesper Bank		
	Jan Mathiasen		
	Steen Secher	DEN	52.70
4	Lawrie Smith		
	Edward Leask		
	Jeremy Richards	GBR	67.10

Star Class
1	Michael McIntyre		
	Bryn Vaile	GBR	64.70
2	Mark Reynolds		
	Hal Haenel	USA	76.00
3	Torben Grael		
	Nelson Falcao	BRA	78.00

FD Class
1	Jorgen Bojsen-Moller		
	Christian Gronborg	DEN	43.10
2	Olepetter Pollen		
	Erik Bjorkum	NOR	58.40
3	Frank McLaughlin		
	John Millen	CAN	66.40
6	Roger Yeoman		
	Neal McDonald	GBR	99.70

Finn Class
1	Jose Doreste	ESP	78.10
2	Peter Holmberg	ISV	80.40
3	John Cutler	NZL	61.00
4	Stuart Childerley	GBR	70.70

Tornado Class
1	Jean-Yves Le Deroff		
	Nicolas Henard	FRA	46.00
2	Christopher Timms		
	Rex Sellers	NZL	51.40
3	Lars Grael		
	Clinio Freitas	BRA	54.10
8	Robert White		
	Jeremy Newman	GBR	100.10

Division II Class
1	Bruce Kendall	NZL	50.40
2	Jan D Boersma	AHO	58.70
3	M Gebhardt	USA	65.00
14	Simon Goody	GBR	106.00

470 Class
1	Thierry Peponnet		
	Luc Pillot	FRA	51.70
2	Tynou Tyniste		
	Toomas Tyniste	URS	82.00
3	John Shadden		
	Charlie McKee	USA	69.00
15	Jason Belben		
	Andrew Hemmings	GBR	150.00

Women
470 Class
1	Allison Jolly		
	Lynne Jewell	USA	54.70
2	Marit Soderstrom		
	Birgitta Bengtsson	SWE	61.00
3	Larissa Moskalenko		
	Irina Chounikhovskaya	URS	59.40
15	Debra Jarvis		
	Susan Hay	GBR	135.40

We don't just stand by and watch.

GRAND METROPOLITAN

....adding value

OLYMPIC GAMES

A POTTED HISTORY

Barcelona's Games of the XXVth Olympiad looks set to be the world's greatest sporting festival. More sports, more athletes and more nations will gather together than ever before.

A slow boat east across the Mediterranean from Barcelona would bring you eventually to Greece - spiritual home of this great sporting spectacle. For a thousand years from 776 BC to 395 AD feuding Greek tribes laid down their weapons and competed in an Olympic festival containing sports and the arts.

On sacred ground at Olympia the Games, part of a religious gathering to honour the gods and goddesses of Greek mythology, encompassed a range of sports including running, boxing, pentathlon, wrestling and chariot races. Competitors and spectators were exclusively male. If a woman broke this rule she would be thrown to her death over a nearby cliff.

In 394 AD Roman Emperor Theodorius banned all pagan festivals including the Ancient Games. But the ideals involved were revived centuries later.

First an Englishman, Robert Dover, set up his own "Olympick Games" in Gloucestershire. People of all classes enjoyed a series of traditional games and sports in an almost unbroken run from 1612 to 1852. Just as those Games were fading a Shropshire doctor, William Brookes, started the "Wenlock Olympics", at Much Wenlock, to revive the ideals of the Ancient Games on similar lines to its "Dover Games" precedent.

In 1890, as in previous years, a colourful procession set off through the streets. Amongst the procession, as guest of William Brookes, was a French visitor, Baron Pierre de Coubertin.

Coubertin wanted to regenerate the physical education curriculum in France. He was also attracted by the morality, traditions, character and honesty of the Ancient Games. He pressed his case around the world and in 1894 called together an International Sports Congress at the Sorbonne in Paris. During the congress, on 23rd June, the International Olympic Committee was formed and it was decided to hold a revived Olympic Games in Athens in 1896.

Olympic Games are not only affected by world trends but they can reflect them as well. The 1936 Games were awarded to Berlin before Adolf Hitler was in power. As the Games app-roached Josef Goebbels convinced Hitler that it would be an excellent PR vehicle. Many countries nearly boycotted the Games due to the political policy of Germany.

The star of the 1936 Games was Jesse Owens, the black American athlete, who won 4 gold medals in the 100m, 200m, long jump and the 4x100m relay much to the displeasure of Hitler.

The first television coverage of the Games also came in 1936. However, it was only broadcast on closed circuit to 28 special halls, including local cinemas in Berlin. The first global broadcast occured at the 1960 Rome Games.

After six years of war and two uncelebrated Olympic Games in 1940 and 1944 the world was looking forward to a "peaceful" gathering of the Olympic countries.

A postal vote in 1946 gave the 1948 Olympic Games to London. Britain still had food, petrol and building rationing. Therefore, the Games became known as the "austerity Games". The Organising Committee built nothing. A cinder running track was laid inside Wembley Stadium and

The 1948 Olympic Stadium, Wembley, London.

other venues were adapted.

Both the 1968 and the 1972 Olympic Games, in Mexico and Munich respectively, were to be marred by politics.

Mexico was the first third-world country to host the Games. Mexican students decided that the world's media should be used to express their anger at the government for holding political prisoners.

Demonstrations for the release of these prisoners turned into bloody riots and at least 200 students were killed. Amidst this turmoil an American athlete, Bob Beamon, set a world record in the long jump at 8.90m. This phenomenal leap stood as a world record until 1991.

Political factors entered the Olympic arena again in 1972 at the Munich Games. On 5th September eight Arab terrorists broke into the Israeli team headquarters. The terrorists killed two Israelis immediately and another nine were murdered after a rescue attempt, by German police, failed at the airport. The Olympic family was stunned.

Gaston Reiff of Belgium takes the 1948 5000m title.

The Soviet Union's invasion of Afghanistan in December 1979 ultimately disrupted the 1980 Olympic Games in Moscow. A number of non-communist nations decided to impose a boycott. Great Britain accepted the invitation. At the Opening Ceremony only the British Olympic Association General Secretary, Dick Palmer, marched in to represent Great Britain.

Tit-for-tat politics came into play at the 1984 Olympic Games with a last minute boycott by the Soviet Union and other socialist countries. The standard of competition was effected at both Games by the boycotts.

The birth of commercialisation for the Olympic Movement came at the 1984 Olympic Games in Los Angeles when a profit of US$215 million was made. In comparison the estimated expenditure for the 1976 Games in Montreal was US$310 million and the final bill came to US$1400 million. The 1988 Games in Seoul made a record profit of US$288 million.

The 1988 Games in Seoul, Korea, were the second to be held in a third-world country since 1896. With 237 events in 23 sports the Games will be remembered for their efficiency and outstanding facilities.

They also unified the Olympic movement after some troubled years.

Munich in 1972.

Year	Venue	Nations	Athletes	GB Team	Sports	No. of Sports
1896	Athens	13	311	8	Athletics, cycling, fencing, gymnastics, shooting, swimming, tennis, weightlifting, wrestling.	9
1900	Paris	22	1330	103	Archery, athletics, cricket, crocquet, cycling, equestrian, fencing, football, golf, gymnastics, polo, rowing, rugby, shooting, swimming, tennis, yachting.	17
1904	St. Louis	12	625	1	Archery, athletics, boxing, fencing, football, golf, gymnastics, lacrosse, roque, rowing, swimming, tennis, weightlifting, wrestling.	14
1906	Athens	20	884	52	Athletics, cycling, fencing, football, gymnastics, rowing, shooting, swimming, tennis, weightlifting, wrestling.	11
1908	London	23	2035	721	Archery, athletics, boxing, cycling, fencing, football, gymnastics, hockey, ice skating, jeu de paume, lacrosse, motorboating, polo, rackets, rowing, rugby, shooting, swimming, tennis, wrestling, yachting.	21
1912	Stockholm	28	2547	293	Athletics, cycling, equestrian, fencing, football, gymnastics, modern pentathlon, rowing, shooting, swimming, tennis, wrestling, yachting.	13
1920	Antwerp	29	2692	231	Archery, athletics, boxing, cycling, equestrian, fencing, football, gymnastics, hockey, ice hockey, ice skating, modern pentathlon, polo, rowing, rugby, shooting, swimming, tennis, weightlifting, wrestling, yachting.	21
1924	Paris	44	3092	247	Athletics, boxing, cycling, equestrian, fencing, football, gymnastics, hockey, modern pentathlon, polo, rowing, rugby, shooting, swimming, tennis, weightlifting, wrestling, yachting.	17
1928	Amsterdam	46	3014	211	Athletics, boxing, cycling, equestrian, fencing, football, gymnastics, hockey, modern pentathlon, rowing, swimming, weightlifting, wrestling, yachting.	14
1932	Los Angeles	37	1408	71	Athletics, boxing, cycling, equestrian, fencing, gymnastics, hockey, modern pentathlon, rowing, shooting, swimming, weightlifting, wrestling, yachting.	14
1936	Berlin	49	4066	205	Athletics, basketball, boxing, canoeing, cycling, equestrian, fencing, football, gymnastics, handball, hockey, modern pentathlon, polo, rowing, shooting, swimming, weightlifting, wrestling, yachting.	19
1948	London	59	4099	313	Athletics, basketball, boxing, canoeing, cycling, equestrian, fencing, football, gymnastics, hockey, modern pentathlon, rowing, shooting, swimming, weightlifting, wrestling, yachting.	17

Year	Venue	Nations	Athletes	GB Team	Sports	No. of Sports
1952	Helsinki	69	4925	257	Athletics, basketball, boxing, canoeing, cycling, equestrian, fencing, football, gymnastics, hockey, modern pentathlon, rowing, shooting, swimming, weightlifting, wrestling, yachting.	17
1956	Melbourne (equestrian in Stockholm)	72	3342	189	Athletics, basketball, boxing, canoeing, cycling, equestrian, fencing, football, gymnastics, hockey, modern pentathlon, rowing, shooting, swimming, weightlifting, wrestling, yachting.	17
1960	Rome	83	5348	253	Athletics, basketball, boxing, canoeing, cycling, equestrian, fencing, football, gymnastics, hockey, modern pentathlon, rowing, shooting, swimming, weightlifting, wrestling, yachting.	17
1964	Tokyo	93	5140	205	Athletics, basketball, boxing, canoeing, cycling, equestrian, fencing, football, gymnastics, hockey, judo, modern pentathlon, rowing, shooting, swimming, volleyball, weightlifting, wrestling, yachting.	19
1968	Mexico City	112	5531	223	Athletics, basketball, boxing, canoeing, cycling, equestrian, fencing, football, gymnastics, hockey, modern pentathlon, rowing, shooting, swimming, volleyball, weightlifting, wrestling, yachting.	18
1972	Munich	122	7156	308	Archery, athletics, basketball, boxing, canoeing, cycling, equestrian, fencing, football, gymnastics, handball, hockey, judo, modern pentathlon, rowing, shooting, swimming, volleyball, weightlifting, wrestling, yachting.	21
1976	Montreal	88	6085	225	Archery, athletics, basketball, boxing, canoeing, cycling, equestrian, fencing, football, gymnastics, handball, hockey, judo, modern pentathlon, rowing, shooting, swimming, volleyball, weightlifting, wrestling, yachting.	21
1980	Moscow	81	5326	230	Archery, athletics, basketball, boxing, canoeing, cycling, equestrian, fencing, football, gymnastics, handball, hockey, judo, modern pentathlon, rowing, shooting, swimming, volleyball, weightlifting, wrestling, yachting.	21
1984	Los Angeles	140	7078	362	Archery, athletics, basketball, boxing, canoeing, cycling, equestrian, fencing, football, gymnastics, handball, hockey, judo, modern pentathlon, rowing, shooting, swimming, volleyball, weightlifting, wrestling, yachting.	21
1988	Seoul	159	8465	386	Archery, athletics, basketball, boxing, canoeing, cycling, equestrian, fencing, football, gymnastics, handball, hockey, judo, modern pentathlon, rowing, shooting, swimming, table tennis, tennis, volleyball, weightlifting, wrestling, yachting.	23
1992	Barcelona				Archery, athletics, badminton, baseball, basketball, boxing, canoeing, cycling, equestrian, fencing, football, gymnastics, handball, hockey, judo, modern pentathlon, rowing, shooting, swimming, table tennis, tennis, volleyball, weightlifting, wrestling, yachting.	25

1984
(LOS ANGELES)

1988
(SEOUL)

1992
(BARCELONA)

Backing the Games
Leading the Competition

Worldwide Sponsor of the 1992 Olympic Games

Brother International Europe Ltd · Brother House · 1 Tame Street · Audenshaw · Manchester · M34 5JE · Tel: 061·330 6531 · Fax: 061·330 5520
Jones + Brother · Shepley Street · Audenshaw · Manchester M34 5JD · Tel: 061·330 6531 · Fax: 061·308 3281

ATHLETICS – Men

Event	Time/Dist	Competitor	Country	Year
100m	9.92	Carl Lewis	USA	1988
200m	19.75	Joe Deloach	USA	1988
400m	43.86	Lee Evans	USA	1968
800m	1:43.00	Joaquim Cruz	BRA	1984
1500m	3:32.53	Sebastian Coe	GBR	1984
5000m	13:05.59	Said Aouita	MOR	1984
10,000m	27:21.47	Brahim Boutaib	MOR	1988
110m Hurdles	12.98	Roger Kingdom	USA	1988
400m Hurdles	47.19	Andre Phillips	USA	1988
3,000m Steeplechase	8:05.51	Julius Koriuki	KEN	1988
20km Walk	1hr19:57.00	Jozef Pribilinec	TCH	1988
50km Walk	3hr 38:29.00	Viacheslav Ivanenko	URS	1988
Marathon	2hr 09:21.00	Carlos Lopes	POR	1984
4 x 100m Relay	37.83	Sam Graddy	USA	1984
		Ron Brown		
		Calvin Smith		
		Carl Lewis		
4 x 400m Relay	2:56.16	Vincent Matthews	USA	1968
		Ronald Freeman		
		Larry James		
		Lee Evans		
	2:56.16	Danny Everett	USA	1988
		Stephen Lewis		
		Kevin Robinzine		
		Butch Reynolds		
High Jump	2.38	Guennadi Avdeenko	URS	1988
Long Jump	8.90	Bob Beamon	USA	1968
Triple Jump	17.61	Hristo Markov	BUL	1968
Pole Vault	5.90	Sergey Bubka	URS	1988
Shot	22.47	Ulf Timmerman	GDR	1988
Discus	68.82	Jurgen Schult	GDR	1988
Javelin	94.58	Miklos Nemeth	HUN	1976
Javelin (New)	85.90	Jan Zelezny	TCH	1988
Hammer	84.80	Serguei Litvinov	URS	1988
Decathlon	8797pts	Daley Thompson	GBR	1984

ATHLETICS – Women

Event	Time/Dist	Competitor	Country	Year
100m	10.54	Florence Griffith-Joyner	USA	1988
200m	21.34	Florence Griffith-Joyner	USA	1988
400m	48.64	Olga Bryzguina	URS	1988
800m	1:53.50	Nadezhda Olizarenko	URS	1980
1500m	3:53.96	Paula Ivan	ROM	1980
3000m	8:26.53	Tatiana Samolenko	URS	1988
10,000m	31:05.21	Olga Bondarenko	URS	1988
100m Hurdles	12.38	Jordana Donkova	BUL	1988
400m Hurdles	53.17	Debra Flintoff-King	AUS	1988
4 x 100m Relay	41.60	Romy Muller	GDR	1980
		Barbel Wockel		
		Ingrid Auerswald		
		Marlies Gohr		
4 x 400m Relay	3:15.18	Tatiana Ledovskaya	URS	1988
		Olga Nazarova		
		Maria Pinigina		
		Olga Bryzguina		
Marathon	2hr 24:52.00	Joan Benoit	USA	1984
High Jump	2.02	Louise Ritter	USA	1988
Long Jump	7.40	Jackie Joyner-Kersee	USA	1988
Shot	22.41	Ilona Slupianek	GDR	1980
Discus	72.30	Martina Hellmann	GDR	1988
Javelin	74.68	Petra Felke	GDR	1988
Pentathlon	5083pts	Nadezhda Tkachenko	URS	1980
Heptathlon	7291pts	Jackie Joyner-Kersee	USA	1988

CYCLING

Event	Time/Dist	Competitor	Country	Year
1,000m time trial	1:02.995	Lothar Thoms	GDR	1980
4,000m ind pursuit	4:32.00	Ginataoutas Umatas	URS	1988
4,000m team pursuit	4:14.64	Viktor Manakov	URS	1980
		Valery Movchan		
		Vladimir Osokin		
		Vitaly Petrakov		

SWIMMING – Men

Event	Time/Dist	Competitor	Country	Year
50m Freestyle	22.14	Matthew Biondi	USA	1988
100m Freestyle	48.43	Matthew Biondi	USA	1988
200m Freestyle	1:47.25	Duncan Armstrong	AUS	1988
400m Freestyle	3:46.95	Uwe Dassler	GDR	1988
1500m Freestyle	14:58.27	Vladimir Salnikov	URS	1976
100m Backstroke	54.51	David Berkoff	USA	1988
200m Backstoke	1:58.99	Rick Carey	USA	1984
100m Breaststroke	1:01.65	Steve Lundquist	USA	1984
200m Breaststroke	2:13.34	Victor Davis	CAN	1984
100m Butterfly	53.00	Anthony Nesty	SUR	1988
200m Butterfly	1:56.94	Michael Gross	FRG	1988
200m Ind Medley	2:00.17	Tamas Darnyi	HUN	1988
400m Ind Medley	4:14.75	Tamas Darnyi	HUN	1988
4 x 100m Freestyle Relay	3:16.53	Christopher Jacobs	USA	1988
		Troy Dalbey		
		Thomas Jager		
		Matthew Biondi		
4 x 200m Freestyle Relay	7:12.51	Troy Dalbey	USA	1988
		Matthew Cetlinski		
		Douglas Gjertsen		
		Matthew Biondi		
4 x 100m Medley Relay	3:36.93	David Berkoff	USA	1988
		Richard Schroeder		
		Matthew Biondi		
		Christopher Jacobs		

CURRENT OLYMPIC RECORDS

SWIMMING – Women

Event	Time/Dist	Competitor	Country	Year	Event	Time/Dist	Competitor	Country	Year
50m Freestyle	25.49	Kristin Otto	GDR	1988	200m Ind Medley	2:12.59	Daniela Hunger	GDR	1988
100m Freestyle	54.79	Barbara Krause	GDR	1980	400m Ind Medley	4:36.29	Petra Schneider	GDR	1980
200m Freestyle	1:57.65	Heiki Friedrich	GDR	1988	4 x 100m Freestyle	3:40.63	Kristin Otto	GDR	1988
400m Freestyle	4:03.85	Janet Evans	USA	1988	Relay		Katrin Meissner		
800m Freestyle	8:20.20	Janet Evans	USA	1988			Daniela Hunger		
100m Backstroke	1:00.86	Rica Reinsich	GDR	1980			Manuela Stellmach		
200m Backstroke	2:09.29	Krisztina Egerszegi	HUN	1988	4 x 100m Medley	4:03.74	Kristin Otto	GDR	1988
100m Breaststroke	1:07.95	Tania Dangalakova	BUL	1988	Relay		Silke Horner		
200m Breaststroke	2:26.71	Silka Moerner	GDR	1988			Birte Weigang		
100m Butterfly	59.00	Kristin Otto	GDR	1988			Katrin Meissner		
200m Butterfly	2:06.90	Mary Meagher	USA	1984					

WEIGHTLIFTING

Weight	KG	Competitor	Country	Year	Weight	KG	Competitor	Country	Year
52kg	270.0	Sevdalin Marionov	BUL	1988	82.5kg	400.0	Y Vardanyan	URS	1980
56kg	292.5	Oxen Mirzonian	URS	1988	90kg	412.5	Anatoli Khrapatyi	URS	1988
60kg	342.5	Naim Suleymanoglu	TUR	1988	100kg	425.0	Pavel Kouznetsov	URS	1988
67.5kg	342.5	Y Roussev	BUL	1980	110kg	455.0	Yuri Zakharevitch	URS	1988
75kg	375.0	Borislav Guidikov	BUL	1988	+110kg	462.5	Alexandre Kourlovitch	URS	1988

A record celebration in Seoul.

WORLD RECORDS

As at 26th February 1992

SWIMMING - Men

Event		Time	Competitor	Country	Year
50m	Freestyle	0:21.81	Tom Jager	USA	24.3.90
100m	Freestyle	0:48.42	Matthew Biondi	USA	10.8.88
200m	Freestyle	1:46.69	Giorgio Lamberti	ITA	15.8.89
400m	Freestyle	3:46.95	Uwe Dassler	GDR	23.9.88
800m	Freestyle	7:46.60	Kieren Perkins	AUS	16.2.92
1,500m	Freestyle	14:50.36	Jeorg Hoffman	GER	13.1.91
100m	Backstroke	0:53.93	Jeffrey Rouse	USA	25.8.91
200m	Backstroke	1:56.57	Martin Zubero	ESP	23.11.91
100m	Breaststroke	1:01.29	Norbert Rozsa	HUN	26.8.91
200m	Breaststroke	2:10.60	Mike Barrowman	USA	13.1.91
100m	Butterfly	0:52.84	Pablo Morales	USA	23.8.91
200m	Butterfly	1:55.69	Melvin Stewart	USA	12.1.91
200m	Ind Medley	1:59.36	Tamas Darnyi	HUN	13.1.91
400m	Ind Medley	4:12.36	Tamas Darnyi	HUN	8.1.91
4x100m Freestyle Relay		3:16.53	Chris Jacobs Troy Dalbey Tom Jager Matthew Biondi	USA	23.9.88
4x200m Freestyle Relay		7:12.51	Troy Dalbey Matthew Cetlinski Doug Gjertsen Matthew Biondi	USA	21.9.88
4x100m Medley Relay		3:36.93	David Berkoff Richard Schroeder Matthew Biondi Chris Jacobs	USA	25.9.88

* Subject to ratification by FINA

SWIMMING - Women

Event		Time	Competitor	Country	Year
50m	Freestyle	0:24.98	Yang Wen Yi	CHN	11.4.88
100m	Freestyle	0:54.73	Kristin Otto	GDR	19.8.86
200m	Freestyle	1:57.55	Heike Freidrich	GDR	18.6.86
400m	Freestyle	4:03.85	Janet Evans	USA	22.9.88
800m	Freestyle	8:16.22	Janet Evans	USA	20.8.89
1500m	Freestyle	15:52.10	Janet Evans	USA	22.3.88
100m	Backstroke	1:00.31	Krisztina Egerszegi	HUN	22.8.91
200m	Backstroke	2:06.62	Krisztina Egerszegi	HUN	25.8.92
100m	Breaststroke	1:07.91	Silke Horner	GDR	21.8.87
200m	Breaststroke	2:26.71	Silke Horner	GDR	21.9.88
100m	Butterfly	0:57.93	Mary Meagher	USA	16.8.81
200m	Butterfly	2:05.96	Mary Meagher	USA	13.8.81
200m	Ind Medley	2:11.73	Ute Gewewniger	GDR	4.7.81
400m	Ind Medley	4:36.10	Petra Schneider	GDR	1.8.82
4x100m Freestyle Relay		3:40.57	Kristin Otto Manuela Stellmach Sabina Schulze Heike Friedrich	GDR	19.8.86
4x200m Freestyle Relay		7:55.47	Manuela Stellmach Astrid Strauss Anke Mohring Heike Friedrich	GDR	18.8.87
4x100m Medley Relay		4:03.69	Ina Kleber Sylvia Gerasch Ines Geissler Birgit Meineke	GDR	24.8.84

As at 23rd March 1992

ATHLETICS - Men

Event	Time/Dist	Competitor	Country	Year
100m	9.86	Carl Lewis	USA	1991
200m	19.72	Pietro Mennea	ITA	1979
400m	43.29	Butch Reynolds	USA	1988
800m	1:41.73	Sebastian Coe	GBR	1981
1500m	3:29.46	Said Aouita	MOR	1985
1 Mile	3:46.32	Steve Cram	GBR	1985
5000m	12:58.39	Said Aouita	MOR	1987
10Km	27:08.23	Arturo Barrios	MEX	1989
110m Hurdles	12.92	Roger Kingdom	USA	1989
400m Hurdles	47.02	Edwin Moses	USA	1983
3000m Steeplechase	8:05.35	Peter Koech	KEN	1989
20Km Walk	1hr18:13.00	Pavol Blazek	TCH	1990
50Km Walk	3hr37:41.00	Andrey Perlov	URS	1989
Marathon	2hr06:50.00	Belayneh Dinsamo	ETH	1988
4x100m Relay	37.50	Andre Cason Leroy Burrell Dennis Mitchell Carl Lewis	USA	1991
4x400 Relay	2:56.16	Vincent Matthews Ronald Freeman Larry James Lee Evans	USA	1968
	2:56.16	Danny Everett Carl Lewis Kevin Robinzine Butch Reynolds	USA	1988
High Jump	2.44	Javier Sotomayor	CUB	1989
Pole Vault	6.10	Sergey Bubka	CIS*	1991
Long Jump	8.95	Mike Powell	USA	1991
Triple Jump	17.97	Willie Banks	USA	1985
Shot Put	23.12	Randy Barnes	USA	1990
Discus	74.08	Jurgen Schult	GER	1986
Hammer	86.74	Yuriy Sedykh	URS	1986
Javelin	91.46	Steve Backley	GBR	1992
Decathlon	8847pts	Daley Thompson	GBR	1984

CIS* = Commonwealth of Independent States, previously URS

As at 23rd March 1992

ATHLETICS – Women

Event	Time/Dist	Competitor	Country	Year	Event	Time/Dist	Competitor	Country	Year
100m	10.49	Florence Griffith-Joyner	USA	1988	4x400m Relay	3:15.17	Tatiana Ledovskaya Olga Nazarova Maria Pinigina Olga Bryzgina	URS	1988
200m	21.34	Florence Griffith-Joyner	USA	1988					
400m	47.60	Marita Koch	GER	1985	Marathon	2:21.06	Ingrid Kristiansen	NOR	1985
800m	1:53.28	Jarmila Kratochvilova	TCH	1983	High Jump	2.09	Stefka Kostadinova	BUL	1987
1500m	3:52.47	Tatyana Kazankina	URS	1980	Long Jump	7.52	Galina Chistyakova	URS	1988
1 Mile	4:15.61	Paula Ivan	ROM	1989	Triple Jump	14.95	Inessa Kravets	URS	1991
3000m	8:22.62	Tatyana Kazankina	URS	1984	Shot Put	22.63	Natalya Lisovskaya	URS	1987
10,000m	30:13.74	Ingrid Kristiansen	NOR	1986	Discus	76.80	Gabriele Reinsch	GER	1988
100m Hurdles	12.21	Yordanka Donkova	BUL	1988	Javelin	80.00	Petra Meier	GER	1988
400m Hurdles	52.94	Marina Stepanova	URS	1986	Heptathlon	7291pts	Jackie Joyner-Kersee	USA	1988
10Km Walk	41.30	Kerry Junna	AUS	1988					
4x100m Relay	41.37	Silke Gladisch Sabine Rieger Ingrid Auerswald Marlies Gohr	GDR	1985					

CIS* = Commonwealth of Independent States, previously URS

EUROPEAN RECORD SUPPLEMENT

Event	Time/Dist	Competitor	Country	Year	Event	Time/Dist	Competitor	Country	Year
MEN					4x400m Relay	2:57.53	Roger Black Derek Redmond John Regis Kriss Akabusi	GBR	1991
100m	9.92	Linford Christie	GBR	1991					
400m	44.33	Thomas Schonlebe	GER	1987					
1500m	3:29.67	Steve Cram	GBR	1985					
5000m	13:00.41	David Moorcroft	GBR	1982	High Jump	2.42	Patrik Sjoberg	SWE	1987
10Km	27:13.81	Fernando Mamede	POR	1984	Long Jump	8.86	Robert Emmiyan	URS	1987
110m Hurdles	13.08	Colin Jackson	GBR	1990	Triple Jump	17.92	Khristo Markov	BUL	1987
400m Hurdles	47.48	Harald Schmid	GER	1982/7	Shot Put	23.06	Ulf Timmermann	GER	1988
3000m Steeplechase	8:07.62	Joseph Mahmoud	FRA	1984	**WOMEN**				
Marathon	2:07.12	Carlos Lopes	POR	1985	100m	10.81	Marlies Gohr	GER	1983
4x100m Relay	37.79	Max Moriniere Daniel Sangouma Jean-Charles Trouabal Bruno Marie-Rose	FRA	1990	200m	21.71	Marita Koch	GER	1979/84
						21.71	Heike Drechsler	GER	1986
					10Km Walk	42.16	Alina Ivanova	URS	1989
					Heptathlon	7007pts	Larisa Nikitina	URS	1989

Jackie Joyner-Kersee: Heptathlon world record holder.

ARCHERY

MEN
1900

Au Cordon Dore -50m	Henri Herouin	FRA
Au Cordon Dore - 33m	Hubert van Innis	BEL
Au Chapelet - 50m	Eugene Mougin	FRA
Au Chapelet - 33m	Hubert van Innis	BEL
Herse	Emmanuel Foulon	FRA
Pyramide	Emile Frumiaux	FRA

1904

Double York Round - 100, 80 & 60 yards	Philip Bryant	USA
Double American Round - 60, 50 & 40 yards	Philip Bryant	USA
Team Round - 60 yards	Potomac Archers	USA

1908

York Round - 100, 80 & 60 yards	William Dod	GBR
Continental Style - 50m	E G Griscot	FRA

1920

Small birds - ind	Edmond van Moer	BEL
Small birds - team		BEL
Large bird - ind	Edouard Cloetens	BEL
Large bird - team		BEL
Moving target - 28m ind	Hubert van Innis	BEL
Moving target - 28m team		BEL
Moving target - 33m - ind	Hubert van Innis	BEL
Moving target - 33m - team		BEL
Moving target - 50m - ind	Julien Brule	FRA
Moving target 50m - team		BEL

Double FITA Round

1972	John Williams	USA	2528 pts
1976	Darrell Pace	USA	2571 pts
1980	Tomi Poikolainen	FIN	2455 pts
1984	Darrell Pace	USA	2616 pts
1988	Jay Barrs	USA	338 pts (2605)
	Team	KOR	

WOMEN
1904

Double National Round - 50, 40, 30 yards.	Lida Howell	USA
Double Columbia Round - 60, 50 yards	Lida Howell	USA
Team Round - 60, 50 yards	Cincinatti Archery Club	USA
1908 National Round - Ind	Queenie Newall	GBR

Double FITA Round

1972	Doreen Wilber	USA	2424 pts
1976	Luann Ruon	USA	2499 pts
1980	Keto Losaberidze	KOR	2568 pts
1988	Kim Soo-Hyung	KOR	344 pts (2683)
	Team	KOR	

ATHLETICS

(Prior to 1972 automatic timings in the shorter distances to one-hundreths of a second are shown additionally, where known.)

MEN
100m

1896	Thomas Burke	USA	12.0
1900	Frank Jarvis	USA	11.0
1904	Archie Hahn	USA	11.0
1906	Archie Hahn	USA	11.2
1908	Reginald Walker	SAF	10.8
1912	Ralph Craig	USA	10.8
1920	Charles Paddock	USA	10.8
1924	Harold Abrahams	GBR	10.6
1928	Percy Williams	CAN	10.8
1932	Eddie Tolan	USA	10.3 (10.38)
1936	Jesse Owens	USA	10.3
1948	Harrison Dillard	USA	10.3
1952	Lindy Remigino	USA	10.4 (10.79)
1956	Bobby Joe Morrow	USA	10.5 (10.62)
1960	Armin Hary	GER	10.2 (10.32)
1964	Bob Hayes	USA	10.0 (10.6)
1968	James Hines	USA	9.9 (9.95)
1972	Valeriy Borzov	URS	10.14
1976	Hasely Crawford	TRI	10.06
1980	Allan Wells	GBR	10.25
1984	Carl Lewis	USA	9.99
1988	Carl Lewis	USA	9.92

200m

1900	Walter Tewkesbury	USA	22.2
1904	Archie Hahn	USA	21.6
1908	Robert Kerr	CAN	22.6
1912	Ralph Craig	USA	21.7
1920	Allen Woodring	USA	22.0
1924	Jackson Scholz	USA	21.6
1928	Percy Williams	CAN	21.8
1932	Eddie Tolan	USA	21.2 (21.12)
1936	Jesse Owens	USA	20.7
1948	Mel Patton	USA	21.1
1952	Andrew Stanfield	USA	20.7 (20.81)
1956	Bobby Joe Morrow	USA	20.6 (20.75)
1960	Livio Berruti	ITA	20.5 (20.62)
1964	Henry Carr	USA	20.3 (20.36)
1968	Tommie Smith	USA	19.8 (19.83)
1972	Valeriy Borzov	URS	20.00
1976	Don Quarrie	JAM	20.23
1980	Pietro Mennea	ITA	20.19
1984	Carl Lewis	USA	19.80
1988	Joe DeLoach	USA	19.75

400m

1896	Thomas Burke	USA	54.2
1900	Maxwell Long	USA	49.4
1904	Harry Hillman	USA	49.2
1906	Paul Pilgrim	USA	53.2
1908	Wyndham Halswelle	GBR	50.0
1912	Charles Reidpath	USA	48.2
1920	Bevil Rudd	SAF	49.6
1924	Eric Liddell	GBR	47.6
1928	Ray Barbuti	USA	47.8
1932	William Carr	USA	46.2 (46.28)
1936	Archie Williams	USA	46.5 (46.66)
1948	Arthur Wint	JAM	46.2
1952	George Rhoden	JAM	45.9 (46.09)
1956	Charles Jenkins	USA	46.7 (46.85)
1960	Otis Davis	USA	44.9 (45.07)
1964	Mike Larrabee	USA	45.1 (45.15)
1968	Lee Evans	USA	43.8 (43.86)
1972	Vince Matthews	USA	44.66
1976	Alberto Juantorena	CUB	44.26
1980	Viktor Markin	URS	44.60
1984	Alonzo Babers	USA	44.27
1988	Steve Lewis	USA	43.87

' Re-run ordered after John Carpenter (USA) disqualified in first final.
Only Halswelle showed up and "walked over" for the title

800m

1896	Edwin Flack	AUS	2.11.0
1900	Alfred Tysoe	GBR	2:01.2
1904	James Lightbody	USA	1:56.0
1906	Paul Pilgrim	USA	2:01.5
1908	Mel Sheppard	USA	1:52.8
1912	James Meredith	USA	1:51.9

PAST GOLD MEDALLISTS

1920	Albert Hill	GBR	1:53.4
1924	Douglas Lowe	GBR	1:52.4
1928	Douglas Lowe	GBR	1:51.8
1932	Thomas Hampson	GBR	1:49.7
1936	John Woodruff	USA	1:52.9
1948	Mal Whitfield	USA	1:49.2
1952	Mal Whitfield	USA	1:49.2
1956	Tom Courtney	USA	1:47.7
1960	Peter Snell	NZL	1:46.3
1964	Peter Snell	NZL	1:45.1
1968	Ralph Doubell	AUS	1:44.3
1972	Dave Wottle	USA	1:45.9
1976	Alberto Juantorena	CUB	1:43.5
1980	Steve Ovett	GBR	1:45.4
1984	Joaquim Cruz	BRA	1:43.00
1988	Paul Ereng	KEN	1:43.45

1500m

1896	Edwin Flack	AUS	4:33.2
1900	Charles Bennett	GBR	4:06.2
1904	James Lightbody	USA	4:05.4
1906	James Lightbody	USA	4:12.0
1908	Mel Sheppard	USA	4:03.4
1912	Arnold Jackson	GBR	3:56.8
1920	Albert Hill	GBR	4:01.8
1924	Paavo Nurmi	FIN	3:53.6
1928	Harri Larva	FIN	3:53.2
1932	Luigi Beccali	ITA	3:51.2
1936	Jack Lovelock	NZL	3:47.8
1948	Henry Eriksson	SWE	3:49.8
1952	Josef Barthel	LUX	3:45.1
1956	Ron Delany	IRL	3:41.2
1960	Herb Elliott	AUS	3:35.6
1964	Peter Snell	NZL	3:38.1
1968	Kipchoge Keino	KEN	3:34.9
1972	Pekka Vasala	FIN	3:36.3
1976	John Walker	NZL	3:39.2
1980	Sebastian Coe	GBR	3:38.4
1984	Sebastian Coe	GBR	3:32.53
1988	Peter Rono	KEN	3:35.96

5000m

1912	Hannes Kolehmainen	FIN	14:36.6
1920	Joseph Guillemot	FRA	14:55.6
1924	Paavo Nurmi	FIN	14:31.2
1928	Ville Ritola	FIN	14:38.0
1932	Lauri Lehtinen	FIN	14:30.0
1936	Gunnar Hockert	FIN	14:22.2
1948	Gaston Reiff	BEL	14:17.6
1952	Emil Zatopek	TCH	14:06.6
1956	Vladimir Kuts	URS	13:39.6
1960	Murray Halberg	NZL	13:43.4
1964	Bob Schul	USA	13:48.8
1968	Mohamed Gammoudi	TUN	14:05.0
1972	Lasse Viren	FIN	13:26.4
1976	Lasse Viren	FIN	13:24.8
1980	Miruts Yifter	ETH	13:21.0
1984	Said Aouita	MAR	13:05.59
1988	John Ngugi	KEN	13:11.70

10,000m

1906	Henry Hawtrey	GBR	26:11.8
1908	Emil Voight	GBR	25:11.2
1912	Hannes Kolehmainen	FIN	31:20.8
1920	Paavo Nurmi	FIN	31:45.8
1924	Ville Ritola	FIN	30:23.2
1928	Paavo Nurmi	FIN	30:18.8
1932	Janusz Kusocinski	POL	30:11.4
1936	Ilmari Salminen	FIN	30:15.4

1948	Emil Zatopek	TCH	29:59.6
1952	Emil Zatopek	TCH	29:17.0
1956	Vladimir Kuts	URS	28:45.6
1960	Pyotr Bolotnikov	URS	28:32.2
1964	Billy Mills	USA	28:24.4
1968	Naftali Temu	KEN	29:27.4
1972	Lasse Viren	FIN	27:38.4
1976	Lasse Viren	FIN	27:44.4
1980	Miruts Yifter	ETH	27:42.7
1984	Alberto Cova	ITA	27:47.54
1988	Brahim Boutaib	MAR	27:21.46

Marathon

1896	Spyridon Louis	GRE	2h58:50
1900	Michel Theato	FRA	2h59:45
1904	Thomas Hicks	USA	3h28:35
1906	William Sherring	CAN	2h51:23.6
1908	John Hayes	USA	2h55:18.4
1912	Kenneth McArthur	SAF	2h36:54.8
1920	Hannes Kolehmainen	FIN	2h32:35.8
1924	Albin Stenroos	FIN	2h41:22.6
1928	Mohamed El Ouafi	FRA	2h32:57
1932	Juan Carlos Zabala	ARG	2h31:36
1936	Sohn Kee-Chung	JPN	2h29:19.2
1948	Delfo Cabrera	ARG	2h34:51.6
1952	Emil Zatopek	TCH	2h23:03.2
1956	Alain Mimoun	FRA	2h25:00
1960	Abebe Bikila	ETH	2h15:16.2
1964	Abebe Bikila	ETH	2h12:11.2
1968	Mamo Wolde	ETH	2h20:26.4
1972	Frank Shorter	USA	2h12:19.8
1976	Waldemar Cierpinski	GDR	2h09.55.0
1980	Waldemar Cierpinski	GDR	2h11:03
1984	Carlos Lopes	POR	2h09:21
1988	Gelindo Bordin	ITA	2h10:32

3000m Steeplechase

1900[1]	George Orton	CAN	7:34.4
1900[2]	John Rimmer	GBR	12:58.4
1904[3]	James Lightbody	USA	7:39.6
1908[4]	Arthur Russell	GBR	10:47.8
1920	Percy Hodge	GBR	10:00.4
1924	Ville Ritola	FIN	9:33.6
1928	Toivo Loukola	FIN	9:21.8
1932[5]	Volmari Iso-Hollo	FIN	10:33.4
1936	Volmari Iso-Hollo	FIN	9:03.8
1948	Tore Sjostrand	SWE	9:04.6
1952	Horace Ashenfelter	USA	8:45.4
1956	Chris Brasher	GBR	8:41.2
1960	Zdzslaw Krzyszkowiak	POL	8:34.2
1964	Gaston Roelants	BEL	8:30.8
1968	Amos Biwott	KEN	8:51.0
1972	Kipchoge Keino	KEN	8:23.6
1976	Anders Garderud	SWE	8:08.0
1980	Bronislaw Malinowski	POL	8:09.7
1984	Julius Korir	KEN	8:11.80
1988	Julius Kariuki	KEN	8:05.51

[1] 2500m;
[2] 4000m;
[3] 2590m;
[4] 3200m;
[5] 3460m in final

110m Hurdles

1896	Thomas Curtis	USA	17.6
1900	Alvin Kraenslein	USA	15.4
1904	Frederick Schule	USA	16.0
1906	Robert Leavitt	USA	16.2
1908	Forrest Smithson	CAN	15.0

Year	Name	Country	Mark
1912	Frederick Kelly	USA	15.1
1920	Earl Thomson	CAN	14.8
1924	Daniel Kinsey	USA	15.0
1928	Sydney Atkinson	SAF	14.8
1932	George Saling	USA	14.6 (14.57)
1936	Forrest Towns	USA	14.2
1948	William Porter	USA	13.9
1952	Harison Dillard	USA	13.7 (13.91)
1956	Lee Calhoun	USA	13.5 (13.70)
1960	Lee Calhoun	USA	13.8 (13.98)
1964	Hayes Jones	USA	13.6 (13.67)
1968	Willie Davenport	USA	13.3 (13.33)
1972	Rod Milburn	USA	13.24
1976	Guy Drut	FRA	13.30
1980	Thomas Munkelt	GDR	13.39
1984	Roger Kingdom	USA	13.20
1988	Roger Kingdom	USA	12.98

400m Hurdles

Year	Name	Country	Mark
1900	Walter Tewksbury	USA	57.6
1904	Harry Hillman	USA	53.0
1908	Charles Bacon	USA	55.0
1920	Frank Loomis	USA	54.0
1924	Morgan Taylor	USA	52.6
1928	Lord Burghley	GBR	53.4
1932	Bob Tisdall	IRL	51.7 (51.67)
1936	Glenn Hardin	USA	52.4
1948	Roy Cochran	USA	51.1
1952	Charlie Moore	USA	50.8 (51.06)
1956	Glenn Davis	USA	50.1 (50.29)
1960	Glenn Davis	USA	49.3 (49.51)
1964	Rex Cawley	USA	49.6
1968	David Hemery	GBR	48.1 (48.12)
1972	John Akii-Bua	UGA	47.82
1976	Edwin Moses	USA	47.64
1980	Volker Beck	GDR	48.70
1984	Edwin Moses	USA	47.75
1988	Andre Phillips	USA	47.19

4x100m Relay

Year	Country	Mark
1912	GBR	42.4
1920	USA	42.2
1924	USA	41.0
1928	USA	41.0
1932	USA	40.0 (40.10)
1936	USA	39.8
1948	USA	40.6
1952	USA	40.1 (40.26)
1956	USA	39.5 (39.60)
1960	GER	39.5 (39.66)
1964	USA	39.0 (39.06)
1968	USA	38.2 (38.24)
1972	USA	38.19
1976	USA	38.33
1980	URS	38.26
1984	USA	37.83
1988	URS	38.19

4x400m Relay

Year	Country	Mark
1908	USA	3:29.4
1912	USA	3:16.6
1920	GBR	3:22.2
1924	USA	3:16.0
1928	USA	3:14.2
1932	USA	3:08.2 (3:08.14)
1936	GBR	3:09.0
1948	USA	3:10.4
1952	JAM	3:03.9 (3:04.4)
1956	USA	3:04.8
1960	USA	3:02.2 (3:02.37)
1964	USA	3:00.7
1968	USA	3:56.1 (2:56.16)
1972	KEN	2:59.83
1976	USA	2:58.65
1980	URS	3:01.08
1984	USA	2:57.91
1988	USA	2:56.16

20km Walk

Year	Name	Country	Mark
1956	Leonid Spirin	URS	1h31:27.4
1960	Vladimir Golubnichiy	URS	1h34:07.2
1964	Ken Matthews	GBR	1h29:34.0
1968	Vladimir Golubnichiy	URS	1h33:58.4
1972	Peter Frenkel	GDR	1h26:42.4
1976	Daniel Bautista	MEX	1h24:40.6
1980	Maurizio Damilano	ITA	1h23:35.5
1984	Ernesto Canto	MEX	1h23:13
1988	Jozef Pribilinec	TCH	1h19:57

50km Walk

Year	Name	Country	Mark
1932	Thomas Green	GBR	4h50:10
1936	Harold Whitlock	GBR	4h30:41.1
1948	John Ljunggren	SWE	4h41:52
1952	Giudeppe Dordoni	ITA	4h28:07.8
1956	Norman Read	NZL	4h30:42.8
1960	Don Thompson	GBR	4h25:30.0
1964	Abdon Pamich	ITA	4h11:12.4
1968	Christoph Hohne	GDR	4h20:13.6
1972	Bernd Kannenberg	FRG	3h56:11.6
1980	Hartwig Gauder	GDR	3h49:24
1984	Raul Gonzalez	MEX	3h47:26
1988	Vyacheslav Ivanenko	URS	3h38:29

High Jump

Year	Name	Country	Mark
1896	Ellery Clark	USA	1.81m
1900	Irving Baxter	USA	1.90m
1904	Samuel Jones	USA	1.80m
1906	Con Leahy	GBR	1.77m
1908	Harry Porter	USA	1.905m
1912	Alma Richards	USA	1.93m
1920	Richmond Landon	USA	1.94m
1924	Harold Osborn	USA	1.98m
1928	Robert King	USA	1.94m
1932	Duncan McNaughton	CAN	1.97m
1936	Cornelius Johnson	USA	2.03m
1948	John Winter	AUS	1.98m
1952	Walt David	USA	2.04m
1956	Charlie Dumas	USA	2.12m
1960	Robert Shavlakadze	URS	2.16m
1964	Valeriy Brumel	URS	2.18m
1968	Dick Fosbury	USA	2.24m
1972	Yuriy Tarmak	URS	2.23m
1976	Jacek Wszola	POL	2.25m
1980	Gerd Wessig	GDR	2.36m
1984	Dietmar Mogenburg	FRG	2.35m
1988	Gennadi Avdeenko	URS	2.38m

Pole Vault

Year	Name	Country	Mark
1896	William Hoyt	USA	3.30m
1900	Irving Baxter	USA	3.30m
1904	Charles Dovrak	USA	3.50m
1906	Fernand Gonder	FRA	3.40m
1908	Edward Cooke	USA	3.70m
	Alfred Gilbert	USA	3.70m
1912	Harry Babcock	USA	3.95m
1920	Frank Foss	USA	4.09m
1924	Lee Barnes	USA	3.95m
1928	Sabin Carr	USA	4.20m
1932	William Miller	USA	4.31m

PAST GOLD MEDALLISTS

1936	Earle Meadows	USA	4.35m
1948	Guinn Smith	USA	4.30m
1952	Bob Richards	USA	4.55m
1956	Bob Richards	USA	4.56m
1960	Don Bragg	USA	4.70m
1964	Fred Hansen	USA	5.10m
1968	Bob Seagren	USA	5.40m
1972	Wolfgang Nordwig	GDR	5.50m
1976	Tadeusz Slusarski	POL	5.50m
1980	Wladislaw Kozakiewicz	POL	5.78m
1984	Pierre Quinon	FRA	5.75m
1988	Sergey Bubka	URS	5.90m

Long Jump

1896	Ellery Clark	USA	6.35m
1900	Alvin Kraenslein	USA	7.18m
1904	Myer Prinstein	USA	7.34m
1906	Myer Prinstein	USA	7.20m
1908	Francis Irons	USA	7.48m
1912	Albert Gutterson	USA	7.60m
1920	William Pettersson	SWE	7.15m
1924	William DeHart Hubbard	USA	7.44m
1928	Edward Hamm	USA	7.73m
1932	Ed Gordon	USA	7.64m
1936	Jesse Owens	USA	8.06m
1948	Willie Steele	USA	7.82m
1952	Jerome Biffle	USA	7.57m
1956	Greg Bell	USA	7.83m
1960	Ralph Boston	USA	8.12m
1964	Lynn Davies	GBR	8.07m
1968	Bob Beamon	USA	8.90m
1972	Randy Williams	USA	8.24m
1976	Arnie Robinson	USA	8.35m
1980	Lutz Dombrowski	GDR	8.54m
1984	Carl Lewis	USA	8.54m
1988	Carl Lewis	USA	8.72m

Triple Jump

1896	James Connolly	USA	13.71m
1900	Myer Prinstein	USA	14.47m
1904	Myer Prinstein	USA	14.35m
1906	Peter O'Connor	GBR	14.07m
1908	Tim Ahearne	GBR	14.91m
1912	Gustaf Lindblom	SWE	14.76m
1920	Viho Tuulos	FIN	14.50m
1924	Anthony Winter	AUS	15.52m
1928	Miklo Oda	JPN	15.21m
1932	Chuhei Nambu	JPN	15.72m
1936	Naoto Tajima	JPN	16.00m
1948	Arne Ahman	SWE	15.40m
1952	Adhemar Ferreira da Silva	BRA	16.22m
1956	Adhemar Ferreira da Silva	BRA	16.35m
1960	Jozef Schmidt	POL	16.81m
1964	Jozef Schmidt	POL	16.85m
1968	Viktor Saneyev	URS	17.39m
1972	Viktor Saneyev	URS	17.35m
1976	Viktor Saneyev	URS	17.29m
1980	Jaak Uudmae	URS	17.35m
1984	Al Joyner	USA	17.26m
1988	Khristo Markov	BUL	17.61m

Shot Put

1896	Robert Garrett	USA	11.22m
1900	Richard Sheldon	USA	14.10m
1904	Ralph Rose	USA	14.80m
1906	Martin Sheridan	USA	12.32m
1908	Ralph Rose	USA	14.21m
1912	Patrick McDonald	USA	15.34m
1920	Ville Porhola	FIN	14.81m

1924	Clarence Houser	USA	14.99m
1928	John Kuck	USA	15.87m
1932	Leo Sexton	USA	16.00m
1936	Hans Woellke	GER	16.20m
1948	Wilbur Thompson	USA	17.12m
1952	Parry O'Brien	USA	17.41m
1956	Parry O'Brien	USA	18.57m
1960	Bill Nieder	USA	19.68m
1964	Dallas Long	USA	20.33m
1968	Randy Matson	USA	20.54m
1972	Wladyslaw Komar	POL	21.18m
1976	Udo Beyer	GDR	21.05m
1980	Volodimir Kiselyev	URS	21.35m
1984	Alessandro Andrei	ITA	21.26m
1988	Ulf Timmermann	GDR	22.47m

Discus

1896[1]	Robert Garrett	USA	29.15m
1900	Rudolf Bauer	HUN	36.04m
1904	Martin Sheridan	USA	39.28m
1906	Martin Sheridan	USA	41.46m
1908	Martin Sheridan	USA	40.89m
1912	Armas Taipale	FIN	45.21m
1920	Elmer Niklander	FIN	44.68m
1924	Clarence Houser	USA	46.15m
1928	Clarence Houser	USA	47.32m
1932	John Anderson	USA	49.49m
1936	Ken Carpenter	USA	50.48m
1948	Adolfo Consolini	ITA	52.78m
1952	Sim Iness	USA	55.03m
1956	Al Oerter	USA	56.36m
1960	Al Oerter	USA	59.18m
1964	Al Oerter	USA	61.00m
1968	Al Oerter	USA	64.78m
1972	Ludvik Danek	TCH	64.40m
1976	Mac Wilkins	USA	67.50m
1980	Viktor Rashchupkin	URS	66.64m
1984	Rolf Danneberg	FRG	66.60m
1988	Jurgen Schult	GDR	68.82m
	[1] From 2.50m square		

Hammer

1900	John Flanagan	USA	49.73m
1904	John Flanagan	USA	51.23m
1908	John Flanagan	USA	51.92m
1912	Matt McGarth	USA	54.74m
1920	Patrick Ryan	USA	52.87m
1924	Fred Tootell	USA	53.29m
1928	Patrick O'Callaghan	IRL	51.39m
1932	Patrick O'Callaghan	IRL	53.92m
1936	Kerl Hein	GER	56.49m
1948	Imre Nemeth	HUN	56.07m
1952	Jozsef Csermak	HUN	60.34m
1956	Harold Connolly	USA	63.19m
1960	Vasiliy Rudenkov	URS	67.10m
1964	Romuald Klim	URS	69.74m
1968	Gyula Zsivotzky	HUN	73.36m
1972	Anatoliy Bondarchuk	URS	75.50m
1976	Yuriy Sedykh	URS	77.52m
1980	Yuriy Sedykh	URS	81.80m
1984	Juha Tiainen	FIN	78.08m
1988	Sergey Litvinov	URS	84.80m

Javelin

1906	Erik Lemming	SWE	53.90m
1908	Erik Lemming	SWE	54.82m
1912	Erik Lemming	SWE	60.64m
1920	Jonni Myyra	FIN	65.78m
1924	Jonni Myyara	FIN	62.96m

1928	Erik Lundkvist	SWE	66.60m
1932	Matti Jarvinen	FIN	72.71m
1936	Gerhard Stock	GER	71.84m
1948	Tapio Rautavaara	FIN	69.77m
1952	Cyrus Young	USA	73.78m
1956	Egil Danielsen	NOR	85.71m
1960	Viktor Tsibulenko	URS	84.64m
1964	Pauli Nevala	FIN	82.66m
1968	Janis Lusis	URS	90.10m
1972	Klaus Woltermann	FRG	90.48m
1976	Miklos Nemeth	HUN	94.58m
1980	Dainis Kula	URS	91.20m
1984	Arton Harkonen	FIN	86.76m
1988	Tapio Korjus	FIN	84.26m

Decathlon

1904	Thomas Kiely	GBR	6036pts
1912	Hugo Wieslander	SWE	5965pts
1920	Helge Lovland	NOR	5803pts
1924	Harold Osborn	USA	6476pts
1928	Paavo Yrjola	FIN	6587pts
1932	Jim Bausch	USA	6735pts
1936	Glenn Morris	USA	7254pts
1948	Bob Mathias	USA	6628pts
1952	Bob Mathias	USA	7592pts
1956	Milt Campbell	USA	7614pts
1960	Rafer Johnson	USA	7926pts
1964	Willi Holdorf	GER	7794pts
1968	Bill Toomey	USA	8144pts
1972	Nikolai Avilov	URS	8466pts
1976	Bruce Jenner	USA	8634pts
1980	Daley Thompson	GBR	8522pts
1984	Daley Thompson	GBR	8847pts
1988	Christian Schenk	GDR	8488pts

The scores for decathlon since 1912 have been recalculated on the current 1984 tables for purposes of comparison.

WOMEN

100m

1928	Elizabeth Robinson	USA	12.2
1932	Stanislawa Walasiewicz	POL	11.9
1936	Helen Stephens	USA	11.5
1948	Fanny Blankers-Koen	HOL	11.9
1952	Marjorie Jackson	AUS	11.5 (11.67)
1956	Betty Cuthbert	AUS	11.5 (11.82)
1960	Wilma Rudolph	USA	11.0 (11.18)
1964	Wyoma Tyus	USA	11.4 (11.49)
1968	Wyoma Tyus	USA	11.0 (11.08)
1972	Renate Stecher	GDR	11.07
1976	Annegret Richter	FRG	11.08
1980	Ludmila Kondratyeva	URS	11.06
1984	Evelyn Ashford	USA	10.97
1988	Florence Griffith-Joyner	USA	10.54

200m

1948	Fanny Blankers-Koen	HOL	24.4
1952	Marjorie Jackson	AUS	23.7 (23.89)
1956	Betty Cuthbert	AUS	23.4 (23.55)
1960	Wilma Rudolph	USA	24.0 (24.13)
1964	Edith Maguire	USA	23.0 (23.05)
1968	Irena Szewinska	POL	22.5 (22.58)
1972	Renate Stecher	GDR	22.40
1976	Barbel Eckert	GDR	22.37
1980	Barbel Wockel	GDR	22.03
1984	Valerie Brisco-Hooks	USA	21.81
1988	Florence Griffith-Joyner	USA	21.34

400m

1964	Bette Cuthbert	AUS	52.0 (52.01)
1968	Colette Besson	FRA	52.0 (52.03)
1972	Monika Zehrt	GDR	51.08

1976	Irena Szewinska	POL	49.29
1980	Marita Koch	GDR	48.88
1984	Valerie Brisco-Hooks	USA	48.83
1988	Olga Bryzguina	URS	48.65

800m

1928	Lina Radke	GER	2:16.8
1960	Lyudmila Shevtsova	URS	2:04.3
1964	Ann Packer	GBR	2:01.1
1968	Madeline Manning	USA	2:00.9
1972	Hildegard Falck	FRG	1:58.6
1976	Tatyana Kazankina	URS	1:54.9
1980	Nadyezda Olizarenko	URS	1:53.5
1984	Doina Melinte	ROM	1:57.60
1988	Sigrun Wodars	GDR	1:56.10

1500m

1972	Lyudmila Bragina	URS	4:01.4
1976	Tatyana Kazankhina	URS	4:05.5
1980	Tatyana Kazankhina	URS	3:56.6
1984	Gabriella Dorio	ITA	4:03.25
1988	Paula Ivan	ROM	3:53.96

3000m

1984	Maricica Puica	ROM	8:35.96
1988	Tatyana Samolenko	URS	8:26.53

10,000m

1988	Olga Bondarenko	URS	31:05.21

Marathon

1984	Joan Benoit	USA	2h24:52
1988	Rosa Mota	POR	2h25:40

100m Hurdles

1932	Mildred Didrikson	USA	11.7
1936	Trebisonda Valla	ITA	11.7 (11.75)
1948	Fanny Blankers-Koen	HOL	11.2
1952	Shirley de la Hunty	AUS	10.8 (11.01)
1956	Shirley de la Hunty	AUS	10.7 (10.96)
1960	Irina Press	URS	10.8 (10.93)
1964	Karin Balzer	GER	10.5 (10.54)
1968	Maureen Caird	AUS	10.3 (10.39)
1972	Annelie Ehrhardt	GDR	12.59
1976	Johanna Schaller	GDR	12.77
1980	Vera Komisova	URS	12.56
1984	Benita Fitzgerald-Brown	USA	12.84
1988	Yordanka Donkova	BUL	12.38

over 80m hurdles 1932-68

400m Hurdles

1984	Nawal El Moutawakel	MAR	54.61
1988	Debbie Flintoff-King	AUS	53.17

4x100m Relay

1928		CAN	48.4
1932		USA	47.0 (46.86)
1936		USA	46.9
1948		HOL	47.5
1952		USA	45.9 (46.14)
1956		AUS	44.5 (44.65)
1960		USA	44.5 (44.72)
1964		POL	43.6 (43.69)
1968		USA	42.8 (42.88)
1972		FRG	42.81
1976		GDR	42.55
1980		GDR	41.60
1984		USA	41.65
1988		USA	41.98

4x400m Relay

1972		GDR	3:22.95
1976		GDR	3:19.23
1980		URS	3:20.12
1984		USA	3:18.29
1988		URS	3:15.17

PAST GOLD MEDALLISTS

High Jump
1928	Ethel Catherwood	CAN	1.59m
1932	Jean Shiley	USA	1.66m
1936	Ibolya Csak	HUN	1.60m
1948	Alice Coachman	USA	1.68m
1952	Esther Brand	SAF	1.67m
1956	Milderd McDaniel	USA	1.76m
1960	Iolanda Balas	ROM	1.85m
1964	Iolanda Balas	ROM	1.90m
1968	Miloslava Rezkova	TCH	1.82m
1972	Ulrike Meyfarth	FRG	1.92m
1976	Rosemarie Ackermann	GDR	1.93m
1980	Sara Simeoni	ITA	1.97m
1984	Ulrike Meyfarth	FRG	2.02m
1988	Louise Ritter	USA	2.03m

Long Jump
1948	Olga Gyarmati	HUN	5.69m
1952	Yvette Williams	NZL	6.24m
1956	Elzbieta Krzensinska	POL	6.35m
1960	Vera Krepkina	URS	6.37m
1964	Mary Rand	GBR	6.76m
1968	Viorica Viscopoleanu	ROM	6.82m
1972	Heidemarie Rosedahl	FRG	6.78m
1976	Angela Voight	GDR	6.72m
1980	Tatyana Kolpakova	URS	7.06m
1984	Anisoara Stanciu	ROM	6.96m
1988	Jackie Joyner-Kersee	USA	7.40m

Shot Put
1948	Micheline Ostermeyer	FRA	13.75m
1952	Galina Sybina	URS	15.28m
1956	Tamara Tyshkevich	URS	16.59m
1960	Tamara Press	URS	17.32m
1964	Tamara Press	URS	18.14m
1968	Margitta Gummel	GDR	19.61m
1972	Nadyezda Chizhova	URS	21.03m
1976	Ivanka Khristova	BUL	21.16m
1980	Ilona Slupianek	GDR	22.41m
1984	Claudia Losch	FRG	20.48m
1988	Natalya Lisovskaya	URS	22.24m

Discus
1928	Helena Konopacka	POL	39.62m
1932	Lilian Copeland	USA	40.58m
1936	Gisela Mauermayer	GER	47.63m
1948	Micheline Ostermeyer	FRA	41.92m
1952	Nina Romashkova	URS	51.42m
1956	Olga Fikotova	TCH	53.69m
1960	Nina Ponomaryeva	URS	55.10m
1964	Tamara Press	URS	57.25m
1968	Lia Manoliu	ROM	58.28m
1972	Faina Malnik	URS	66.62m
1976	Evelin Schlaak	GDR	69.00m
1980	Evelin Jahl	GDR	69.96m
1984	Ria Stalman	HOL	65.36m
1988	Martina Hellmann	GDR	72.30m

Javelin
1932	Mildred Didrikson	USA	43.68m
1936	Tilly Fleischer	GER	45.18m
1948	Herma Bauma	AUT	45.57m
1952	Dana Zatopkova	TCH	50.47m
1956	Inese Jaunzeme	URS	53.86m
1960	Elvira Ozolina	URS	55.98m
1964	Mihaela Penes	ROM	60.64m
1968	Angela Nemeth	HUN	60.36m
1972	Ruth Fuchs	GDR	63.88m
1976	Ruth Fuchs	GDR	65.94m
1980	Maria Colon	CUB	68.40m
1984	Tessa Sanderson	GBR	69.56m
1988	Petra Felke	GDR	74.68m

Pentathlon
1964	Irina Press	URS	5246pts
1968	Ingrid Becker	FRG	5098pts
1972	Mary Peters	GBR	4801pts
1976	Siegrun Siegl	GDR	4745pts
1980	Nadyezda Tkachenko	URS	5083pts

Heptathlon
1984	Glynis Nunn	AUS	6387pts
1988	Jackie Joyner-Kersee	USA	7291pts

BASKETBALL

MEN
1936	USA
1948	USA
1952	USA
1956	USA
1960	USA
1964	USA
1968	USA
1972	URS
1976	USA
1980	YUG
1984	USA
1988	URS

WOMEN
1976	URS
1980	URS
1984	USA
1988	USA

BOXING

Light-Flyweight-48kg
1968	Francisco Rodriguez	VEN
1972	Gyorgy Gedo	HUN
1976	Jorge Hernandez	CUB
1980	Shamil Sabirov	URS
1984	Paul Gonzales	USA
1988	Ivailo Hristov	BUL

Flyweight -51kg
1904	George Finnegan	USA
1920	Frank Di Gennara	USA
1924	Fidel La Barba	USA
1928	Antal Kocsis	HUN
1932	Istvan Enekes	HUN
1936	Willi Kaiser	GER
1948	Pascual Perez	ARG
1952	Nathan Brooks	USA
1956	Terence Spinks	GBR
1960	Gyula Torok	HUN
1964	Fernando Atzori	ITA
1968	Ricardo Delgado	MEX
1972	Gheorghi Kostadinov	BUL
1976	Leo Randolph	USA
1980	Peter Lessov	BUL
1984	Steve McCrory	USA
1988	Kim Kwang-Sun	KOR

Bantamweight-54kg
1904	Oliver Kirk	USA
1908	Henry Thomas	GBR
1920	Clarence Walker	SAF

PAST GOLD MEDALLISTS

146

1924	William Smith	SAF
1928	Vittorio Tamagnini	ITA
1932	Horace Gwynne	CAN
1936	Ulderico Sergo	ITA
1948	Tibor Csik	HUN
1952	Pentti Hamalainen	FIN
1956	Wolfgang Behrendt	GER
1960	Oleg Grigoryev	URS
1964	Takao Sakurai	JPN
1968	Varleriy Sokolov	URS
1972	Orlando Martinez	CUB
1976	Yong Jo Gu	PRK
1980	Juan Hernandez	CUB
1984	Maurizio Stecca	ITA
1988	Kennedy McKinney	USA

Featherweight-57kg

1904	Oliver Kirk	USA
1908	Richard Gunn	GBR
1920	Paul Fritsch	FRA
1924	John Fields	USA
1928	Lambertus van Kalveren	HOL
1932	Carmelo Robledo	ARG
1936	Oscar Casanovas	ARG
1948	Ernesto Formenti	ITA
1952	Jan Zachara	TCH
1956	Vladimir Safronov	URS
1960	Francesco Musso	ITA
1964	Stanislav Stepashkin	URS
1968	Antonio Roldan	MEX
1972	Boris Kuznetsov	URS
1976	Angel Herrera	CUB
1980	Rudi Fink	GDR
1984	Meldrick Taylor	USA
1988	Giovanni Parisi	ITA

Lightweight -60kg

1904	Harry Spanger	USA
1908	Frederick Grace	GBR
1920	Samuel Mosberg	USA
1924	Hans Nielsen	DEN
1928	Carlo Orlandi	ITA
1932	Lawrence Stevens	SAF
1936	Imre Harangi	HUN
1948	Gerald Dreyer	SAF
1952	Aureliano Bolognesi	ITA
1956	Richard McTaggart	GBR
1960	Kazimierz Pazdzior	POL
1964	Jozef Grudzien	POL
1968	Ronald Harris	USA
1972	Jan Szczepanksi	POL
1976	Howard Davis	USA
1980	Angel Herrera	CUB
1984	Pernell Whitaker	USA
1988	Andreas Zulow	GDR

Light-Welterweight-63.5kg

1952	Charles Adkins	USA
1956	Vladimir Yengibarvan	URS
1960	Bohumil Nemecek	TCH
1964	Jerzy Kulej	POL
1968	Jerzy Kulej	POL
1972	Ray Seales	USA
1976	Ray Leonard	USA
1980	Patrizio Oliva	ITA
1984	Jerry Page	USA
1988	Vyacheslav Janovski	URS

Welterweight-67kg

1904	Albert Young	USA
1920	Albert Schneider	CAN
1924	Jean Delarge	BEL
1928	Edward Morgan	NZL
1932	Edward Flynn	USA
1936	Sten Suvio	FIN
1948	Julius Torma	TCH
1952	Zygmunt Chychia	POL
1956	Nicholae Lince	ROM
1960	Giovanni Benvenuti	ITA
1964	Marian Kasprzyk	POL
1968	Manfred Wolke	GDR
1972	Emilio Correa	CUB
1976	Jochen Bachfeld	GDR
1980	Andrew Aldama	CUB
1984	Mark Breland	USA
1988	Robert Wangila	KEN

Light-Middleweight-71kg

1952	Laszlo Papp	HUN
1956	Laszlo Papp	HUN
1960	Wilbert McClure	USA
1964	Boris Lagutin	URS
1968	Bors Lagutin	URS
1972	Dieter Kottysch	FRG
1976	Jerzy Rybicki	POL
1980	Armando Martinez	CUB
1984	Frank Tate	USA
1988	Park Si-Hun	KOR

Middleweight-75kg

1904	Charles Mayer	USA
1908	John Douglas	GBR
1920	Harry Mallin	GBR
1924	Harry Mallin	GBR
1928	Piero Toscani	ITA
1932	Carmen Barth	USA
1936	Jean Despeaux	FRA
1948	Laszlo Papp	HUN
1952	Floyd Patterson	USA
1956	Gennadiy Schatkov	URS
1960	Edward Crook	USA
1964	Valeriy Popentschenko	URS
1968	Christopher Finnegan	GBR
1972	Vyatcheslav Lemechev	URS
1976	Michael Spinks	USA
1980	Jose Gomez	CUB
1984	Shin Joon-Sup	KOR
1988	Henry Maske	GDR

Light-Heavyweight-81kg

1920	Edward Eagan	USA
1924	Harry Mitchell	GBR
1928	Victor Avendano	ARG
1932	David Carstens	SAF
1936	Roger Michelot	FRA
1948	George Hunter	SAF
1952	Norvel Lee	USA
1956	James Boyd	USA
1960	Cassius Clay	USA
1964	Cosimo Pinto	ITA
1968	Dan Poznyak	URS
1972	Mate Parlov	YUG
1976	Leon Spinks	USA
1980	Slobodan Kacar	YUG
1984	Anton Josipovic	YUG
1988	Andrew Maynard	USA

Heavyweight-91kg

1904	Samuel Berger	USA	
1908	A L Oldham	GBR	
1920	Ronald Rawson	GBR	
1924	Otto von Porat	NOR	
1928	Arturo Rodriguez Jurado	ARG	
1932	Santiago Lovell	ARG	
1936	Herbert Runge	GER	
1948	Rafael Iglesias	ARG	
1952	Hayes Edward Sanders	USA	
1956	Peter Rademacher	USA	
1960	Franco de Piccoli	ITA	
1964	Joe Frazier	USA	
1968	George Foreman	USA	
1972	Teofilo Stevenson	CUB	
1976	Teofilo Stevenson	CUB	
1980	Teofilo Stevenson	CUB	
1984	Henry Tillman	USA	
1988	Ray Mercer	USA	

Super-Heavyweight+91kg

1984	Tyrell Biggs	USA	
1988	Lennox Lewis	CAN	

CANOEING

MEN
Kayak
500m K1

1976	Vasile Diba	ROM	1:46.41
1980	Vladimir Parfenovich	URS	1:43.43
1984	Ian Ferguson	NZL	1:47.84
1988	Zsolt Gyulay	HUN	1:44.82

1000m K1

1936	Gregor Hradetsky	AUT	4:22.9
1948	Gert Fredriksson	SWE	4:33.2
1952	Gert Fredriksson	SWE	4:07.9
1956	Gert Fredriksson	SWE	4:12.8
1960	Erik Hansen	DEN	3:53.00
1964	Rolf Peterson	SWE	3:57.13
1968	Mihaly Hesz	HUN	4:02.63
1972	Aleksandr Shaparenko	URS	3:48.06
1976	Rudiger Helm	GDR	3:48.20
1980	Rudiger Helm	GDR	3:48.77
1984	Alan Thompson	NZL	3:45.73
1988	Greg Barton	USA	3:55.27

10,000m K1

1936	Ernst Krebs	GER	46.01.6
1948	Gert Fredriksson	SWE	50:47.7
1952	Thorvald Stromberg	FIN	47:22.8
1956	Gert Fredriksson	SWE	47:43.4

500m K2

1976		GDR	1:35.87
1980		URS	1:32.38
1984		NZL	1:34.21
1988		NZL	1:33.98

1000m K2

1936		AUT	4:03.8
1948		SWE	4:07.3
1952		FIN	3:51.1
1956		GER	3:49.6
1960		SWE	3:34.7
1964		SWE	3:38.4
1968		URS	3:37.54
1972		URS	3:31.23
1976		URS	3:29.01

1980		URS	3.26.72
1984		CAN	3:24.22
1988		USA	3:32.42

10000m K2

1936		GER	41:45.0
1948		SWE	46:09.4
1952		FIN	44:21.3
1956		HUN	43:37.0

1000m K4

1964		URS	3:14.67
1968		NOR	3:14.38
1972		URS	3:14.02
1976		URS	3:08.69
1980		GDR	3:13.76
1984		NZL	3:02.28
1988		HUN	3:00.30

500m C1

1976	Aleksandr Rogov	URS	1:59.23
1980	Sergey Postrekhin	URS	1:53.37
1984	Larry Cain	CAN	1:57.01
1988	Olaf Heukrodt	GDR	1:56.42

1000m C1

1936	Francis Arnyot	CAN	5:32.1
1948	Josef Holocek	TCH	5:42.0
1952	Josef Holocek	TCH	4:56.3
1956	Leon Rotman	ROM	5:05.3
1960	Janos Parti	HUN	4:33.93
1964	Jurgen Eschert	GER	4:35.14
1968	Tibor Tatai	HUN	4:36.14
1972	Ivan Patzaichin	ROM	4:08.94
1976	Matija Ljubek	YUG	4:09.51
1980	Lubomir Lubenov	BUL	4:12.38
1984	Ulrich Eicke	FRG	4:06.32
1988	Ivan Klementyev	URS	4:12.78

10000m C1

1948	Frantisek Capek	TCH	62:05.2
1952	Frank Havens	USA	57:41.1
1956	Leon Rotman	ROM	56:41.0

500m C2

1976		URS	1:45.81
1980		HUN	1:43.39
1984		YUG	1:43.67
1988		URS	1:41.77

1000m C2

1936		TCH	4:50.1
1948		TCH	5:07.1
1952		DEN	4:38.3
1956		ROM	4:47.4
1960		URS	4:17.94
1964		URS	4:04.64
1968		ROM	4:07.18
1972		URS	3:52.60
1976		URS	3:52.76
1980		ROM	3:47.65
1984		ROM	3:40.60
1988		URS	3:48.36

10000m C2

1936		TCH	50:33.5
1948		USA	55:55.4
1952		FRA	54:08.3
1956		URS	54:02.4

4x500m K1 Relay

1960		GER	7:39.43

Slalom
K1

1972	Siegbert Horn	GDR	268.56

C1

1972	Reinhard Eiben	GDR	315.84

C2

1972		GDR	310.68

WOMEN
Kayak
K1

1948	Karen Hoff	DEN	2:31.9
1952	Sylvi Saimo	FIN	2:18.4
1956	Yelisaveta Dementyeva	URS	2:18.9
1960	Antonina Seredina	URS	2:08.08
1964	Ludmila Khvedosyuk	URS	2:12.87
1968	Ludmila Pinayeva	URS	2:11.09
1972	Yulia Ryabchinskaya	URS	2:03.17
1976	Carola Zirzow	GDR	2:01.05
1980	Birgit Fischer	GDR	1:57.96
1984	Agneta Andersson	SWE	1:58.72
1988	Vania Guecheva	BUL	1:55.19

500m K2

1960		URS	1:54.76
1964		GER	1:56.95
1968		FRG	1:56.44
1972		URS	1:53.50
1976		URS	1:51.15
1980		GDR	1:43.88
1984		SWE	1:45.25
1988		GDR	1:43.46

500m K4

1984		ROM	1:38.34
1988		GDR	1:40.78

Slalom
K1

1972	Angelika Bahmann	GDR	364.50

CYCLING

MEN
1000m Time-Trial

1896[1]	Paul Masson	FRA	24.0
1900	Francesco Verri	ITA	22.8
1928	Willy Falck-Hansen	DEN	1:14.4
1932	Edgar Gray	AUS	1:13.0
1936	Arie Van Vliet	HOL	1:12.0
1948	Jacques Dupont	FRA	1:13.5
1952	Russell Mockridge	AUS	1:11.1
1956	Leandro Faggin	ITA	1:09.8
1960	Sante Gaiardoni	ITA	1:07.27
1964	Patrick Sercu	BEL	1:09.59
1968	Pierre Trentin	FRA	1:03.91
1972	Niels-Christian Fredborg	DEN	1:06.44
1976	Klaus-Jurgen Grunke	GDR	1:05.93
1980	Lothar Thomas	GDR	1:02.955
1984	Fredy Schmidtke	FRG	1:-6.10
1988	Alexsandr Kiritchenko	URS	1:04.499

[1] Event held over 333.333m

1000m Sprint

1896[1]	Paul Masson	FRA	4:56.0
1900[1]	Georges Tallandier	FRA	2:52.0
1906	Francesco Verri	ITA	1:42.2
1920	Maurice Peeters	HOL	1:38.3
1924[2]	Lucien Michard	FRA	12.8
1928	Rene Beaufrand	FRA	13.2
1932	Jacobus van Egmond	HOL	12.6
1936	Toni Merkens	GER	11.8
1948	Mario Chella	ITA	12.0

1952	Enzo Sacchi	ITA	12.0
1956	Michel Rousseau	FRA	11.4
1960	Sante Gaiardoni	ITA	11.1
1964	Giovanni Pettenella	ITA	13.69
1968	Daniel Morelon	FRA	10.68
1972	Daniel Morelon	FRA	11.25
1976	Anton Tkac	TCH	10.78
1980	Lutz Hesslich	GDR	11.40
1984	Marks Gorski	USA	10.49
1988	Lutz Hesslich	GDR	

[1] Held over 2000m
[2] Since 1924 only times over last 200m of the event have been recorded

4000m Ind Pursuit

1964	Jiri Daler	TCH	5:04.75
1968	Daniel Rebillard	FRA	4:41.71
1972	Knut Knudsen	NOR	4:45.74
1976	Gregor Braun	GDR	4:47.61
1980	Robert Dill-Bundi	SUI	4:35.66
1984	Steve Hegg	USA	4:39.35
1988	Gintaoutas Umaras	URS	4:32.00

4000m Team Pursuit

1908[1]		GBR	2:18.6
1920		ITA	5:20.0
1924		ITA	5:15.0
1928		ITA	5:01.8
1932		ITA	4:53.0
1936		FRA	4:45.0
1948		FRA	4:57.8
1952		ITA	4:46.1
1956		ITA	4:37.4
1960		ITA	4:30.90
1964		GER	4:35.67
1968		DEN	4:22.44
1972		FRG	4:22.14
1976		FRG	4:21.06
1980		URS	4:15.70
1984		AUS	4:25.99
1988		URS	4:13.31

[1] Event held over 1810.5m

2000mTandem

1906		GBR	2:57.0
1908		FRA	3:07.8
1920		GBR	2:34.4
1924		FRA	12.6
1928		HOL	11.8
1932		FRA	12.0
1936		GER	11.8
1948		ITA	11.3
1952		AUS	11.0
1956		AUS	10.8
1960		ITA	10.7
1964		ITA	10.75
1968		FRA	9.83
1972		URS	10.52

Individual Points Race

1984	Roger Llegems	BEL	
1988	Dan Frost	DEN	

Team Road Race

1912		SWE	44h35:33.6
1920		FRA	19h16:43.2
1924		FRA	19h30:14.0
1928		DEN	15h09:14.0
1932		ITA	7h27.15.2
1936		FRA	7h39:16.2
1948		BEL	15h58:17.4
1952		BEL	15h20:46.6
1956		FRA	22 points

PAST GOLD MEDALLISTS

Road Team Time-Trial

1960		ITA	2h14:33.53
1964		HOL	2h26:31.19
1968		HOL	2h07:49.06
1972		URS	2h22:17.8
1976		URS	2h08:53.0
1980		URS	2h01:21.7
1984		ITA	1h58:28.0
1988		GDR	1h57:47.7

Individual Road Race

1896	Aristidis Konstantinidis	GRE	3h22:31.0
1906	Fernand Vast	FRA	2h41:28.0
1912	Rudoph Lewis	SAF	10h42:39.0
1920	Harry Stenqvist	SWE	4h40:01.8
1924	Armand Blanchonnet	FRA	6h20:48.0
1928	Henry Hansen	DEN	4h47:18.0
1932	Attilio Pavesi	ITA	2h28:05.6
1936	Robert Charpentier	FRA	2h33:05.0
1948	Jose Bevaert	FRA	5h18:12.6
1952	Andre Nouvelle	BEL	5h06:03.4
1956	Ercole Baldini	ITA	5h21:17.0
1960	Viktor Kapitonov	URS	4h20:37.0
1964	Mario Zanin	ITA	4h39:51.63
1968	Pierfranco Vianelli	ITA	4h41:25.24
1972	Hennie Kuiper	HOL	4h14:37.0
1976	Bernt Johansson	SWE	4h46.52.0
1980	Sergey Sukhoruchenkov	URS	4h48:28.9
1984	Alexi Grewal	USA	4h59:57.0
1988	Olaf Ludwig	GDR	4h32:22.0

The Individual Road Race has been held over various distances.

WOMEN

Sprint

1988	Erika Saloumae	URS	

Individual Road Race

1984	Connie Carpenter-Phinney	USA	2:11.14
1988	Monique Knol	HOL	2:00.52

Event held over 79.2km in 1984; 82km in 1988

EQUESTRIAN

Show Jumping

1900	Aime Haegeman	Benton II	BEL	
1912	Jean Cariou	Mignon	FRA	186pts
1920	Tommaso Lequio	Trebecco	ITA	2 faults
1924	Alphonso Gemuseus		SUI	6 faults
1928	Frantisek Venura	Eliot	TCH	no faults
1932	Takeichi Nishi	Uranus	JPN	8 faults
1936	Kurt Hasse	Tora	GER	4 faults
1948	Humberto Mariles Cortes			
		Arete	MEX	6.25 faults
1952	Pierre Jonqueres d'Oriola			
		Ali Baba	FRA	no faults
1956	Hans Gunter Winkler	Halla	GER	4 faults
1960	Raimondo d'Inzeo	Posillipo	ITA	12 faults
1964	Pierre Jonqueres d'Oriola			
		Lutteur	FRA	9 faults
1968	William Steinkraus	Snowbound	USA	4 faults
1972	Graziano Mancinelli	Ambassador	ITA	8 faults
1976	Alwin Schockemohle	Warwick Rex	FRG	0 faults
1980	Jan Kowalczyk	Artemor	POL	8 faults
1984	Joe Fargis	Touch of Class	USA	4 faults
1988	Pierre Durand	Jappeloup	FRA	1.25 faults

Show Jumping Team

1912		SWE	545 pts
1920		SWE	14 faults
1924		SWE	42.25 pts
1928		ESP	4 faults
1932[1]			
1936		GER	44 faults
1948		MEX	34.25 faults
1952		GBR	40.75 faults
1956		GER	40 faults
1960		GER	46.50 faults
1964		GER	68.50faults
1968		CAN	102.75 faults
1972		FRG	32 faults
1976		FRA	40 faults
1980		URS	16 faults
1984		USA	12 faults
1988		FRG	17.25 faults

[1] There was a team competition but no nation completed the course

Dressage Team

1928		GER	669.72 pts
1932		FRA	2828.75 pts
1936		GER	5074 pts
1948		FRA	1269 pts
1952		SWE	1597.5 pts
1956		SWE	2475 pts
1964		GER	2558 pts
1968		FRG	2699 pts
1972		URS	5095 pts
1976		FRG	5155 pts
1980		URS	4383 pts
1984		FRG	4955 pts
1988		FRG	4302 pts

Dressage Ind

1912	Carl Bonde	Emperor	SWE	15 pts
1920	Janne Lundblad	Uno	SWE	27 237 pts
1924	Ernst Linder	Piccolo-mini	SWE	276.4 pts
1928	Carl von Langen	Draufganger	GER	237.42 pts
1932	Xavier Lesage	Taine	FRA	1031.25 pts
1936	Heinz Pollay	Kronos	GER	1760 pts
1948	Hans Moser	Hummer	SUI	492.5 pts
1952	Henri St Cyr	Master Rufus	SWE	561 pts
1956	Henri St Cyr	Juli	SWE	860 pts
1960	Sergey Filatov	Absent	URS	2144 pts
1964	Henri Chammartin	Woermann	SUI	1504 pts
1968	Ivan Kizimov	Ikhov	URS	1572 pts
1972	Liselott Linsenhoff	Piaff	FRG	1229 pts
1976	Christine Stuckelberger		SUI	1486 pts
1980	Elisabeth Theurer	Mon Cherie	AUT	1370 pts
1984	Reiner Klimke	Ahlerich	FRG	1504 pts
1988	Nicole Uphoff	Rembrandt 24	FRG	1521 pt

Three-Day Event

1912	Axel Nordlander	Lady Artist	SWE	46.59 pts
1920	Helmer Morner	Germania	SWE	1775 pts
1924	Adolph van der Voort van Zijp,			
		Silver Piece	HOL	1976 pts
1928	Charles Pahud de Mortanges			
		Marcroix	HOL	1969.82 pts
1932	Charles Pahud de Mortanges			
		Marcroix	HOL	1813.83 pts
1936	Ludwig Stubbendorff	Nurmi	GER	37.7 faults
1948	Bernard Chevallier	Aiglonne	FRA	+4 pts
1952	Hans von Blixen-Finecke			
		Jubal	SWE	28.33 faults
1956	Petrus Kastenman	Illuster	SWE	66.53 faults
1960	Lawrence Morgan	Salad Days	AUS	+7.15 pts
1964	Mauro Checcoli	Surbean	ITA	64.40 pts
1968	Jean-Jacques Guyon	Pitou	FRA	38.86 pts

1972	Richard Meade	Laurieston	GBR	57.73 pts
1976	Edmund Coffin	Bally-Cor	USA	114.99 pts
1980	Fererico Roman	Rossinan	ITA	108.60 pts
1984	Mark Todd	Charisma	NZL	51.60 pts
1988	Mark Todd	Charisma	NZL	42.60 pts

Three-Day Event Team

1912			SWE	139.06 pts
1920			SWE	5057.5 pts
1924			HOL	5297.5 pts
1928			HOL	5865.68 pts
1932			USA	5038.08 pts
1936			GER	676.75 pts
1948			USA	161.50 pts
1952			SWE	221.49 pts
1956			GBR	355.48 pts
1960			AUS	128.18 pts
1964			ITA	85.80 pts
1968			GBR	175.93 pts
1972			GBR	95.53 pts
1976			USA	441.00 pts
1980			URS	457.00 pts
1984			USA	186.00 pts
1988			FRG	225.95 pts

FENCING

MEN
Foil

1896	Emile Gravelotte	FRA	4 wins
1900	Emile Cost	FRA	6 wins
1904	Ramon Fonst	CUB	3 wins
1906	Georges Dillon-Kavanagh	FRA	d.n.a
1912	Nedo Nadi	ITA	7 wins
1920	Nedo Nadi	ITA	10 wins
1924	Roger Ducret	FRA	6 wins
1928	Lucien Gaudin	FRA	9 wins
1932	Gustavo Marzi	ITA	9 wins
1936	Giulio Gaudini	ITA	7 wins
1948	Jean Buhan	FRA	7 wins
1952	Christian d'Oriola	FRA	8 wins
1956	Christain d'Oriola	FRA	6 wins
1960	Viktor Zhdanovich	URS	7 wins
1964	Egon Franke	POL	3 wins
1968	Ion Drimba	ROM	4 wins
1972	Witold Woyda	POL	5 wins
1976	Fabio Dal Zotto	ITA	4 wins
1980	Vladimir Smirnov	URS	5 wins
1984	Mauro Numa	ITA	
1988	Stefano Cerioni	ITA	

Epee

1900	Ramon Fonst	CUB	
1904	Ramon Fonst	CUB	3 wins
1906	Georges de la Falaise	FRA	d.n.a
1908	Gaston Alibert	FRA	5 wins
1912	Paul Anspach	BEL	6 wins
1920	Armand Massard	FRA	9 wins
1924	Charles Delporte	BEL	8 wins
1928	Lucien Gaudin	FRA	8 wins
1932	Gaincarlo Cornaggia-Medici	ITA	8 wins
1936	Franco Riccardi	ITA	5 wins
1948	Luigi Cantone	ITA	7 wins
1952	Edoardo Mangiarotti	ITA	7 wins
1956	Carlo Pavesi	ITA	5 wins
1960	Giuseppe Delfino	ITA	5 wins
1964	Grigoriy Kriss	URS	2 wins
1968	Gyozo Kulcsar	HUN	4 wins

1972	Csaba Fenyvesi	HUN	4 wins
1976	Alexander Pusch	FRG	3 wins
1980	Johan Harmenberg	SWE	4 wins
1984	Philippe Boisse	FRA	
1988	Arnd Schmitt	FRG	

Sabre

1896	Jean Georgiadis	GRE	4 wins
1900	Georges de la Falaise	FRA	d.n.a
1904	Manuel Diaz	CUB	4 wins
1906	Jean Georgiadis	GRE	d.n.a
1908	Jeno Fuchs	HUN	6 wins
1912	Jeno Fuchs	HUN	6 wins
1920	Nedo Nadi	ITA	11 wins
1924	Sandor Posta	HUN	5 wins
1928	Odon Tersztyanszky	HUN	9 wins
1932	Gyorgy Piller	HUN	8 wins
1936	Endre Kabos	HUN	7 wins
1948	Aladar Gerevich	HUN	7 wins
1952	Pal Kovacs	HUN	8 wins
1956	Rudolf Karpati	HUN	6 wins
1960	Rudolf Karpati	HUN	5 wins
1964	Tibor Pezsa	HUN	2 wins
1968	Jerzy Pawlowski	POL	4 wins
1972	Viktor Sidiak	URS	4 wins
1976	Viktor Krovopouskov	URS	5 wins
1980	Viktor Krovopouskov	URS	5 wins
1984	Jean Francois Lamour	FRA	
1988	Jean Francois Lamour	FRA	

Epee - Team

1906			FRA	
1908			FRA	
1912			BEL	
1920			ITA	
1924			FRA	
1928			ITA	
1932			FRA	
1936			ITA	
1948			FRA	
1952			ITA	
1956			ITA	
1960			ITA	
1964			HUN	
1968			HUN	
1972			HUN	
1976			SWE	
1980			FRA	
1984			FRG	
1988			FRA	

Sabre - Team

1906			GER	
1908			HUN	
1912			HUN	
1920			ITA	
1924			ITA	
1928			HUN	
1932			HUN	
1936			HUN	
1948			HUN	
1952			HUN	
1956			HUN	
1960			HUN	
1964			URS	
1968			URS	
1972			ITA	
1976			URS	
1980			URS	
1984			ITA	
1988			HUN	

Foil - Team

1904	USA/CUB
1920	ITA
1924	FRA
1928	ITA
1932	FRA
1936	ITA
1948	FRA
1952	FRA
1956	ITA
1960	URS
1964	URS
1968	FRA
1972	POL
1976	FRG
1980	FRA
1984	FRA
1988	URS

WOMEN
Foil

1924	Ellen Osiier	DEN	5 wins
1928	Helene Mayer	GER	7 wins
1932	Ellen Preis	AUT	9 wins
1936	Ilona Elek	HUN	6 wins
1948	Ilona Elek	HUN	6 wins
1952	Irene Camber	ITA	5 wins
1956	Gillian Sheen	GBR	6 wins
1960	Heidi Schmid	GER	6 wins
1964	Ildiko Uilaki-Reito	HUN	2 wins
1968	Elena Novikova	URS	4 wins
1972	Antonella Ragno-Lonzi	ITA	4 wins
1976	Ildiko Schwarczenberger	HUN	4 wins
1980	Pascale Trinquet	FRA	4 wins
1984	Jujie Luan	CHN	
1988	Anja Fichtel	FRG	

Foil Team

1960	URS
1964	HUN
1968	URS
1972	URS
1976	URS
1980	FRA
1984	FRG
1988	FRG

FOOTBALL

1900	GBR
1904	CAN
1906	DEN
1908	GBR
1912	GBR
1920	BEL
1924	URU
1928	URU
1936	ITA
1948	SWE
1952	HUN
1956	URS
1960	YUG
1964	HUN
1968	HUN
1972	POL
1976	GDR
1980	TCH

1984	FRA
1988	URS

GYMNASTICS

MEN — Pts
Team

		Pts
1904	USA	374.43
	AUT	374.43
1906	NOR	19.00
1908	SWE	438
1912	ITA	265.75
1920	ITA	359.835
1924	ITA	839.058
1928	SUI	1718.625
1932	ITA	541.850
1936	GER	657.430
1948	FIN	1358.3
1952	URS	575.4
1956	URS	568.25
1960	JPN	575.20
1964	JPN	577.95
1968	JPN	575.90
1972	JPN	571.25
1976	JPN	576.85
1980	URS	589.60
1984	USA	591.40
1988	URS	593.350

Ind All-Round

1900	Gustave Sandras	FRA	302
1904	Julius Lennard	AUT	69.90
1906*	Pierre Paysse	FRA	97
1906	Pierre Paysse	FRA	116
1908	Alberto Braglia	ITA	317.0
1912	Alberto Braglia	ITA	135.0
1920	Giorgio Zampori	ITA	88.35
1924	Leon Stukelj	YUG	110.340
1928	Georges Miez	SUI	247.500
1932	Romeo Neri	ITA	140.625
1936	Alfred Schwarzmann	GER	113.100
1948	Veikko Huhtanen	FIN	229.7
1952	Viktor Chukarin	URS	115.70
1956	Viktor Chukarin	URS	114.25
1960	Boris Shakhlin	URS	115.95
1964	Yukio Endo	JPN	115.95
1968	Sawao Kato	JPN	115.90
1972	Sawao Kato	JPN	114.650
1976	Nikolay Andrianov	URS	116.650
1980	Aleksandr Dityatin	URS	118.650
1984	Koji Gushiken	JPN	118.700
1988	Vladimir Artemov	URS	119.125

* Two competitions held in this year.

Floor

1932	Istvan Pelle	HUN	9.60
1936	Georges Miez	SUI	18.666
1948	Ferenc Pataki	HUN	38.7
1952	William Thoresson	SWE	19.25
1956	Valentin Muratov	URS	19.20
1960	Nobuyuki Aihara	JPN	19.450
1964	Franco Menichelli	ITA	19.45
1968	Sawao Kato	JPN	19.475
1972	Nikolay Andrianov	URS	19.175
1976	Nikolay Andrianov	URS	19.450
1980	Roland Bruckner	GDR	19.750
1984	Li Ning	CHN	19.925
1988	Sergey Kharikov	URS	19.925

Parallel Bars

1896	Alfred Flatow	GER	d.n.a.
1904	George Eyser	USA	44
1924	August Guttinger	SUI	21.63
1928	Ladislav Vacha	TCH	18.83
1932	Romeo Neri	ITA	18.97
1936	Konrad Frey	GER	19.067
1948	Michael Reusch	SUI	39.5
1952	Hans Eugster	SUI	19.65
1956	Viktor Chukarin	URS	19.20
1960	Boris Shakhlin	URS	19.40
1964	Yukio Endo	JPN	19.675
1968	Akinori Nakayama	JPN	19.475
1972	Sawao Kato	JPN	19.475
1976	Sawao Kato	JPN	19.675
1980	Aleksandr Tkachev	URS	19.775
1984	Bart Conner	USA	19.950
1988	Vladimir Artemov	URS	19.925

Pommel Horse

1896	Jules Zutter	SUI	d.n.a
1904	Anton Heida	USA	42
1924	Josef Wilhelm	SUI	21.23
1928	Hermann Hanggi	SUI	1975
1932	Istvan Pelle	HUN	19.07
1936	Konrad Frey	GER	19.333
1948	Paavo Aaltonen	FIN	38.7
	Veikko Huhtanen	FIN	38.7
	Heikki Savolainen	FIN	38.7
1952	Viktor Chukarin	URS	19.50
1956	Boris Shakhlin	URS	19.25
1960	Eugen Ekman	FIN	19.375
	Boris Shakhlin	URS	19.375
1964	Miroslav Cerar	YUG	19.525
1968	Miroslav Cerar	YUG	19.325
1972	Viktor Klimenko	URS	19.125
1976	Zoltan Magyar	HUN	19.700
1980	Zoltan Magyar	HUN	19.925
1984	Li Ning	CHN	19.950
	Peter Vidmar	USA	19.950
1988	Lubomir Gueraskov	URS	19.950
	Zsolt Borkai	HUN	19.950
	Dmitry Bilozertchev	URS	19.950

Rings

1896	Ioannis Mitropoulos	GRE	d.n.a.
1904	Herman Glass	USA	45
1924	Franco Martino	ITA	21.553
1928	Leon Skutelji	YUG	19.25
1932	GeorgeGulack	USA	18.97
1936	Alois Hudec	TCH	19.433
1948	Karl Frei	SUI	39.60
1952	Grant Shaginyan	URS	19.75
1956	Albert Azaryan	URS	1935
1960	Albert Azaryan	URS	19.725
1964	Takuji Hayata	JPN	19.475
1968	Akinori Nakayama	JPN	19.450
1972	Akinori Nakayama	JPN	19.350
1976	Nilolay Andrianov	URS	19.650
1980	Aleksandr Dityatin	URS	19.857
1984	Koji Gushiken	JPN	19.850
	Li Ning	CHN	19.850
1988	Holger Behrendt	GDR	19.925
	Dmitry Bilozertchev	URS	19.925

Horizontal Bar

1896	Hermann Weingartner	GER	d.n.a.
1904	Anton Heida	USA	40
	Edward Hennig	USA	40
1924	Leon Strukelj	YUG	19.730
1928	George Miez	SUI	19.17
1932	Dallas Bixler	USA	18.33
1936	Aleksanteri Saarvala	FIN	19.367
1948	Josef Stalder	SUI	39.7
1952	Jack Gunthard	SUI	19.55
1956	Takashi Ono	JPN	19.60
1960	Takashi Ono	JPN	19.60
1964	Boris Shakhlin	URS	19.625
1968	Mikhail Voronin	URS	19.550
	Akinori Nakayama	JPN	19.550
1972	Mitzuo Tsukahara	JPN	19.725
1976	Mitsuo Tsukahara	JPN	19.675
1980	Stoyan Deltchev	BUL	19.825
1984	Shinje Morisue	JPN	20.00
1988	Vladimir Artemov	URS	19.900
	Valeriy Lyukhine	URS	19.900

Horse Vault

1896	Carl Schuhmann	GER	d.n.a.
1904	Anton Heida	USA	36
	George Eyser	USA	36
1924	Frank Kriz	USA	9.98
1928	Eugen Mack	SUI	9.58
1932	Savino Guglielmetti	ITS	18.03
1936	Alfred Schwarzmann	GER	19.200
1948	Paavo Aaltonen	FIN	39.10
1952	Viktor Chukarin	URS	19.20
1956	Helmuth Bantz	GER	18.85
	Valentin Muratov	URS	18.85
1960	Takashi Ono	JPN	19.350
	Boris Shakhlin	URS	19.350
1964	Haruhio Yamashita	JPN	19.600
1968	Mikhail Voronin	URS	19.000
1972	Klaus Koste	GDR	18.850
1976	Nikolay Andrianov	URS	19.450
1980	Nikolay Andrianov	URS	19.825
1984	Lou Yun	CHN	19.950
1988	Lou Yun	CHN	19.875

WOMEN

Team

1928		HOL	316.75
1936		GER	506.50
1948		TCH	445.45
1952		URS	527.03
1956		URS	444.80
1960		URS	382.320
1964		URS	380.890
1968		URS	382.85
1972		URS	380.50
1976		URS	390.35
1980		URS	394.90
1984		ROM	392.20
1988		URS	395.475

Ind All-Round

1952	Maria Gorokhovskaya	URS	76.78
1956	Larissa Latynina	URS	74.933
1960	Larissa Latynina	URS	77.031
1964	Vera Caslavska	TCH	77.564
1968	Vera Caslavska	TCH	78.25
1972	Ludmilla Tourischeva	URS	77.025
1976	Nadia Comaneci	ROM	70.275
1980	Yelena Davydova	URS	70.150
1984	Mary Lou Retton	USA	79.175
1988	Yelena Chouchounova	URS	79.662

Asymmetrical Bars

1952	Margit Korondi	HUN	19.40
1956	Agnes Keleti	HUN	18.966
1960	Polina Astakhova	URS	19.616
1964	Polina Astakhova	URS	19.332
1968	Vera Caslavska	TCH	19.650
1972	Karin Janz	GDR	19.675
1976	Nadia Comaneci	ROM	20.00
1980	Maxi Gnauck	GDR	19.875
1984	Ma Yanhong	CHN	19.950
	Julianne McNamara	USA	19.950
1988	Daniela Silivas	ROM	20.00

Beam

1952	Nina Bocharova	URS	19.22
1956	Agnes Keleti	HUN	18.80
1960	Eva Bosakova	TCH	19.283
1964	Vera Caslavska	TCH	19.449
1968	Natalya Kuchinskaya	URS	19.650
1972	Olga Korbut	URS	19.575
1976	Nadia Comaneci	ROM	19.950
1980	Nadia Comaneci	ROM	19.800
1984	Simona Pauca	ROM	19.800
	Ecaterina Szabo	ROM	19.800
1988	Daniela Silivas	ROM	19.924

Floor

1952	Agnes Keleti	HUN	19.36
1956	Larissa Latynina	URS	18.733
	Agnes Keleti	HUN	18.733
1960	Larissa Latynina	URS	19.583
1964	Larissa Latynina	URS	19.599
1968	Larissa Petrik	URS	19.675
	Vera Caslavska	TCH	19.675
1972	Olga Korbut	URS	19.575
1976	Nelli Kim	URS	19.850
1980	Nelli Kim	URS	19.875
	Nadia Comaneci	ROM	19.875
1984	Ecaterina Szabo	ROM	19.975
1988	Daniela Silivas	ROM	19.937

Horse Vault

1952	Yekaterina Kalinchuk	URS	19.20
1956	Larissa Latynina	URS	18.833
1960	Margarita Nikolayeva	URS	19.316
1964	Vera Caslavska	TCH	19.483

HANDBALL

MEN

1936		GER
1972		YUG
1976		URS
1980		GDR
1984		YUG
1988		URS

WOMEN

1976		URS
1980		URS
1984		YUG
1988		KOR

HOCKEY

MEN

1908		England[1]
1920		England[2]

1928		IND
1932		IND
1936		IND
1948		IND
1952		IND
1956		IND
1960		PAK
1964		IND
1968		PAK
1972		FRG
1976		NZL
1980		IND
1984		PAK
1888		GBR

WOMEN

1980		ZIM
1984		HOL
1988		AUS

[1] Great Britain had four teams entered.
[2] Great Britain represented by England team.

JUDO

Open Category

1964	Antonius Geesink	HOL
1972	Willen Ruska	HOL
1976	Haruki Uemura	JPN
1980	Dietmar Lorenz	GDR
1984	Yasuhiro Yamashita	JPN

+ 95kg

1980	Angelo Parisi	FRA
1984	Hitoshi Saito	JPN
1988	Hitoshi Saito	JPN

-95kg

1980	Robert Van de Walle	BEL
1984	Ha Hyoung-Zoo	KOR
1988	Aurelio Miguel	BRA

-86kg

1980	Jurg Rotheisberger	SUI
1984	Peter Seisenbacher	AUT
1988	Peter Seisenbacher	AUT

-78kg

1980	Shota Khabaleri	URS
1984	Frank Wieneke	FRG
1988	Waldemar Legien	POL

-71kg

1980	Ezio Gamba	ITA
1984	Ahn Byeong-Keun	KOR
1988	Marc Alexandre	FRA

-65kg

1980	Nikolai Solodukhin	URS
1984	Yoshiyuki Matsuoka	JPN
1988	Lee Kyung-Keun	KOR

-60kg

1980	Thierry Rey	FRA
1984	Shinji Hosokawa	JPN
1988	Kim Jae-Yup	KOR

MODERN PENTATHLON

Individual

1912	Gosta Lilliehopok	SWE	27
1920	Gustaf Dyrssen	SWE	18

1924	Bo Lindman	SWE	18
1928	Sven Thofelt	SWE	47
1932	Johan Gabriel Oxenstierna	SWE	32
1936	Gotthard Handrick	GER	31.5
1948	Willie Grut	SWE	16
1952	Lars Hall	SWE	32
1956	Lars Hall	SWE	4843
1960	Ferenc Nemeth	HUN	5024
1964	Ferenc Torok	HUN	5024
1968	Bjorn Ferm	SWE	4964
1972	Andras Balczo	HUN	5412
1976	Janusz Pyciak-Peciak	POL	5520
1980	Anatoliy Starostin	URS	5568
1984	Daniel Massala	ITA	5469
1988	Janos Martinek	HUN	5404

Team

1952	HUN	116
1956	URS	13690.5
1960	HUN	14863
1964	URS	14961
1968	HUN	14325
1972	URS	15968
1976	GBR	15559
1980	URS	16126
1984	ITA	16060
1988	HUN	15886

ROWING

MEN
Single Sculls

1900	Henri Barrelet	FRA	7:35.6
1904	Frank Geer	USA	10:08.5
1906	Gaston Delaplane	FRA	5:53.4
1908	Harry Blackstaffe	GBR	9:26.0
1912	William Kinnear	GBR	7:47.6
1920	John Kelly	USA	7:35.0
1924	Jack Beresford	GBR	7:49.2
1928	Henry Pearce	AUS	7:11.0
1932	Henry Pearce	AUS	7:44.4
1936	Gustav Schafer	GER	8:21.5
1948	Mervyn Wood	AUS	7:24.4
1952	Yuriy Tyukalov	URS	8:12.8
1956	Vyacheslav Ivanov	URS	8:02.5
1960	Vyacheslav Ivanov	URS	7:13.96
1964	Vyacheslav Ivanov	URS	8:22.51
1968	Henri Jan Wienese	HOL	7:47.80
1972	Yuriy Malishev	URS	7:10.12
1976	Pertti Karpinnen	FIN	7:29.03
1980	Pertti Karpinnen	FIN	7:09.61
1984	Pertti Karpinnen	FIN	7:00.24
1988	Thomas Lange	GDR	6:49.86

Double Sculls

1904	USA	10:03.2
1920	USA	7:09.0
1924	USA	7:45.0
1928	USA	6:41.4
1932	USA	7:17.4
1936	GBR	7:20.8
1948	GBR	6:51.3
1952	ARG	7:32.2
1956	URS	7:24.0
1960	TCH	6:47.50
1964	URS	7:10.66
1968	URS	6:51.82
1972	URS	7:07.77
1976	NOR	7:13.20
1980	GDR	6:24.33
1984	USA	6:36.87
1988	HOL	6:21.13

Coxless Quadruple Sculls

1976	GDR	6:18.65
1980	GDR	5:49.81
1984	FRG	5:57..55
1988	ITA	5:53.37

Coxless Pairs

1908	GBR	9:43.0
1924	HOL	8:19.4
1928	GER	7:06.4
1932	GBR	8:00.0
1936	GER	8:16.1
1948	GBR	7:21.1
1952	USA	8:20.7
1956	USA	7:55.4
1960	URS	7:02.01
1964	CAN	7:32.94
1968	GDR	7:26.56
1972	GDR	6:53.16
1976	GDR	7:23.31
1980	GDR	6:48.01
1984	ROM	6:45.39
1988	GBR	6:36.84

Coxed Pairs

1900	HOL	7:34.2
1906[1]	ITA I	4:23.0
1906[2]	ITA	7:32.4
1920	ITA	7:56.0
1924	SUI	8:39.0
1928	SUI	7:42.6
1932	USA	8:25.8
1936	GER	8:36.39
1948	DEN	8:00.5
1952	FRA	8:28.6
1956	USA	8:26.1
1960	GER	7:29.14
1964	USA	8:21.23
1968	ITA	8:04.81
1972	GDR	7:17.25
1976	GDR	7:58.99
1980	GDR	7:02.54
1984	ITA	7:05.99
1988	ITA	6:58.79

[1] Over 1000m
[2] Over 1600m

Coxless Fours

1904	USA	9:53.8
1908	GBR	8:34.0
1924	GBR	7:08.6
1928	GBR	6:36.0
1932	GBR	6:58.2
1936	GER	7:01.8
1948	ITA	6:39.0
1952	YUG	7:16.0
1956	CAN	7:08.8
1960	USA	6:26.26
1964	DEN	6:59.30
1968	GDR	6:39.18
1972	GDR	6:24.27
1976	GDR	6:37.42
1980	GDR	6:08.17
1984	NZL	6:03.48
1988	GDR	6:03.11

Coxed Fours

1900		GER	5:59.0
1900		FRA	7:11.0
1906		ITA	8:13.0
1912		GER	6:59.4
1920		SUI	6:54.0
1924		SUI	7:18.4
1928		ITA	6:47.8
1932		GER	7:19.0
1936		GER	7:16.2
1948		GER	6:50.3
1952		USA	7:33.4
1956		ITA	7:19.4
1960		GER	6:39.12
1964		GER	7:00.44
1968		NZL	6:45.62
1972		FRG	6:31.85
1976		URS	6:40.22
1980		GDR	6:14.51
1984		GBR	6:18.64
1988		GDR	6:10.74

Eights

1900		USA	6:09.8
1904		USA	7:50.0
1908		GBR	7:52.0
1912		GBR	6:15.0
1920		USA	6:02.6
1924		USA	6:33.4
1928		USA	6:03.2
1932		USA	6:37.6
1936		USA	6:25.4
1948		USA	5:56.7
1952		USA	6:25.9
1956		USA	6:35.2
1960		GER	5:57.18
1964		USA	6:18.23
1968		FRG	6:07.00
1972		NZL	6:08.94
1976		GDR	5:58.29
1980		GDR	5:49.05
1984		CAN	5:41.32
1988		FRG	5:46.05

WOMEN

Single Sculls

1976	Christine Scheiblich	GDR	4:05.56
1980	Sandra Toma	ROM	3:40.69
1984	Valeria Racila	ROM	3:40.68
1988	Jutta Behrednt	GDR	7:47.19

Double Sculls

1976		BUL	3:44.36
1980		URS	3:16.27
1984		ROM	3:2.6.75
1988		GDR	7:00.48

Coxed Quadruple Sculls

1976		GDR	3:29.99
1980		GDR	3:15.32
1984		ROM	3:14.11
1988		GDR	6:21.06

Coxless Pairs

1976		BUL	4:01.22
1980		GDR	3:30.49
1984		ROM	3:32.60
1988		ROM	7:28.13

Coxed Fours

1976		GDR	3:45.08

1980		GDR	3:19.27
1984		ROM	3:19.30
1988		GDR	6:56.00

Eights

1976		GDR	3:33.32
1980		GDR	3:03.32
1984		USA	2:59.80
1988		GDR	6:15.17

SHOOTING

MEN

Free Pistol (50 m)

1896	Sumner Paine	USA	442
1900	Karl Roderer	SUI	503
1906	Georgios Orphanidis	GRE	221
1912	Alfred Lane	USA	499
1920	Karl Frederick	USA	496
1936	Torsten Ullmann	SWE	559
1948	Edwin Vazquez Cam	PER	545
1952	Huelet Benner	USA	553
1956	Pentti Minnosvuo	FIN	556
1960	Aleksey Gushchin	URS	560
1964	Vaino Markkanen	FIN	560
1968	Grigory Kossykh	URS	562
1972	Ragnar Skanakar	SWE	567
1976	Uwe Potteck	GDR	573
1980	Aleksandr Melentyev	URS	581
1984	Xu Haifeng	CHN	566
1988	Sorin Babii	ROM	(566+94) 660

Rapid-Fire Pistol

1896	Jean Pharangoudis	GRE	344
1900	Maurice Larrouy	FRA	58
1906	Maurice Lecoq	FRA	250
1908	Paul van Asbroeck	BEL	490
1912	Alfred Lane	USA	287
1920	Guiherme Paraense	BRA	274
1924	Paul Bailey	USA	18
1932	Renzo Morigi	ITA	36
1936	Cornelius van Oyen	GER	36
1948	Karoy Takacs	HUN	580
1952	Karoly Takacs	HUN	579
1956	Stefan Petrescu	ROM	587
1960	William McMillan	USA	587
1964	Penttii Linnosvuo	FIN	592
1968	Jozef Zapedzki	POL	593
1972	Jozef Zapedzki	POL	593
1976	Norbert Klaar	GDR	597
1980	Corneliu Ion	ROM	596
1984	Takeo Kamachi	JPN	595
1988	Afanasi Kouzmine	URS	(598+100) 698

Small-bore Rifle (Prone)

1908	A A Carnell	GBR	387
1912	Frederick Hird	USA	194
1920	Lawrence Nuesslein	USA	391
1924	Pierre Coquelin de Lisle	FRA	398
1932	Bertil Ronnmark	SWE	294
1936	Willy Rogeberg	NOR	300
1948	Arthur Cook	USA	599
1952	Josif Sarbu	ROM	400
1956	Gerald Ouellette	CAN	600
1960	Peter Kohnke	GER	590
1964	Laszlo Hammerl	HUN	597

1968	Jan Kurka	TCH	598
1972	Li Ho Jun	PRK	599
1976	Karl heinz Smieszek	FRG	599
1980	Karoly Varga	HUN	599
1984	Edward Etzel	USA	599
1988	Miroslav Varga	TCH (600+103.9) 703.9	

Small-bore Rifle -3-Positions

1952	Erling Kongshaug	NOR	1164
1956	Anatoliy Bogdanov	URS	1172
1960	Viktor Shamburkin	URS	1149
1964	Lones Wigger	USA	1164
1968	Bernd Klingner	FRG	1157
1972	John Writer	USA	1166
1976	Lanny Bassham	USA	1162
1980	Viktor Vlasov	URS	1173
1984	Malcolm Cooper	GBR	1173
1988	Malcolm Cooper	GBR(1180+99.3) 1279.3	

Running Game Target

1900	Louis Debray	FRA	20
1972	Lakov Zhelezniak	URS	569
1976	Aleksandr Gazov	URS	579
1980	Igor Sokolov	URS	589
1984	Li Yuwei	CHN	587
1988	Tor Heiestad	NOR	(591+98) 689

Trap

1900	Roger de Barbarin	FRA	17
1906[1]	Gerald Merlin	GBR	24
1906[2]	Sidney Merlin	GBR	15
1908	Walter Ewing	CAN	72
1912	James Graham	USA	96
1920	Marke Arie	USA	95
1924	Gyula Halasy	HUN	98
1952	George Genereux	CAN	192
1956	Galliano Rossini	ITA	195
1960	Ion Dumitrescu	ROM	192
1964	Ennio Mattarelli	ITA	198
1968	Robert Braithwaite	GBR	198
1972	Angelo Scalzone	ITA	199
1976	Don Haldeman	USA	190
1980	Luciano Giovanetti	ITA	198
1984	Luciano Giovanetti	ITA	192
1988	Dmitriy Monakov	URS	(197+25) 222

[1] single shot
[2] double shot

Skeet

1968	Evgeny Petrov	URS	198
1972	Konrad Wirnhier	FRG	195
1976	Josef Panacek	TCH	198
1980	Hans Kjeld Rasmussen	DEN	196
1984	Matthew Dryke	USA	198
1988	Axel Wegner	GDR	(198+24) 222

Air Pistol

1988	Taniou Kiriakov	BUL (585+102.9) 687.9	

Air Rifle

1984	Phillippe Herberle	FRA	589
1988	Goran Maksimovic	YUG (594+101.6) 695.6	

WOMEN

Sport Pistol

1984	Linda Thom	CAN	585
1988	Nino Saloukvadze	URS	(591+99) 690

Standard Rifle

1984	Wu Xiaoxuan	CHN	581
1988	Silvia Sperber	FRG	(590+95.6) 685.6

Air Pistol

1988	Jasna Sekaric	YUG (389+100.5) 489.5	

Air Rifle

1984	Pat Spurgin	USA	393
1988	Irina Chilova	URS	(395+103.5) 498.5

SWIMMING

MEN

50m Freestyle

1988	Matthew Biondi	USA	22.14

100m Freestyle

1896	Alfred Hajos	HUN	1:22.2
1904[1]	Zoltan Halmay	HUN	1:02.8
1906	Charles Daniels	USA	1:13.4
1908	Charles Daniels	USA	1:05.6
1912	Duke Kahanamoku	USA	1:03.4
1920	Duke Kahanamoku	USA	1:01.4
1924	Johnny Weissmuller	USA	59.0
1928	Johnny Weissmuller	USA	58.6
1932	Yasuji Miyazaki	JPN	58.2
1936	Ferenc Csik	HUN	57.6
1948	Walter Ris	USA	57.3
1952	Clarke Scholes	USA	57.4
1956	Jon Henricks	AUS	55.4
1960	John Devitt	AUS	55.2
1964	Don Schollander	USA	53.4
1968	Mike Wendon	AUS	52.2
1972	Mark Sptiz	USA	51.22
1976	Jim Montgomery	USA	49.99
1980	Jorg Woithe	GDR	50.40
1984	Ambrose Gaines	USA	49.80
1988	Matthew Biondi	USA	48.63

[1] 100 yards

200m Freestyle

1900	Frederick Lane	AUS	2:25.2
1904[2]	Charles Daniels	USA	2:4.2
1968	Mike Wenden	AUS	1:55.2
1972	Mark Spitz	USA	1:52.78
1976	Bruce Furniss	USA	1:50.29
1980	Sergey Kopliakov	URS	1:49.81
1984	Michael Gross	FRG	1:47.44
1988	Duncan Armstrong	AUS	1:47.25

[2] 200 yards

400m Freestyle

1896[1]	Paul Neuman	AUT	8:12.6
1904[2]	Charles Daniels	USA	6:16.2
1906	Otto Scheff	AUT	6:23.8
1908	Henry Taylor	GBR	5:36.8
1912	George Hodgson	CAN	5:24.4
1920	Norman Ross	USA	5:26.8
1924	Johnny Weissmuller	USA	5:04.2
1928	Alberto Zorilla	ARG	5:01.6
1932	Buster Crabbe	USA	4:48.4
1936	Jack Medica	USA	4:44.5
1948	William Smith	USA	4:41.0
1952	Jean Boiteaux	USA	4:30.7
1956	Murray Rose	AUS	4:27.3
1960	Murray Rose	AUS	4:18.3
1964	Don Schollander	USA	4:12.2
1968	Mike Burton	USA	4:09.0
1972	Brad Cooper	AUS	4:00.27
1976	Brian Goodell	USA	3:51.93
1980	Vladimir Salnikov	URS	3:51.31
1984	Georgio Di Carlo	USA	3:51.23
1988	Uwe Dassler	GDR	3:46.95

[1] 500m
[2] 440yds

1500m Freestyle

1896[1]	Alfred Hajos	HUN	18:22.2
1900[2]	John Jarvis	GBR	13:40.2
1904[3]	Emil Rausch	GER	27.18.2
1906[3]	Henry Taylor	GBR	28.28.0
1908	Henry Taylor	GBR	22:48.4
1912	George Hodgson	CAN	22:00.0
1920	Norman Ross	USA	22:23.2
1924	Andrew Chapman	AUS	20:06.6
1928	Arne Borg	SWE	19:51.8
1932	Kusuo Kitamura	JPN	19:12.4
1936	Noboru Terada	JPN	19:13.7
1948	James McLane	USA	19:18.5
1952	Ford Konno	USA	18:30.0
1956	Murray Rose	AUS	17:58.9
1960	John Konrads	AUS	17:19.6
1964	Bob Windle	USA	17:01.7
1968	Mike Burton	USA	16:38.9
1972	Mike Burton	USA	15.52.58
1976	Brian Goodall	USA	15:02.40
1980	Vladimir Salnikov	URS	14:58.27
1984	Michael O'Brien	USA	15:05.20
1988	Vladimir Salnikov	URS	15.00.40

[1] 1200m
[2] 1000m
[3] 1 mile

100m Breaststroke

1968	Don McKenzie	USA	1:07.7
1972	Nobutaka Taguchi	JPN	1:04.94
1976	John Hencken	USA	1:03.11
1980	Duncan Goodhew	GBR	1:03.34
1984	Steve Lundquist	USA	1:01.65
1988	Adrian Moorhouse	GBR	1:02.04

200m Breaststroke

1908	Frederick Holman	GBR	3:09.2
1912	Walter Bathe	GER	3:01.8
1920	Haken Malmroth	SWE	3:04.4
1924	Robert Skelton	USA	2:56.5
1928	Yoshiyuki Tsuruta	JPN	2:48.8
1932	Yoshiyuki Tsuruta	JPN	2:45.4
1936	Tetsuo Hamuro	JPN	2:42.5
1948	Joseph Verdeur	USA	2:39.3
1952	John Davies	AUS	2:34.4
1956	Masaru Furukawa	JPN	2:34.7
1960	William Mulliken	USA	2:37.4
1964	Ian O'Brien	AUS	2:27.8
1968	Felipe Munoz	MEX	2:28.7
1972	John Hencken	USA	2:21.55
1976	David Wilkie	GBR	2:15.11
1980	Robertas Shulpa	URS	2:15.85
1984	Victor Davis	CAN	2:13.34
1988	Jozsef Szabo	HUN	2:13.52

100m Backstroke

1904	Walter Brack	GER	1:16.8
1908	Arno Bieberstein	GER	1:24.6
1912	Harry Hebner	USA	1:21.2
1920	Warren Kealoha	USA	1:15.2
1924	Warren Kealoha	USA	1:13.2
1928	George Kojac	USA	1:08.2
1932	Masaji Kiyokawa	JPN	1:08.6
1936	Adolf Kiefer	USA	1:05.9
1948	Allen Stack	USA	1:06.4
1952	Yoshinobu Oyakawa	USA	1:05.4
1956	David Thiele	AUS	1:02.2
1960	David Thiele	AUS	1:01.9
1968	Roland Matthes	GDR	58.7
1972	Roland Matthes	GDR	56.58
1976	John Naber	USA	55.49
1980	Bengt Baron	SWE	56.53
1984	Richard Carey	USA	55.79
1988	Daichi Suzuki	JPN	55.05

200m Backstroke

1900	Ernst Hoppenberg	GER	2:47.0
1964	Jed Graef	USA	2:10.3
1968	Roland Matthes	GDR	2:09.6
1972	Roland Matthes	GDR	2:02.82
1976	John Naber	USA	1:59.19
1980	Sandor Wladar	HUN	2:01.93
1984	Richard Carey	USA	2:00.23
1988	Igor Polianski	URS	1:59.37

100m Butterfly

1968	Doug Russell	USA	55.9
1972	Mark Spitz	USA	54.27
1976	Matt Vogel	USA	54.35
1980	Par Arvidsson	SWE	54.92
1984	Michael Gross	FRG	53.08
1988	Anthony Nesty	SUR	53.00

200m Butterfly

1956	William Yorzyk	USA	2:19.3
1960	Mike Troy	USA	2:12.8
1964	Kevin Berry	AUS	2:06.6
1968	Carl Robie	USA	2:08.7
1972	Mark Spitz	USA	2:00.70
1976	Mike Bruner	USA	1:59.23
1980	Sergey Fesenko	URS	1:59.76
1984	Jon Sieben	AUS	1:57.04
1988	Michael Gross	FRG	1:56.94

200m Ind Medley

1968	Charles Hickcox	USA	2:12.0
1972	Gunnar Larsson	SWE	2:07.17
1984	Alex Baumann	CAN	2:01.42
1988	Tamas Darnyi	HUN	2:00.17

400m Ind Medley

1968	Richard Roth	USA	4:45.4
1968	Charles Hickcox	USA	4:48.4
1972	Gunnar Larsson	SWE	4:31.98
1976	Rod Strachan	USA	4:23.68
1980	Aleksandr Sidorenko	URS	4:22.89
1984	Alex Baumann	CAN	4:17.41
1988	Tamas Darnyi	HUN	4:14.75

4x100m Freestyle Relay

1964		USA	3:33.2
1968		USA	3:31.7
1972		USA	3:26.42
1984		USA	3:19.03
1988		USA	3:16.53

4x200m Freestyle Relay

1906		HUN	16:52.4
1908		GBR	10:55.6
1912		AUS/NZL	10:11.6
1920		USA	10:04.4
1924		USA	9:53.4
1928		USA	9:36.2
1932		JPN	8:58.4
1936		JPN	8:51.5
1948		USA	8:46.0
1952		USA	8:31.1
1956		AUS	8:23.6
1960		USA	8:10.2
1964		USA	7:52.1
1968		USA	7:52.3
1972		USA	7:35.78
1976		USA	7:23.22

1980		URS	7:23.50
1984		USA	7:15.69
1988		USA	7:12.51

4x100m Medley Relay

1960		USA	4:05.4
1964		USA	4:38.5
1968		USA	3:54.9
1972		USA	3:48.16
1976		USA	3:42.22
1980		AUS	3:45.70
1984		USA	3:39.30
1988		USA	3:36.93

WOMEN

50m Freestyle

1988	Kristin Otto	GDR	25:49

100m Freestyle

1912	Fanny Durack	AUS	1:22.2
1920	Ethelda Beleibtrey	USA	1:13.6
1924	Ethel Lackie	USA	1:12.4
1928	Albina Osipowich	USA	1:11.0
1932	Helene Madison	USA	1:06.8
1936	Henrika Masenbroek	HOL	1:05.9
1948	Greta Andersen	DEN	1:06.3
1952	Katalin Szoke	HUN	1:06.8
1956	Dawn Fraser	AUS	1:02.0
1960	Dawn Fraser	AUS	1:01.2
1964	Dawn Fraser	AUS	59.5
1968	Jan Henne	USA	1:00.0
1972	Sandra Neilson	USA	58.59
1976	Kornelia Ender	GDR	55.65
1980	Barbara Krause	GDR	54.79
1984	Carrie Steinseifer/	USA/	55.92
	Nancy Hogshead	USA	55.92
1988	Kristin Otto	GDR	54.93

200m Freestyle

1968	Debbie Meyer	USA	2:10.5
1972	Shane Gould	AUS	2:03.56
1976	Kornelia Ender	GDR	1:59.26
1980	Barbara Krause	GDR	1:58.33
1984	Mary Wayte	USA	1:59.23
1988	Heike Friedrich	GDR	1:57.65

400m Freestyle

1920	Ethelda Bleibtrey	USA	4:34.0
1924	Martha Norelius	USA	6:02.2
1928	Martha Norelius	USA	5:42.8
1932	Helene Madison	USA	5:28.5
1936	Henrika Mastenbroek	HOL	5:26.4
1948	Ann Curtis	USA	5:17.8
1952	Valeria Gyenge	HUN	5:12.1
1956	Lorraine Crapp	USA	4:54.6
1960	Chris von Saltza	USA	4:50.6
1964	Virginia Duenkel	USA	4:43.3
1968	Debbie Meyer	USA	4:31.8
1972	Shane Gould	AUS	4:19.04
1976	Petra Thuemer	GDR	4:09.89
1980	Ines Diers	GDR	4:08.76
1984	Tiffany Cohen	USA	4:07.10
1988	Janet Evans	USA	4:03.85

800m Freestyle

1968	Debbie Meyer	USA	9:24.0
1972	Keena Rothhammer	USA	8:53.68
1976	Petra Thuemer	GDR	8:37.14
1980	Michelle Ford	AUS	8:28.9
1984	Tiffany Cohen	USA	8:24.95
1988	Janet Evans	USA	8:20.20

100m Breaststroke

1968	Djurdjica Bjedov	YUG	1:15.8

1972	Catherine Carr	USA	1:13.58
1976	Hannelore Anke	GDR	1:11.16
1980	Ute Geweniger	GDR	1:10.22
1984	Petra Van Staveren	HOL	1:09.88
1988	Tania Dangalakova	URS	1:07.95

200m Breaststroke

1924	Lucy Morton	GBR	3:33.2
1928	Hilde Schrader	GER	3:12.6
1932	Claire Dennis	AUS	3:06.3
1936	Hideko Maehata	JPN	3:03.6
1948	Petronella van Vliet	HOL	2:57.2
1952	Eva Szekely	HUN	2:51.7
1956	Ursula Happe	GER	2:53.1
1960	Anita Lonsborough	GBR	2:49.5
1964	Galina Prozumenshchikova	URS	2:46.4
1968	Sharon Wichman	USA	2:44.4
1972	Beverly Whitfield	AUS	2:41.7
1976	Marina Kosheveya	URS	2:33.35
1980	Lina Kachushite	URS	2:29.54
1984	Anne Ottenbrite	CAN	2:30.38
1988	Silke Horner	GDR	2:26.71

100m Backstroke

1924	Sybil Bauer	USA	1:23.2
1928	Marie Braun	HOL	1:22.0
1932	Eleanor Holm	USA	1:19.4
1936	Dina Senff	HOL	1:18.9
1948	Karen Harup	DEN	1:14.4
1952	Joan Harrison	SAF	1:14.3
1956	Judy Grinham	GBR	1:12.9
1960	Lynn Burke	USA	1:09.3
1964	Cathy Ferguson	USA	1:07.7
1968	Kaye Hall	USA	1:06.2
1972	Melissa Belote	USA	1:05.78
1976	Ulrike Richter	GDR	1:01.83
1980	Rica Reinisch	GDR	1:00.86
1984	Theresa Andrews	USA	1:02.55
1988	Kristin Otto	GDR	1:00.89

200m Backstroke

1968	Lillian Watson	USA	2:24.8
1972	Melissa Belote	USA	2:19.19
1976	Ulrike Richter	GDR	2:13.43
1980	Rica Reinisch	GDR	2:11.77
1984	Jolanda De Rover	HOL	2:12.38
1988	Krisztina Egerszegi	HUN	2:09.29

100m Butterfly

1956	Shelley Mann	USA	1:11.0
1960	Carolyn Schuler	USA	1:09.5
1964	Sharon Stouder	USA	1:04.7
1968	Lynette McClements	AUS	1:05.5
1972	Mayumi Aoki	JPN	1:03.34
1976	Kornelia Ender	GDR	1:00.13
1980	Caren Metschuck	GDR	1:00.42
1984	Mary T Meagher	USA	59.26
1988	Kristin Otto	GDR	59.00

200m Butterfly

1968	Ada Kok	HOL	2:24.7
1972	Karen Moe	USA	2:15.57
1976	Andrea Pollock	GDR	2:11.41
1980	Ines Geissler	GDR	2:10.44
1984	Mary T Meagher	USA	2:06.90
1988	Kathleen Nord	GDR	2:09.51

200m Ind Medley

1968	Claudia Kolb	USA	2:24.7
1972	Shane Gould	AUS	2:23.07
1984	Tracy Caulkins	USA	2:12.64
1988	Daniela Hunger	GDR	2:12.59

400m Ind Medley

1964	Donna de Verona	USA	5:18.7
1968	Claudia Kolb	USA	5:08.5
1972	Gail Neall	AUS	5:02.97
1976	Ulrike Tauber	GDR	4:42.77
1980	Petra Schneider	GDR	4:36.29
1984	Tracy Caulkins	USA	4:39.24
1988	Janet Evans	USA	4:37.76

4x100m Freestyle Relay

1912	GBR	5:52.8
1920	USA	5:11.6
1924	USA	4:58.8
1928	USA	4:47.6
1932	USA	4:38.0
1936	HOL	4:36.0
1948	USA	4:29.2
1952	HUN	4:24.4
1956	AUS	4:17.1
1960	USA	4:08.9
1964	USA	4:03.8
1968	USA	4:02.5
1972	USA	3:55.19
1976	USA	3:44.82
1980	GDR	3:42.71
1984	USA	3:43.43
1988	GDR	3:40.63

4x100m Medley Relay

1960	USA	4:41.1
1964	USA	4:33.9
1968	USA	4:28.3
1972	USA	4:20.75
1976	GDR	4:07.95
1980	GDR	4:06.67
1984	USA	4:08.34
1988	GDR	4:03.74

DIVING

MEN

Springboard

1908	Albert Zurner	GER	85.5
1912	Paul Gunther	GER	79.23
1920	Louis Kuehn	USA	675.4
1924	Albert White	USA	696.4
1928	Pete Desjardins	USA	185.04
1932	Michael Galitzen	USA	161.38
1936	Richard Degener	USA	163.57
1948	Bruce Harlan	USA	163.64
1952	David Browning	USA	205.29
1956	Robert Clotworthy	USA	159.56
1960	Gary Tobian	USA	170.00
1964	Kenneth Sitzberger	USA	159.90
1968	Bernard Wrightson	USA	170.15
1972	Vladimir Vasin	URS	594.09
1976	Philip Boggs	USA	619.05
1980	Alexsandr Portnov	URS	905.025
1984	Greg Louganis	USA	754.41
1988	Greg Louganis	USA	730.80

Highboard

1904	George Sheldon	USA	12.66
1906	Gottlob Walz	GER	156.00
1908	Hjalmar Johansson	SWE	83.75
1912	Erik Adlerz	SWE	73.94
1920	Clarence Pinkston	USA	100.67
1924	Albert White	USA	97.46
1928	Pete Desjardins	USA	98.74
1932	Harold Smith	USA	124.80
1936	Marshall Wayne	USA	113.58
1948	Samuel Lee	USA	130.05
1952	Samuel Lee	USA	156.28
1956	Joaquin Capilla Perez	MEX	152.44
1960	Robert Webster	USA	165.56
1964	Robert Webster	USA	148.58
1968	Klaus Dibaisi	ITA	164.18
1972	Klaus Dibiasi	ITA	504.12
1976	Klaus Dibiasi	ITA	600.51
1980	Falk Hoffmann	GDR	835.650
1984	Greg Louganis	USA	710.91
1988	Greg Louganis	USA	638.61

WOMEN

Springboard

1920	Aileen Riggin	USA	539.9
1924	Elizabeth Becker	USA	474.5
1928	Helen Meany	USA	78.62
1932	Georgia Coleman	USA	87.52
1936	Marjorie Gestring	USA	89.27
1948	Victoria Draves	USA	108.74
1952	Patricia McCormick	USA	147.30
1956	Patricia McCormick	USA	142.36
1960	Ingrid Kramer	GER	155.81
1964	Ingrdi Kramer-Engel	GER	145.00
1968	Sue Gossick	USA	150.77
1972	Micki King	USA	450.03
1976	Jennifer Chandler	USA	506.19
1980	Irina Kalinina	URS	725.910
1984	Sylvie Bernier	CAN	530.70
1988	Gao Min	CHN	580.23

Highboard

1912	Greta Johansson	SWE	39.9
1920	Stefani Fryland-Clausen	DEN	34.6
1924	Caroline Smith	USA	10.5
1928	Elizabeth Pinkston	USA	31.6
1932	Dorothy Poynton	USA	40.26
1936	Dorotny Poynton-Hill	USA	33.93
1948	Victoria Draves	USA	68.87
1952	Patricia McCormick	USA	79.37
1956	Patricia McCormick	USA	84.85
1960	Ingrid Kramer	GER	91.28
1964	Lesley Bush	USA	99.80
1968	Milena Duchkova	TCH	109.59
1972	Ulrika Knape	SWE	390.00
1976	Elena Vaytsekhovskaya	URS	406.59
1980	Martina Jaschke	GDR	596.250
1984	Zhou Jihong	CHN	435.51
1988	Xu Yanmei	CHN	445.20

SYNCHRONISED SWIMMING

Solo

1984	Tracie Ruiz	USA	198.467
1988	Carolyn Waldo	CAN	200.150

Duet

1984		USA	195.584
1988		CAN	197.717

PAST GOLD MEDALLISTS

WATERPOLO

1900	GBR
1904	USA
1908	GBR
1912	GBR
1920	GBR
1924	FRA
1928	GER
1932	HUN
1936	HUN
1948	ITA
1952	HUN
1956	HUN
1960	ITA
1964	HUN
1968	YUG
1972	URS
1976	HUN
1980	URS
1984	YUG
1988	YUG

TABLE TENNIS

MEN
Singles

1988	Yoo Nam-Kyu	KOR

Doubles

1988		CHN

WOMEN
Singles

1988	Chen Jing	CHN

Doubles

1988		KOR

TENNIS

MEN
Singles

1896	John Boland	GBR
1900	Hugh Doherty	GBR
1904	Beals Wright	USA
1906	Max Decugis	FRA
1908	Josiah Ritchie	GBR
1908*	Wentworth Gore	GBR
1912	Charles Winslow	SAF
1912*	Andre Gobert	FRA
1920	Louis Raymond	SAF
1924	Vicent Richards	USA
1988	Miloslav Mecir	TCH

Doubles

1896		GBR/GER
1900		GBR
1904		USA
1906		FRA
1908		GBR
1908*		GBR
1912		SAF
1912*		FRA
1920		GBR
1924		USA
1988		USA

Mixed Doubles

1900		GBR
1906		FRA
1912		GER
1912*		GBR
1920		FRA
1924		USA

WOMEN
Singles

1900	Charlotte Cooper	GBR
1906	Esmee Simiriotou	GRE
1908	Dorothea Chambers	GBR
1908*	Gwen Eastlake-Smith	GBR
1912	Marguerite Broquedis	FRA
1912*	Ethel Hannam	GBR
1920	Suzanne Lenglen	FRA
1924	Helen Wills	USA
1988	Steffi Graf	FRG

Doubles

1920		GBR
1924		USA
1988		USA

*   Indoor tournaments

VOLLEYBALL

MEN

1964	URS
1968	URS
1972	JPN
1976	POL
1980	URS
1984	USA
1988	USA

WOMEN

1964	JPN
1968	URS
1972	URS
1976	JPN
1980	URS
1984	CHN
1988	URS

WEIGHTLIFTING

Flyweight	**-52kg**		
1972	Zygmunt Smalcerz	POL	337.5 kg
1976	Aleksandr Voronin	URS	242.5kg
1980	Kanybek Osmonoliev	URS	245kg
1984	Zeng Gyogiang	CHN	235kg
1988	Sevdalin Marinov	BUL	270kg
Bantamweight-56kg			
1948	Joseph de Pietro	USA	307.5kg
1952	Ivan Udodov	URS	315kg
1956	Charles Vinci	USA	342.5kg
1960	Charles Vinci	USA	345kg
1964	Aleksey Vakhoni	URS	357.5kg
1968	Mohammad Nassiri	IRN	367.5kg
1972	Imre Foldi	HUN	377.5kg
1976	Norair Nuikyan	BUL	262.5kg
1980	Daniel Nunez	CUB	275kg
1984	Wu Shude	CHN	267.5kg
1988	Oxen Mirzoyan	URS	292.5kg

Featherweight-60kg

1920	Frans de Haes	BEL	220kg
1924*	Pierino Gabetti	ITA	402.5kg
1928	Franz Andrysek	AUT	287.5kg
1932	Raymond Suvigny	FRA	287.5kg
1936	Anthony Terlazzo	USA	312.5kg
1948	Mahmoud Fayad	EGY	332.5kg
1952	Rafael Chimishkyan	URS	337.5kg
1956	Isaac Berger	USA	352.5kg
1960	Yevgeniy Minayev	URS	372.5kg
1964	Yoshinobu Miyake	JPN	397.5kg
1968	Yoshinobu Miyake	JPN	392.5kg
1972	Norair Nurikyan	BUL	402.5kg
1976	Nikolai Kolesnikov	URS	285kg
1980	Viktor Mazin	URS	290kg
1984	Chen Weigiang	CHN	282.5kg
1988	Naim Suleymanoglu	TUR	342.5kg

Lightweight -67.5kg

1920	Alfred Neuland	EST	257.5kg
1924	Edmond Decottignies	FRA	440kg
1928	Kurt Helbig	GER	322.5kg
	Hans Haas	AUT	322.5kg
1932	Rene Duverger	FRA	325kg
1936	Anwar Mohammed Mesbah	EGY	342.5kg
	Robert Fein	AUT	342.5kg
1948	Ibrahim Shams	EGY	360kg
1952	Tommy Kono	USA	362.5kg
1956	Igor Rybak	URS	380kg
1960	Viktor Bushuyev	URS	397.5kg
1964	Waldemar Baszanowski	POL	432.5kg
1968	Waldemar Baszanowski	POL	437.5kg
1972	Mukharbi Kirzhinov	URS	460kg
1976	Pyotr Korol	URS	305kg
1980	Yanko Rusev	BUL	342.5kg
1984	Yao Jingyuan	CHN	320kg
1988	Joachim Kunz	GDR	340kg

Middleweight-75kg

1920	Henri Gance	FRA	245kg
1924	Carlo Galimberti	ITA	492.5kg
1928	Roger Francois	FRA	335kg
1932	Rudolf Isamay	GER	345kg
1936	Khadr El Thouni	EGY	387.5kg
1948	Frank Spellman	USA	390kg
1952	Peter George	USA	400kg
1956	Fyodor Boganovski	URS	420kg
1960	Aleksandr Kurinov	URS	437.5kg
1964	Hans Zdrazila	TCH	445kg
1968	Viktor Kurentsov	URS	475kg
1972	Yordan Bikov	BUL	485kg
1976	Yordan Bikov	BUL	335kg
1980	Asen Zlatev	BUL	360kg
1984	Karl-Heinz Radschinsky	FRG	340kg
1988	Borislav Guidkov	BUL	375kg

Light-Heavyweight-82.5kg

1920	Ernest Cadine	FRA	290kg
1924*	Charles Rigourlot	FRA	502.5kg
1928	Said Nossier	EGY	355kg
1932	Louis Hostin	FRA	372.5kg
1936	Louis Hostin	FRA	372.5kg
1948	Stanley Stancyk	USA	417.5kg
1952	Trofim Lomakin	URS	417.5kg
1956	Tommy Konc	USA	447.5kg
1960	Ireneusz Palmski	POL	442.5kg
1964	Rudolf Plukfeider	URS	475kg
1968	Boris Selitshky	URS	485kg
1972	Leif Jenssen	NOR	507.5kg
1976	Valeriy Shary	URS	365kg

1980	Yurik Vardanyan	URS	400kg
1984	Petre Becheru	ROM	355kg
1988	Israil Arsamakov	URS	377.5kg

Middle-Heavyweight-90kg

1952	Norbert Schemansky	USA	445kg
1956	Arkadiy Vorobyev	URS	462.5kg
1960	Arkadiy Vorobyev	URS	472.5kg
1964	Vladimir Golovanov	URS	487.5kg
1968	Kaarlo Kangasniemi	FIN	517.5kg
1972	Andon Nikolov	BUL	525kg
1976	David Rigert	URS	382.5kg
1980	Peter Baczako	HUN	377.5kg
1984	Nicu Vlad	ROM	392.5kg
1988	Anatoly Khrapatiy	URS	412.5kg

Up to 100kg

1980	Ota Zaremba	TCH	395kg
1984	Rolf Milser	FRG	385kg
1988	Pavel Kuznetsov	URS	425kg

Heavyweight-110kg

1896[1]	Launceston Eliot	GBR	71kg
1896[2]	Viggo Jensen	DEN	111.5kg
1904[3]	Oscar Osthoff	USA	48pts
1904[2]	Perikles Kakousis	GRE	111.58kg
1906[1]	Josef Steinbach	AUT	76.55kg
1906[2]	Dimitrios Tofalos	GRE	142.5kg
1920	Filippo Bottino	ITA	270kg
1924	Giuseppe Tonani	ITA	517.5kg
1928	Josef Stassbergr	GER	372.5kg
1932	Jaroslav Skobla	TCH	380kg
1936	Josef Manger	AUT	410kg
1948	John Davis	USA	452.2kg
1952	John Davis	USA	460kg
1956	Paul Anderson	USA	500kg
1960	Yuriy Vlasov	URS	537.5kg
1964	Leonid Zhabotinsky	URS	572.5kg
1968	Leonid Zhabotinsky	URS	572.5kg
1972	Jan Talts	URS	580kg
1976	Yuriy Zaitsev	URS	385kg
1980	Leonid Taranenko	URS	422.5kg
1984	Norberto Oberburger	ITA	390kg
1988	Yuriy Zakharevich	URS	455kg

1 one-hand lift
2 two-hand lift
3 dumbell lift

Super-Heavyweight+110kg

1972	Vasiliy Alexeyev	URS	640kg
1976	Vasiliy Alexeyev	URS	440kg
1980	Sultan Rakhmanov	URS	440kg
1984	Dinko Lukin	AUS	412.5kg
1988	Alexsandr Kurlovich	URS	462.5kg

* aggregate of 5 lifts

WRESTLING

Freestyle -	**Light Flyweight**	**-48 kg**	
1904	Robert Curry		USA
1972	Roman Dmitriev		URS
1976	Khassan Issaev		BUL
1980	Claudio Pollio		ITA
1984	Robert Weaver		USA
1988	Takashi Kobayashi		JPN
Freestyle-	**Flyweight**	**-52kg**	
1904	George Mehnert		USA
1948	Lennart Vitala		FIN
1952	Hasan Gemici		TUR
1956	Mirian Tsalkalamanidze		URS
1960	Ahmet Bilek		TUR

Year	Name	Country		Year	Name	Country
1964	Yoshikatsu Yoshida	JPN		1932	Jack van Bebber	USA
1968	Shigeo Nakata	JPN		1936	Frank Lewis	USA
1972	Kiyomi Kato	JPN		1948	Yasar Dogu	TUR
1976	Yuji Takada	JPN		1952	William Smith	USA
1980	Anatoliy Beloglazov	URS		1956	Mitsuo Ikeda	JPN
1984	Saban Trstena	YUG		1960	Douglas Blubaugh	USA
1988	Mitsuru Sato	JPN		1964	Ismail Ogan	TUR
Freestyle - Bantamweight -57kg				1968	Mahmut Atalay	TUR
1904	Isidor Niflot	USA		1972	Wayne Wells	USA
1908	George Mehnert	USA		1976	Jiichiro Date	JPN
1924	Kustaa Pihlajamaki	FIN		1980	Valentin Raitchev	BUL
1928	Kaarlo Makinen	FIN		1984	David Schultz	USA
1932	Robert Pearce	USA		1988	Kenneth Monday	USA
1936	Odon Zombori	HUN		**Freestyle Middleweight -82kg**		
1948	Nasuk Akar	TUR		1908	Stanley Bacon	GBR
1952	Shohachi Ishii	JPN		1920	Eino Leino	FIN
1956	Mustafa Dagistanli	TUR		1924	Fritz Hagmann	SUI
1960	Terrence McCann	USA		1928	Ernst Kyburz	SUI
1964	Yojiro Uetake	JPN		1932	Ivar Johansson	SWE
1968	Yojiro Uetake	JPN		1936	Emile Poilve	FRA
1972	Hideaki Yanagide	JPN		1948	Glen Brand	USA
1976	Vladimir Yumin	URS		1952	David Tsimakuridze	URS
1980	Sergey Beloglazov	URS		1956	Nikola Stantschev	BUL
1984	Hideyaki Tomiyama	JPN		1960	Hasan Gungor	TUR
1988	Sergey Beloglazov	URS		1964	Prodan Gardschev	BUL
Freestyle - Featherweight -62kg				1968	Boris Gurevich	URS
1904	Benjamin Bradshaw	USA		1972	Leven Tediashvili	URS
1908	George Dole	USA		1976	John Peterson	USA
1920	Charles Ackerly	USA		1980	Ismail Abilov	BUL
1924	Robin Reed	USA		1984	Mark Schultz	USA
1928	Allie Morrison	USA		1988	Han Myung-Woo	KOR
1932	Hermanni Pihajamaki	FIN		**Freestyle Light-Heavyweight -90kg**		
1936	Kustaa Pihlajamaki	FIN		1920	Anders Larsson	SWE
1948	Gazanfer Bilge	TUR		1924	John Spellman	USA
1952	Bayram Sit	TUR		1928	Thure Sjostedt	SWE
1956	Shozo Sasahara	JPN		1932	Peter Mehringer	USA
1960	Mustafa Dagistanli	TUR		1936	Knut Fridell	SWE
1964	Osamu Watanabe	JPN		1948	Henry Wittenberg	USA
1968	Masaaki Kaneko	JPN		1952	Wiking Palm	SWE
1972	Zagalav Adbulbekov	URS		1956	Gholam Reza Tahkti	IRN
1976	Yang Jung-Mo	KOR		1960	Ismet Atli	TUR
1980	Magomedgasan Abushev	URS		1964	Aleksandr Medved	URS
1984	Randy Lewis	USA		1968	Ahmet Ayik	TUR
1988	John Smith	USA		1972	Ben Peterson	USA
Freestyle Lightweight -68kg				1976	Levan Tedishvili	URS
1904	Otton Boehm	USA		1980	Sanasar Oganesyan	URS
1908	George de Relwyskow	GBR		1984	Ed Banach	USA
1920	Kalle Anttila	FIN		1988	Makharbek Khadartsev	URS
1924	Russell Vis	USA		**Freestyle Heavyweight -100kg**		
1928	Osvald Kapp	EST		1904	Bernhuff Hansen	USA
1932	Charles Pancome	FRA		1908	George O'Reilly	GBR
1936	Karoly Karpati	HUN		1920	Robert Roth	SUI
1948	Celal Atik	TUR		1924	Harry Steele	USA
1952	Olle Anderberg	SWE		1928	Johan Richtoff	SWE
1956	Emamali Habibi	IRN		1932	Johan Richtoff	SWE
1960	Shelby Wilson	USA		1936	Kristjan Palusalu	EST
1964	Enyu Valtschev	BUL		1948	Gyula Bobis	HUN
1968	Abdollah Movahed Ardabili	IRN		1952	Arsen Mekoksihvili	URS
1972	Dan Gable	USA		1956	Hamit Kaplan	TUR
1976	Pavel Pinigin	URS		1960	Wilfried Dietrich	GER
1980	Saipulla Absaidov	URS		1964	Aleksandr Ivanitsky	URS
1984	You In-Tak	KOR		1968	Aleksandr Medved	URS
1988	Arsen Fadzayev	URS		1972	Ivan Yaragin	URS
Freestyle Welterweight -74kg				1976	Ivan Yaragin	URS
1904	Charles Erikson	USA		1980	Ilya Mate	URS
1924	Hermann Gehri	SUI		1984	Lou Banach	USA
1928	Arvo Haavisto	FIN		1988	Vasile Puscasu	ROM

Freestyle	Super-Heavyweight	+100kg
1972	Aleksandr Medved	URS
1976	Sosian Andiev	URS
1980	Sosian Andiev	URS
1984	Bruce Baumgartner	USA
1988	David Gobedjichvili	URS
Greco-Roman	**Light-Flyweight**	**-48kg**
1972	Gheorghe Berceanu	ROM
1976	Aleksey Shumakov	URS
1980	Zaksylik Ushkempirov	URS
1984	Vincenzo Mazenza	ITA
1988	Vincenzo Mazenza	ITA
Greco-Roman	**Flyweight**	**-52kg**
1948	Pietro Lombardi	ITA
1952	Boris Gurevich	URS
1956	Nikolai Solovyov	URS
1960	Dumitru Piryulescu	ROM
1964	Tsutomu Hanahara	JPN
1968	Petar Kirov	BUL
1972	Petar Kirov	BUL
1976	Vitaliy Konstantinov	URS
1980	Vakhtang Blagidze	URS
1984	Atsuji Miyahara	JPN
1988	Jon Ronningen	NOR
Greco-Roman	**Bantamweight**	**- 57kg**
1924	Eduard Putsep	EST
1928	Kurt Leucht	GER
1932	Jakob Brendel	GER
1936	Marton Lorincz	HUN
1948	Kurt Pettersen	SWE
1952	Imre Hodos	HUN
1956	Konstantin Vyrupayev	URS
1960	Oleg Karavayev	URS
1964	Masamitsu Ichiguchi	JPN
1968	Janos Varga	HUN
1972	Rustem Kazakov	URS
1976	Pertti Ukkola	FIN
1980	Shamil Serikov	URS
1984	Pasquale Passarelli	FRG
1988	Andras Sike	HUN
Greco-Roman	**Featherweight**	**-63kg**
1912	Kaarlo Koskelo	FIN
1920	Oskari Friman	FIN
1924	Kallo Antila	FIN
1928	Voldemar Vali	EST
1932	Giovanni Gozzi	ITA
1936	Yasar Erkan	TUR
1948	Mehmet Oktav	TUR
1952	Yakov Punkin	URS
1956	Rauno Makinen	FIN
1960	Muzahir Sille	TUR
1964	Imre Polyak	HUN
1968	Roman Rurua	URS
1972	Gheorghi Markov	BUL
1976	Kazimierz Lipien	POL
1980	Stilianos Migiakis	GRE
1984	Kim Weon-Kee	KOR
1988	Kamandear Madjidov	URS
Greco-Roman	**Lightweight**	**-68kg**
1906	Rudolf Watz	AUT
1908	Enrico Porro	ITA
1912	Eemil Ware	FIN
1920	Eemil Ware	FIN
1924	Oskari Friman	FIN
1928	Lajos Keresztes	HUN
1932	Erik Malmberg	SWE

1936	Lauri Koskela	FIN
1948	Gustaf Freij	SWE
1952	Shazam Safin	URS
1956	Kyosti Lentonen	FIN
1960	Avtandil Koridza	URS
1964	Kazim Avvaz	TUR
1968	Munji Mumermura	JPN
1972	Shamii Khisamutdinov	URS
1976	Suren Naibandyan	URS
1980	Stefan Rusu	ROM
1984	Vlado Lisjak	YUG
1988	Levon Djoulfalakian	URS
Greco-Roman	**Welterweight**	**-74kg**
1932	Ivar Johansson	SWE
1936	Rudolf Svedberg	SWE
1948	Gosta Andersson	SWE
1952	Miklos Szilvasi	HUN
1956	Mithat Bayrak	TUR
1960	Mithat Bayrak	TUR
1964	Anatoliy Kolesov	URS
1968	Rudolf Vesper	GDR
1972	Vitezslav Macha	TCH
1976	Anatoliy Bykov	URS
1980	Ferenc Kocsis	HUN
1984	Jonko Salomaki	FIN
1988	Kim Young-Nam	KOR
Greco-Roman	**Middleweight**	**-82kg**
1906	Verner Weckman	FIN
1908	Frithiof Martensson	SWE
1912	Claes Johansson	SWE
1920	Carl Westergren	SWE
1924	Eduard Weterlund	SWE
1928	Vaino Kokkinen	FIN
1932	Vaino Kokkinen	FIN
1936	Ivar Johansson	SWE
1948	Axel Gronberg	SWE
1952	Axel Gronberg	SWE
1956	Givi Kartiziya	URS
1960	Dimiter Dobrev	BUL
1964	Branislav Simic	YUG
1968	Lothar Metz	GDR
1972	Csaba Hegedus	HUN
1976	Momir Petkovic	YUG
1980	Gennadiy Korban	URS
1984	In Draica	ROM
1988	Mikhail Mamiachvili	URS
Greco-Roman	**Light-Heavyweight**	**-90kg**
1908	Verner Weckman	FIN
1912	-¹	
1920	Claes Johansson	SWE
1924	Carl Westergren	SWE
1928	Ibrahim Moustafa	EGY
1932	Rudolf Svensson	SWE
1936	Axel Cadler	SWE
1948	Karl-Erik Nilsson	SWE
1952	Kaelpo Grondahl	FIN
1956	Valentin Nikolayev	URS
1960	Tevfik Kis	TUR
1964	Boyan Radev	BUL
1968	Boyan Radev	BUL
1972	Valeriy Rezantsev	URS
1976	Valeriy Rezantsev	URS
1980	Norbert Nottny	HUN
1984	Steven Fraser	USA
1988	Atanas Komchev	BUL

¹ Ahlgren (SWE) and Bohling (FIN) declared equal second after nine hours of wrestling

Greco-Roman	Heavyweight	-100kg
1896	Carl Schumann	GER
1906	Soren Jensen	DEN
1908	Richard Weisz	HUN
1912	Yrjo Saarela	FIN
1920	Adolf Lindfors	FIN
1924	Henri Deglane	FRA
1928	Rudolf Svensson	SWE
1932	Carl Westergren	SWE
1936	Kristian Palusalu	EST
1948	Ahmet Kirecci	TUR
1952	Johannes Kotkas	URS
1956	Anatoliy Parfeno	URS
1960	Ivan Bogdan	URS
1964	Istvan Kozma	HUN
1968	Istvan Kozma	HUN
1972	Nicolae Matinescu	ROM
1976	Nikolai Bolboshin	URS
1980	Gheorghi Raikov	BUL
1984	Vasile Andrei	ROM
1988	Andrzej Wronski	POL

Greco-Roman	Super-Heavyweight	+100kg
1972	Anatoliy Roschin	URS
1976	Aleksandr Kolchinsky	URS
1980	Aleksandr Kolchinsky	URS
184	Jeffrey Blatnick	USA
1988	Aleksandr Kareline	URS

YACHTING

MEN

Finn

1920[1]	Franciscus Hin	Johannes Hin	HOL
1920[2]	F A Richards	T Hedberg	GBR
1924[3]	Leon Huybrechts	BEL	
1928[4]	Sven Thorell	SWE	
1932[5]	Jacques Lebrun	FRA	
1936[6]	Daniel Kagchelland	HOL	
1948[7]	Paul Elvstrom	DEN	
1952[8]	Paul Elvstrom	DEN	
1956	Paul Elvstrom	DEN	
1960	Paul Elvstrom	DEN	
1964	Willi Kuhweide	GER	
1968	Valentin Mankin	URS	
1972	Serge Maury	URS	
1976	Jochen Schumann	GDR	
1980	Esko Rechardt	FIN	
1984	Russell Coutts	NZL	
1988	Jose Luis Doreste	ESP	

[1] 12-foot dinghy, no bronze medal
[2] 18-foot dinghy no silver and bronze medals.
[3] Meulan class 12-foot dinghy.
[4] International 12-foot class.
[5] Snowbird class.
[6] International Olympia class.
[7] Firefly class.
[8] Since 1952 Finn class.

Boardsailing Class

1984	Steve Van Den Berg	HOL
1988	Bruce Kendall	NZL

International Soling

1972	USA
1976	DEN
1980	DEN
1984	USA
1988	GDR

International 470

1976	FRG
1980	BRA
1984	ESP
1988	FRA

International Tornado

1976	GBR
1980	BRA
1984	NZL
1988	FRA

International Star

1932	USA
1936	GER
1948	USA
1952	ITA
1956	USA
1960	URS
1964	BAH
1968	USA
1972	AUS
1980	URS
1984	USA
1988	GBR

Flying Dutchman

1956[1]	NZL
1960	NOR
1964	NZL
1968	GBR
1972	GBR
1976	FRG
1980	ESP
1984	USA
1988	DEN

WOMEN

International 470

1988	USA

DAILY PROGRAMME OF EVENTS

All times given are local **Barcelona** times. Barcelona is one hour ahead of the **UK**.

19.00	Football	Prelims	Barcelona
21.00	Football	Prelims	Sabadell, Zaragoza, Valencia

10.00	Opening ceremony		Montjuic

08.30	Shooting	10m air rifle prelims **(w)**	Camp de Tir
09.00	Cycling	100km team time trial **FINAL (m)**	Circuit de l'A-17
	Modern pentathlon	Fencing	Palau de la Metal-lurgia
	Shooting	Skeet prelims **(o)**	Camp de Tir
09.30	Basketball	Prelims **(m)**	Badalona
10.00	Diving	Platform prelims **(w)**	Piscina Montjuic
	Hockey	Pool **(m)**	Terrassa
	Swimming	100m free hts **(w)**	Picornell
		100m breast hts **(m)**	
		400m medley hts **(w)**	
		200m free hts **(m)**	
	Wrestling (Greco-roman)	52, 68 & 100kg elim	INEFC, Montjuic
10.30	Baseball	Prelims	Villadecans & l'Hospitalet
	Shooting	10m air rifle **FINAL (w)**	Camp de Tir
	Volleyball	Prelims **(m)**	Palau d'Esports
11.30	Basketball	Prelims **(m)**	Badalona
	Gymnastics	Team **(w)**	Sant Jordi
	Shooting	50m free pistol prelims **(m)**	Camp de Tir
12.30	Weightlifting	Up to 52kg Grp C	Pavello L'Espanya Industrial
13.00	Boxing	Prelims	Pavello Club Joventut
	Volleyball	Prelims **(m)**	Palau d'Esports
14.30	Basketball	Prelims **(m)**	Badalona
15.00	Diving	Platform prelims **(w)**	Piscina Montjuic
	Shooting	50m free pistol **FINAL (m)**	Camp de Tir
	Volleyball	Prelims **(m)**	Pavello Vall d'Hebron
	Weightlifting	Up to 52kg Grp B	Pavello L'Espanya Industrial
16.30	Basketball	Prelims **(m)**	Badalona
17.00	Hockey	Pool **(m)**	Terrassa
17.00	Wrestling (Greco-roman)	52, 68 & 100kg elim	INEFC, Montjuic
17.30	Cycling	Ind road race **FINAL (w)**	Sant Sadurni d'Anoia
17.30	Volleyball	Prelims **(m)**	Pavello Vall d'Hebron
18.00	Baseball	Prelims	Villadecans & l'Hospitalet

DAILY PROGRAMME OF EVENTS

All times given are local Barcelona times. Barcelona is one hour ahead of the UK.

18.00	Swimming	100m free **FINAL (w)**	Picornell
		100m breast **FINAL (m)**	
		400m medley **FINAL (w)**	
		200m free **FINAL (m)**	
18.30	Weightlifting	Up to 52kg Grp C **FINAL**	Pavello L'Espanya Industrial
19.00	Boxing	Prelims	Pavello Club Joventut
	Football	Prelims	Zaragoza & Sabadell
	Hockey	Pool **(m)**	Terrassa
	Volleyball	Prelims **(m)**	Palau d'Esports
20.00	Gymnastics	Team **(w)**	Sant Jordi
20.30	Basketball	Prelims **(m)**	Badalona
21.00	Football	Prelims	Barcelona & Valencia
21.30	Volleyball	Prelims **(m)**	Palau d'Esports
22.30	Basketball	Prelims **(m)**	Badalona

08.00	Rowing	Coxless fours hts **(w)**	Banyoles
		Double sculls hts **(w)**	
		Coxless pairs hts **(w)**	
		Coxed fours hts **(m)**	
		Double sculls hts **(m)**	
		Coxless pairs hts **(m)**	
		Single sculls hts **(m)**	
08.30	Equestrian	3-day event - dressage **(o)**	Real Club de Polo
09.00	Shooting	Skeet prelims **(o)**	Camp de Tir
		25m sport pistol prelims **(w)**	Camp de Tir
	Shooting	10m air rifle prelims **(m)**	Camp de Tir
09.30	Basketball	Prelims **(m)**	Badalona
	Swimming	100m fly hts **(m)**	Picornell
		200m free hts **(w)**	
		400m medley hts **(m)**	
		200m breast hts **(w)**	
		4x200m free relay hts **(m)**	
10.00	Handball	Prelims **(m)**	Palau d'Esports, Granollers
	Wrestling (Greco-roman)	48, 52, 68, 74, 100, 130kg elims	INEFC, Montjuic
11.00	Gymnastics	Team **(m)**	Sant Jordi
11.30	Basketball	Prelims **(m)**	Badalona
	Handball	Prelims **(m)**	Palau d'Esports, Granollers
12.00	Modern pentathlon	Swimming	Picornell

167

DAILY PROGRAMME OF EVENTS

All times given are local Barcelona times. Barcelona is one hour ahead of the UK.

12.30	Shooting	10m air rifle **FINAL (m)**	Camp de Tir
	Weightlifting	Up to 56kg Grp C	Pavello L'Espanya Industrial
13.00	Boxing	Prelims	Pavello Club Joventut
	Yachting	Race 1	Port Olimpic
14.00	Shooting	25m sport pistol **FINAL (w)**	Camp de Tir
14.30	Basketball	Prelims **(m)**	Badalona
	Handball	Prelims **(m)**	Palau d'Esports, Granollers
15.00	Baseball	Prelims	Viladecans
	Diving	Platform **FINAL (w)**	Piscina Montjuic
	Gymnastics	Team **(m)**	Sant Jordi
	Weightlifting	Up to 56kg Grp B	Pavello L'Espanya Industrial
15.30	Equestrian	3-day event - dressage **(o)**	Real Club de Polo
16.00	Baseball	Prelims	l'Hospitalet
	Handball	Prelims **(m)**	Palau d'Esports, Granollers
16.30	Basketball	Prelims **(m)**	Badalona
	Judo	Heavyweight prelims & repechage **(m+w)**	Palau Blaugrana
	Modern pentathlon	Shooting	Camp de Tir
17.00	Hockey	Pool **(w)**	Terrassa
	Wrestling (Greco-roman)	48, 52, 68, 74, 100, 130kg elims	INEFC, Montjuic
18.00	Cycling	Ind pursuit elim Rd 1 **(m)**	Velodrom
	Swimming	100m fly **FINAL (m)**	Picornell
		200m free **FINAL (w)**	
		400m medley **FINAL (m)**	
		200m breast **FINAL (w)**	
		4x200m free **FINAL (m)**	
18.30	Weightlifting	Up to 56kg Grp A **FINAL**	Pavello L'Espanya Industrial
19.00	Boxing	Prelims	Pavello Club Joventut
	Football	Prelims	Zaragoza, Sabadell
	Handball	Prelims **(m)**	Palau d'Esports, Granollers
	Hockey	Pool **(w)**	Terrassa
20.00	Cycling	1km time trial **FINAL (m)**	Velodrom
	Gymnastics	Team **(m)**	Sant Jordi
20.30	Basketball	Prelims **(m)**	Badalona
	Handball	Prelims **(m)**	Palau d'Esports, Granollers
21.00	Baseball	Prelims	Viladecans & l'Hospitalet
	Football	Prelims	Barcelona, Valencia
21.30	Judo	Heavyweight s/f & **FINAL (m+w)**	Palau Blaugrana
	Basketball	Prelims **(m)**	Badalona

DAILY PROGRAMME OF EVENTS

All times given are local Barcelona times. Barcelona is one hour ahead of the UK.

TUESDAY, 28TH JULY 1992

08.00	Rowing	Single sculls hts (w)	Banyoles
		Quadruple sculls hts (w)	
		Eights hts (w)	
		Coxed pairs hts (m)	
		Coxless fours hts (m)	
		Quadruple sculls hts (m)	
		Eights hts (m)	
08.30	Equestrian	3 day event - dressage (o)	Real Club de Polo
09.00	Shooting	Skeet s/f (o)	Camp de Tir
		10m air pistol prelims (m)	Camp de Tir
10.00	Badminton	Singles & doubles Rd 1 (m+w)	Pavello Mar Bella
	Cycling	Sprint elim Rd 1 (m+w)	Velodrom
	Diving	Springbd. prelims (m)	Piscina Montjuic
	Hockey	Pool (m)	Terrassa
	Swimming	400m free hts (w)	Picornell
		100m free hts (m)	
		100m back hts (w)	
		200m back hts (m)	
		4x100m free relay hts (w)	
	Tennis	Singles Rd 1 (m+w)	Vall d'Hebron
	Wrestling (Greco-roman)	48, 52, 57, 62, 68, 74, 82, 90, 100, 130kg elim	INEFC, Montjuic
10.30	Volleyball	Prelims (m)	Palau Esports
11.00	Modern pentathlon	Cross country	Circuit de Cros
11.30	Gymnastics	Team (w)	Sant Jordi
12.30	Shooting	10m air pistol FINAL (m)	Camp de Tir
	Weightlifting	Up to 60kg Grp C	Pavello L'Espanya Industrial
13.00	Boxing	Prelims	Pavello Club Joventut
	Volleyball	Prelims (m)	Palau Esports
	Yachting	Race 2 (m+w) & (o)	Port Olimpic
14.00	Shooting	Skeet FINAL (o)	Camp de Tir
15.00	Baseball	Prelims	Viladecans
	Diving	Springbd prelims (m)	Piscina Montjuic
	Volleyball	Prelims (m)	Pavello Vall d'Hebron
	Weightlifting	Up to 60kg Grp B	Pavello L'Espanya Industrial
16.00	Baseball	Prelims	l'Hospitalet
16.30	Judo	Half-heavyweight prelims & repechage (m+w)	Palau Blaugrana
17.00	Badminton	Singles & doubles Rd 1 (m+w)	Pavello Mar Bella
	Hockey	Pool (m)	Terrassa
	Wrestling (Greco-roman)	57, 62, 74, 82, 90kg. elim	INEFC, Montjuic

DAILY PROGRAMME OF EVENTS

All times given are local Barcelona times. Barcelona is one hour ahead of the UK.

17.30	Volleyball	Prelims **(m)**	Pavello Vall d'Hebron
18.00	Cycling	Ind pursuit,sprint,ind points - elim **(m+w)**	Velodrom
	Swimming	400m free **FINAL (w)**	Picornell
		100m free **FINAL (m)**	
		100m back **FINAL (w)**	
		200m back **FINAL (m)**	
		4x100m free relay **FINAL (w)**	
18.30	Weightlifting	Up to 60kg Grp A **FINAL**	Pavello L'Espanya Industrial
19.00	Boxing	Prelims	Pavello Club Joventut
	Football	Prelims	Zaragoza & Sabadell
	Hockey	Pool **(m)**	Terrassa
	Volleyball	Prelims **(m)**	Palau Esports
	Wrestling (Greco-roman)	52, 68, 100kg **FINAL**	INEFC, Montjuic
20.00	Gymnastics	Team **FINAL (w)**	Sant Jordi
	Table tennis	Doubles groups **(m+w)**	Estacio del Nord
21.00	Baseball	Prelims	Viladecans & l'Hospitalet
	Football	Prelims	Barcelona & Valencia
21.30	Judo	Half-heavyweight s/f & **FINAL (m+w)**	Palau Blaugrana
	Volleyball	Prelims **(m)**	Palau Esports

08.00	Rowing	Coxless fours rep **(w)**	Banyoles
		Double sculls rep **(w)**	
		Coxless pairs rep **(w)**	
		Coxed fours rep **(m)**	
		Double sculls rep **(m)**	
		Coxless pairs rep **(m)**	
		Single sculls rep **(m)**	
08.30	Equestrian	3-day event - endurance **(o)**	El Circuit d'Hipica
09.00	Shooting	50m free rifle prelims **(m)**	
		25m rapid fire pistol prelims **(m)**	Camp de Tir
09.30	Basketball	Prelims **(m)**	Badalona
10.00	Badminton	Singles & doubles Rd 2 **(m+w)**	Pavello Mar Bella
	Handball	Prelims **(m)**	Palau d'Esports, Granollers
	Modern pentathlon	Riding	Real Club de Polo

DAILY PROGRAMME OF EVENTS

All times given are local Barcelona times. Barcelona is one hour ahead of the UK.

10.00	Swimming	400m free hts **(m)**	Picornell
		100m fly hts **(w)**	
		200m breast hts **(m)**	
		100m breast hts **(w)**	
		4x100m free relay hts **(m)**	
		800m free hts **(w)**	
	Table tennis	Singles groups **(w)**	Estacio del Nord
	Tennis	Singles Rd.1 **(m+w)**	Vall d'Hebron
	Wrestling (Greco-roman)	48, 57, 62, 74, 82, 90, 130kg elims	INEFC, Montjuic
10.30	Volleyball	Prelims **(w)**	Palau Esports
11.00	Gymnastics	Team **(m)**	Sant Jordi
11.30	Basketball	Prelims **(m)**	Badalona
	Handball	Prelims **(m)**	Palau d'Esports, Granollers
12.30	Shooting	50m free rifle **FINAL (m)**	Camp de Tir
	Weightlifting	Up to 67.5kg Grp C	Pavello L'Espanya Industrial
13.00	Boxing	Prelims	Pavello Club Joventut
	Volleyball	Prelims **(w)**	Palau Esports
	Yachting	Race 3	Port Olimpic
14.30	Basketball	Prelims **(m)**	Badalona
	Handball	Prelims **(m)**	Palau d'Esports, Granollers
15.00	Baseball	Prelims	Viladecans
	Diving	Springbd **FINAL (m)**	Piscina Montjuic
	Gymnastics	Team **(m)**	Sant Jordi
	Weightlifting	Up to 67.5kg Grp B	Pavello L'Espanya Industrial
16.00	Baseball	Prelims	l'Hospitalet
	Handball	Prelims **(m)**	Palau d'Esports, Granollers
16.30	Basketball	Prelims **(m)**	Badalona
	Judo	Middleweight prelims & repechage **(m+w)**	Palau Blaugrana
17.00	Badminton	Singles & doubles Rd 2 **(m+w)**	Pavello Mar Bella
	Hockey	Pool **(w)**	Terrassa
	Modern pentathlon	Riding	Real Club de Polo
	Wrestling (Greco-roman)	57, 62, 82, 90kg elim	INEFC, Montjuic
17.30	Rowing	Single sculls rep **(w)**	Banyoles
		Quadruple sculls rep **(w)**	
		Eights rep **(w)**	
		Coxed pairs rep **(m)**	
		Coxless fours rep **(m)**	
		Quadruple sculls rep **(m)**	
		Eights rep **(m)**	

DAILY PROGRAMME OF EVENTS

All times given are local Barcelona times. Barcelona is one hour ahead of the UK.

18.00	Cycling	Ind pursuit s/f **(m)**	Velodrom
		Sprint elim, repechage and q/f **(m+w)**	
	Swimming	400m free **FINAL (m)**	Picornell
		100m fly **FINAL (w)**	
		200m breast **FINAL (m)**	
		100m breast **FINAL (w)**	
		4x100m free relay **FINAL (m)**	
18.30	Weightlifting	Up to 67.5kg Grp A **FINAL**	Pavello L'Espanya Industrial
19.00	Boxing	Prelims	Pavello Club Joventut
	Football	Prelims	Zaragoza & Sabadell
	Handball	Prelims **(m)**	Palau d'Esports, Granollers
	Hockey	Pool **(w)**	Terrassa
19.00	Volleyball	Prelims **(w)**	Palau Esports
	Wrestling (Greco-roman)	48, 74, 130kg **FINAL**	INEFC, Montjuic
19.30	Cycling	Ind pursuit **FINAL (m)**	Velodrom
20.00	Gymnastics	Team **FINAL (m)**	Sant Jordi
	Table tennis	Doubles groups **(m+w)**	Estacio del Nord
20.30	Basketball	Prelims **(m)**	Badalona
	Handball	Prelims **(m)**	Palau d'Esports, Granollers
21.00	Baseball	Prelims	Viladecans & l'Hospitalet
	Football	Prelims	Barcelona & Valencia
21.30	Judo	Middleweight s/f & **FINAL (m+w)**	Palau Blaugrana
	Volleyball	Prelims **(w)**	Palau Esports
22.30	Basketball	Prelims **(m)**	Badalona

08.00	Rowing	Coxless fours s/f **(w)**	Banyoles
		Double sculls s/f **(w)**	
		Coxless pairs s/f **(w)**	
		Coxed fours s/f **(m)**	
		Double sculls s/f **(m)**	
		Coxless pairs s/f **(m)**	
		Single sculls s/f **(m+w)**	
09.00	Fencing	Ind foil prelims **(w)**	Palau Metal-lurgia
	Shooting	25m rapid fire pistol prelims **(m)**	Camp de Tir
		50m standard rifle prelims **(w)**	
	Table tennis	Singles groups **(m+w)**	Estacio del Nord
10.00	Badminton	Singles Rd 2 & doubles Rd 1 **(m+w)**	Pavello Mar Bella
	Handball	Prelims **(w)**	Palau d'Esports, Granollers

All times given are local Barcelona times. Barcelona is one hour ahead of the UK.

THURSDAY, 30TH JULY 1992

10.00	Hockey	Pool **(m)**	Terrassa
	Swimming	200m fly hts **(m)**	Picornell
		200m medley hts **(w)**	
		100m back hts **(m)**	
		4x100m medley relay hts **(w)**	
		50m free hts **(m)**	
		1500m free hts **(m)**	
	Tennis	Singles Rd 2 & doubles Rd 1 **(m+w)**	Vall d'Hebron
	Wrestling (Greco-roman)	57, 62, 82 & 90kg elims	INEFC, Montjuic
10.30	Volleyball	Prelims **(m)**	Palau Esports
11.00	Basketball	Prelims **(w)**	Badalona
11.30	Handball	Prelims **(w)**	Palau d'Esports, Granollers
12.30	Shooting	50m standard rifle **FINAL (w)**	Camp de Tir
	Weightlifting	Up to 75kg Grp C	Pavello L'Espanya Industrial
13.00	Basketball	Prelims **(w)**	Badalona
	Boxing	Prelims	Pavello Club Joventut
	Volleyball	Prelims **(m)**	Palau Esports
	Yachting	Race 4	Port Olimpic
14.00	Shooting	25m rapid fire pistol **FINAL (m)**	Camp de Tir
15.00	Handball	Prelims **(w)**	Palau d'Esports, Granollers
	Volleyball	Prelims **(m)**	Pavello Vall d'Hebron
	Weightlifting	Up to 75kg Grp B	Pavello L'Espanya Industrial
16.30	Handball	Prelims **(w)**	Palau d'Esports, Granollers
	Judo	Half-middleweight prelims & repechage **(m+w)**	Palau Blaugrana
17.00	Badminton	Singles Rd 2 & doubles Rd 1 **(m+w)**	Pavello Mar Bella
	Equestrian	3-day event - jumping **FINAL (o)**	Real Club de Polo
	Hockey	Pool **(m)**	Terrassa
	Wrestling (Greco-roman)	57, 62, 82 & 90kg **FINAL**	INEFC, Montjuic
17.30	Volleyball	Prelims **(m)**	Pavello Vall d'Hebron
18.00	Cycling	Team & ind pursuit elim & q/f **(m+w)**	Velodrom
		Sprint s/f **(m+w)**	
	Swimming	200m fly **FINAL (m)**	Picornell
		200m medley **FINAL (w)**	
		50m free **FINAL (m)**	
		800m free **FINAL (w)**	
		100m back **FINAL (m)**	
		4x100m medley relay **FINAL (w)**	
18.30	Weightlifting	Up to 75kg Grp A **FINAL**	Pavello L'Espanya Industrial
19.00	Boxing	Prelims	Pavello Club Joventut

DAILY PROGRAMME OF EVENTS

All times given are local Barcelona times. Barcelona is one hour ahead of the UK.

THURSDAY, 30TH JULY 1992

19.00	Football	Prelims	Zaragoza & Sabadell
	Hockey	Pool **(m)**	Terrassa
	Table tennis	Doubles groups **(m+w)**	Estacio del Nord
	Volleyball	Prelims **(m)**	Palau Esports
20.00	Basketball	Prelims **(w)**	Badalona
	Fencing	Ind foil **FINAL (w)**	Palau Metal-lurgia
	Gymnastics	All-round **FINAL (w)**	Sant Jordi
21.00	Football	Prelims	Barcelona & Valencia
21.30	Judo	Half-middleweight s/f & **FINAL (m+w)**	Palau Blaugrana
	Volleyball	Prelims **(m)**	Palau Esports
21.40	Table tennis	Singles groups **(m)**	Estacio del Nord
22.00	Basketball	Prelims **(w)**	Badalona

FRIDAY, 31ST JULY 1992

08.00	Rowing	Single sculls s/f **(w)**	Banyoles
		Quadruple sculls s/f **(w)**	
		Eights s/f **(w)**	
		Coxed pairs s/f **(m)**	
		Coxless fours s/f **(m)**	
		Quadruple sculls s/f **(m)**	
		Eights s/f **(m+w)**	
09.00	Archery	70m & 60m qual **(w)**	Vall d'Hebron
	Fencing	Ind foil prelims **(m)**	Palau Metal-lurgia
	Shooting	50m free rifle prelims **(m)**	Camp de Tir
		10m running target prelims **(m)**	
		Trap prelims **(o)**	
	Table tennis	Singles groups **(m+w)**	Estacio del Nord
09.30	Athletics	100m Rd 1 **(w)**	Montjuic
	Basketball	Prelims **(m)**	Badalona
10.00	Athletics	Shot put qual **(m)**	Montjuic
	Badminton	Singles Rd 3, doubles Rd 2 **(m+w)**	Pavello Mar Bella
	Handball	Prelims **(m)**	Palau d'Esports, Granollers
	Swimming	200m fly hts **(w)**	Picornell
		200m medley hts **(m)**	
		200m back hts **(w)**	
		4x100m medley hts **(m)**	
		50m free hts **(w)**	
	Tennis	Singles Rd 2 & doubles Rd 1 **(m+w)**	Vall d'Hebron

DAILY PROGRAMME OF EVENTS

All times given are local Barcelona times. Barcelona is one hour ahead of the UK.

10.30	Athletics	100m Rd 2 **(m)**	Montjuic
	Volleyball	Prelims **(w)**	Palau Esports
11.30	Athletics	800m Rd 1 **(w)**	Montjuic
	Basketball	Prelims **(m)**	Badalona
	Handball	Prelims **(m)**	Palau d'Esports, Granollers
12.30	Weightlifting	Up to 82.5kg Grp C	Pavello L'Espanya Industrial
13.00	Archery	90m & 70m qual **(m)**	Vall d'Hebron
	Boxing	Last 16	Pavello Club Joventut
	Volleyball	Prelims **(w)**	Palau Esports
	Yachting	Reserve races and race 5	Port Olimpic
14.30	Basketball	Prelims **(m)**	Badalona
	Handball	Prelims **(m)**	Palau d'Esports, Granollers
15.00	Baseball	Prelims	Viladecans
	Weightlifting	Up to 82.5kg Grp B	Pavello L'Espanya Industrial
15.30	Shooting	50m free rifle **FINAL (m)**	Camp de Tir
16.00	Baseball	Prelims	l'Hospitalet
	Handball	Prelims **(m)**	Palau d'Esports, Granollers
16.30	Basketball	Prelims **(m)**	Badalona
	Judo	Lightweight prelims & repechage **(m+w)**	Palau Blaugrana
17.00	Badminton	Singles Rd 3, doubles Rd 2 **(m+w)**	Pavello Mar Bella
18.00	Athletics	Javelin qual **(w)**	Montjuic
	Cycling	Team **(m)** & ind pursuit s/f **(w)**	Velodrom
		Sprint **FINAL (m+w)**	
	Swimming	200m fly **FINAL (w)**	Picornell
		200m medley **FINAL (m)**	
		50m free **FINAL (w)**	
		1500m free **FINAL (m)**	
		200m back **FINAL (w)**	
		4x100m medley **FINAL (m)**	
18.05	Athletics	100m Rd 2 **(w)**	Montjuic
18.10	Athletics	High jump qual **(m)**	Montjuic
18.30	Weightlifting	Up to 82.5kg Grp A **FINAL**	Pavello L'Espanya Industrial
18.35	Athletics	100m Rd 2 **(m)**	Montjuic
19.00	Athletics	Shot put **FINAL (m)**	Montjuic
	Boxing	Last 16	Pavello Club Joventut
	Handball	Prelims **(m)**	Palau d'Esports, Granollers
	Table tennis	Doubles q/f **(w)**	Estacio del Nord
	Volleyball	Prelims **(w)**	Palau Esports
19.05	Athletics	800m Rd 1 **(m)**	Montjuic

DAILY PROGRAMME OF EVENTS

All times given are local Barcelona times. Barcelona is one hour ahead of the UK.

19.15	Athletics	20km walk **FINAL (m)** (start)	Passeig de la Zona Franca
19.30	Athletics	Javelin qual **(w)**	Montjuic
19.50	Athletics	3000m Rd 1 **(w)**	Montjuic
20.00	Cycling	Team pursuit **FINAL (m)**	Velodrom
		Ind pursuit **FINAL (w)**	
		Ind points race **FINAL** (50km) **(m)**	
	Fencing	Ind foil **FINAL (m)**	Palau Metal-lurgia
	Gymnastics	All-round **FINAL (m)**	Sant Jordi
	Table tennis	Doubles groups **(m)**	Estacio del Nord
20.30	Basketball	Prelims **(m)**	Badalona
	Handball	Prelims **(m)**	Palau d'Esports, Granollers
20.50	Athletics	10,000m ht 1 **(m)**	Montjuic
21.00	Baseball	Prelims	Viladecans & l'Hospitalet
21.20	Table tennis	Singles groups **(w)**	Estacio del Nord
21.30	Judo	Lightweight s/f & **FINAL (m+w)**	Palau Blaugrana
	Volleyball	Prelims **(w)**	Palau Esports
21.35	Athletics	10,000m ht 2 **(m)**	Montjuic
22.30	Basketball	Prelims **(m)**	Badalona

07.50	Rowing	FINAL B:	Banyoles
		Coxless fours **(w)**	
		Double sculls **(w)**	
		Coxless pairs **(w)**	
		Coxed fours **(m)**	
		Double sculls **(m)**	
		Coxless pairs **(m)**	
		Single sculls **(m)**	
09.00	Archery	50m & 30m qual **(w)**	Vall d'Hebron
	Canoeing (slalom)	K1 **FINAL (w)** & C1 **FINAL (m)**	La Seu d'Urgell
	Fencing	Ind epee prelims **(m)**	Palau de la Metal-lurgia
	Shooting	10m air pistol prelims **(w)**	Camp de Tir
		10m running target prelims **(m)**	
		Trap prelims **(o)**	
	Table tennis	Singles groups **(m)**	Estacio del Nord

DAILY PROGRAMME OF EVENTS

All times given are local Barcelona times. Barcelona is one hour ahead of the UK.

09.10	Rowing	**FINAL** A:	Banyoles
		Coxless fours **(w)**	
		Double sculls **(w)**	
		Coxless pairs **(w)**	
		Coxed fours **(m)**	
		Double sculls **(m)**	
		Coxless pairs **(m)**	
		Single sculls **(m)**	
09.30	Athletics	Heptathlon (100m hurdles)	Montjuic
	Water polo	Prelims	Piscina Montjuic
10.00	Athletics	400m Rd 1 **(m)**	Montjuic
	Badminton	Singles Rd 3 & doubles Rd 2 **(m+w)**	Pavello Mar Bella
	Diving	Springbd prelims **(w)**	Piscina Montjuic
	Handball	Prelims **(w)**	Palau d'Esports, Granollers
	Hockey	Pool **(m)**	Terrassa
	Tennis	Singles Rd 3 & doubles Rd 2 **(m+w)**	Vall d'Hebron
10.30	Athletics	Heptathlon (high jump)	Montjuic
	Volleyball	Prelims **(m)**	Palau Esports
11.00	Athletics	400m hurdles Rd 1 **(w)**	Montjuic
	Basketball	Prelims **(w)**	Badalona
	Table tennis	Singles last 16 **(w)**	Estacio del Nord
11.30	Athletics	Hammer qual **(m)**	Montjuic
	Handball	Prelims **(w)**	Palau d'Esports, Granollers
12.00	Shooting	10m air pistol **FINAL (w)**	Camp de Tir
	Table tennis	Singles groups **(m)**	Estacio del Nord
12.30	Weightlifting	Up to 90kg Grp C	Pavello L'Espanya Industrial
13.00	Archery	50m & 30m qual **(m)**	Vall d'Hebron
	Athletics	Hammer qual **(m)**	Montjuic
	Basketball	Prelims **(w)**	Badalona
	Boxing	Last 16	Pavello Club Joventut
	Volleyball	Prelims **(m)**	Palau Esports
	Yachting	Races 5 & 6	Port Olimpic
14.30	Shooting	10m running target **FINAL (m)**	Camp de Tir
15.00	Baseball	Prelims	Viladecans
	Diving	Springbd prelims **(w)**	Piscina Montjuic
	Handball	Prelims **(w)**	Palau d'Esports, Granollers
	Volleyball	Prelims **(m)**	Pavello Vall d'Hebron
	Weightlifting	Up to 90kg Grp B	Pavello L'Espanya Industrial
16.00	Baseball	Prelims	l'Hospitalet

DAILY PROGRAMME OF EVENTS

All times given are local Barcelona times. Barcelona is one hour ahead of the UK.

16.30	Handball	Prelims **(w)**	Palau d'Esports, Granollers
	Judo	Half-lightweight prelims & repechage **(m+w)**	Palau Blaugrana
17.00	Badminton	Singles Rd 3 & doubles Rd 2 **(m+w)**	Pavello Mar Bella
	Hockey	Pool **(m)**	Terrassa
17.30	Athletics	Heptathlon (shot put)	Montjuic
	Volleyball	Prelims **(m)**	Pavello Vall d'Hebron
18.00	Athletics	Triple jump qual **(m)**	Montjuic
18.15	Athletics	100m s/f **(w)**	Montjuic
18.30	Athletics	Marathon **FINAL (w)** (start)	Mataro to Montjuic
	Water polo	Prelims	Piscina Montjuic
	Weightlifting	Up to 90kg Grp A **FINAL**	Pavello L'Espanya Industrial
18.35	Athletics	100m s/f **(m)**	Montjuic
18.55	Athletics	800m Rd 2 **(m)**	Montjuic
19.00	Boxing	Last 16	Pavello Club Joventut
	Football	Q/f	Valencia
	Hockey	Pool **(m)**	Terrassa
	Table tennis	Doubles q/f **(m)**	Estacio del Nord
	Volleyball	Prelims **(m)**	Palau Esports
19.20	Athletics	Javelin **FINAL (w)**	Montjuic
19.25	Athletics	800m s/f **(w)**	Montjuic
19.45	Athletics	100m **FINAL (w)**	Montjuic
20.00	Athletics	100m **FINAL (m)**	Montjuic
	Basketball	Prelims **(w)**	Badalona
	Fencing	Ind. epee **FINAL (m)**	Palau de la Metal-lurgia
	Gymnastics	Apparatus **FINAL (w)**	Sant Jordi
20.15	Athletics	Heptathlon (200m)	Montjuic
21.00	Baseball	Prelims	Viladecans & l'Hospitalet
	Table tennis	Doubles s/f **(w)**	Estacio del Nord
21.15	Athletics	10,000m ht 1 **(w)**	Montjuic
21.30	Football	Q/f	Barcelona
	Judo	Half-lightweight s/f and **FINAL (m+w)**	Palau Blaugrana
	Volleyball	Prelims **(m)**	Palau Esports
21.55	Athletics	10,000m ht 2 **(w)**	Montjuic
22.00	Basketball	Prelims **(w)**	Badalona

All times given are local Barcelona times. Barcelona is one hour ahead of the UK.

SUNDAY, 2ND AUGUST 1992

07.50	Rowing	Final B:	Banyoles
		Single sculls **(w)**	
		Quadruple sculls **(w)**	
		Eights **(w)**	
		Coxed pairs **(m)**	
		Coxless fours **(m)**	
		Quadruple sculls **(m)**	
		Eights **(m)**	
08.00	Equestrian	Team dressage **(o)**	Real Club de Polo
08.30	Cycling	Ind road race **(m)**	Sant Sadurni d'Anoia
09.00	Archery	70m - last 32 & 16 **(w)**	Vall d'Hebron
	Canoeing (slalom)	K1 **(m) FINAL** & C2 **(m) FINAL**	La Seu d'Urgell
	Fencing	Ind sabre prelims **(m)**	Palau de la Metal-lurgia
	Shooting	Trap s/f **(o)**	Camp de Tir
09.10	Rowing	**FINAL A**:	Banyoles
		Single sculls **(w)**	
		Quadruple sculls **(w)**	
		Eights **(w)**	
		Coxed pairs **(m)**	
		Coxless fours **(m)**	
		Quadruple sculls **(m)**	
		Eights **(m)**	
09.30	Basketball	Prelims **(m)**	Badalona
	Water polo	Prelims	Piscina Montjuic
10.00	Athletics	110m hurdles Rd 1 **(m)**	Montjuic
	Badminton	Singles & doubles q/f **(m+w)**	Pavello Mar Bella
	Diving	Platform prelims **(m)**	Piscina Montjuic
	Handball	Prelims **(m)**	Palau d'Esports, Granollers
	Tennis	Singles Rd 3 & doubles Rd 2 **(m+w)**	Vall d'Hebron
10.05	Athletics	Heptathlon (long jump)	Montjuic
10.30	Athletics	Discus qual **(w)**	Montjuic
	Baseball	Prelims	l'Hospitalet & Villadecans
	Volleyball	Prelims **(w)**	Palau Esports
11.00	Athletics	400m Rd 1 **(w)**	Montjuic
	Table tennis	Singles last 16 **(m)**	Estacio del Nord
11.30	Athletics	Discus qual **(w)**	Montjuic
	Basketball	Prelims **(m)**	Badalona
	Handball	Prelims **(m)**	Palau d'Esports, Granollers
12.30	Weightlifting	Up to 100kg Grp C	Pavello L'Espanya Industrial

DAILY PROGRAMME OF EVENTS

All times given are local Barcelona times. Barcelona is one hour ahead of the UK.

13.00	Archery	70m q/f, s/f and **FINAL (w)**	Vall d'Hebron
	Boxing	Last 16	Pavello Club Joventut
	Volleyball	Prelims **(w)**	Palau Esports
	Yachting	Reserve races and race 5	Port Olimpic
14.00	Shooting	Trap **FINAL (o)**	Camp de Tir
14.30	Basketball	Prelims **(m)**	Badalona
	Diving	Platform prelims **(m)**	Piscina Montjuic
	Handball	Prelims **(m)**	Palau d'Esports, Granollers
15.00	Synchronised swimming	Solo prelims	Picornell
	Weightlifting	Up to 100kg Grp B	Pavello L'Espanya Industrial
16.00	Equestrian	Team dressage **(o)**	Real Club de Polo
	Handball	Prelims **(m)**	Palau d'Esports, Granollers
16.30	Athletics	Hammer **FINAL (m)**	Montjuic
	Basketball	Prelims **(m)**	Badalona
	Judo	Extra Lightweight prelims & repechage **(m+w)**	Palau Blaugrana
17.00	Badminton	Singles & doubles q/f **(m+w)**	Pavello Mar Bella
	Hockey	Pool **(w)**	Terrassa
18.00	Athletics	High jump **FINAL (m)**	Montjuic
	Baseball	Prelims	l'Hospitalet & Villadecans
18.25	Athletics	Heptathlon (javelin)	Montjuic
18.30	Athletics	110m hurdles Rd 2 **(m)**	Montjuic
	Water polo	Prelims	Piscina Montjuic
	Weightlifting	Up to 100kg Grp A **FINAL**	Pavello L'Espanya Industrial
19.00	Boxing	Last 16	Pavello Club Joventut
	Football	Q/f	Zaragoza
	Handball	Prelims **(m)**	Palau d'Esports, Granollers
	Hockey	Pool **(w)**	Terrassa
	Volleyball	Prelims **(w)**	Palau Esports
19.15	Athletics	400m Rd 2 **(m)**	Montjuic
19.50	Athletics	400m hurdles s/f **(w)**	Montjuic
20.00	Athletics	Heptathlon (javelin)	Montjuic
	Fencing	Ind sabre **FINAL (m)**	Palau de la Metal-lurgia
	Gymnastics	Apparatus **FINAL (m)**	Sant Jordi
20.20	Athletics	800m s/f **(m)**	Montjuic
	Basketball	Prelims **(m)**	Badalona
	Handball	Prelims **(m)**	Palau d'Esports, Granollers
20.45	Athletics	800m **FINAL (w)**	Montjuic
21.00	Athletics	3000m **FINAL (w)**	Montjuic

DAILY PROGRAMME OF EVENTS

All times given are local Barcelona times. Barcelona is one hour ahead of the UK.

SUNDAY, 2ND AUGUST 1992

21.30	Athletics	Heptathlon (800m)	Montjuic
	Football	Q/f	Barcelona
	Judo	Extra Lightweight s/f & **FINAL (m+w)**	Palau Blaugrana
	Volleyball	Prelims **(w)**	Palau Esports
22.30	Basketball	Prelims **(m)**	Badalona

MONDAY, 3RD AUGUST 1992

08.00	Equestrian	Team dressage **(o)**	Real Club de Polo
09.00	Archery	70m last 32 & 16 **(m)**	Vall d'Hebron
	Canoeing (flatwater)	500m K1,C1,K2,C2 hts **(m+w)**	Castelldefels
09.30	Athletics	Discus qual **(m)**	Montjuic
	Water polo	Prelims	Piscina Montjuic
09.35	Athletics	200m Rd 1 **(w)**	Montjuic
10.00	Badminton	Singles & doubles s/f **(m+w)**	Pavello Mar Bella
	Handball	Prelims **(w)**	Palau d'Esports,Granollers
	Hockey	Pool **(m)**	Terrassa
	Wrestling (freestyle)	52, 68, 100kg elim	INEFC, Montjuic
10.20	Athletics	200m Rd 1 **(m)**	Montjuic
10.30	Volleyball	Prelims **(m)**	Palau Esports
11.00	Athletics	Discus qual **(m)**	Montjuic
	Basketball	Prelims **(w)**	Palau d'Esports Joventut
	Fencing	Team foil prelims **(w)**	Palau de la Metal-lurgia
	Table tennis	Doubles **FINAL (w)**	Estacio del Nord
	Tennis	Singles q/f **(m+w)** & doubles q/f **(m)**	Vall d'Hebron
11.15	Athletics	1500m Rd 1 **(m)**	Montjuic
11.30	Handball	Prelims **(w)**	Palau d'Esports,Granollers
12.15	Athletics	400m hurdles Rd 1 **(m)**	Montjuic
12.30	Weightlifting	Up to 110kg Grp C	Pavello L'Espanya Industrial
13.00	Archery	70m q/f, s/f & **FINAL (m)**	Vall d'Hebron
	Basketball	Prelims **(w)**	Badalona
	Boxing	Q/f	Pavello Club Joventut
	Volleyball	Prelims **(m)**	Palau Esports
	Yachting	Match race and race 7	Port Olimpic
14.30	Diving	Springbd **FINAL (w)**	Piscina Montjuic
15.00	Handball	Prelims **(w)**	Palau d'Esports,Granollers
	Synchronised swimming	Duet prelims	Picornell
	Volleyball	Prelims **(m)**	Pavello Vall d'Hebron
	Weightlifting	Up to 110kg Grp B	Pavello L'Espanya Industrial
16.00	Equestrian	Team dressage **FINAL (o)**	Real Club de Polo

DAILY PROGRAMME OF EVENTS

All times given are local Barcelona times. Barcelona is one hour ahead of the UK.

MONDAY, 3RD AUGUST 1992

16.30	Handball	Prelims **(w)**	Palau d'Esports,Granollers
17.00	Badminton	Singles & doubles s/f **(m+w)**	Pavello Mar Bella
	Canoeing (flatwater)	500m K1,C1,K2,C2 rep **(m+w)**	Castelldefels
	Hockey	Pool **(m)**	Terrassa
	Wrestling (freestyle)	52, 68, 100kg elim	INEFC, Montjuic
17.30	Volleyball	Prelims **(m)**	Pavello Vall d'Hebron
18.00	Athletics	110m hurdles s/f **(m)**	Montjuic
18.20	Athletics	200m Rd 2 **(w)**	Montjuic
18.30	Water polo	Prelims	Piscina Montjuic
	Weightlifting	Up to 110kg Grp A **FINAL**	Pavello L'Espanya Industrial
18.45	Athletics	200m Rd 2 **(m)**	Montjuic
18.50	Athletics	Discus **FINAL (w)**	Montjuic
19.00	Hockey	Pool **(m)**	Terrassa
	Table tennis	Singles q/f **(w)**	Estacio del Nord
	Volleyball	Prelims **(m)**	Palau Esports
19.10	Athletics	400m Rd 2 **(w)**	Montjuic
19.30	Athletics	Triple jump **FINAL (m)**	Montjuic
19.35	Athletics	400m s/f **(m)**	Montjuic
19.50	Athletics	10km walk **FINAL (w)** (start)	Passeig de la Zona Franca to Montjuic
20.00	Basketball	Prelims **(w)**	Badalona
	Boxing	Q/f	Pavello Club Joventut
20.05	Athletics	110m hurdles **FINAL (m)**	Montjuic
20.45	Athletics	3000m steeple Rd 1 **(m)**	Montjuic
21.00	Table tennis	Doubles s/f **(m)**	Estacio del Nord
21.30	Athletics	400m hurdles **FINAL (w)**	Montjuic
	Volleyball	Prelims **(m)**	Palau Esports
21.45	Athletics	10,000m **FINAL (m)**	Montjuic
22.00	Basketball	Prelims **(w)**	Badalona

TUESDAY, 4TH AUGUST 1992

08.00	Equestrian	Team jumping **(o)**	Real Club de Polo
09.00	Archery	Team 70m last 16, q/f, s/f & **FINAL (w)**	Vall d'Hebron
	Canoeing (flatwater)	1000m K1,C1,K1,C2,K4 hts **(m)** 500m K4 hts **(w)**	Castelldefels
	Fencing	Team foil prelim **(m)**	Palau Metal-lurgia
09.30	Basketball	Classification **(m)**	Badalona
	Hockey	Classification **(w)**	Terrassa

DAILY PROGRAMME OF EVENTS

All times given are local Barcelona times. Barcelona is one hour ahead of the UK.

TUESDAY, 4TH AUGUST 1992

10.00	Handball	Prelims **(m)**	Palau d'Esports, Granollers
	Wrestling (freestyle)	48,52,68,74,100,130kg elims	INEFC, Montjuic
11.00	Badminton	Singles & doubles **FINAL (m+w)**	Pavello Mar Bella
	Fencing	Team foil prelim **(w)**	Palau Metal-lurgia
	Table tennis	Doubles **FINAL (m)**	Estacio del Nord
	Tennis	Singles s/f **(m+w)** & doubles q/f **(w)**	Vall d'Hebron
11.30	Basketball	Classification **(m)**	Badalona
	Handball	Prelims **(m)**	Palau d'Esports, Granollers
12.30	Weightlifting	Over 110kg Grp C	Pavello L'Espanya Industrial
13.00	Archery	Team 70m last 16, q/f, s/f & **FINAL (m)**	Vall d'Hebron
	Boxing	Q/f	Pavello Club Joventut
	Yachting	Match race	Port Olimpic
14.30	Basketball	Q/f **(m)**	Badalona
	Handball	Prelims **(m)**	Palau d'Esports, Granollers
15.00	Diving	Platform **FINAL (m)**	Piscina Montjuic
	Equestrian	Team jumping **FINAL (o)**	Real Club de Polo
	Weightlifting	Over 110kg Grp B	Pavello L'Espanya Industrial
16.00	Baseball	S/f	l'Hospitalet
	Handball	Prelims **(m)**	Palau d'Esports, Granollers
16.30	Basketball	Q/f **(m)**	Badalona
	Volleyball	Final 7-8 **(w)**	Pavello Vall d'Hebron
17.00	Canoeing (flatwater)	1000m K1,C1,K1,C2,K4 rep **(m)**	Castelldefels
		500m K4 rep **(w)**	
	Hockey	S/f **(w)**	Terrassa
	Wrestling (freestyle)	48,52,68,74,100,130kg elims	INEFC, Montjuic
18.15	Hockey	Classification **(w)**	Terrassa
18.30	Weightlifting	Over 110kg Grp A **FINAL**	Pavello L'Espanya Industrial
19.00	Handball	Prelims **(m)**	Palau d'Esports, Granollers
	Table tennis	Singles q/f **(m)**	Estacio del Nord
	Volleyball	Q/f **(w)**	Pavello Vall d'Hebron
19.30	Hockey	S/f **(w)**	Terrassa
20.00	Boxing	Q/f	Pavello Club Joventut
	Fencing	Team foil **FINAL (w)**	Palau Metal-lurgia
20.30	Basketball	Q/f **(m)**	Badalona
	Handball	Prelims **(m)**	Palau d'Esports, Granollers
21.00	Baseball	S/f	Viladecans
	Table tennis	Singles s/f **(w)**	Estacio del Nord
21.30	Volleyball	Q/f **(w)**	Pavello Vall d'Hebron
22.30	Basketball	Q/f **(m)**	Badalona

DAILY PROGRAMME OF EVENTS

All times given are local Barcelona times. Barcelona is one hour ahead of the UK.

08.00	Synchronised swimming	Figures	Picornell
09.00	Athletics	Decathlon (100m)	Montjuic
	Canoeing (flatwater)	500m K1,C1,K2,C2 s/f **(m)**	Castelldefels
		500m K1 & K2 s/f **(w)**	
	Equestrian	Ind dressage **FINAL (o)**	Real Club de Polo
	Fencing	Team epee prelims **(m)**	Palau Metal-lurgia
09.30	Athletics	Pole vault qual **(m)**	Montjuic
	Hockey	Classification **(m)**	Terrassa
	Water polo	Prelims	Piscina de Montjuic
10.00	Athletics	1500m Rd 1 **(w)**	Montjuic
	Wrestling (freestyle)	48,52,57,62,68,74,82,90,100,130kg elim	INEFC, Montjuic
10.05	Athletics	Decathlon (long jump)	Montjuic
10.30	Volleyball	Q/f **(m)**	Sant Jordi
10.45	Athletics	100m hurdles Rd 1 **(w)**	Montjuic
11.00	Basketball	Classification **(w)**	Badalona
	Fencing	Team foil prelims **(m)**	Palau Metal-lurgia
	Table tennis	Singles **FINAL (w)**	Estacio del Nord
	Tennis	Singles s/f **(w)** & doubles s/f **(m)**	Vall d'Hebron
11.45	Athletics	Decathlon (shot put)	Montjuic
13.00	Basketball	S/f **(w)**	Badalona
	Volleyball	Q/f **(m)**	Sant Jordi
15.00	Volleyball	Final 11-12 **(m)**	Pavello Vall d'Hebron
16.00	Baseball	Final 3-4	l'Hospitalet
17.00	Hockey	Classification & s/f **(m)**	Terrassa
17.00	Wrestling (freestyle)	57,62,74,82,90kg elim	INEFC, Montjuic
17.30	Athletics	Shot put qual **(w)**	Montjuic
	Volleyball	Final 9-10 **(m)**	Pavello Vall d'Hebron
	Water polo	Prelims	Piscina de Montjuic
17.35	Athletics	Decathlon (high jump)	Montjuic
18.00	Athletics	100m hurdles Rd 2 **(w)**	Montjuic
18.30	Athletics	200m hurdles s/f **(w)**	Montjuic
18.35	Athletics	Long jump qual **(m)**	Montjuic
18.50	Athletics	200m s/f **(m)**	Montjuic
19.00	Football	S/f	Valencia
	Volleyball	Q/f **(m)**	Sant Jordi
	Wrestling (freestyle)	52,68 and 100kg **FINAL**	INEFC, Montjuic
19.15	Athletics	400m hurdles s/f **(m)**	Montjuic
19.30	Athletics	Discus **FINAL (m)**	Montjuic
	Hockey	Classification & s/f **(m)**	Terrassa

DAILY PROGRAMME OF EVENTS

All times given are local Barcelona times. Barcelona is one hour ahead of the UK.

19.35	Athletics	400m s/f (w)	Montjuic
19.50	Athletics	3000m steeple s/f	Montjuic
20.00	Basketball	Classification (w)	Badalona
	Fencing	Team foil **FINAL** (m)	Palau Metal-lurgia
	Table tennis	Singles s/f (m)	Estacio del Nord
20.20	Athletics	400m **FINAL** (m)	Montjuic
20.35	Athletics	200m **FINAL** (w)	Montjuic
20.50	Athletics	200m **FINAL** (m)	Montjuic
21.00	Baseball	**FINAL**	l'Hospitalet
21.05	Athletics	800m **FINAL** (m)	Montjuic
21.20	Athletics	Decathlon (400m)	Montjuic
21.30	Football	S/f	Barcelona
	Volleyball	Q/f (m)	Sant Jordi
21.45	Athletics	5000m Rd I (m)	Montjuic
22.00	Basketball	S/f (w)	Badalona

09.00	Athletics	Decathlon (110m hurdles)	Montjuic
	Basketball	Places 9-12 (m)	Badalona
	Canoeing (flatwater)	1000m K1,C1,K2,C2,K4 s/f (m)	Castelldefels
		500m K4 s/f (w)	
	Fencing	Team sabre prelims (m)	Palau Metal-lurgia
09.30	Athletics	High jump qual (w)	Montjuic
	Hockey	Final 5-8 (w)	Terrassa
	Water polo	Prelims	Piscina Montjuic
10.00	Athletics	Decathlon (discus) qual	Montjuic
	Wrestling (freestyle)	48,57,62,74,82,90,130kg elim	INEFC, Montjuic
10.05	Athletics	Long jump qual (w)	Montjuic
10.30	Volleyball	Final 5-6 (w)	Pavello Vall d'Hebron
11.00	Fencing	Team epee prelims (m)	Palau Metal-lurgia
	Table tennis	Singles **FINAL** (m)	Estacio del Nord
	Tennis	Singles s/f (m) & doubles s/f (w)	Vall d'Hebron
11.30	Athletics	Decathlon (discus) qual	Montjuic
13.00	Athletics	Decathlon (pole vault)	Montjuic
	Boxing	S/f	Pavello Club Joventut
	Volleyball	Classification (m)	Pavello Vall d'Hebron
14.00	Handball	S/f (w)	Palau d'Esports, Granollers
14.30	Basketball	Classification (m)	Badalona
15.00	Synchronised swimming	Solo **FINAL**	Picornell

DAILY PROGRAMME OF EVENTS

All times given are local Barcelona times. Barcelona is one hour ahead of the UK.

16.00	Gymnastics	Rhythmic prelims **(w)**	Palau d'Esports
	Handball	S/f **(w)**	Palau d'Esports, Granollers
16.30	Basketball	S/f **(m)**	Badalona
	Volleyball	Classification **(m)**	Pavello Vall d'Hebron
17.00	Hockey	Final 5-12 **(m)**	Terrassa
	Wrestling (freestyle)	57,62,82,90kg elim	INEFC, Montjuic
17.30	Athletics	Decathlon (javelin)	Montjuic
	Water polo	Prelims	Piscina Montjuic
18.00	Athletics	100m hurdles s/f **(w)**	Montjuic
18.15	Hockey	Final 5-8 **(w)**	Terrassa
18.30	Athletics	400m **FINAL (w)**	Montjuic
18.45	Athletics	Decathlon (javelin)	Montjuic
18.50	Athletics	Long jump **FINAL (m)**	Montjuic
19.00	Athletics	400m hurdles **FINAL (m)**	Montjuic
	Handball	S/f **(m)**	Palau d'Esports, Granollers
	Volleyball	S/f **(w)**	Sant Jordi
	Wrestling (freestyle)	48,74 & 130kg	INEFC, Montjuic
19.20	Athletics	1500m s/f **(w)**	Montjuic
19.30	Hockey	Final 5-12 **(m)**	Terrassa
19.45	Athletics	1500m s/f **(m)**	Montjuic
20.00	Fencing	Team epee **FINAL (m)**	Palau Metal-lurgia
20.10	Athletics	100m hurdles **FINAL (w)**	Montjuic
20.30	Athletics	5000m s/f **(m)**	Montjuic
	Basketball	Classification **(m)**	Badalona
21.00	Handball	S/f **(m)**	Palau d'Esports, Granollers
21.15	Athletics	Decathlon (1500m) **FINAL**	Montjuic
21.30	Volleyball	S/f **(w)**	Sant Jordi
22.30	Basketball	S/f **(m)**	Badalona

07.30	Athletics	50km walk **FINAL (m)** start	Passeig de la Zona Franca
09.00	Canoeing (flatwater)	500m K1,C1,K2,C2 **FINAL (m)**	Castelldefels
		500m K1, K2 **FINAL (w)**	
	Handball	Final 7-8 **(w)**	Palau d'Esports, Granollers
09.30	Athletics	4x100m relay Rd 1 **(m)**	Montjuic
	Equestrian	Ind jumping qual **(o)**	Real Club de Polo
	Hockey	Final 5-12 **(m)**	Terrassa
09.35	Athletics	Javelin qual **(m)**	Montjuic

All times given are local Barcelona times. Barcelona is one hour ahead of the UK.

FRIDAY, 7TH AUGUST 1992

10.00	Athletics	4x100m relay Rd 1 **(w)**	Montjuic
	Wrestling (freestyle)	57,62,82,90kg elim	INEFC, Montjuic
10.30	Athletics	4x400m relay Rd 1 **(m)**	Montjuic
	Volleyball	S/f **(m)**	Sant Jordi
10.45	Athletics	Javelin qual **(m)**	Montjuic
11.00	Basketball	Places 5-6 **(w)**	Badalona
	Fencing	Team sabre prelims **(m)**	Palau Metal-lurgia
	Handball	Final 5-6 **(w)**	Palau d'Esports, Granollers
	Tennis	Doubles **FINAL (m)**	Vall d'Hebron
13.00	Basketball	Places 3-4 **(w)**	Badalona
	Boxing	S/F	Pavello Club Joventut
	Volleyball	Final 3-4 **(w)**	Sant Jordi
14.00	Handball	Final 11-12 **(m)**	Palau d'Esports, Granollers
	Tennis	Singles **FINAL (w)**	Vall d'Hebron
15.00	Synchronised swimming	Duet **FINAL**	Picornell
	Volleyball	Final 7-8 **(m)**	Pavello Vall d'Hebron
16.00	Gymnastics	Rhythmic prelims **(w)**	Palau d'Esports
	Handball	Final 9-10 **(m)**	Palau d'Esports, Granollers
16.30	Equestrian	Ind jumping qual **(o)**	Real Club de Polo
17.00	Athletics	Pole vault **FINAL**	Montjuic
	Hockey	Final 3-4 **(w)**	Terrassa
	Wrestling (freestyle)	57,62,82,90kg **FINAL**	INEFC, Montjuic
17.30	Volleyball	Final 5-6 **(m)**	Pavello Vall d'Hebron
18.15	Hockey	Final 5-12 **(m)**	Terrassa
18.55	Athletics	Shot put **FINAL (w)**	Montjuic
19.00	Athletics	4x100m relay s/f **(w)**	Montjuic
	Handball	Final 7-8 **(m)**	Palau d'Esports, Granollers
	Volleyball	S/f **(m)**	Sant Jordi
19.15	Athletics	Long jump **FINAL (w)**	Montjuic
19.30	Athletics	4x100m relay s/f **(m)**	Montjuic
	Hockey	**FINAL (w)**	Terrassa
20.00	Athletics	4x400m relay Rd 1 **(w)**	Montjuic
	Basketball	Places 7-8 **(w)**	Badalona
	Fencing	Team sabre **FINAL (m)**	Palau Metal-lurgia
	Football	Final 3-4	Barcelona
20.30	Athletics	4x400m relay s/f **(m)**	Montjuic
21.00	Athletics	3000m steeple **FINAL**	Montjuic
	Handball	Final 5-6 **(m)**	Palau d'Esports, Granollers
21.20	Athletics	10,000m **FINAL (w)**	Montjuic

All times given are local Barcelona times. Barcelona is one hour ahead of the UK.

FRIDAY, 7TH AUGUST 1992

21.30	Volleyball	**FINAL (w)**	Sant Jordi
22.00	Basketball	**FINAL (w)**	Badalona

SATURDAY, 8TH AUGUST 1992

09.00	Canoeing (flatwater)	1000m K1,C1,K2,C2,K4 **FINAL (m)** 500m k4 **FINAL (w)**	Castelldefels
09.30	Water polo	Classification	Piscina Montjuic
10.00	Boxing	**FINALS**	Pavello Club Joventut
	Handball	Final 3-4 **(w)**	Palau d'Esports, Granollers
11.00	Basketball	Places 5-6 **(m)**	Badalona
	Tennis	Doubles **FINAL (w)**	Vall d'Hebron
12.00	Handball	**FINAL (w)**	Sant Jordi
13.00	Basketball	Places 3-4 **(m)**	Badalona
14.00	Tennis	Singles **FINAL (m)**	Vall d'Hebron
15.00	Handball	Final 3-4 **(m)**	Palau d'Esports, Granollers
16.00	Gymnastics	Rhythmic **FINAL (w)**	Palau d'Esports
17.00	Handball	**FINAL (m)**	Sant Jordi
	Hockey	Final 3-4 **(m)**	Terrassa
17.30	Water polo	Classification & s/f	Piscina Montjuic

DAILY PROGRAMME OF EVENTS

All times given are local Barcelona times. Barcelona is one hour ahead of the UK.

18.30	Athletics	High jump **FINAL (w)**	Montjuic
18.55	Athletics	Javelin **FINAL (m)**	Montjuic
19.00	Athletics	4x100m relay **FINAL (w)**	Montjuic
19.20	Athletics	4x100m relay **FINAL (m)**	Montjuic
19.30	Athletics	1500m **FINAL (w)**	Montjuic
	Hockey	**FINAL (m)**	Terrassa
20.00	Basketball	Places 7-8 **(m)**	Badalona
	Football	**FINAL**	Barcelona
20.15	Athletics	1500m **FINAL (m)**	Montjuic
20.40	Athletics	5000m **FINAL (m)**	Montjuic
21.15	Athletics	4x400m relay **FINAL (w)**	Montjuic
21.45	Athletics	4x400m relay **FINAL (m)**	Montjuic
22.00	Basketball	**FINAL (m)**	Badalona

09.00	Equestrian	Ind jumping **FINAL (o)** Course A	Real Club de Polo
	Water polo	Classification	Piscina Montjuic
10.00	Boxing	**FINALS**	Pavello Club Joventut
10.30	Volleyball	Final 3-4 **(m)**	Sant Jordi
13.00	Volleyball	**FINAL (m)**	Sant Jordi
13.30	Equestrian	Ind jumping **FINAL (o)** Course B	Real Club de Polo
14.00	Water polo	Classification and **FINAL**	Piscina Montjuic
18.30	Athletics	Marathon **FINAL (m)** (start)	Mataro to Montjuic
21.30	Closing ceremony		Montjuic

Monday Mail
Tuesday Mail
Wednesday Mail
Thursday Mail
Friday Mail
Saturday Mail
&
The Mail
ON SUNDAY

The everyday special occasion

THE
PEOPLE

*SOME OF THE NAMES TO LOOK OUT FOR
ON BRITAIN'S TEAM IN BARCELONA

*All names are provisional.
Final selections will be on 10 July 1992.

Joanne Edens

b: 01.10.67 Kings Lynn
l: Coventry, West Midlands
o: Computer Programmer
s: Married
cb: Leamington Spa AS
ch: Stuart Edens
ht: 172 cm, 5'8"
wt: 60 kg, 9 st 6 lb

Joanne finished 7th in the Olympic final in 1988. A year later she picked up an eleventh place at the world championships in Switzerland. And two years ago she was fifth at the european championships where she set a world record for the 30m target of 357 out of a possible 360 points. In 1991 Joanne was disappointed with her 25th placing at the world championships in Poland. Joanne has married since the 1988 Games. Her maiden name was Franks.

Pauline Edwards

b: 23.04.49 Dartford
l: Epsom, Surrey
o: Computer analyst
s: Single
cb: Atkins Archers
ht: 162 cm, 5'4"
wt: 56 kg, 8 st 11 lb

Pauline is one of Britain's longest-serving Olympians. She was a bronze medallist at the world championships in 1973 after competing in the Munich Olympic Games of 1972. In Seoul she was 17th in the individual event and 5th in the team competition. At the 1990 european championships in Barcelona she finished 23rd. Pauline sits on the National Olympic Committee as an athlete representative.

Steven Hallard

b: 22.02.65 Rugby
l: Rugby, Warwickshire
o: CAD Design Draughtsman
s: Married
cb: Dunlop
ch: Barry Farndon
ht: 188 cm, 6'2"
wt: 100 kg, 15 st 11 lb

This Warwickshire archer followed up his team Olympic bronze medal from Seoul with a silver medal in the individual event at the world championships in 1989 in Switzerland. Since then he has finished 10th in the 1990 european and 12th in the 1991 world championships. Steven must go to Barcelona as one of Britain's leading medal contenders.

Richard Priestman

b: 16.07.55 Liverpool
l: Preston, Lancashire
o: Bank official
s: Single
cb: Nethermoss Archers
ch: B Jewell
ht: 180 cm, 5'11"
wt: 66 kg, 10 st 6 lb

Richard competed at his first Olympic Games in 1984 before winning bronze in the men's team event in Seoul four years ago. A year after Seoul he picked up a tenth place in the individual event at the world championships in Switzerland. In Barcelona, Richard will be hoping to better his 28th place in the world championships in Poland last year.

In Barcelona the team is also likely to include: **Alison Williamson, Peter Armstrong, Martin Evans, Dale Hughes** and **Simon Terry**. The team manager will be **David Clarke**.

Marcus Adam

b: 28.02.68 London
l: London
s: Single
cb: Belgrave Harriers
ch: John Isaacs
ht: 185cm, 6'1"
wt: 82kg, 12st 13lb

Marcus Adam is amongst Britain's burgeoning ranks of world class sprinters. He took the 1990 Commonwealth Games gold at 200m easing out his England team-mates John Regis and Ade Mafe. In that same year Marcus also reached the semi-finals of the european championships 200m and took sprint relay silver. In 1989 Marcus became AAA and UK champion over 200m. His personal best going into the 1991 world athletics championships was 20.63 for 200m.

Kriss Akabusi

b: 28.11.58 London
l: Southampton, Hants
s: Married
cb: Team Solent
ch: Michael Whittingham
ht: 185cm, 6'1"

You have to look as far back as the 1984 Olympic Games to find the beginning of Kriss Akabusi's medal-winning streak. The conquering hero - who took individual 400m hurdles bronze and 400m relay gold at the 1991 world championships - was an Olympic silver medallist in Los Angeles in the 400m relay. Since that time he has added euro-pean and commonwealth individual gold at 400m hurdles and a 400m commonwealth relay title - all in 1990. At the 1988 Olympic Games, Kriss finished sixth in the 400m hurdles final. Since switching from 400m flat to the hurdles Kriss has broken the British record. His personal best is 47.86.

Steve Backley

b: 12.02.69 Sidcup
l: Bexley, Kent
o: Student (Loughborough)
s: Single
cb: Cambridge Harriers
ch: John Trower
ht: 196cm, 6'4"
wt: 95kg, 14st 13lb

For almost four years nearly everything which Steve Backley touched with his javelin turned to gold. It all began with a european junior gold in 1987, continued with the UK title in 1989; the world student title in 1989 and 1991; common-wealth and european gold in 1990. Steve was also busy, meanwhile, setting a series of world records - which he holds (23.3.92) at 91.46m. But it all went wrong, for Britain's field event star, in Tokyo at the world championships last year when he failed to reach the final. Steve will wish to wipe that memory away with a medal in Barcelona.

Roger Black

b: 31.03.66 Portsmouth
l: Bishops Waltham, Herts
s: Single
cb: Team Solent
ch: Michael Whittingham
ht: 190cm, 6'3"
wt: 79kg, 12st 6lb

Roger Black had the world at his feet at the end of 1986. He was senior commonwealth and euro-pean champion at 400m and 400m relay just a year after finishing a junior career with a european individual gold. Then came serious injury and a long, long lay-off. But by 1990 the world knew that Roger was back. He regained the european senior title and added the relay for good measure in Split. And at the 1991 world championships he missed individual gold by a whisker in the 400m final before coming home with gold from the 400m relay. The Barcelona stage awaits.

ATHLETICS

Christina Cahill

b: 25.03.57 Northolt
l: Bradford on Avon, Wilts
s: Married
cb: Gateshead Harriers & AC
ch: Sean Cahill
ht: 163cm, 5'4"
wt: 49kg, 7st 10lb

Christina tends to be one of Britain's unsung heroines. Yet she has featured in nearly every major international event for her country since 1978 when she finished 11th in the Commonwealth Games 800m. In 1988 she produced her best Olympic result of all-time with a 4th place in the 1500m final. That was two places better than four years earlier in Los Angeles. In 1990 Christina took silver at the Commonwealth Games 1500m and was 10th in the european championships at the same distance. She did not qualify from the heats at last year's world championships.

Linford Christie

b: 02.04.60 St. Andrews
l: London
s: Single
cb: Thames Valley Harriers
ch: Ronald Roddan
ht: 189cm, 6'2"
wt: 77kg, 12st 2lb

For the last six years Linford Christie has held centre-stage amongst Britain's world-class sprinters. A 1986 european championships 100m gold triggered off a run which has included: european gold a second time as well as european bronze in the 200m in 1990; commonwealth silver and gold at 100m in 1986 and 90; european sprint relay silver and bronze in 1986 and 90; world sprint relay bronze in 1991 and 1990 commonwealth bronze in the same event. All that, without mentioning Linford's Olympic 100m and sprint relay silvers from Seoul in 1988. And he ran 9.92 in Tokyo in the 100m race of all-time to finish fourth.

Stephen Cram

b: 14.10.60 Gateshead
l: Morpeth, Northumberland
s: Married
cb: Jarrow & Hebburn AC
ch: James Hedley
ht: 186cm, 6'1"
wt: 69kg, 10st 12lb

Steve's recent performances might not make him a current, major world force. But who can discount, particularly if he is injury-free, the Jarrow man who has twice been european 1500m champion - 1982 and 1986 - and who became world title-holder in 1983 at the same distance. In 1986 Steve was double commonwealth gold medallist at 800 and 1500m - adding to the 1500m title he won in Brisbane in 1982. At the 1991 world championships Steve did not qualify from the semi-final. But Barcelona could await the athlete who twice finished fourth in Olympic finals - in 1984 and 1988 at 1500m.

Peter Elliott

b: 9.10.62 Rawmarsh
l: Rotherham, South Yorks
s: Single
cb: Rotherham
ch: Kim McDonald
ht: 185cm, 6'0"
wt: 65kg, 10st 3lb

Who can forget the grimace on Peter Elliott's face in Seoul as he crossed the line to collect Olympic silver in the 1500m. It was a gritty performance from a man who that morning had had a series of pain-killing injections and who later needed surgery for the injury. And Peter was also kept out of the 1991 world championships by injury. Between times, though, he has made space for a commonwealth gold in Auckland in 1990 and the european cup title in 1991. Only Morceli, the current world champion, ran faster than Peter last year. Barcelona could offer up a fascinating duel.

Dalton Grant

b: 08.04.66 London
l: London
s: Single
cb: Haringey AC
ch: Elzbieta Krezesinka
ht: 186cm, 6'1"
wt: 74kg, 11st 9lb

Dalton is Britain's effervescent and leading high-jumper. And he is a "nearly-man" of British athletics having finished fourth at each of the 1990 european, 1991 world and 1989 world indoor championships. His major event medals have been gold at the european cup in 1989 and silver at the 1991 Commonwealth Games. The 1991 UK champion is hoping to hold his late run of form last season into Olympic competition.

Sally Gunnell

b: 29.07.66 Chigwell
l: Patcham, East Sussex
s: Single
o: Solicitors clerk
cb: Essex Ladies
ch: Bruce Longden
ht: 167cm, 5'6"
wt: 56kg, 8st 11lb

In Seoul, four years ago, Sally Gunnell placed fifth in the semi-finals of the 400m hurdles. At that stage she had only recently stepped up from the shorter hurdles distance. Her progress over the four year gap can be measured in precious medal - the silver she won at the 1991 world champion-ships. In the Tokyo final she also set a personal best of 53.16. A little more work on the final stride patterns for the double commonwealth medallist - in the 100m and 400m hurdles in 1986 and 1990 respectively - could see a gold for Britain in Barcelona.

Colin Jackson

b: 18.02.67 Cardiff
l: Cardiff, South Glamorgan
s: Single
cb: Brecon AC
ch: Malcolm Arnold
ht: 182cm, 6'0"
wt: 73kg, 11st 7lb

Colin Jackson won Olympic silver in the men's 110m hurdles in Seoul. And Britain will be hoping that he has cause to celebrate once more in Spain. Knee and hamstring problems forced him to pull out of the 1991 world championships at the last minute. But Colin has an impressive career record at 110m hurdles. In 1987 he took bronze in the world championships following a common-wealth silver in 1986. He turned the latter into gold in 1990. Indoors, the Welshman has world silver and european gold from 1989. He has been AAA champion four times and set four european records with a best of 13.08.

Anthony Jarrett

b: 13.08.68 Enfield
l: London
s: Single
cb: Haringey AC
ch: John Isaacs
ht: 188cm, 6'2"
wt: 80kg, 12st 8lb

Tony ran the 110m hurdles race of his life in Tokyo at the world championships last year to take bronze for himself and Britain. His medal marked a new confidence from the talented athlete who has often run in the shadow of his team-mates and rivals Colin Jackson and Jon Ridgeon. Tony was 6th in the Olympic final in 1988. Since then he has taken commonwealth, european and european indoor silver - all in 1990. Back in 1987 he was european junior gold medal-list. Barcelona could signal a continuing break-through for Tony.

Linda Keough

b: 26.12.63 Hackney
l: Thames Ditton, Surrey
s: Single
o: Clerk
cb: Basingstoke & Mid Hants AC
ch: James Spooner
ht: 174cm, 5'9"
wt: 61kg, 9st 9lb

Nigerian Fatimat Yusuf came from nowhere to spoil a potentially golden moment for Linda at the 1990 Commonwealth Games in Auckland. So she settled for silver but hit back with 400m relay gold. The girl from Thames Ditton has been UK no.1 at 400m almost permanently since 1985. But for illness she might have snatched a medal in Split at the 1990 europeans. In Barcelona Linda will be looking to qualify for the later stages.

Jason Livingston

b: 17.03.71 Croydon
l: Thornton Heath, Surrey
s: Single
cb: Shaftesbury-Barnet Harriers
ch: Ronald Roddan
ht: 168cm, 5'6"
wt: 70kg, 11st 0lb

Jason proved at the european indoor championships in early 1992 that he is ready to challenge the best of British and world sprinters. He took the 60m title which had belonged to Linford Christie. 1990 was the year that Jason - once nicknamed "baby Ben" after his teen-years hero Ben Johnson - made his senior British debut. In that same year he was world junior 100m silver medallist. At the 1991 world seniors in Tokyo he went out in the heats in 10.57 but watch out for some fast action from Jason in Olympic year.

Adeoye Mafe

b: 12.11.66 Isleworth
l: London
s: Single
ch: Ronald Roddan
ht: 185cm, 6'1"
wt: 77kg, 12st 2lb

Ade had an outstandingly successful early career. He came 8th in the 200m at the Olympic Games in 1984 and took silver in the european indoor championships in 1984. Then injury struck and he did not return until he won the latter event in 1989. Since that time he has picked up world indoor silver at 200m in 1989, world indoor and commonwealth bronze in 1990. For Barcelona he could target either the 200m or the 400m.

Eamonn Martin

b: 09.10.58 Basildon
l: Basildon, Essex
s: Married
o: Ford test engineer
cb: Basildon AC
ch: Mel Batty
ht: 183cm, 6'0"
wt: 68kg, 10st 10lb

Eamonn Martin will want to forget Seoul and the 1988 Olympic Games. He went out in the 5000m semi-finals and did not finish the 10,000m. It was a powerful disappointment for the man who is rarely challenged on the domestic distance running scene. In Barcelona Eamonn will be looking for the kind of form which gave him commonwealth gold at 10,000m in Auckland, holding off a strong African challenge. At the Tokyo world championships Eamonn was 15th in the 10,000m and at the 1990 europeans he placed 13th - equal to his Olympic finish in the 1984 5,000m.

ATHLETICS

Elizabeth McColgan

b: 24.05.64 Dundee
l: Dundee, Tayside
s: Married
cb: Dundee Hawkhill Harriers AC
ch: John Anderson
ht: 168cm, 5'6"
wt: 46kg, 7st 3lb

This feisty Scottish mum exhausted worldwide superlatives last year. She broke a top-class field from the front to win the world 10,000m title on a steamy Tokyo night in September. Then she made a spectacular marathon debut by winning in New York. Her successes were the latest in a line of medals which include Olympic silver from Seoul four years ago and double commonwealth gold from 1986 and 1990 - all at 10,000m. At the 1986 europeans, Liz finished 7th and then came 5th at the world championships in 1987.

Fiona May

b: 12.12.69 Slough
l: Derby
s: Single
o: College student
cb: Derby Ladies AC
ch: Jon Rosenthal
ht: 182cm, 5'11"
wt: 62kg, 9st 11lb

Fiona May jumped, quite literally, out of the junior ranks and into a sixth place in the Olympic final in Seoul in 1988. Earlier that year she signalled her potential with gold at the world junior championships in Canada. Her success there was in addition to a 1987 european junior gold and a 1986 world junior silver. 1990, though, did not start so well for the Derby girl with the sunny personality. She was tipped for gold and only got bronze at the Auckland Commonwealth Games. And at the europeans she finished 7th. In Barcelona, this 1991 UK and WAAA champion will be looking for a return to world-class form.

Yvonne Murray

b: 14.10.64 Edinburgh
l: Musselburgh, East Lothian
s: Single
cb: Edinburgh AC
ch: Tommy Boyle
ht: 172cm, 5'8"
wt: 51kg, 8st 0lb

Yvonne Murray appeared perfectly prepared for the 3000m rostrum in Tokyo at last year's world championships. The Seoul Olympic bronze medallist could only apologise to the nation for her ultimate demise. But, no doubt, she will now be doubly determined to return to form in Barcelona. Yvonne has the proven capability. She was european champion and commonwealth silver medallist in 1990 and 1989 world cup champion. And the european gold in Split made her the first British woman to win a european track title for 21 years.

Tom McKean

b: 27.10.63 Bellshill
l: Motherwell, Strathclyde
s: Married
ch: Tommy Boyle
ht: 183cm, 6'0"
wt: 71kg, 11st 3lb

Tom had a miserable time in Seoul four years ago in the 800m. He was disqualified in the heats. That was a disappointment for the Scot who two years earlier had taken silver in the Stuttgart european championships But Tom has since hit back with title successes at the european cup in 1989 and 1991, making a unique competitive hat-trick. He was not best pleased with his 1990 common-wealth performance finishing 7th - a long way from his silver medal-winning form of 1986. Tom silenced many of his critics with european gold in 1990. He will be looking for a similar Olympic performance.

ATHLETICS

John Regis

b: 13.10.66 London
l: London
s: Single
ch: Belgrave Harriers
cb: John Isaacs
ht: 181cm, 5'11"
wt: 88kg, 13st 12lb

John is an incredible hulk of a man. But he did not truly move athletics mountains until the european championships in 1990 - a meeting at which he won four medals including gold in the 200m, bronze in the 100m together with 400m relay gold and sprint relay silver. That was a popular performance, particularly after John had come so close to winning the world 200m title in 1987 before fading to a bronze. In Auckland at the 1990 Commonwealth Games he started favourite, too, but ended up with silver in the 200m. At the world championships John was part of Britain's winning 400m relay team.

Derek Redmond

b: 03.09.65 Bletchley
l: Towcester, Northants
s: Single
cb: Birchfield Harriers
ch: Tony Hadley
ht: 183cm, 6'0"
wt: 64kg, 10st 1lb

Derek has had a tough career. After a promising start - including a european 4th place in the 400m in 1986 the likeable Birchfield harrier had injuries which kept him out of two commonwealth, one Olympic and one european championships teams. Tokyo, in 1991, brought a major consolation with a gold medal from the 400m relay.

Kirsty Wade

b: 06.08.62 Girvan
l: Rowlands Gill, Tyne & Wear
s: Married
cb: Blaydon Harriers AC
ch: Harry Wilson/Tony Wade
ht: 170cm, 5'7"
wt: 54kg, 8st 8lb

Kirsty was a world championships 1500m finalist in 1991, coming sixth. That marked a return to form for the double 1986 commonwealth champion - at 800m and 1500m - who took time out in 1989 to have a baby daughter. Back in 1982 Kirsty also won a commonwealth title for Wales at 800m - the first of her countrywomen to win a track title in the history of the Games. In 1987 she won the european cup 1500m in Prague.

Matthew Yates

b: 04.02.69 Rochford
l: Basildon, Essex
s: Single
cb: Newham & Essex Beagles
ch: Mike Yates
ht: 190cm, 6'3"
wt: 76kg, 12st 0lb

Matthew is a newcomer who dares to tread where some of Britain's athletics "greats" have gone before in the middle distance events. He upstaged a Coe swansong in Auckland by taking a bronze medal at 800m. In the same year he was eighth in the european championships 800m. Matthew became european indoor champion early in Olympic year. After a disappointing world championships he has his sights set on Barcelona.

ATHLETICS

Julie Bradbury

b: 12.02.67 Oxford
l: Didcot, Oxfordshire
o: Admin Assistant
s: Single
ch: Mark Methven
ht: 175 cm, 5'9"
wt: 64 kg, 10 st 1 lb

This talented singles and doubles player caught the public eye in early 1991 with a shock victory in the national singles championships. Since then she has also formed a successful doubles partnership with Gillian Clark. The duo were All England semi-finalists in March of this year and quarter-finalists in the Japan Open.

Stephen Butler

b: 27.09.63 Coventry
l: Coventry, West Midlands
o: Sportsman
s: Single
ht: 185 cm, 6'1"
wt: 78 kg, 12 st 4 lb

Nicknamed "Turbo", Steve is a player who has had an exciting career but one plagued by injuries. This season he has already won the Canadian and US Open singles. In 1990 he took a bronze medal in the european championships. Steve's greatest win was over the then world champion Icuk Sugiarto in the 1984 Thomas Cup.
Currently fighting off a leg thrombosis to make the Olympics.

Gillian Clark

b: 02.09.61 Baghdad
l: London
o: Badminton player
s: Single
cb: Wimbledon & the David Lloyd Club
ch: Lee Jae Bok
ht: 176 cm, 5'9"
wt: 68 kg, 10 st 10 lb

Twice a commonwealth gold medallist (team) and three times european women's doubles champion, Gillian is one of England's greatest international players of all time. She has won more caps for her country than any other female - having over-taken another famous Gillian - Gilks - this season. A world bronze medallist in 1983, Gillian was also a semi-finalist at the 1992 All England champion-ships with Julie Bradbury. Now a leading medal contender in Barcelona.

Gillian Gowers

b: 09.04.64 Hornchurch
l: Welwyn Garden City, Hertfordshire
o: Badminton player
s: Single
cb: Gosling
ch: Barbara Beckett
ht: 157 cm, 5'2"
wt: 55 kg, 8 st 9 lb

Gillian is set to play doubles for Britain in Barcelona with Sara Sankey. The duo were semi-finalists at the 1992 All England championships. With past partners, Gillian has been one of the world's greatest doubles exponents picking up commonwealth and european gold in the women's doubles and a 1985 world bronze in the mixed. Gillian has also twice been an All England women's doubles finalist and winner of the Japan Open title.

Darren Hall

b: 25.10.65 Walthamstow
l: London
o: Badminton player
s: Single
ch: Ray Stevens
ht: 180 cm, 5'11"
wt: 71 kg, 11 st 3 lb

Darren is a fast and exciting singles player. He narrowly missed taking a record sixth national singles title earlier this year. In Auckland in 1990 he won commonwealth team gold and individual bronze. But his greatest triumph came in 1988 when he became european champion. He beat Morten Frost in the final to become the first Englishman to take the title.

Sara Sankey

b: 29.09.67 Southport
l: Southport, Merseyside
o: Housewife
s: Married 1 child
cb: Churchtown BC
ht: 170 cm, 5'7"
wt: 68 kg, 10 st 10 lb

When Sara is not busy looking after her son, Scott, she is winning badminton titles. This current commonwealth women's doubles champion also won the same event at the 1991 Dutch and Canadian Opens. In partnership with Gillian Gowers, Sara reached the semi-final of the All England Open in 1991 and 1992. This year they were narrowly beaten by the top Chinese pairing and will be looking for revenge in Barcelona.

Fiona Smith

b: 13.11.63 Farnborough
l: Guildford, Surrey
o: Badminton player
s: Married 1 child
cb: Wimbledon
ch: Mark Elliott
ht: 167 cm, 5'6"
wt: 56 kg, 8 st 11 lb

Fiona was a triple gold medallist at the 1990 Commonwealth Games in the women's singles and doubles and the team events. And, in the same year, she reached the final of the european championships singles. Since then she has taken a year out to have a baby but still returned to take the national singles title earlier this year - her sixth in the event.

Helen Troke

b: 07.11.64 Southampton
s: Single
cb: Lanz SC and Bitterne LC
ch: Brian Hooper
ht: 172 cm, 5'8"
wt: 63 kg, 9 st 13 lb

Over the last decade Helen has been one of Europe's main threats to far eastern dominance of women's singles. She was a world bronze medallist in 1983, twice commonwealth champion - in 1982 and 1986 - and european title-holder in 1984 and 1986. More recently she reached the semi-finals of the 1991 Japan Open and won the Scottish Open title in 1990. Has battled back to fitness after snapping her achilles tendon two years ago.

Look out, too, in Barcelona for Anders Nielsen - All England men's singles quarter-finalist this March - and Joanne Muggeridge a feisty singles player from Kent. Team manager will be former european champion Stephen Baddeley.

BADMINTON

Adrian Dodson

b: 20.9.70 Guyana
l: London
o: Boxer
cb: St Pancras and London ABA

Adrian boxed for Guyana in the 63.5kg class at the Seoul Olympic Games of 1988. He reached the third round before losing. Since then he has moved to Britain and changed his surname by deed poll from Carew to Dodson. Adrian won the 1990 ABA title in the 67kg class. He boxed and won for England against Sweden in December 1991 at 71kg. His only other international for his country came against Denmark, again in 1991, but he lost his fight.

Mark Edwards

b: 15.09.63 London
l: Lee-on-Solent, Hampshire
o: Royal Marine Commando
s: Married 1 child
cb: Royal Navy
ch: Tony Bevel
ht: 178 cm, 5'10"
wt: 76 kg, 12 st 0 lb

This 1990 commonwealth bronze medallist at middleweight was the ABA champion in 1988 and 1991. He also took a silver medal at the Canada Cup in 1989. Mark won his 1991 ABA title after a 14-month lay-off. His hobbies are cross country running and ten pin bowling.

Paul Ingle

b: 22.06.72 Scarborough
l: Scarborough, Yorkshire
o: Building labourer
s: Single
cb: Scarborough ABC
ch: T Johnson, Ian Irwin
ht: 162 cm, 5'4"
wt: 51 kg, 8 st 0 lb

Paul is the 1991 ABA champion in the 51kg weight category. In 1991 he won a bronze medal at the world junior championships as well as taking gold at the Canada cup. A year earlier he was a silver medallist at the "multi-nations" tournament. His hobbies are football and table tennis. .

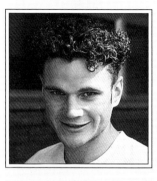

John Irwin

b: 31.05.69 Mexbrough
l: Doncaster, South Yorkshire
o: Joiner
s: Single
cb: Tom Hill YC ABC
ch: Steven Phillips
ht: 170 cm, 5'7"
wt: 57 kg, 9 st 0 lb

John went to Auckland for the 1990 Commonwealth Games and came back with a gold medal from the featherweight category. A year later he proved his international status by reaching the quarter-finals of the world championships. John is the 1991 ABA champion. His hobbies are football, swimming and mountain-biking.

Look out, too, in Barcelona for world junior silver medallist Robin Reid and world junior gold medallist Alan Vaughan. Team manager will be Joe Lewis and the coach will be Ian Irwin.

Eric Jamieson
Flatwater
b: 11.08.61 Kilwinning
l: Guildford, Surrey
o: Construction Manager
s: Married
cb: Wey Kayak Club
ht: 190 cm, 6'3"
wt: 85 kg, 13 st 5 lb

Eric was Britain's best performer at the 1988 Olympic Games. He made two finals - Canadian singles at 500 and 1000m - and finished ninth in both. Four years earlier he also took seventh place in the Olympic Canadian doubles 500m final. In 1985 Eric was ninth in the world championships 500m. His hobbies are DIY, catamaran sailing and most sports.

Richard Fox
Slalom
b: 05.06.60 Winsford, Somerset
l: West Bridgford, Notts
o: Marketing Consultant
s: Married
cb: Nottingham Kayak Club
ch: Hugh Mantle
ht: 177 cm, 5'10"
wt: 70 kg, 11 st 0 lb

Britain has very few world champions - and even fewer who have won the title four times. Richard Fox, however, did just that in 1981, 83, 85 and 89 in the canoe slalom men's kayak singles. He was also overall winner of the seven-race series world cup in 1988, 89 and 91. Richard has been a member of the Sports Council and sits on the BOA competitors council. He is one of Britain's brightest medal prospects for the 1992 Olympic Games.

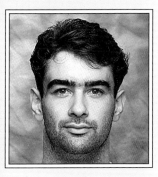

Gareth Marriott
Slalom
b: 14.07.70 Mansfield
l: Holme Pierrepont, Nottinghamshire
o: Athlete/Student
s: Single
ch: Hugh Mantle
ht: 184 cm, 6'0"
wt: 72 kg, 11 st 5 lb

Gareth began to make his mark internationally when he won the world junior canadian singles title in 1988. A year later he took sixth place in the senior world championships. In 1990 he won gold at the pre-worlds and followed that with gold at the pre-Olympics in 1991. He was also the world cup overall champion in 1991. Gareth goes to Barcelona hoping to atone for a poor showing in the world championships last year.

Shaun Pearce
Slalom
b: 13.12.69 Reading
l: Basford, Nottinghamshire
o: Assistant Shop Manager
s: Single
cb: Newbury Canoe Club
ch: Hugh Mantle
ht: 172 cm, 5'8"
wt: 71 kg, 11 st 3 lb

Shaun Pearce ousted his Barcelona team-mate Richard Fox from the title slot by becoming the world kayak singles champion in 1991. Both men are now rivals for the gold medal at the Games. Shaun began his international career by winning the world junior kayak singles title in 1987. On the 1990/91 world cup race series he picked up a bronze and a gold medal. When he's not canoeing or working, Shaun likes to play golf.

Look out, too, in Barcelona for the Train family in the flatwater canoeing and Richard Fox's sister, Rachel, in the canoe slalom. Team manager will be Steve Jackson.

CANOEING

Eddie Alexander

b: 10.08.64 Huntly, Aberdeenshire
l: Bovingdon, Hertfordshire
o: Engineer, BP Engineering
s: Single
cb: City of Edinburgh R.C.
ht: 179 cm, 5'10"
wt: 78 kg, 12 st 4 lb

Eddie proved that he is one of the world's best sprint cyclists when he finished 4th at the 1988 Olympic Games in Seoul. Two years later he was disappointed with a fifth placing in the 1990 Commonwealth Games final after picking up a bronze four years earlier. Eddie's best world championship result to date was a ninth place in the 1986 final.

Christopher Boardman

b: 26.08.68 Clatterbridge, Wirral
l: Hoylake, Wirral
o: Frame Design Consultant
s: Married 2 children
cb: Manchester Wheelers
ch: Peter Keen
ht: 175 cm, 5'9"
wt: 72 kg, 11 st 5 lb

Christopher is the 1991 British 4000m individual pursuit champion. His club, Manchester Wheelers, also took the team title at the same championships. For Christopher it was a repeat of the same double triumph in 1989. This bronze medallist at the 1986 Commonwealth Games could be a medal chance for Britain in Barcelona. He qualified in fifth place for the 1991 world championships in Stuttgart but finished ninth - a result he will be looking to improve at the Games.

Sally Dawes

b: 27.06.73
l: Arnold, Nottinghamshire
o: Unemployed
s: Single
cb: Leicester RC
ht: 165 cm, 5'5"
wt: 55 kg, 8 st 9 lb

Sally has qualified for the Olympic Games after picking up a silver medal in the world junior championships in 1991 in the women's road race. At the same event she was also a semi-finalist in the individual pursuit. In 1990 she represented England at the Commonwealth Games and used the experience well before going out in the heats. She could be one of Britain's brightest future prospects.

Simon Lillistone

b: 13.02.69 Shrewsbury
l: Shrewsbury, Salop
o: Student
s: Single
cb: Team Haverhill
ch: Peter Keen
ht: 183 cm, 6'0"
wt: 76 kg, 12 st 0 lb

If Simon performs well at the pre-Games trials he could be a competitor in both the individual points race and the team pursuit. And in Barcelona Simon will be hoping to add another major Games medal to the bronze he took in Auckland for the team pursuit at the 1990 Commonwealth Games. Since Auckland he has won the 1991 national title at 50km points and a national silver medal in the team time trial. At the 1991 world championships he was part of the team which finished 11th for Britain in the team time trial.

David Broome
Show Jumping
b: 01.03.40 Cardiff
s: Married 3 children
ht: 180 cm, 5'11"
wt: 86 kg, 13 st 8 lb

David Broome's Olympic career began in 1960 in Rome when he took individual bronze - a feat he repeated eight years later in Mexico City. He competed in 1964 and 72, too, but was then barred as a "professional". Changes to the eligibility rules brought him back in 1988. So Barcelona will be his sixth Olympic Games. In Seoul he finished fourth individually on Countryman. David won world team gold in 1978 and European team silver in 1983 and 1991. He is also a six times winner of the King George V cup at the Royal International Horse Show.

Karen Dixon
3-day event
b: 17.09.64
l: Barnard Castle, County Durham
s: Married
ch: Elaine Straker
o.f.: Father in Law, Robert Dixon, bobsleigh gold 1964.

Karen's international career blossomed first in 1983 when she won European junior individual silver at Burghley. In 1988 she finished fifth at Badminton and was selected for the Olympic Games in Seoul where she finished 19th individually and took team silver. Since Seoul Karen has had a 6th, 9th and 10th place at Badminton in 1989, 90 and 91 respectively. Last year Karen married Andrew Dixon. Her maiden name was Straker.

Virginia Leng
3-day event
b: 01.02.55 Malta
l: Chippenham, Wiltshire
o: Director of P&N Company
s: Single
ch: Dorothy Willis
ht: 167 cm, 5'6"
wt: 54 kg, 8 st 7 lb

Few Olympic competitors have a better international record than Ginny Leng. She was world individual champion in 1986, european champion in 1985, 87 and 89. And Burghley winner from 1984-87 and 1989. At Badminton she recorded two victories in 1985 and 1989. Barcelona marks Ginny's third Olympic Games. In 1984 she took individual bronze and team silver and four years later she added a second team silver to her collection in Seoul. Ginny was kept out of the 1990 europeans with a broken ankle but came back a year later to win team silver.

Jennie Loriston-Clarke
Dressage
b: 22.01.43 Charmouth
l: Brockenhurst, Hampshire
o: Housewife and journalist
s: Married 2 children
cb: Dressage Supporters Club
ch: Ferdi Eilberg

Jennie was a bronze medallist at the 1978 world championships. She also finished fifth in the world cup placings overall in both 1990 and 1991. At the world equestrian games in Stockholm in 1990 she was 13th - one place better than her Olympic result of 14th in Seoul in 1988. Jenny has consistently been Britain's top dressage performer. In 1991 she took fourth place at the european championships. Jenny did not compete at the 1984 Olympic Games because her horse had a virus infection.

EQUESTRIAN

Nick Skelton

Show Jumping

b: 30.12.57 Bedworth
o: Farmer
s: Married 2 children
ht: 177 cm, 5'10"
wt: 76 kg, 12 st 0 lb

Nick Skelton placed fourth on Apollo four years ago in Seoul in the individual competition. Two years earlier he was a bronze medallist in the world championships individually as well as winning team silver. Nick repeated his individual world bronze in 1990. With Britain's european championships teams, Nick has won team gold in 1985 and 1987 as well as silver last year. But he considers his three consecutive Hickstead Derby wins as his greatest achievement of all time.

Robert Smith

Show Jumping

b: 12.07.61 Shipley
l: Bingley, Yorkshire
o: Show Jumper
s: Married
ht: 182 cm, 6'0"
wt: 89 kg, 14 st 0 lb

Robert Smith has a string of world grand prix wins to his name spread from 1984 - 1991 and in venues from Aachen to Toronto. Riding Video, Robert won the King George V Cup at the age of just 17 in 1979. Robert was short-listed but did not make either the 1984 or 1988 Olympic Games.

Ian Stark

3-day event

b: 22.02.54
l: Selkirk
o: Owns Livery Yard
s: Married 2 children
ch: Ferdi Eilberg

Ian Stark leads Britain's 3-day eventers in Barcelona. He was a world individual and team silver medallist at the 1990 championships. And he followed that up by individual and team gold at the european championships a year later. In Seoul, in 1988, Ian was individual silver medallist and led the team to a medal of the same colour. A year later he won european individual gold for the first time to add to his silver medal in 1987 and a bronze in 1985. Ian has twice been champion at Badminton - in 1986 and 1988.

John Whitaker

Show Jumping

b: 05.08.55 Huddersfield
l: Huddersfield
o: Show Jumping/Farming
s: Married 3 children
ht: 170 cm, 5'7"
wt: 64 kg, 10 st 1 lb

In 1984 John collected a team silver at the Los Angeles Games. Four years later he was unable to compete. Milton's owners would not let their horse travel that far. For Barcelona, however, they have relented. And John must be a gold medal contender. He was the 1990 and 1991 world cup winner, european individual and team gold medallist in 1989 and world individual bronze medallist in 1990. His major championships medal tally also includes five other european medals and a world team bronze and silver in 1982 and 1986 respectively.

William Gosbee

b: 20.05.61 London
l: London
o: PR Manager
s: Single
cb: Salle Boston
ch: Tomasz Walicki
ht: 170 cm, 5'7"
wt: 67 kg, 10 st 8 lb

Billy has competed at the last two Olympic Games. In Los Angeles in 1984 he came 22nd individually but the team ended up fifth. Four years later in Seoul he went out in the fourth of the elimination series of the individual foil and the team came tenth. The Seoul results were disappointing for Billy as he had picked up two top five placings in world cups leading up to the Games. He will be looking to make amends in Barcelona.

Fiona McIntosh

b: 24.06.60 Edinburgh
l: London
o: Teacher
s: Single
ch: Ziemowit Wojciechowski
ht: 170 cm, 5'7"
wt: 61 kg, 9 st 9 lb

Fiona is the current British women's foil champion. And in 1990 she picked up a gold medal in the commonwealth championships and the De Beaumont International. She fenced in Seoul but went out in the third round. At the 1984 Olympic Games Fiona finished 24th individually. Her hobbies include driving, eating out and travelling. Fiona also plays county hockey for Surrey.

Donald McKenzie

b: 03.06.60 Edinburgh
l: Edinburgh, Lothian
o: Civil Servant
s: Single
cb: Meadowbank Fencing Club
ht: 172 cm, 5'8"
wt: 60 kg, 9 st 6 lb

Donnie fenced in Seoul for Britain and made it through to the elimination stage of the competition where he went out in the first series. A year later he became the British champion at foil. His best world cup results to date have included a 9th placing in 1986 and a 13th placing in 1990. In 1986 he won the gold medal at the British Open (Leon Paul) cup. Donnie will be hoping to fly the British flag against stiff opposition in Barcelona.

Stephen Paul

Epee

b: 28.09.54 London
l: London
o: Manager
s: Married 2 children
cb: Salle Paul
ch: Ziemowit Wojciechowski
wt: 80 kg, 12 st 8 lb

Stephen recently returned to top class fencing in Britain after several years living and working in Australia. Back in 1979, 80 and 83 he was the British epee champion and also won the world-class Martini International in 1980 - the first British title success in the event for 20 years. Whilst in Australia he picked up the Australian epee title in 1984, 89 and 90. Stephen last competed for Britain in the 1980 and 84 Olympic Games where he reached the quarter-finals on both occasions.

FENCING

Terence Bartlett

b: 02.12.63 Southampton
l: Southampton, Hampshire
o: Unemployed
s: Single
cb: Lilleshall NSC
ch: Edmund Van Hoof
ht: 175 cm, 5'9"
wt: 71 kg, 11 st 3 lb

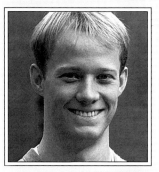

Terry Bartlett is the effervescent men's team captain. He competed at the Olympic Games of 1984 and 1988, finishing 36th and 71st overall respectively. Terry was also a member of England's Commonwealth Games team in Auckland in 1990. In 1991 he played his part in Britain's twelfth place at the world championships in Indianapolis - a result which put them into the 1992 Olympic Games with a full men's team for the first time. Terry recovered from major shoulder surgery to compete in 1991.

David Cox

b: 20.06.70 Johannesburg
l: Liverpool, Merseyside
o: Gymnastics coach
s: Single
cb: City of Liverpool
ht: 170 cm, 5'7"
wt: 62 kg, 9 st 11 lb

David went to Auckland as part of England's team in 1990 and came back with a silver medal from the team event. Two years earlier he became British champion in the floor exercise. In 1991 he won overall gold at the Kodak Cup and competed in the Seiko grand prix where he finished 11th overall. David's 16th place in the european junior championships in 1988 remains the best ever placing for a Briton in the event.

James May

b: 30.01.68 Seaton, Devon
l: Wolverhampton, West
    Midlands
o: RAF Officer
s: Single
cb: Bristol Hawks Gymnastic
    Club
ch: Stephen May
ht: 175 cm, 5'9"
wt: 77 kg, 12 st 2 lb

James May picked up a hatful of medals when he went to the Commonwealth Games in 1990 in Auckland. Two bronzes came from his performance in the overall and pommel horse competitions. He followed that with silver medals on both the rings and in the team event. But the pinnacle came with individual gold in the vault. In that same year James narrowly missed a bronze at the european championships, finishing fourth. He was also part of Britain's team which qualified for Barcelona at the world championships in Indianapolis in 1991.

Neil Thomas

b: 06.04.68 Chirk
l: Newport, Shropshire
o: Unemployed
s: Single
ch: Edmund Van Hoof
ht: 162 cm, 5'4"
wt: 61 kg, 9 st 9 lb

Neil is Britain's outstanding gymnast going into the Barcelona Games. At the 1991 world championships he came sixth in the floor final and 27th overall. And at the 1990 european championships he became the first British medallist for decades when he took bronze in the vault. Before that, in Auckland, at the Commonwealth Games, he was gold medallist in the floor exercises. Neil proved that 1990 was a very good year by adding the British national title. He was injured last year and could not defend his title. But look out for British Olympic history in the making in Barcelona.

Robert Clift

b: 01.08.62 Newport Gwent
l: Orpington, Kent
o: Banker
s: Married
cb: East Grinstead Hockey
Club
ch: Bram Van Asselt
ht: 182 cm, 5'11"
wt: 77 kg, 12 st 2 lb

This unassuming banker from Kent is a likely candidate for the British captaincy in Barcelona. His qualifications for the job, of course, include a gold medal from the Seoul Games of 1988. Before that Robert's career had read like a tale of three silvers - in the Champions Trophy of 1985, the world cup of 1986 and the european cup of 1987. He will be hoping that the team make up for recent poor form with a run of success in Spain.

Victoria Dixon

b: 05.08.59 Ormskirk
l: Thurston, Suffolk
o: Maths teacher
s: Single
cb: Ipswich Ladies Hockey
Club
ch: Dennis Hay
ht: 170 cm, 5'7"
wt: 73 kg, 11 st 7 lb

Vicky Dixon was part of the women's team in Seoul in 1988, narrowly missing out in the bronze medal play-off. Since then she has doubled her number of GB caps to 63 and helped her country win gold at the european cup in 1991 following a silver in the same event in 1987. At the 1990 world cup, Vicky was part of the team which finished fourth overall.

Russell Garcia

b: 20.06.70 Portsmouth
l: Portsmouth, Hampshire
o: Sports Consultant
s: Single
cb: Havant Hockey Club
ch: Norman Hughes
ht: 177 cm, 5'10"
wt: 73 kg, 11 st 7 lb

Russell created all-time Olympic history in Seoul as the youngest ever hockey gold medallist at the age of 18 years and 103 days. Now he is an established member of the team. Since Seoul he has won a bronze medal in the european cup and was part of the side that finished 5th in the 1990 world cup in Lahore. Russell plays for Havant in the national league.

Sean Kerly

b: 29.01.60 Tankerton
l: Reigate, Surrey
o: Sales & marketing manager
s: Married 2 children
cb: Canterbury
ht: 180 cm, 5'11"
wt: 80 kg, 12 st 8 lb

Sean is the prolific goal-scoring centre forward who featured in both of Britain's recent Olympic Games campaigns - to take unexpected bronze in 1984 and a gold in 1988. His charisma on the pitch is unmistakeable and Britain will be hoping that he is on form in Barcelona. Over the last four years Sean has won a bronze medal in the european cup and helped his team to a fifth placing in the world cup. Back in 1986 he was a double silver medallist at the world and european cups. Sean now plays for second division Canterbury in the national league.

HOCKEY

Mary Nevill

b: 12.03.61 Gansworth
l: Coleorton, Leicestershire
o: Lecturer
s: Married
cb: Leicester ladies
ch: Dennis Hay
ht: 158 cm, 5'2"
wt: 58 kg, 9 st 2 lb

Mary Nevill is Britain's stalwart captain who has made over 80 international appearances. She was part of the team which finished fourth in Seoul at the last Olympic Games. And she helped her country to european cup gold only last year. Mary would also have gone to Los Angeles in 1984 if Britain had not lost to the USA by a single goal in the qualifying tournament. In 1987 she won european championships silver as part of the England team. Her hobbies include many sports and dining out. She is a lecturer in sports science.

Jon Potter

b: 19.11.63 London
l: York
o: Marketing Manager
s: Single
cb: Hounslow
ht: 172 cm, 5'8"
wt: 10 st 10 lb

Jon is Great Britain's most-capped male player with 109 international appearances to his credit. He was part of the nation's bronze medal-winning team at the Olympic Games in Los Angeles in 1984. And he returned to take gold with the team in 1988. Jon was also a world silver medallist in 1984, european silver medallist in 1986 and took world bronze in 1987 and 1991. He captained Hounslow to the National League title in 1989/90.

Alison Ramsay

b: 16.04.59 London
l: Perth, Tayside
o: Solicitor
s: Married
cb: Glasgow Western Ladies
ch: Dennis Hay, Neil Menzies
ht: 167 cm, 5'6"
wt: 56 kg, 8 st 11 lb

When Alison goes training for the Olympic Games she enlists the support of her collie dog. And when she competes or trains with Great Britain she invariably has a long trip to make down from Perth. But that does not seem to trouble the Scot with the sunny personality who hopes to make up in Barcelona for her semi-final disappointment in Seoul four years ago. She will be Britain's vice-captain in Barcelona and already has over 80 GB caps and more than a century of Scottish caps to her name.

Jane Sixsmith

b: 05.09.67 Sutton Coldfield
l: Sutton Coldfield
o: Payroll clerk
s: Single
cb: First Personnel Sutton
    Coldfield
ch: Dennis Hay
ht: 160 cm, 5'3"
wt: 57 kg, 9st 0lb

This talented winger has played for Great Britain on almost sixty occasions in an international career which began just prior to the Seoul Games. Her energetic style reflects a bubbly personality. Jane was part of the team which won european gold for England in 1991 and a silver medal in the same event in 1987. At the 1990 world cup she was part of the team which finished fourth - the identical placing to Britain's Olympic effort in 1988.

Look out, too, in Barcelona for many more members of Britain's 1988 men's gold medal-winning team. Team manager will be Bernard Cotton (men) and Di Batterham (women).

Diane Bell

-61kg (women)
b: 11.10.63 Corbridge
l: High Wycombe, Bucks
s: Single
cb: Fairholme Judo
ch: Roy Inman
ht: 156 cm, 5'1"
wt: 61 kg, 9 st 9 lb

When the Olympic curtain is raised in Barcelona Diane Bell will be hoping to convert demonstration gold from 1988 into the real thing. She has the right to be confident. Twice a world champion, in 1986 and 1987, Diane picked up silver at the worlds in Barcelona in 1991 - all in the under-61kg weight category. And she has also been a three-times european champion in 1984, 86 and 88. When she is not puzzling her opponents on the mat, Diane likes to try her hand at crosswords as relaxation.

Karen Briggs

-48kg (women)
b: 11.04.63
l: Hull, Humberside
o: Sports development
s: single
cb: Kingston Fairholme
ch: Mike Joyce, Roy Inman
ht: 5'0"
wt: 48kg 7st 10lb

Karen Briggs is noted for her determination. She has come back from numerous injuries to take the world title in 1982, 1984 and 1986. In 1991 she lost in the world championships final to Cecile Nowak of France. But Sharon struck back earlier this year to defeat the same opponent in the final of the Tournoi de Paris. Barcelona could prove a fascinating duel between the two. Briggs, meanwhile, has also been european champion on numerous occasion including 1982, 83, 84, 86 and 87.

Loretta Cusack

-52kg (women)
b: 12.07.63 London
l: Edinburgh
o: Sports teacher
s: Married
cb: Edinburgh
ch: George Kerr, Colin McIver
ht: 154 cm, 5'1"
wt: 52 kg, 8 st 3 lb

Loretta, nee Doyle, was world champion in 1982 in the under-52kg category. She followed that in 1983 with a european gold. More recently she took gold in the 1990 Commonwealth Games in Auckland for Scotland and at the US Open in 1991. A double silver medallist in the european championships individual and team events last year, Loretta is as self-possessed off the tatami as in competition. She is married to William Cusack, currently a member of the Great Britain Olympic men's squad. She devotes some of her spare time to working with mentally-handicapped children in sport.

Elvis Gordon

+95Kg and open
b: 23.06.53 Hanover
l: Wolverhampton, West Midlands
o: Unemployed
s: Single
cb: Wolverhampton Judo Club
ch: Mac Abbotts
ht: 188 cm, 6'2"
wt: 132 kg, 20 st 11 lb

Gargantuan Elvis Gordon was so angry at being mistaken for a coach at the recent German Open that he went on to prove his continuing youth by winning a silver medal. The style was typical of a man who won world silver in 1987 in the open category, european gold in 1988 and double commonwealth gold in Auckland in 1990. He will be hoping to make Barcelona a dramatic swansong before, perhaps, fulfilling apparent appearances as a coach.

JUDO

For key to abbreviations: see page 239

211

Kate Howey

-66kg (women)

b: 31.05.73 Andover
l: Andover, Hants
o: Unemployed
s: Single
cb: Kent Invicta JudoKwai
ch: Alan Roberts
ht: 160 cm, 5'3"
wt: 66 kg, 10 st 6 lb

Kate Howey is the youngster to watch for in Barcelona. She has made dramatic international progress in the last three years. In 1989 she was gold medallist in the junior european champion-ships under 66kg category - a result she followed up with gold at world junior level a year later. In 1990 she returned to the junior europeans to mount a successful title defence. And then added european senior silver in both 1990 and 1991. Finally, she established herself as an Olympic medal contender when she took bronze at the 1991 senior world championships.

Sharon Lee

+72 Kg (women)

b: 13.03.63 Birmingham
l: Birmingham, West Midlands
o: Assistant Sport Leader
s: Single
cb: Great Barr Judo Club
ch: Roy Inman
ht: 175 cm, 5'9"
wt: 72 kg, 11 st 5 lb

Sharon Lee was one of England's stars at the 1990 Commonwealth Games picking up double gold in the over-72kg and open categories. A year earlier she became world silver medallist in the same weight band and has since added 1990 european gold to her tally. Now Sharon is hungry for medals in Barcelona as part of potentially Britain's most successful Olympic squad of all time.

Sharon Rendle

-52Kg (women)

b: 18.06.66 Drypool, Hull
l: Grimsby, South
      Humberside
o: Unemployed
s: Single
cb: Grimsby Judo Club
ch: Terry Alltoft
ht: 150 cm, 4'11"
wt: 55 kg, 8 st 9 lb

Sharon Rendle soaked up the Olympic atmos-phere and a gold medal from the sidelines in Seoul as part of a demonstration event in women's judo. This time it is all for real. And Sharon goes to Barcelona as world silver medallist. Her loss in 1991 will have been a disappointment for the girl who won the world title in 1987 and 1989 at under-52kg. When Sharon is not training or competing she likes to read and watch old Bette Davis films.

Densign White

-86kg

b: 21.12.61 Wolverhampton
l: Wolverhampton, West
      Midlands
o: Student
s: Single
cb: Wolverhampton Mander's
ch: Mac Abbotts
ht: 180 cm, 5'11"
wt: 86 kg, 13 st 8 lb

Densign White has a delightfully sunny personality but is a tough fighter in competition. He was a gold medallist at the 1990 Commonwealth Games, silver medallist at the 1987 and 1988 european championships and a european bronze medallist in 1990. At the Olympic Games, four years ago, he went out at the quarter-final stage - a result he will be looking to beat this time round. Densign is one of a strong West Midlands squad in British judo. He also competed at the 1984 Games.

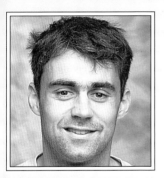

Graham Brookhouse

b: 19.06.62 Birmingham
l: Birmingham
o: Sportsman
s: Single
cb: Spartan
ch: Robert Phelps, Paul Willis
ht: 182cm 6'0"
wt: 73kg

Graham was part of Britain's bronze medal-winning side at the 1988 Olympic Games in Seoul. Individually, in 1988, he finished 20th. At the national championships he has twice been silver medallist - in 1990 and 1991 - but won the title in 1989. Last year Graham placed 17th in the european championships in Italy. At the beginning of 1992 Graham picked up a team silver medal in the Australia Cup in Melbourne. His hobbies are surfing and meeting people.

Dominic Mahony

b: 26.04.64 Plymouth
l: Alverstoke, Hants
o: Army officer
s: Single
ht: 190cm 6' 3"
wt: 13st 0lb

Dominic came into modern pentathlon from the sport of fencing in 1980. In 1987 he won a world team bronze and followed that up in Seoul as part of Britain's bronze medal-winning trio there. Mahony carried a knee injury through those Games. At the last British championships he finished third overall. And in early 1992 he ended up fifth individually in the Australia Cup whilst the team took a silver medal. His best world championships result to date was a sixth place in 1987. Mahony hopes for a return to form in Barcelona. His hobbies are movies, music and military history.

Richard Phelps

b: 19.04.61 Gloucester
l: Upton St Leonard, Glos
o: Iron reclamation business
s: Single
cb: Spartan
ch: Robert Phelps (Uncle)
ht: 185cm 6'1"
wt: 75kg 11st 3lb

Richard is the country's leading modern pentath-lete. He won the national championships in July 1991. At the Olympic Games in 1984 he came fourth individually but he had to wait until 1988 for a medal - a bronze in the team event. This was an addition to the bronze medals Richard won at the 1987 world and european champion-ships. In that same year he also finished 7th individually at the world championships. In both 1989 and 1990 Richard improved that world placing to fifth in Hungary and Lathi, Finland, respectively. He is Britain's best chance of an individual medal in 1992.

Miriam Batten

b: 04.11.64 Dartford
l: London
o: Retail buyer
s: Single
cb: Thames rowing club
ch: Panagis Michaels, Peter Proudley
ht: 173 cm, 5'8"
wt: 66 kg, 10 st 6 lb

Miriam Batten rows with Fiona Freckleton in a coxless pairs partnership which snapped up a bronze medal in the 1991 world championships in Vienna - putting them in the history books as the first British women's crew ever to win a medal at a world championships. It also makes them potential Barcelona medallists. Miriam learnt her craft at Southampton University guided by coach Peter Proudley. Since then she has won two silver and one gold medal at the national championships. At the 1990 and 1991 world championships she achieved two ninth places in the coxless four and eight respectively.

Katharine Brownlow

b: 16.08.64 Altrincham
l: London
o: Student/Part-time Work
s: Single
cb: Thames Rowing Club
ch: Gill Bond, David Lister
ht: 172 cm, 5'8"
wt: 60 kg, 9 st 6 lb

Katie has been one of Britain's top lightweight rowers who will make the move up to the heavyweight divisions in Barcelona. She is likely to stroke the eight if fully recovered from back surgery over the winter. Katie has put together an impressive world championships series including a 5th place in 1988, a 4th in 1989 and a silver medal in 1991 - all in the lightweight coxless fours. Currently studying a technical translators' course, Katie is a former employee of the British Olympic Association technical department.

Martin Cross

b: 19.07.57 London
l: Hampton, Middlesex
o: History Teacher
s: Married 1 child
cb: Thames Tradesmens RC
ch: Martin Aitken
ht: 187 cm, 6'2"
wt: 89 kg, 14 st 0 lb

Martin is rowing's equivalent of perpetual motion. He is a history teacher at Hampton School, secretary of the Hampton Labour party and an athlete representative on the National Olympic Committee - as well as being a double Olympic medallist, husband and father. His medals came as a bronze in 1980 in the coxless fours, followed by gold in the coxed fours in Los Angeles in 1984. He competed in Seoul, finishing fourth in the coxed four. And at world championship level the likeable middlesex man has a silver medal, from the coxless pairs in 1985 and a bronze medal, from the eight in 1991, to his credit.

Fiona Freckleton

b: 06.11.60 Chelmsford Essex
l: London
o: Maths teacher
s: Single
cb: Westminster School BC
ch: Panagis Michaels
ht: 172 cm, 5'8"
wt: 69 kg, 10 st 12 lb

Fiona, who started rowing at Oxford in 1979, is currently maths teacher and rowing coach at Westminster School. At the 1991 world rowing championships in Vienna she won a bronze medal in the coxless pairs with Miriam Batten and added a sixth place in the women's eight. A year earlier she was ninth at the worlds in a coxless four. In 1986 Fiona rowed for Scotland in the Commonwealth Games. And in 1982/83 she was stroke of the Oxford women's boat race eight.

Matthew Pinsent

b: 10.10.70 Holt Norfolk
l: Portsmouth, Hampshire
o: Geography student
s: Single
cb: Leander
ch: Jurgen Grobler
ht: 195 cm, 6'5"
wt: 98 kg, 15 st 6 lb

Matthew's world championships race to fame started in 1988 with world junior coxless pairs gold. He moved from there to a bronze in the senior coxed four in 1989, a bronze in the coxless pairs in 1990 and gold in the same event in 1991. He goes to Barcelona as gold medal favourite in the coxless pairs with Steven Redgrave - one of the biggest names in the business. Matthew also has two boat race wins to his credit. When he has any time away from studies at Oxford and rowing, Matthew likes to play golf.

Steven Redgrave

b: 23.03.62 Marlow
l: Marlow, Buckinghamshire
o: Sports consultant
s: Married 1 child
cb: Leander
ch: Jurgen Grobler
ht: 195 cm, 6'5"
wt: 100 kg, 15 st 11 lb

It is hard to know where to start with this man's international success record. He already possesses three Olympic medals - two golds from the 1984 coxed four and the 1988 coxless pairs together with bronze in the Seoul coxed pairs. In 1986 he also scored a hat-trick of commonwealth golds at single scull, the coxed pairs and fours. His world championship medals include three golds from the 1987 and 1991 coxless pairs and the 1986 coxed pairs. And between 1987 and 1990 he added two silvers and a bronze to his world tally. After the 1988 Olympic Games his partnership with Andy Holmes split up and Steven now rows with Matthew Pinsent. If Redgrave wins gold in Barcelona he will be the first Briton to win three Olympic golds in a row since two water-polo players who won their third golds in 1920.

Richard Stanhope

b: 27.04.57 Blackpool
l: London
o: Building Surveyor
s: Single
cb: Leander & Royal Chester RC
ch: Jurgen Grobler, Martin Aitken
ht: 189 cm, 6'2"
wt: 84 kg, 13 st 3 lb

Richard will be competing in his fourth Olympic Games in Barcelona in a career which began with a silver medal from the eight in 1980. In 1988 in Seoul he was in the men's eight which finished fourth. At world championships level he has won two medals split by a ten year gap - silver in the 1981 eight and bronze in the 1991 eight. He has represented Great Britain at every world championships between those dates except 1984 and 1990. Richard also won a commonwealth silver in 1986 in the men's eight. Last year he was in the winning boat in the Grand Challenge Cup at Henley Royal Regatta. And he has won the Head of River eight on four separate occasions.

ROWING

Adrian Breton

Rapid Fire Pistol
b: 04.10.62 Guernsey
l: Guernsey
o: Telephone Engineer
s: Married 2 children
cb: Guernsey Rifle Club
ch: R Prevel, Albert Redhead
ht: 170 cm, 5'7"
wt: 73 kg, 11 st 7 lb

Adrian went to the 1988 Olympic Games as a last-minute qualifier and finished 24th. But the Guernsey man came up trumps for his island home two years later in Auckland when he won commonwealth gold. And Adrian continued his international improvement later in 1990 with an 11th place in the world championships and an 8th place in the world cup. The latter event, in Zurich, also gave him the British record for rapid-fire pistol. When he is not training or competing Adrian likes to swim, read and listen to music.

David Chapman

Skeet
b: 30.10.63
l: Baldock, Hertfordshire
o: Butcher
s: Married
ht: 179 cm, 5'10"
wt: 75 kg, 11 st 11 lb

David was first in the 1990 trials and set a British record of 564pts from a possible total of 600. He was part of England's Commonwealth Games squad in 1990. And in 1989 he picked up no fewer than four national titles – two English and two British. David went to the 1984 Olympic Games in Los Angeles where he finished 15th. He missed out in 1988 – a victim of international quota restrictions. He will be hoping to make up for that in Barcelona.

Diane Le Grelle

Skeet
b: 04.05.52 Ekeren, Belgium
o: Housewife
ch: Ian Coley, Joseph Neville
ht: 168 cm, 5'6"
wt: 60 kg, 9 st 6 lb

Diane will make Olympic history in Barcelona as the first British woman to have qualified directly for a place in the open event of skeet. Equally, she will cause quite a stir because for 20 years she competed for Belgium before making the change to Britain. Diane attempted to make that transfer in time for Seoul but failed. She will be looking to make up for lost time in Barcelona and could be a medal prospect after finishing fourth in the 1991 european skeet championships.

John Rolfe

Rapid fire Pistol
b: 16.06.60
l: Southampton, Hants
o: Artist
s: Single
cb: Marylebone
ch: Albert Redhead
ht: 172 cm, 5'8"
wt: 67 kg, 10 st 8 lb

John was national rapid fire pistol champion in both 1988 and 1990. At the Commonwealth Games in Auckland two years ago he won a bronze medal in the team pistol event and came fourth individually. At the commonwealth championships of both 1988 and 1989 John won individual gold. He also took the title and equalled the British record at the 1990 GBPC championships. John was delighted at qualifying first amongst British pistol shooters for the 1992 Olympic Games – having missed out on both 1988 Olympic and recent world championships selections.

Madeleine Campbell

b: 18.08.64 Portsmouth
l: Aylesbury, Buckinghamshire
o: Bank clerk
s: Married
cb: Portsmouth Northsea, Maxwell
ch: Chris Nesbit, Mick Wakely
ht: 180 cm, 5'11"
wt: 59 kg, 9 st 4 lb

Madeleine Campbell was disappointed at not making the 1988 Olympic Games team so she made up for it by taking a bronze medal two years later at the Commonwealth Games in Auckland at 100m butterfly. At the 1991 european championships she finished fourth in the same event. Madeleine was also world grand prix 100m butterfly champion last season. Her husband, Iain, competed in the 1984 Olympic Games and her sister and brother-in-law, Doug and Nicky Campbell, were also Olympians at the Moscow and Los Angeles Games respectively.

Sharron Davies

b: 01.11.62 Plymouth
l: Crowthorne, Berkshire
o: Interior Design & Fashion Consultant
s: Married
cb: Portsmouth Northsea
ch: Chris Nesbit
ht: 180 cm, 5'11"
wt: 67 kg, 10 st 8 lb

Sharron Davies is the come-back girl on the British team. In 1978 she took commonwealth gold for the 200m and 400m individual medley in Edmonton. The glamour girl of swimming then went on to Olympic silver at 400m in 1980. She also had a fistful of national titles and records. And decided to retire. But 1988 changed all that. She caught big-competition fever once more whilst commentating on the swimming in Seoul. And she started a come-back which has already included commonwealth silver in the 100m freestyle relay in 1990 and a 6th place in the 1989 european championships.

Joanne Deakins

b: 20.11.72 Worcester
l: Evesham, Worcestershire
o: Unemployed
s: Single
cb: Gloucester City SC
ch: Henry Menike, Simon Hillson
ht: 162 cm, 5'4"
wt: 59 kg, 9 st 4 lb

Joanne produced one of her best performances on the road to Barcelona at the european championships last year when she finished fifth in the 200m backstroke. In the same season she also picked up world cup silver again at the 200m backstroke. In 1990 she travelled to Auckland with the Commonwealth Games team and won a silver medal in the medley relay team. Outside swimming, music is Joanne's greatest love.

Michael Fibbens

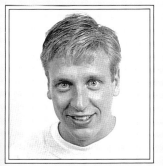

b: 31.05.68 Harlow
l: London
o: Swimmer
s: Single
ht: 198 cm, 6'6"
wt: 87 kg, 13 st 10 lb

Mike won the 1991/92 world cup series in the freestyle sprint category. He took the title in the last meeting of the season this February in Paris. Swimming is a Fibbens family affair. His sister Nicky was a commonwealth medallist in 1986. Mike himself came fourth in the 50m freestyle at the 1990 Commonwealth Games in Auckland and took bronze in the 100m. He swam in the 50m freestyle in Seoul at the Olympic Games before going out in the heats. In 1990 Mike took bronze in the european championships at 50m freestyle. He was British champion at 50 and 100m freestyle in 1989. And Mike has a long-running domestic battle with Mark Foster and Austyn Shortman for the British no.1 slot.

SWIMMING

Mark Foster

b:	12.5.70 Billericay
l:	Southend
o:	Unemployed
s:	Single
cb:	Barnet Copthall
ch:	Dougie Campbell
ht:	6' 5"
wt:	15st 13lb

Mark Foster already has two commonwealth bronze medals to his credit - from the 100m freestyle relay in 1986 and the individual 50m freestyle in 1990. He swam in the latter distance in Seoul but went out in the heats. After that he took an 18-month break. But he has bounced back in 1991/92 with a series of British best swims at 50m freestyle and 50m butterfly. Mark spent much of last season doing battle with his Barnet Copthall team-mate Mike Fibbens and Austyn Shortman for the British 50m freestyle record.

Nick Gillingham

b:	22.01.67 Walsall
l:	Walsall, West Midlands
o:	Sports development officer
s:	Single
cb:	City of Birmingham
ch:	Barry Prime
ht:	185 cm, 6'1"
wt:	73 kg, 11 st 7 lb

In an unassuming and controlled manner Nick Gillingham took silver in the 200m breaststroke at the 1988 Olympic Games in Seoul. A year later he followed that with gold at the same event in the european championships. In 1991 he was back winning european gold once more and setting a new world record of 2:12.55. Nick's second european success was a test of mettle after his own disappointment at his commonwealth games performances in 1990 - where he won silver at 100m and bronze at 200m breaststroke. His hobbies include the arts, photography and old movies.

Martin Harris

b:	21.05.69 London
o:	Unemployed
s:	Single
cb:	Barnet Copthall
ch:	Douglas Campbell
ht:	198 cm, 6'6"

Martin Harris set a British record for the 1500m freestyle in Perth during the 1991 world championships. But his best performances came in the 1991/92 world cup series where he finished fifth overall in the 100m backstroke and sixth in the 50m backstroke. That made up for his disappointment in not making the commonwealth team in 1990. For the 1991 British champion at 100m, a Barcelona medal is the next target. This will be his first Olympic Games.

Paul Howe

b:	08.01.68 Singapore
l:	Burntwood, West Midlands
o:	Sports development
s:	Single
cb:	City of Birmingham, Phoenecians SC
ch:	P Lafontaine, Barry Prime
ht:	183 cm, 6'0"
wt:	81 kg, 12 st 11 lb

Paul has already savoured an Olympic medal ceremony - when he won bronze in the 200m freestyle relay in Los Angeles in 1984. Two years later he added a commonwealth bronze in the same event. Paul swam for England at the 1990 Commonwealth Games and was disappointed not to get a medal.

Zara Long

b:	06.11.70 London
l:	London
o:	Swimming & weights instructor
s:	Single
cb:	Beckenham
ch:	Antony Ross
ht:	172 cm, 5'8"
wt:	66 kg, 10 st 6 lb

When Zara Long went to the Los Angeles Olympic Games in 1984 she was Britain's youngest ever competitor - at the age of thirteen years and 287 days. Zara also competed in the 200m i/m in Seoul four years ago but went out in the heats. At the Commonwealth Games in 1986 Zara collected two silvers in the 100m and 200m freestyle relays. In 1990 in Auckland she finished fifth in the 400m i/m final. Zara is Sharron Davies' main rival domestically having won the 1991 national titles at both 200m and 400m i/m. In her spare time Zara supports Crystal Palace football club.

Adrian Moorhouse

b:	24.05.64 Bradford
l:	Leeds, West Yorkshire
o:	Swimmer
s:	Single
cb:	City of Leeds
ch:	Terry Denison
ht:	187 cm, 6'2"
wt:	87 kg, 13 st 10 lb

The only major title to have eluded Adrian is the world championships - he was disqualified in 1986 in Madrid after "winning" the race. But he made amends in 1988 by taking Olympic gold at 100m breaststroke. In 1989 he became european champion at the same event for the third time and set a world record of 1:01.49. Since 1982 this Leeds-based swimmer has won Commonwealth gold at 100m in 1982 and 90, at 200m in 1982 and 86, silver at 100m in 1986 and two further silvers at 100m medley relay in 1986 and 90. At both the 1991 european and world championships Adrian took silver in the 100m breaststroke.

Robert Morgan

Diving

b:	27.03.67 Cardiff
l:	Lantwit Major, South Glamorgan
o:	Unemployed
s:	Single
cb:	Highgate DC
ch:	Mike Edge
ht:	177 cm, 5'10"
wt:	74 kg, 11 st 9 lb

Robert Morgan is the country's leading diver - following in the slipstream of Chris Snode and hoping to emulate the great Greg Louganis. At the Olympic Games in 1988 he finished 14th in the platform competition. Two years later he followed that with commonwealth gold from the highboard. And in 1991 he won european championship bronze - again from the highboard.

Paul Palmer

b:	18.10.74 Lincoln
l:	Lincoln
o:	Student
s:	Single
cb:	City of Lincoln Pentaqua
ch:	Ian Turner
ht:	192 cm, 6'4"
wt:	85 kg, 13 st 5 lb

1991 was a great year for Paul Palmer. He took three golds in the european junior championships at 200m, 400m and 1500m freestyle. No wonder Paul lists the event, which took place in Antwerp, as his best ever result. He will be looking to make a successful transition from the junior to the senior ranks in Barcelona.

SWIMMING

Karen Pickering

b: 19.12.71 Brighton
l: Ipswich
o: Student
s: Single
cb: Ipswich SC
ch: Dave Champion
ht: 175cm 5' 9"
wt: 9st 0lb 58kg

Karen gave herself an early Christmas present in 1991 when she created history by becoming the first British woman to win all five freestyle titles - from 50m to 800m - at the national winter short course championships in Barnet. She is ranked in the world's top ten at 200m. Karen swam at both the world and european championships in 1991. And now she has her sights firmly set on Barcelona.

Katharine Read

b: 30.06.69 Great Yarmouth
l: London
o: Swimmer
s: Single
cb: Barnet Copthall
ch: Douglas Campbell
ht: 177 cm, 5'10"
wt: 60 kg, 9 st 6 lb

In her own words Kathy Read had a "bad year" in 1990. But she bounced back last year to reach the final of the european championships 200m backstroke, finishing sixth. At the same meeting she also came ninth in the 100m backstroke. And she became the 1991 British long course champion at all three backstroke distances. It was her most successful year since 1986 when she took commonwealth silver at 200m and was British champion at the same distance.

Grant Robins

b: 21.05.69 Portsmouth
l: Portsmouth, Hampshire
o: Trainee accountant
s: Single
cb: Portsmouth Northsea
ch: Chris Nesbit
ht: 183 cm, 6'0"
wt: 84 kg, 13 st 3 lb

Grant Robins was disappointed not to miss out on Olympic selection in 1988. So he will be hoping for better things in Barcelona. In 1990 Grant was part of the England Commonwealth Games team and finished fifth in the 200m backstroke. A year earlier he had picked up three national titles - at 100 and 200m backstroke and 200m individual medley. Grant works for Olympic sponsors Grant Thornton.

Austyn Shortman

b: 24.10.72 London
l: Bristol, Avon
o: Student
s: single
cb: Bristol Central SC
ch: Mike Shortman
ht: 188cm 6'2"
wt: 76kg 12st 0lb

Austyn swam for England at the Commonwealth Games in 1990 where he won silver with the 100m medley team. His performance there was a personal best by over a second which made him the first British man to break 50 seconds for the 100m. Individually, he finished seventh in the 100m freestyle and did not qualify for the 50m final. In 1991 Austyn went to Perth to the world championships but went out in the heats. Over the 1991/92 season, however, he has broken the British 50m record.

Ian Wilson

b: 19.12.70 Sunderland
l: Sunderland, Tyne & Wear
o: Student
s: Single
cb: Borough of Sunderland ASC
ch: Mike Richards
ht: 185 cm, 6'1"
wt: 72 kg, 11 st 5 lb

Ian comes from a swimming family. His sister Lynne was a "B" finalist in the 200m butterfly in 1988 in Seoul. But the tall north-easterner is beginning to make a name of his own. He started last year by finishing 4th in the 1500m freestyle at the world championships in Perth, setting a new British record. Then he lowered that record to 15:03.72 at the european championships in Bonn and took a silver medal in the process. At the world student games in Sheffield he added a gold medal to his collection - again in the 1500m freestyle. He will be looking to continue the pattern in Barcelona.

Natasha Haynes

Synchronised swimming
b: 26.10.69 London
l: Bristol, Avon
s: Single
cb: Bristol Central SC
ch: Georgie Coombs, Caroline Francis
ht: 180 cm, 5'11"

Natasha Haynes lists weightlifting and triathlons amongst her hobbies - a sign of just how fit you need to be to compete at top class synchronised swimming. Natasha has competed for her country in the last year at the world and european championships. She is the current British no.3.

Kerry Shacklock

Synchronised swimming
b: 30.10.71 Wokingham
l: Yately, Surrey
s: Single
cb: Rushmoor SSC
ch: Mike Firmin
ht: 172 cm, 5'8"
wt: 57 kg, 9 st 0 lb

This is the girl whose neck injury - sustained in a fall - made the national news two years ago because she was girlfriend to javelin thrower Steve Backley. The second-hand attention will not have pleased Kerry - she is a top-class sports-woman in her own right - nor did the injury which kept her out of the 1991 world championships. But Kerry recovered in time to take the national title last year and finish fifth in the european championships. At the 1990 Commonwealth Games she took silver in the solo discipline.

Laila Vakil

Synchronised swimming
b: 21.03.74 Northcamp
l: Farnborough, Hampshire
o: Student
s: Single
cb: Rushmoor
ch: Carolyn Wilson
ht: 165 cm, 5'5"
wt: 49 kg, 7 st 10 lb

Laila has had a good two years leading up to her Olympic selection. She took world junior silver in 1991 and european junior bronze in 1990. At the senior european and world championships last year she finished 18th and 49th respectively. Laila is the current British no.2.

SWIMMING

Alan Cooke

b: 23.03.66 Clay Cross
l: Chesterfield
s: Married
cb: Flakenberg (Sweden)
ht: 170cm 5'7"
wt: 63.5kg 10st 0lb

This fast counter-attacker has been national champion twice and represented England at four world and european championships. In 1988 he took team silver at the europeans. And a year later he became commonwealth champion. In 1991 he produced the win of the world championships by beating world no.2 Mikael Appelgren in the first round.

Andrea Holt

b: 11.11.70 Radcliffe
l: Bury, Lancashire
o: Full Time Player & Coach
s: Single
cb: NFD Grove
ch: Wilton Holt
ht: 169 cm, 5'7"
wt: 58 kg, 9 st 2 lb

Andrea had her best year yet in 1991 when she won the national singles title and took over the England no.1 ranking for the first time. She also had a number of good tournament wins at home and beat the european champion in the Italian Open. Andrea plays in both the British and French national leagues.

Lisa Lomas

b: 09.03.67 Dunstable
l: Luton, Bedfordshire
o: Table tennis player
s: Single
cb: Molndals BTK
ht: 170 cm, 5'7"
wt: 61 kg, 9 st 9 lb

This defensive style player was national champion in 1985 and remains the top-ranked British player internationally. In 1986 she won a bronze medal at the european championships in Prague. Lisa has also been national doubles champion twice and was in England's 1991 world championships squad.

Carl Prean

b: 20.08.67 Newport IOW
l: Ryde IOW
o: Table tennis player
s: Single
cb: Saarbrucken (Germany)
ch: Stellan Bengtsson
ht: 184cm 6'1"
wt: 80kg 12st 9lb

Carl is the 1991 national singles champion. He returned from playing in the German bundesliga to take the title. Back in 1983 Carl took world team silver. He followed that with european team silver in 1988. In 1985 he also became european junior and top 12 champion. His career wins include a victory over world champion Jorgen Persson.

TABLE TENNIS

Andrew Castle

b: 15.11.63 Epsom
l: London
s: Single
ch: Warren Jacques
ht: 188cm, 6'2"
wt: 74kg, 11st 9lb

Andrew provided a magical moment at Wimbledon on his return from a tennis scholarship in America when he took the seeded Swede Mats Wilander to five sets on no.1 court. Since that time he has been amongst the top-ranked British players and won the national title in 1991. Last year he also qualified for the Australian and US Opens. He played in the Olympic Games in 1988 but went out in the second round of the singles.

Jo Durie

b: 27.02.60
l: Winchmore Hill, Avon
s: Single
ch: Allan Jones
ht: 183cm, 6'0"
wt: 68kg, 10st 10lb

Jo would like more than anything NOT to be Britain's no.1 and current national champion. She would like to see new British talent rising up the ranking lists. But her wish has yet to be fulfilled. In the meantime she remains the only one of the current crop of leading domestic players to have scaled the heights of the world's top five (in 1983). Injuries have plagued her career. Yet she enjoyed a resurgence of form last year, reaching the final at the Newport Rhode Island tournament and the fourth round of the US Open. In her spare time Jo supports Bristol City FC.

Monique Javer

b: 22.7.67
l: California
s: Single
ht: 178cm, 5'10"
wt: 63kg, 10st 0lb

Monique was brought up in America but has an English mother. Her British eligibility was sanctioned in 1988 - the year she won her first "pro" tournament (in Singapore) and broke into the world's top 100 for the first time. 1990 proved her best year to date with a tournament quarter-final in Tokyo and third round in Singapore as well as moving through the early rounds of the French and US Opens. At the end of that year she also won two vital singles matches to help Britain into the final of the european cup.

Chris Wilkinson

b: 05.01.70
l: Southampton, Hants
s: Single
ch: Jonathan Smith

Chris caused an early stir in Olympic year when he won two of the British satellite tournaments upsetting Jeremy Bates along the way. The current British no.3 turned professional in 1988 and is now ranked in the top 250 in the world. He made his senior British debut in 1989 in the european cup and in 1991 he played in the Davis cup for the first time winning his singles rubber against Poland.

Andrew Davies

b: 17.07.67 Newport
l: Caldicot, Gwent
o: Carpenter
s: Single
cb: Caldicot School
ch: K Price
ht: 188 cm, 6'2"
wt: 110 kg, 17 st 5 lb

Andrew Davies will want to forget the 1988 Olympic Games. He failed to make a total in Seoul But the next year he bounced back to take a second place at the world championships. At last year's world championships he was seventh in the 110kg category - a repeat performance of his 1987 result. Andrew also finished 6th at the 1988 european championships.

Raymond Kopka

b: 20.12.71 Nitra
l: London
o: Purchase ledger assistant
s: Single
cb: Crystal Palace NSC
ch: Mark Lemenager
ht: 185 cm, 6'1"
wt: 100 kg, 15 st 11 lb

Raymond is an exciting new lifter for Britain internationally. At the 1991 world championships he finished 12th in the 110kg category with a total of 337.5kg. And he proved that 1991 was a very good year by taking a gold medal in the British junior championships with a total of 330kg and a silver in the senior domestic event with 337.5kg. Raymond also took european junior bronze last year and now has his sights firmly set on an Olympic debut in Barcelona. When he is not working or lifting, Raymond likes to read James Herbert novels.

Peter May

b: 18.06.66 Enfield
l: Enfield
o: Weights instructor
s: Married
cb: Old Wheatsheaf
ch: Ron Taylor
ht: 180 cm, 5'11"
wt: 90 kg, 14 st 2 lb

Peter was disappointed not to take gold in the 100kg class at the 1990 Commonwealth Games - instead he had to settle for silver. Four years earlier Peter had also won commonwealth bronze - but in the 82.5kg category. At the last Olympic Games Peter competed in the 100kg class and finished 13th. At last year's world championships he was 10th in the 82.5kg category. He will be hoping to stay in the world's top ten when the competition starts in Barcelona. Peter's hobbies are graphic design, motor bikes and boxing.

David Morgan

b: 30.09.64 Cambridge
l: Cambridge
o: Unemployed
s: Single
cb: Shelford WLC
ht: 172 cm, 5'8"
wt: 82 kg, 12 st 13 lb

David Morgan is the "nearly" man of British weightlifting. At both the 1984 and 1988 Olympic Games he finished fourth in the 75kg and 82.5kg categories respectively. But if David missed the podium at Olympic level he has made sure of the top slot at three consecutive Commonwealth Games from 1982 to 1990. And in 1987 David took european bronze. During his junior career the Cambridge man also took a world junior silver in 1984.

Look out, too, in Barcelona for **Andrew Saxton** and **Mark Thomas**. Team manager will be **Wally Holland** and **John Lear** is the team coach.

WEIGHT LIFTING

For key to abbreviations: see page 239

Graeme English

90kg

b: 25.09.64 Kilsyth
l: East Kilbride
o: Joiner
s: Single
ht: 180 cm, 5'11"
wt: 93 kg, 14 st 9 lb

British wrestlers will find the new qualifying rules for the Olympic Games a very tough hurdle. But if Graeme English - the inappropriately named Scot - makes the grade he will be looking to improve on his 9th placing in Seoul four years ago. This 1986 commonwealth bronze medallist has consistently been British and Scottish champion in his weight category over the past six years.

Calum McNeil

b: 30.04.66 Glasgow
l: Glasgow
o: Chartered accountant
s: single
cb: Milngavie AWC
ch: Nick Cipriano, D Scott
ht: 183cm
wt: 70kg

Calum is the current British no.1 at 68kg freestyle. He won the national title in front of a home crowd in Glasgow in May 1991. At the world championships in Varna, Bulgaria, in October 1991 he finished 10th. Back in September 1989 Calum won silver at the commonwealth championships held in Malta - this time in the 74kg category. Calum is based in Canada to prepare for his Olympic campaign.

Malcolm Morley

b: 01.06.66 Sheffield
l: Chesterfield, Derbyshire
o: Police Officer
s: Single
cb: YMCA - Manchester
ch: Fitzlloyd Walker
ht: 180 cm, 5'11"
wt: 83 kg, 13 st 1 lb

Malcolm competed in the 1990 world championships in the in the 82kg category and came 10th. That is the sort of result he will be seeking in Barcelona. When he is not competing and training, Malcolm's hobbies are running and weightlifting.

Fitzlloyd Walker

b: 07.03.57 Kingston, Jamaica
l: Stretford, Manchester
o: Teacher
s: Married 3 children
cb: YMCA - Manchester
wt: 74 kg, 11 st 9 lb

Fitzlloyd Walker has been a British team stalwart for many years. He competed in the 1988 Olympic Games in the 74kg class but went out in the second round. This Manchester man has also won 13 British championships in his career. In his spare time he likes to play badminton and fives.

WRESTLING

Stuart Childerley

b: 17.2.66 Lowestoft
l: Southampton
o: Sportsman
s: single
cb: Royal Southern
ch: John Derbyshire
ht: 5' 11"
wt: 93kg   14st 8lb

Stuart took pre-Olympic gold in 1987 in Pusan. But he could not quite repeat the performance during the 1988 Games when he finished 4th. In 1988, too, he placed fifth in the world championships in Brazil despite a bad bout of food poisoning. Stuart was world and european youth champion in 1984 and has been sailing since the age of four. He was first tactician on "Indulgence" during the 1989 Admiral's Cup.

Barrie Edgington

b: Sandhurst, Berks
    (aged: 25)
l: Hayling Island

Barrie's win at the 1992 world championships in Singapore in January means that Britain must have a good chance of a medal in the Olympic lechner - windsurfing - class. A year earlier Barrie also won the european title and finished sixth in the pre-Olympics. He learnt his craft as a teenager when his family moved to Hayling Island. Since then he has also won several national titles.

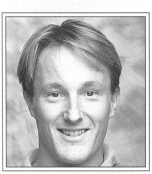

Andrew Hemmings

b: 09.08.64 Reading
l: Gosport, Hampshire
o: Unemployed
s: Single
cb: Hayling Island & Stokes Bay
ch: Rob Andrews
ht: 181 cm, 5'11"
wt: 72 kg, 11 st 5 lb

Andy Hemmings, together with Jason Belbin, upset the, then, reigning world champions Nigel Buckley and Pete Newlands, to snatch the 470 class slot in Seoul. Now Hemmings is back with a new partner, Paul Brotherton, and they look set to do the same thing. Andy and Paul came third in the world championships in Brisbane in December 1991 and Andy is a former world 420 class champion - a title he won in 1983. In 1985 he was also world silver medallist and european champion in the fireball class.

Penny Way

b: 03.04.62 Bristol
l: Christchurch, Dorset
o: Windsurfer/Author/
    Housewife
s: Married
cb: Christchurch Sailing Club
ch: Rob Andrews
ht: 169 cm, 5'7"
wt: 55 kg, 8 st 9 lb

If Olympic golds could be awarded now on past merit Penny Way would be the first in the queue where women's windsurfing is concerned. She has been Olympic champion three times in 1986, 90 and 91. But a recent hiccough came when she lost her title in 1992 to a combination of a Frenchwoman, strong winds and a bout of influenza. There is no doubt, however, that this determined Dorset sailor - who has also won world silver in 1989 and world bronze in 1987 and 1988 - will want to re-establish supremacy on Olympic waters in Spain.

FLY THE FLAG

AT GRANT THORNTON WE'RE HELPING PEOPLE TO REACH FOR GOLD

As business advisers and chartered accountants, helping people to achieve their personal ambitions is something we do every day. That's why Grant Thornton are proud to be associated with the British Olympic team, with their ideals and sporting endeavours. In helping to raise funds and organise support through our 45 offices across the country, we hope we have been able to communicate some of their enthusiasm – and their ideals – to a wider audience.

We would like to thank all those involved and wish the team every success.

Grant Thornton

Grant Thornton, the UK member firm of
Grant Thornton International, is authorised by the Institute of Chartered Accountants
in England and Wales to carry on investment business.

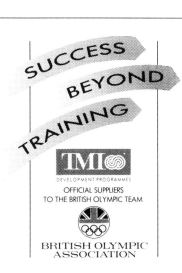

OFFICIAL SUPPLIERS
TO THE BRITISH OLYMPIC TEAM

BRITISH OLYMPIC
ASSOCIATION

TMI
supporting
Britain's Olympic
teams in
Barcelona and
Albertville in
1992

THE VESTEY GROUP

wishes the British Olympic Team
the very best of luck
when they "Go for Gold"

BARCELONA 1992

Results

DATE /SPORT	NAME	COUNTRY	RESULT /SCORE /TIME

BARCELONA 1992

Results

DATE /SPORT	NAME	COUNTRY	RESULT /SCORE /TIME

BARCELONA 1992
Results

DATE /SPORT	NAME	COUNTRY	RESULT /SCORE /TIME

The World's No 1 Building Society

wishes the British Olympic Team

a successful Olympic Games

in Barcelona 1992.

World Class

Best wishes from a
World Class company to a World Class event.

BARCELONA 1992

Results

DATE /SPORT	NAME	COUNTRY	RESULT /SCORE /TIME

RANK XEROX

THREE YEAR OFFICE PLANNER

1992

MOST SUPPLIERS ONLY GIVE A 6 MONTH GUARANTEE.

OPTED FOR ANOTHER FIRM'S 1 YEAR GUARANTEE IN JAN? IT'S ABOUT TO RUN OUT.

1993

IF YOU'RE NOT HAPPY WITH YOUR MACHINE AFTER 18 MONTHS, TOUGH LUCK (UNLESS IT'S A RANK XEROX).

1994

RANK XEROX. NO ONE ELSE OFFERS A 3 YEAR, NO QUIBBLE, MACHINE REPLACEMENT GUARANTEE.

A little reminder for people who didn't buy a Rank Xerox machine.

We hate to rub it in, but we're the only company to offer a 3 year, no quibble, machine replacement guarantee with our service agreement.

Not to mention the unique Rank Xerox Finance Code of Conduct which guarantees no hidden extra rates.

How come we're the only ones to offer such a generous package?

Could it be that no other company has as much faith its equipment?

**Rank Xerox
The Document Compan**

Call us free on 0800 010 766

BARCELONA 1992

Results

DATE /SPORT	NAME	COUNTRY	RESULT /SCORE /TIME

COUNTRY ABBREVIATIONS

AFG	Afghanistan	ECU	Ecuador	LAO	Laos	SAF	South Africa
AHO	Netherlands Antilles	EGY	Egypt	LAT	Latvia	SAM	Western Samoa
ALB	Albania	ESA	El Salvador	LBA	Libya	SEN	Senegal
ALG	Algeria	ESP	Spain	LBR	Liberia	SEY	Seychelles
AND	Andora	EST	Estonia	LES	Lesotho	SIN	Singapore
ANG	Angola	ETH	Ethiopia	LIB	Lebanon	SLE	Sierra Leone
ANT	Antigua	FIJ	Fiji	LIE	Liechtenstein	SMR	San Marino
ARG	Agentina	FIN	Finland	LIT	Lithuania	SOL	Solomon Islands
ARU	Aruba	FRA	France	LUX	Luxembourg	SOM	Somalia
ASA	American Samoa	GAB	Gabon	MAD	Madagascar	SRI	Sri Lanka
AUS	Australia	GAM	Gambia	MAR	Morocco		(ex Ceylon)
AUT	Austria	GBR	Great Britain	MAS	Malaysia	SUD	Sudan
BAH	Bahamas	GEQ	Equatorial Guinea	MAW	Malawi	SUI	Switzerland
BAN	Bangladesh	GER[1]	Germany	MDV	Maldives	SUR	Surinam
BAR	Barbados	GHA	Ghana	MEX	Mexico	SWE	Sweden
BEL	Belgium		(ex Gold Coast)	MGL	Mongolia	SWZ	Swaziland
BEN	Benin	GRE	Greece	MLI	Mali	SYR	Syria
BER	Bermuda	GRN	Grenada	MLT	Malta	TAN	Tanzania
BHU	Bhutan	GUA	Guatemala	MON	Monaco	TCH	Czechoslovakia
BIZ	Belize	GUI	Guinea	MOZ	Mozambique	THA	Thailand
	(ex British Honduras)	GUM	Guam	MRI	Mauritius	TGA	Tonga
BOL	Bolivia	GUY	Guyana	MTN	Mauritania	TOG	Togo
BOT	Botswana		(ex British Guiana)	MYA	Myanmar	TPE	Taipei
BRA	Brazil	HAI	Haiti	NAM	Namibia		(ex Formosa/Taiwan)
BRN	Bahrain	HKG	Hong Kong	NCA	Nicaragua	TRI	Trinidad & Tobago
BRU	Brunei	HOL	Netherlands	NEP	Nepal	TUN	Tunisia
BUL	Bulgaria	HON	Honduras	NGR	Nigeria	TUR	Turkey
BUR	Burkina Faso	HUN	Hungary	NIG	Niger	UAE	United Arab Emirates
CAF	Central African	INA	Indonesia	NOR	Norway	UGA	Uganda
	Republic	IND	India	NZL	New Zealand	URS	Soviet Union
CAN	Canada	IRL	Ireland	OMA	Oman	URU	Uruguay
CAY	Cayman Islands	IRI	Iran	PAK	Pakistan	USA	United States
CGO	Congo	IRQ	Iraq	PAN	Panama	VAN	Vanuatu
CHA	Chad	ISL	Iceland	PAR	Paraguay	VEN	Venezuela
CHI	Chile	ISR	Israel	PER	Peru	VIE	Vietnam
CHN	China	ISV	Virgin Islands	PHI	Philippines	VIN	St Vincent and
CIV	Ivory Coast	ITA	Italy	PNG	Papua New Guinea		the Grenadines
CMR	Cameroun	IVB	British Virgin Islands	POL	Poland	YAM	Yemen
COK	Cook Islands	JAM	Jamaica	POR	Portugal	YUG	Yugoslavia
COL	Colombia	JOR	Jordan	PRK	Democratic People's	ZAI	Zaire
CRC	Costa Rica	JPN	Japan		Republic of Korea	ZAM	Zambia
CUB	Cuba	KEN	Kenya	PUR	Puerto Rico	ZIM	Zimbabwe
CYP	Cyprus	KOR	Korea	QAT	Qatar		
DEN	Denmark	KSA	Kingdom of	ROM	Romania		
DJI	Djibouti		Saudi Arabia	RSA[2]	South Africa		
DOM	Dominican Republic	KUW	Kuwait	RWA	Rwanda		

[1] 1948-1991 - FRG = Federal Repubic of Germany GDR = German Democratic Republic
[2] Prior to 1992, SAF = South Africa, thereafter the new abbreviation is RSA.

COMPETITOR DATA SECTION

b:	Date and place of birth
l:	Current residence
o:	Occupation
s:	Marital status
cb:	Club
ch:	Coach
ht:	Height
wt:	Weight
of:	Olympic family

EVENT ABBREVIATIONS

(m)	men
(w)	women
(o)	open
elim	elimination
F	medal event (final)
grp	group
hts	heats
ind	individual
prelims	preliminaries
pts	points
q or qual	qualifying
q/f	quarter-final
rd	round
rep	repechage
s/f	semi-final

RESULTS ABBREVIATIONS

d/q	Disqualified
dna	Data not available
DNF	Did not finish
DNS	Did not start
KO	Knock-out
NOR	New Olympic Record
nta	No time available
NWR	New World Record
RSC	Received standing count
WO	Walk-over

MEASUREMENT ABBREVIATIONS

Times:	hr	= hour
	1h48:32.065	
	(1 hour 48 minutes 32.065 seconds)	
Distance:	km	= kilometre
	m	= metre
Height:	cm	= centimetres
	' "	= feet and inches
Weight:	kg	= kilogrammes
	st lb	= stones and pounds

SCHEDULE TO A VIEW

PROGRAMME OF THE XXVth OLYMPIAD IN BARCELONA 1992

	JULY								AUGUST								
	24	25	26	27	28	29	30	31	1	2	3	4	5	6	7	8	9
Opening ceremony		O															
Archery								O	O	O	O	O					
Athletics								O	O	O	O		O	O	O	O	O
Badminton					O	O	O	O	O	O	O	O					
Baseball			O	O	O			O	O	O			O	O			
Basketball			O	O		O	O	O	O	O	O	O	O	O	O	O	
Boxing			O	O	O	O	O	O	O	O	O	O		O	O	O	O
Canoeing								O	O	O	O	O	O	O	O	O	
Cycling			O	O	O	O	O	O		O							
Equestrian					O	O	O	O		O	O	O			O		O
Fencing							O	O	O	O	O	O	O	O	O		
Football	O		O	O	O	O	O		O	O			O		O	O	
Gymnastics			O	O	O	O	O	O	O	O			O	O	O		
Handball				O		O	O	O	O	O	O	O		O	O	O	
Hockey			O	O	O	O	O		O	O	O	O	O	O	O	O	
Judo				O	O	O	O	O	O	O							
Modern pentathlon			O	O	O	O											
Rowing					O	O	O	O	O	O							
Shooting			O	O	O	O	O	O	O	O							
Swimming			O	O	O	O	O	O									
Diving			O	O	O	O			O	O	O	O					
Synchronised swimming										O	O		O	O	O		
Water polo									O	O	O		O	O		O	O
Table tennis					O	O	O	O	O	O	O	O	O				
Tennis					O	O	O	O	O	O	O	O	O	O	O		
Volleyball				O		O	O	O	O	O	O	O	O	O	O		O
Weightlifting			O	O	O	O	O	O	O	O	O						
Wrestling			O	O	O	O			O	O	O	O					
Yachting					O	O	O	O	O	O	O	O					
Basque Pelota*		O	O	O	O	O	O	O	O	O	O	O	O				
Roller Hockey*		O	O	O	O	O			O	O	O	O	O	O	O		
Taekwondo*											O	O	O				
Closing ceremony																	O
	24	25	26	27	28	29	30	31	1	2	3	4	5	6	7	8	9

* Demonstration sports